THE WELFARE STATE

ECONOMISTS OF THE TWENTIETH CENTURY

General Editors: Mark Perlman, *University Professor of Economics, University of Pittsburgh* and Mark Blaug, *Professor Emeritus, University of London, Consultant Professor, University of Buckingham and Visiting Professor, University of Exeter*

This innovative series comprises specially invited collections of articles and papers by economists whose work has made an important contribution to economics in the late twentieth century.

The proliferation of new journals and the ever-increasing number of new articles make it difficult for even the most assiduous economist to keep track of all the important recent advances. By focusing on those economists whose work is generally recognized to be at the forefront of the discipline, the series will be an essential reference point for the different specialisms included.

A list of published and future titles in this series is printed at the end of this volume.

The Welfare State

The Selected Essays of Assar Lindbeck

Volume II

Assar Lindbeck

Professor of International Economics
Institute for International Economic Studies
University of Stockholm, Sweden

Edward Elgar

Published by
Edward Elgar Publishing Limited
Gower House
Croft Road
Aldershot
Hants GU11 3HR
England

Edward Elgar Publishing Company
Old Post Road
Brookfield
Vermont 05036
USA

A CIP catalogue record for this book is available from the British Library

ISBN 1 85278 720 1 (Volume I)
     1 85278 721 X (Volume II)
     1 85278 603 5 (2-volume set)

Printed and Bound in Great Britain by
Hartnolls Limited, Bodmin, Cornwall.

Contents

Preface

This book of essays on the welfare state is the second volume of my selected published papers; the first dealt with macroeconomics. As in the first volume, I have endeavoured to include only papers that may be of some general interest. Because of space limitations, joint papers are excluded; their titles may be found in the reference list at the end of the Introduction. Technical papers on methodology have also been excluded.

Assar Lindbeck
Institute for International Economic Studies
University of Stockholm

Introduction*

In view of the ambitious welfare state policies in Sweden, it is hardly surprising that Swedish economists have devoted considerable effort to analysing various aspects of the modern welfare state. I perceive the term 'welfare state' as referring, in particular, to four basic features of government policies in modern Western societies: (i) attempts by the government to enhance the economic security of citizens in general, largely by way of social security systems; (ii) political ambitions to redistribute income to low-income groups by transfers in cash or in kind, sometimes accompanied by attempts to make the overall distribution of disposable income more even; (iii) efforts by the government to provide and control various types of services to households ('public consumption'); and (iv) attempts to change the distribution of factor incomes by way of price regulation, tariffs and subsidies, particularly perhaps in the housing and agricultural sectors.

My own involvement in welfare state issues is probably a result of my family background, as my father was in charge of the social welfare administration (*socialvårdskonsulent*) in the northern provinces of Sweden, where I saw much poverty in my childhood. I also met many politicians, in particular Social Democrats, in my home; so this, perhaps, is the background for my lifetime interest in politics. These childhood experiences probably explain my habit of often having kept one foot in the political sphere during my career as an academic economist – to begin with in student politics, later on as an economic adviser to the government and the Central Bank of Sweden. As a consequence, I have often studied economic policy from a combined position as an insider and an outsider in political decision-making. But every time I have had an opportunity to choose, more permanently, between political or administrative work and an academic life, I have always chosen the latter.

My endeavours to analyse welfare state problems as a scholar started with studies of price regulation in housing and agriculture. A joint project with Ragnar Bentzel and Ingemar Ståhl, sponsored by the Industrial Institute for Economic and Social Research in Stockholm, resulted in a small book on rent control, *Bostadsbristen – en studie av prisbildningen på bostadsmarknaden* (The Housing Shortage – A Study of Pricing in the Housing Market), 1963. We tried to show that even though rent control tends to redistribute income from landlords to tenants, other redistributional consequences of rent control are rather dubious from the point of view of officially expressed distributional targets. For instance, it is far from clear that low-income groups are favoured by a system of permanent excess demand in most of the housing stock ('housing shortage'), as apartments in such a situation are distributed by informal rationing, which in reality means that personal contacts become a crucial factor. Moreover, low-income groups cannot easily compete on the black market that is one of the unavoidable consequences of rent control.

* I am grateful to Thorvaldur Gylfason, Lars Jonung, Torsten Persson and Lars E.O. Svensson for very helpful comments on an earlier draft of this Introduction.

I returned to this issue, assisted by Sören Blomquist, in another small book, *Hyreskontroll och bostadsmarknad* (Rent Control and the Housing Market), 1972, again sponsored by the Industrial Institute for Economic and Social Research. The purpose was to analyse various methods of abolishing rent control without the government having to relinquish its fundamental distributional aims. The book was partly inspired by my earlier work as an adviser to the Department of Housing, through which I tried to convince the (social democratic) government of the advantages of removing rent control, particularly if removal would be combined with redistributional measures in the form of taxes and/or subsidies, including taxes on the windfall profits of landlords. Indeed, the government was convinced and introduced a parliamentary proposal for the abolition of rent control in the mid-1960s. The proposal did not, however, include any redistributional measures. This was because the government feared that the general public (i.e., the voters) would blame the tax increase, and hence the government, for the increase in rents, whereas the landlords would be blamed for the rent increase if their taxes were not raised simultaneously!

On this occasion, however, it was not only the government that played party politics. The leader of the opposition, Bertil Ohlin, who had been against rent control for many years, now characterized the proposal as irresponsible, as it did not include any taxes on the windfalls of landlords. The government (on the initiative of the Secretary of the Treasury, Gunnar Sträng) reacted by withdrawing its proposal. Sweden is still (in 1992) stuck with rent control, though in modified form. This course of events certainly helped me understand that 'market imperfections', which have occupied the interest of economists for long periods of time, are often overshadowed by 'political imperfections'.

I also published a number of articles on rent control and housing policy in Swedish. My only article in English on this issue is included as Chapter 8 in this book of essays: 'Rent control as an instrument of housing policy', *The Economic Problems of Housing*, 1967, where it is argued that various officially stated targets of housing policy may be achieved more effectively by instruments other than rent control. Indeed, in my book *The Political Economy of the New Left*, 1971, I proclaimed: 'next to bombing, rent control seems in many cases to be the most efficient technique so far known for destroying cities' (p. 39).

My research next turned to the other major target for price regulation in Western Europe, i.e., the agricultural sector. This research was also sponsored by the Industrial Institute for Economic and Social Research. Again, a basic motive behind such regulation was to redistribute income, although in this case to farmers. An additional motive for price regulation in the agricultural sector was to boost farm output, partly for reasons of national self-sufficiency.

I collaborated with an agricultural economist, Odd Gulbrandsen, on this research. We began by publishing a small book in Swedish, *Mål och medel i jordbruks-politiken* (Ends and Means of Agricultural Policy) in 1966, which focused on the possibility of reaching the stated goals of agricultural policy without using high tariffs and detailed domestic market regulations. The book was to some extent inspired by my participation in the Government Agriculture Committee of 1960. The committee could not be convinced that the existing 'high-price system', based on high tariffs, should be replaced by a so-called 'low-price system', based on world market prices and subsidies to farm production. However, a majority of the committee was prepared to take a modest step in the direction of a 'low-price system'. The government initially took the same position, which I could not help but notice as an adviser to the Secretary of Agriculture. Political protests, however, in particular from farmers and their organizations, made the government retreat from even such an unobtrusive reform. Agricultural protectionism has remained with us in Sweden, approximately unchanged, throughout the decades. It is rather baffling that not only a large group of consumers (tenants in the case of rent control) can induce the government to intervene by price ceilings on their behalf, but also that a small group of producers (farmers) can exert so much influence, by way of high food prices, against the interest of consumers, i.e., the vast majority of voters.

Gulbrandsen and I continued with a major research project, *The Economics of the Agricultural Sector*, published in 1969 (English version in 1973). This was a detailed theoretical and empirical study of agriculture in Sweden, viewed in the context of the international market for agricultural products. We studied the effects of agricultural protectionism in Sweden on incomes and production, including the welfare costs (in terms of producer and consumer surpluses). We also calculated the lowest costs of guaranteeing national self-sufficiency in the case of a prolonged war that would block imports of agricultural products. It turned out that the optimum policy would result in a highly animal-oriented agricultural sector and large storage of some agricultural products, such as sugar, in peacetime. Such an optimal agricultural policy also implied that about one-third of all farm land would be taken out of farming. This book made me about as unpopular among farmers' organizations as the earlier book on rent control had made me among the leaders of the tenants' association.

I also published a number of articles on agriculture in Swedish journals and newspapers. My only article on agriculture in English was 'Swedish agricultural policy in an international perspective', *Skandinaviska Enskilda Banken Quarterly Review*, 1966. The statistics in this article, however, are too dated to be included in the present volume.

Regional policy was another controversial topic in Sweden in the 1960s and 1970s. In response to the proposals of a government committee in 1964 to subsidize declining regions in Sweden, particularly in the north, I was asked by the Government to suggest alternatives. I tried to base my proposals on the notion of agglomeration externalities. The basic line of reasoning was published in an article entitled 'Location policy', *Skandinaviska Enskilda Banken Quarterly Review*, 1964. However, this article is too closely related to specific Swedish examples to be suitable for publication here. The final policy proposal of the government, which I helped formulate as an 'instant expert' on regional economics at the Department of Interior, could perhaps be regarded as a compromise between these two approaches.

In the 1970s and 1980s, the focus of my work on welfare state problems shifted to issues such as social security, income transfers, public consumption and progressive taxation. One example is a rather extensive study for the OECD in 1975, 'Inequality and redistributional policy issues, principles and Swedish experience', which (largely because of its length) is not included in this book. The purpose of the study was to compare alternative methods of redistribution policy or, more specifically, to discuss objectives, methods and problems of redistribution policy. The analysis was designed to provide some background information for answering questions such as how far public authorities and other organizations can go along the various routes of redistribution policies in mixed economies without running into serious problems. The inspiration for my interest in these issues – concerns that I have not yet been able to abandon – was derived largely from Swedish reality and the Swedish policy debate. The majority of the papers in this volume deal, in fact, with similar problems. All these papers were written after 1970, when I moved from the Stockholm School of Economics (*Handelshögskolan*) to the University of Stockholm, where I replaced Gunnar Myrdal as professor of International Economics and Director of the Institute for International Economic Studies (IIES).

This volume is organized in three sections. The first consists of two articles on the driving forces behind the modern welfare state. 'The changing role of the national state' (Chapter 1), *Kyklos*, 1975, concerns the emergence of the nation-state and its development into a modern welfare state. The paper is a result of a research project on 'The Internationalization Process' at the IIES in Stockholm in the 1970s. A basic idea in the paper is that several important economic and political issues of today may be conceived as the result of tensions between increased internationalization of the economic system and gradually increased ambitions regarding national welfare states. One example is contemporary tendencies towards protectionism and mercantilism.

The second article (Chapter 2), 'Redistribution policy and the expansion of the public sector', *Journal of Public Economics*, 1985, was written for a 'Nobel Symposium' in 1984 on the political economy of the public sector. It is argued in the paper that the most important driving forces behind the modern welfare state, and the related expansion of public sector spending, are redistributional considerations. During the first part of this century, life-cycle and insurance-type redistributional considerations seem to have dominated redistribution policy, particularly in terms of the consequences for the expansion of public spending. More recently, however, 'fragmented horizontal redistributions' among various minority groups have probably been the most important mechanisms.

The analysis also indicates that it may be misleading to regard redistribution policy as being executed deliberately and systematically by some 'social planner', such as a uniform group of politicians or a political party. Rather, redistributions via the state may be seen as the unplanned final result of a great number of separate, uncoordinated policy actions. The most constructive approach is probably to regard redistribution policy as the outcome of competition for votes among political parties. I have, accordingly, pursued formal analysis of the politics of redistribution in a number of joint theoretical articles with Jörgen W. Weibull. Indeed, whatever useful contributions I have made in the field of formal analysis of political equilibrium are largely the result of my cooperation with Jörgen.

We first modelled the politics of redistribution among socio-economic groups in the paper 'Balanced-budget redistribution as the outcome of political equilibrium', *Public Choice*, 1987. The analysis was followed up in a working paper, 'A model of political equilibrium in representative democracy', 1992. It was shown that different 'policy-motivated' political parties will, in general, adopt varying policy positions in equilibrium; under certain qualifications, the equilibrium outcome will lie between the preferred policy of the most popular party and a certain type of utilitarian optimum. The smaller the popularity bias among the parties, the closer the equilibrium policy will be to this utilitarian optimum.

Moreover, in a paper entitled 'Altruism and time consistency: The economics of fait accompli', *Journal of Political Economy*, 1988, we analysed the strategic and intertemporal interaction between economic agents who have 'overlapping' concerns, such as altruistic concerns for each other's welfare. We showed how the presence of such common concerns may lead to socially inefficient outcomes, in which one economic agent 'free-rides' on the other's concern. We also briefly discussed how this inefficiency and free-riding may be mitigated, such as by compulsory social security systems.

Part II of this book consists of six articles on various 'economic' consequences of the modern welfare state, in particular the effects on work and saving, and on the division of labour among markets, government and family. The first of these articles (Chapter 3), 'Interpreting income distributions in a welfare state: The case of Sweden', *European Economic Review*, 1983, highlights the drastic difference between the distribution of factor incomes and disposable incomes in modern welfare states, illustrated by statistics from Sweden. The implication is that the distribution of purchasing power, and hence probably also 'economic well-being', in a welfare state like Sweden is not tightly connected with the contributions of households in the production system. As a consequence, there are wide marginal wedges between factor costs for firms and factor rewards for households which are bound to distort the allocation of resources. It is also shown that economic inequality is drastically exaggerated when income statistics are not adjusted for lifetime differences in working time and in the time-profile of income.

The next essay (Chapter 4), 'Disincentive problems in developed countries', in *Growth and Entrepreneurship*, 1981, is a brief but broad survey of 'welfare statism'. It is pointed out that in combination with economic growth, the buildup of elaborate welfare state systems has civilized our societies considerably, although there is a great deal of apprehension that such systems may in the long run undermine the structure of economic incentives. The same point is elaborated in the paper (Chapter 5), 'Consequences of the advanced welfare state', *The World Economy*, 1988. This essay is an attempt to specify exactly what the main achievements of the modern welfare state are: to have mitigated, or even eliminated, destitution among people with extremely low lifetime incomes; to have evened out lifetime wealth among households in general; to have raised productivity in the national economy by inducing investment in human capital, in particular by subsidizing services such as education and health care for which, at least until recently, the social return seems to have been higher than the return on alternative investments; to have helped individuals reduce economic uncertainty; and to have evened out consumption over the life cycle.

Notwithstanding these major achievements of the modern welfare state, it is reasonable to argue that the marginal contributions of welfare-state spending gradually fall as the level of spending increases – assuming that the most beneficial reforms tend to be made early in the development of the welfare state. At the same time, it is well known that the marginal costs of welfare-state policies tend to rise as the size of the programmes increases. This is due to the fact that various types of distortions in relative prices increase by higher marginal tax rates, which means that the information and incentive content of the price system deteriorates. The tendency of the traditional 'welfare state' to develop into a generalized, free-for-all 'redistribution (or transfer) state' is also considered.

The consequences for work effort are studied more carefully in the essay (Chapter 6), 'Work disincentives in the welfare state', *National Ökonomische Gesellschaft Lectures*, 1981. As the disincentive effects of taxes are related to their *substitution effects* and as taxes finance public expenditures, I emphasize the substitution effects of parallel (i.e., combined) increases in taxes and benefits, rather than the income plus the substitution effects of *isolated* tax changes. Moreover, rather than restricting the discussion to the effects on hours of work in the market, I deal with a broad spectrum of effects on households' use of time – in fact, nine types of effects. These are classified as the effects on (i) the choice between income and leisure (in the sense of recreation); (ii) the pursuit of do-it-yourself work; (iii) production for barter; (iv) the choice of intensity and dexterity (quality) of work; (v) the choice of occupation; (vi) investment in human capital; (vii) the choice of residence (geographical location) by the individual; (viii) the search for tax loopholes, i.e., legal tax avoidance; and (ix) involvement in illegal activities, including illegal tax evasion and cheating on public sector benefits.

The consequences for the supply of labour are analysed more formally in Chapter 7, 'Tax effects versus budget effects on labor supply', *The Economic Inquiry*, 1982. As the analysis, again, deals with the effects of combined changes in taxes and government spending on goods and services, it emphasizes cross substitution effects on the labour supply of changes in public spending on goods and services, or of the subsidization of goods and services provided by private markets. It turns out that several important recent developments in the labour supply behaviour of households are highlighted by such a study of 'budget effects' rather than isolated 'tax effects'.

Jointly with Jörgen W. Weibull, I also wrote some more technical papers on the welfare effects of public spending programmes. In 'Intergenerational aspects of public transfers, borrowing and debt', *Scandinavian Journal of Economics*, 1986, we analysed the intergenerational distribution effects of increased government spending in the context of a two-period life-cycle model with overlapping generations. A specific feature of the model is that in both periods, private wealth enters as an argument in the preference functions of the individual household. It is shown how some fiscal policy actions in this framework favour both of the generations currently living, possibly at the expense of future generations, while other actions generate conflicts between the generations currently living. This analysis was followed up in our paper 'Welfare effects of alternative forms of public spending', *European Economic Review*, 1988, where we analysed the effects, in a second-best world, of three different types of public spending – transfer payments, public consumption and public investment – in a model where household production of services is explicitly modelled. The macroeconomic consequences of such policies were studied in a joint paper with Parameswar Nandakumar, 'Public spending and private services – macroeconomic effects', *Oxford Economic Papers*, 1990.

Part III of this volume contains four papers on some broader consequences for society of the modern welfare state. It opens with a discussion (Chapter 9) on 'Limits to the welfare state', *Challenge*, 1986. It is pointed out that the burgeoning public sector not only alters economic incentives and the distribution of income and wealth, but also changes the role of the family, influences freedom of choice, and makes honesty more 'expensive'. Although the definition of 'limits to the welfare state' is quite debatable, it is likely to include the following three factors: (i) induced inefficiencies in the economic system due to various disincentive effects on the allocation of resources and on productive effort in general; (ii) 'unpopular', and perhaps also partly unexpected, consequences for the role and freedom of choice of the household; and (iii) unwanted implications for the relation between the individual citizen and the state. These issues were also covered in my Lee Kuan Yew Lectures, *The Welfare State – Driving Forces, Functioning and Limits*, 1987. A brief statement on the same issues is the paper 'Is the welfare state in trouble?', *Eastern Economic Review*, 1987.

The consequences of the welfare state for the freedom of choice of the individual are further examined in Chapter 10, 'Individual freedom and welfare state policy', *European Economic Review*, 1988, which was my 'Schumpeter Lecture' at the congress of the European Economic Association in 1987. In economic analysis, the traditional utilitarian argument for individual freedom, including freedom of choice, is 'consequentialist' or 'instrumentalist' in the special sense that decentralized decision-making is defended by its consequences for economic efficiency in production and consumption, and hence also for the *actual* consumption bundles of individuals. However, it is argued in this paper that the individual may also be interested in the *process* by which a certain consumption bundle is achieved, and that, indeed, the individual values the *act of choosing* as such, which implies that freedom of choice also has an 'intrinsic' value. This is an idea which has been in my mind ever since the days (or rather, years) when I waited in vain for an apartment in the housing queue in Stockholm.

I also speculate on some even broader aspects of welfare state policies in the essay (Chapter 11) 'Can pluralism survive?', *The Eleventh Annual William K. McInally Memorial Lecture*, 1977. This paper deals with issues on the borderline between economic analysis and political ideology. It is concerned with the relation between the organization of our economic system and the possibilities of maintaining a highly pluralistic society. This topic, of course, forced me to wander outside the realm of my profession as an economist. I tried to show that pluralism is strongly related to the organization of our economic system, and that some contemporary trends in the economic system constitute a threat to this pluralism. I refer, in particular, to the risk that the traditional division of functions and responsibilities among households, firms, private organizations and public authorities may become less pronounced than earlier. The analysis has a 'Hayekian' flavour, although I take a more positive stance than Hayek on the achievements of the welfare state. Moreover, whereas Hayek regarded far-reaching government interventions in markets and in the lives of households and firms as a threat to democracy, I view it rather as a threat to the 'pluralism' of our democratic system.

The primary explanation for this threat is not that some 'evil forces' are consciously at work to undermine our pluralistic society. Instead, the new trends are mainly more or less unplanned side-effects of developments which, in themselves, are often thought to be great advances, and in fact are often actively promoted by large fractions of the population. I also discuss the possibilities of avoiding such consequences, without giving up important policy objectives.

All these essays were written mainly with conditions in highly developed countries in the 1970s and 1980s in mind. I choose to end this book, however, with a discussion of the role of public spending and taxation policies in poor ('developing') countries (Chapter 12), 'Public finances for developing countries', *Liberalization in the Process of Economic Development*, 1991. Much of the inspiration for this paper came from my experience as a consultant to UNCTAD, UNIDO and, in particular, to The World Bank.

In this paper, I reflect on how the role of public finance changes when developing countries shift their economic philosophy from an attempted planning system to something closer to a market system. It is argued that if a country starts to rely more heavily on markets, economic incentives and decentralized initiatives, the 'classical' roles of government shift to the forefront: infrastructure investment in physical and human capital; the supply of public (collective) goods, including the legal system, education, basic research and environmental protection; and redistributional policies in favour of the poor.

When considering various ways of improving the distribution of income in developing countries, from the point of view of rather universal values, I emphasized in particular: (i) attempts to redistribute the ownership of human capital, financial capital and physical assets in favour of low- and low-middle income groups; (ii) removal of institutional obstacles that prevent these groups from participating in the process of income growth; (iii) redistributional considerations when designing general economic policies; and (iv) fiscal policy actions specifically designed to improve the living standards of people in the above-mentioned groups.

It is also argued that those who, for efficiency reasons, are in favour of outward-oriented development strategies have no reason to be shy about their positions from the point of view of the distribution of income – rather the opposite. Considerable experience in countries such as South Korea and Taiwan illustrate this point, as these countries have demonstrated the possibilities of reconciling efficiency and distributional considerations, both by choosing an outward-looking development strategy and by redistributing the ownership of land and human capital at an early stage.

Swedish economists have often participated extensively in discussions of domestic economic policy, not only in journals but also in the mass media – a tradition from the days of Wicksell, Cassel, Ohlin, Myrdal and Lundberg. I have followed this tradition since the mid-1950s, having published some hundred newspaper articles over the years. Although some of my popular contributions in Swedish magazines and newspapers have dealt with issues in my main field of research, i.e., macroeconomics, the bulk of my intervention has been on issues of the welfare state and the organization of the economic system.

In particular, I have devoted considerable time and effort in trying to clarify to the general public the potential contributions of a well-functioning market system, and the importance of improving, rather than sabotaging, this system. I thought that this was particularly important during the high tide of economic policy interventionism and New Left ideology, from the late 1960s to the late 1970s.

This was the background for my book on *The Political Economy of the New Left* in 1971, even if its immediate inspiration was provided by events at Columbia University where I was visiting professor during the turbulent academic year 1968–69. I gave a lecture on the topic at both Columbia University and MIT, and Paul A. Samuelson was kind enough to convince McGraw Hill that the manuscript of the lecture (in extended form) was worth publishing and to suggest that he should write a preface which, beyond any doubt, helped to make the book a success in terms of circulation.

I cannot be the judge as to whether my writings on economic policy and economic system issues have had much influence on the economic policies actually pursued in Sweden. In light of my general experience, however, it is by influencing the general policy discussion and journalists, rather than by serving as an adviser to the government, that lasting effects may be brought about on policies actually pursued. Politicians are, indeed, highly 'endogenous'; they are 'prisoners' of the general policy discussion in the media, as well as of the ideologies and interests of organized groups in society. To help the government write proposals to parliament is like writing in the sand on an ocean beach: the next wave of fashion in public opinion will wash them away.

I do believe, however, that my warnings about the risks of letting so-called 'wage earner funds' (collective funds controlled by labour unions and politicians) take over the ownership of a large fraction of the Swedish economy strengthened the opposition in Sweden against the radical proposal along these lines by the Confederation of Trade Unions and the Social Democratic Party during the period 1975–91. The stance I took on this issue not only angered my old friends in the Social Democratic Party – including Olof Palme, to whom I had been a personal adviser and sparring partner from the mid-1950s until the defeat of the party in the elections of 1976. It also made me leave the Social Democratic Party in 1981, after having felt increasingly uncomfortable throughout the 1970s with the party's rising sympathies for detailed government intervention in the lives of firms and households.

References

(Selected publications on the welfare state not included in this book)

BOOKS
Bostadsbristen – en studie av prisbildningen på bostadsmarknaden (*The Housing Shortage – A Study of Pricing in the Housing Market*) (with Ragnar Bentzel and Ingemar Ståhl), Almqvist & Wiksell, Stockholm 1963.
Mål och medel i jordbrukspolitiken (*Ends and Means of Agricultural Policy*) (with Odd Gulbrandsen), Industriens Utredningsinstitut, Stockholm 1966.
The Economics of the Agricultural Sector (with Odd Gulbrandsen), Industriens Utrednings-institut, Stockholm 1973, 264 pp. (Swedish ed. 1969).
The Political Economy of the New Left, Harper & Row, New York 1971.
Hyreskontroll och bostadsmarknad (*Rent Control and the Housing Market*), assisted by S. Blomqvist, Almqvist & Wiksell, Stockholm 1972.

The Welfare State – Driving Forces, Functioning and Limits, Three Public Lectures, Lee Kuan Yew Distinguished Visitor Public Lecture Series, 1987.

ARTICLES (IN ENGLISH)
'Location policy', *Skandinaviska Banken Quarterly Review*, No. 2, 1964, 41–50.
'Swedish agricultural policy in an international perspective', *Skandinaviska Enskilda Banken Quarterly Review*, No. 4, 1966, 95–106.
'Inequality and redistributional policy issues, principles and Swedish experience' in *Education, inequality and life chances*, Vol. 2, OECD, Paris 1975, 229–385.
'Intergenerational aspects of public transfers, borrowing and debt' (with Jörgen W. Weibull), *Scandinavian Journal of Economics*, No. 1, 1986.
'Balanced-budget redistribution as the outcome of political equilibrium' (with Jörgen W. Weibull), *Public Choice*, **52**, 1987.
'Is the welfare state in trouble?', *Eastern Economic Journal*, **13** (4), Oct/Dec. 1987.
'Altruism and time consistency: The economics of fait accompli' (with Jörgen W. Weibull), *Journal of Political Economy*, 1988.
'A model of political equilibrium in representative democracy' (with Jörgen W. Weibull), *Journal of Public Economics*, 1992.
'Welfare effects of alternative forms of public spending' (with Jörgen W. Weibull), *European Economic Review*, March 1988.
'Public spending and private services – macroeconomic effects' (with Parameswar Nandakumar), *Oxford Economic Papers*, **42** (3), 1990.

PART I

DRIVING FORCES BEHIND THE WELFARE STATE

[1]

KYKLOS, Vol. 28 – 1975 – Fasc. 1, 23–46

THE CHANGING ROLE
OF THE NATIONAL STATE

Assar Lindbeck*

THE CONSOLIDATION OF THE NATIONAL STATE

The consolidation of the national state is one of the most spectacular developments in modern history – from the emergence of the first national states in Europe during the centuries after the medieval period, to the 'high tide' of nationalism in Europe and on the American continent during the 18th and 19th centuries, and finally to the proliferation of national states in our time, in the wake of the decolonization of the less developed countries.

Usually, the consolidation of national states has meant that central, national governments have gained powers at the expense of *both* foreign political powers *and* local interests, such as cities, municipalities, feudal kingdoms and tribes. There has been some controversy among historians as to what the driving forces behind the consolidation of the national states during previous centuries have been – a desire to obtain military protection against common enemies; an ambition to express solidarity among people with a common historic and cultural heritage; a striving for political power and domination by certain individuals and groups, *etc.* [6,9,10,15,16][1]. However, for an economist, it is tempting to look at the consolidation of the national state partly as a method of reducing the costs and troubles for the mobility of commodities, factors of production (labor as well as physical capital), entrepreneurship, technology, and financial capital within a given geographical area. This was achieved by the national state, perhaps in particular in the early phases of its development, by way of unified economic legislation which con-

* University of Stockholm. Based on a lecture delivered at the Van Leer Jerusalem Foundation, Spring 1974.

1. For a detailed bibliography on nationalism and the history of the national state, see [4].

23

ASSAR LINDBECK

cerned, for instance, rules of contracts and ownership, a common currency and tariff system as well as a coordinated infrastructure with respect to, for instance, communication, water supply, production and distribution of energy, education and research.

From this point of view, we might say that the emergence and consolidation of the national state during previous centuries was partly a political adjustment to the economic forces which required larger integrated areas for production, exchange, entrepreneurship and factor mobility. *Local* regulations, such as those concerning tariffs, transportation fees and laws regarding contracts, production and exchange were replaced by *national* rules. The increased returns to scale in production and marketing, so to speak, created increased returns to scale in the political decision-making process, and *vice versa* [11].

It is hazardous to generalize about long historical periods. However, with the risk of over-simplifying, perhaps we could say that the early buildup of national states in Europe from, say, the 16th to the 18th centuries often went hand in hand with a rather centralistic and interventionist national economic policy. I am, of course, thinking of the mercantilistic period [2, 7, 17]. By the term 'mercantilism' I then mean the ideas and practices of economic policy, including trade policy, that dominated in many European countries from the end of the medieval period to about the time of the industrial revolution. The exact meaning of the term mercantilism has been a source of controversy among economic historians. However, the term usually refers to selective and discriminatory state regulations of production, commerce and trade, often for the purpose of increasing the competitive position, and the exchange reserves, mainly gold, of the national economy relative to other countries[2].

2. The following definition in UNESCO's *Dictionary of the Social Sciences* probably gives just about the greatest common denominator for prevailing opinions of what should be meant by mercantilism: 'The term mercantilism denotes the principle of the mercantile system, sometimes understood as the identification of wealth with money; but more generally, the belief that the economic welfare of the state can only be secured by government regulation of nationalist character' [17]. When later on in the paper I talk about a 'new mercantilism', it is mainly the latter, broader part of the definition of mercantilism that is relevant, *i.e.* government regulations of the economy of a nationalist character, usually in fact by rather selective and discriminatory measures.

THE CHANGING ROLE OF THE NATIONAL STATE

However, we also know from our history books that the period of 'high nationalism' in the 18th and, even more, the 19th century, in contrast to the early period of nationalism, often can be characterized as a combination of nationalism and economic liberalism, manifested by the *removal* of a number of mercantilistic regulations. At the same time, many of the remaining areas of the medieval guild system, which had to a considerable extent survived during the mercantilistic period, were abolished when the new liberal principles of freedom from detailed state regulations of production and trade were formally codified by laws in several European countries during the middle of the 19th century [2, 6, 10, 15, 16]. As we know, these new liberal principles of domestic economic and industrial policies were often combined with a foreign trade policy that was considerably more liberal than earlier, in the sense that many trade restrictions were removed and tariffs often kept on a rather low level.

However, probably more important than the removal of the old regulations – which in some countries were not very efficient devices of influencing the new form of industrial activity that developed during the 19th century, such as the new industrial corporations and the private banks – was that the authorities to a large extent abstained from introducing *new* detailed regulations of the production and exchange operations of these new types of economic organization.

The fact that the nationalism of the 19th century was largely combined with economic liberalism has given contemporary Western societies a heritage of a pronounced division of functions and responsibilities between government and business firms. This implies that the individual firms were 'given' the responsibility for production and exchange decisions, whereas government authorities were in charge of the *general rules* – *i.e.* parts of the general institutional environment – within which firms could operate, as well as being in charge of collective services and services with strong external and distributional effects (schools, basic research, hospitals, *etc.*), infrastructure (communication systems, *etc.*), and social security. It was at a rather late stage of the development that governments also started to assume a major responsibility for the income distribution and, mainly during the post-World War II period, economic stability and growth, the latter responsibility manifested by attempts to influence the volume of investment in physical capital, human capital

25

ASSAR LINDBECK

and technology. Even more recently, the responsibility of the national government for major parts of the institutional and man-made physical environment (the infrastructure) has been extended to a major responsibility also for the natural environment, *i. e.* the ecological system.

This division of functions and responsibilities between firms and public authorities in the economic field has probably been a crucial factor behind the pluralism which, to a varying degree, characterizes the Western societies – not only in the economic field, but in political and cultural matters as well. The emergence of labor unions, free from detailed state control, has added considerably to this pluralism by providing a countervailing force against 'Big Business'; the power of this countervailing force has, of course, been particularly pronounced in the 'full employment society' after the Second World War.

It is rather remarkable that the expansion of the responsibilities of the public sector during the course of this century – in particular after the Second World War – has *largely* taken place within the framework of the above-mentioned 'traditional' division of functions between the national state, firms, and organizations even though public production now is a somewhat larger fraction of GNP than earlier; in most developed countries in the West, it accounts today for between 15 and 25 percent of total output (OECD Statistics).

The pluralistic character of the economic, political and cultural systems in Western Europe and North America is particularly obvious if we compare them with the countries of state capitalism in Eastern Europe (as well as with some less developed countries, LDCs), where a characteristic feature of the economic and political system is just the *absence* of far-reaching division of functions and responsibilities between firms, organizations, and public authorities. Instead we may talk about the *hegemony* of politics over economic matters, including a hegemony of government authorities over firms, and often also over labor unions; and hence over decisions concerning production, exchange, investment, and frequently prices and wages.

RECENT DEVELOPMENTS

It is hazardous to generalize not only about long-term historical trends, such as the development over centuries, but also about recent

THE CHANGING ROLE OF THE NATIONAL STATE

trends. However, most observers would probably agree that the 1930s and early 1940s witnessed a strong deviation from the previously described liberal economic policy, both domestically and in the field of international economic relations. The various national states tried to solve their own domestic problems during the depression of the 1930s and during the Second World War by strengthening the powers of their national governments. In particular, the international interdependence was reduced by measures such as exchange controls, import regulations, high tariffs, competitive devaluations, multiple exchange rates, *etc.* Domestic policies also become more interventionist than earlier, in particular of course during the war, due to the centralized regulations of prices, wages, and the allocation of resources, as well as of the distribution of consumer goods among households.

At the end of the Second World War, a return to a liberal national and international economic system was regarded as unlikely by many experts, including JOHN MAYNARD KEYNES. However, history – as so often – turned in an unexpected direction. The 1950s implied, in fact, a drastic liberalization of economic policy; *within countries,* by way of the removal, or at least liberalization of price and wage controls, and physical regulations of the allocation of resources such as via building controls and rationing of raw materials, consumer goods and capital goods; in the field of *external economic relations* by way of the removal of import controls, the lowering of tariffs and the partial return to convertibility (most dramatically after 1958). Instead of direct, and often strongly discriminatory, regulations, a number of rather *general,* indirect policy tools were introduced: a 'Keynesian' macro policy designed to influence aggregate demand, mainly by way of a more flexible monetary and fiscal policy.

As we know, the liberalization of the *external* economic policies continued, and even accelerated, during the sixties and early seventies, for instance by six rounds of general tariff cuts in the context of bargaining within GATT, and by the formation of wider and wider regional trading blocs. However, parallel with this liberalization of foreign trade, there seems to be a new tendency in the late sixties and early seventies to again return to the exercise of rather detailed government interventions in the *domestic* economy. Hence, we have in recent years witnessed a historically rather unusual com-

27

ASSAR LINDBECK

bination of reduced intervention in the external relations and in-creased intervention in internal economic matters. We shall see that these divergent trends in foreign and domestic economic policies, respectively, are related to each other and that many interesting problems are connected with the interrelations between them.

Is it true, as is sometimes asserted, that we are moving away from the liberal, decentralized market model that has so far dominated the development during the last hundred years (except for the 1930s and the two World Wars), to something more resembling the strongly regulated mercantilistic society which we left behind us during the course of the last century, or maybe to a society more resembling the strongly centralistic systems of state capitalism in Eastern Europe?

To help supply answers to this question, let us consider the follow-ing three problems. First: what are the driving forces behind the new developments? Second: what problems are created for the national states by these developments, *i.e.* how does the development change the role in the economic and political system of the national state? And third: what are the alternative possibilities of dealing with these problems?

NEW FORCES

It may be useful to make a distinction here between (1) international forces and (2) domestic forces, behind contemporary tendencies to a changing role for the national state.

International forces

A celebrated aspect of the technical, economic and cultural develop-ment during the present century, and perhaps in particular during the post-World War II period, is that a great number of human activities have expanded more drastically than earlier across the borders of the national states: research, education, technology, sports, fashion, art, ideology, knowledge and culture in general. This inter-nationalization process is, perhaps, particularly strong for the eco-nomic system, which during the post-World War II period has be-come increasingly international in character, in the sense that the

28

THE CHANGING ROLE OF THE NATIONAL STATE

international mobility of commodities, factors of production, entrepreneurship, technology and financial capital has increased enormously [3, 11].

In other words, the economic system tends to be more and more *international* in character, at the same time as the political system has largely continued to be *national*. Thus, whereas the consolidation of the national state in the 18th and 19th centuries was a logical adjustment of the political system to the geographic expansions of the economic system, the national state today tends to run into trouble just because the economic system, in contrast to the political system, goes on expanding geographically over the borders of existing national states. *Many national and international problems of today can in fact fruitfully be seen in the perspective of the tensions between a more and more internationalized economic system and still mainly nationally based political systems.* What we are experiencing is an increased difficulty in fitting the new international economic forces – brought about by modern technology and modern economic growth – into traditional political concepts and institutions, based on the notion of sovereign national states.

The internationalization process is particularly apparent in the *market system*; in markets for commodities, factors of production, entrepreneurship, technology and financial capital. For instance, export and import play an increasingly important role in nearly every sector of the national economy, and individual consumers and firms can to an increasing extent choose between commodities from the whole world, implying that individual firms are confronted with competitors from more and more nations. The markets are increasingly becoming world markets rather than national markets[3].

3. The fraction of total exports (or imports) to GNP has not expanded drastically during the post-World War II period, in spite of the fact that exports (imports) have substantially increased their share within practically all sectors of the economy. The reason is, of course, that at the same time as nearly every sector has become more international in character, the composition of GNP (in current prices) has shifted to sectors with a small foreign trade content, mainly public services. Thus, aggregate figures over total exports (imports) as a fraction of GNP, 'hide' the fact that firms (outside the public service sector) experience a more and more international environment, and that the same holds for households in their role as consumers [11].

ASSAR LINDBECK

We can also notice a considerable internationalization of a number of important *institutions*, perhaps in particular 'market-oriented' institutions, such as production firms. Production by subsidiaries abroad is, for many nations, expanding about twice as fast as production for the firms' own home markets. While the production volume, measured as Gross National Product, during the 1960s has expanded by some 4 percent per year in most countries, imports and exports have often increased by about 8 percent per year and production by subsidiaries abroad by some 10 or 12 percent per year [3, 5, 11].

A similar internationalization of institutions is occurring in the markets for insurance, travelling, consulting and, perhaps most dramatically, money and credit, for instance by the development of international banks and other international credit institutes, such as those operating in the Eurocurrency and Eurobond markets.

The 'geographical strips' on the world map which define the nations are, in other words, penetrated more and more by economic, technological and cultural forces. In fact, the expansion of multinational economic organizations implies that the world is increasingly dominated by two quite differently organized entities: 'geographically' defined national states, and 'footloose' multinational organizations, such as firms, labor unions and industrial organizations, built up along 'functional' lines, such as industrial branches, or possibly as international conglomerates for a number of different economic activities.

We can also see how the so-called *externalities* of the production system become more and more international in character. Some of the most important externalities today – the pollution of the air and the sea, as well as exploitation of the riches in the oceans (such as fish) and on or below the seabed (minerals and oil) – are not only 'external' with respect to the individual firm but to the individual nation as well. In fact, many of the most important externalities of the production process today are *international externalities*.

The rapid 'internationalization' of the economic system of the western world is partly just a 'catching-up' process from the time before the First World War, as the two world wars and the thirties resulted in a drastic regression in the internationalization process.

THE CHANGING ROLE OF THE NATIONAL STATE

The main *new* features after the Second World War in the internationalization process, as compared to the decades before the First World War, are perhaps (1) the increased importance of international trade within nearly *all* sectors of the economy (except for the growing public service sector), including private services such as banking, insurance, travel, holiday life, consulting, *etc.*; (2) the internationalization of entrepreneurship and technology; and (3) the increasingly international character of the externalities of the production process.

It is also often asserted, perhaps correctly, that many modern economies today are both more *vulnerable* and more *sensitive* to conditions in other countries. They would be more vulnerable in the sense that some strategic factors in the production process are imported from abroad (oil and uranium being obvious examples), and also that a number of large firms, and hence the employment level in these, are extremely dependent on foreign markets. It is also often believed, probably quite rightly, that the international flows of goods, services and factors tend to become more and more *sensitive* to marginal changes (or differences) in economic and political variables between nations [3]. We have seen how interest rate differentials between nations, and expected changes in exchange rates, can generate enormous financial flows between countries. For instance, when the U.S. tried to stimulate the domestic economy during the early sixties through lower interest rates, a major effect was that financial capital was invested abroad rather than in the U.S. in order to attain higher returns. And when West Germany tried several times during the sixties to fight domestic inflation by introducing higher interest rates, a main effect was that the domestic credit market was flooded with liquidity, hence making the restrictive monetary policy actions impotent. We can also notice how, particularly in the fixed exchange rate system of the past (the Bretton Woods system), international inflation 'brutally' crosses the national borders, making national governments rather powerless in domestic price policies. It is also possible that we experience increased sensitivity to the location in the world of highly trained individuals and real investment by firms, in response to differences in, for instance, tax legislation and the general political environment for business activity in various countries.

31

ASSAR LINDBECK

The consequences of the internationalization process can also be seen in other fields of economic policy. For instance, we have noticed a stiffer international competition and a tendency for profit margins in most countries to fall during the course of the 1960s, and the comparative advantage among countries to change more rapidly than earlier. As a consequence, the rate of structural change of many economies has speeded up. A result has been increased structural unemployment and increased regional dispersion of unemployment within countries. We have also noticed a tendency to an increased rate of mergers by firms and in some countries reduced investment incentives, as a response to stiffer competition [11].

What are the *factors* underlying this internationalization of the economic system? Perhaps we could schematically make a distinction here between technological and political factors. On the technological side, the most important factor is perhaps that there seems to have been a *bias* in the technological development in favor of communication and transport, which has about the same effect on world trade as a fall in tariffs. Commodities and services which were not earlier profitable to trade internationally become profitable to trade when transportation costs fell relative to other costs.

The fall in communication costs has occurred not only in the transportation of commodities but also, and perhaps even more, in the communication of messages. The cost of leading organizations over large distances has fallen enormously as a result of developments in telecommunication and data technology. For the first time in history, it has been possible to direct effectively the operations of firms over the entire globe. This is probably one of the main explanations for the rapid expansion of multinational firms. Another technological factor which has boosted the expansion of international firms is that technology, by being more complicated, has also become more *complementary* than earlier to managerial skill. This makes it increasingly profitable to sell technology *in combination* with managerial skill, rather than selling technology separately, for instance by patent rights. In other words, it becomes more profitable to move *packages* of technology and managerial skill between countries, rather than selling the technological knowledge separately [11]. And this 'package' of technology and managerial skill is exactly what is provided by the internationally operating multinational firm. As we

32

THE CHANGING ROLE OF THE NATIONAL STATE

know, the package often also includes two other important components: capital and organization for marketing [5].

Also the increasingly international character of the externalities in the production process is, of course, largely caused by technological developments, when environmental disruptions expand over larger and larger geographical areas.

However, in addition to the technological factors, there are also important *political factors* behind the internationalization of the economic system. The Western countries agreed, after the Second World War, to establish a 'liberal' international economic system built on free trade, reflected for instance in the GATT rules about non-discrimination and 'most-favored nation' clauses.

This ensuing trade liberalization has been an important prerequisite for much of the just-mentioned process of internationalization of markets and market-oriented institutions. This point is supported by the observation that the economic internationalization process has largely been prevented in that sector where trade liberalization has not been implemented: European agriculture.

When politicians, by their own decisions, have contributed to a process of economic internationalization, they have in fact helped to release international economic forces which they cannot control very well, most recently illustrated by international inflation, oil and raw material price increases, balance-of-payments problems and 'turmoil' in markets for foreign exchange. The 'operation domain' of markets and market-oriented organizations, such as firms, more and more exceeds the 'jurisdiction domain' of the national state. This has resulted, as we know, in that the national state, in field after field, has become a less and less effective unit of policy-making. Thus national governments have, like the Wizard's Apprentice, helped to release forces which are beyond their powers to control[4].

---

4. There is *perhaps* a parallel in the military field, where it is often argued that modern technology has made the national state a less efficient unit than earlier for defence, and that this is the main reason for the emergence of systems of 'collective security', composed of agreements between a great number of national states. As military coalitions between nations are hardly anything new in history, the point is perhaps that modern technology has made such coalitions more important than earlier and that they, to be effective, have to comprise a larger number of countries than earlier [8]?

ASSAR LINDBECK

Domestic forces

There are also a number of *domestic* reasons for the contemporary problems of the national state. First of all, the ambitions of governments have greatly increased in economic and social policies, which is perhaps most clearly reflected in the expansion of the size of public budgets. In many developed countries in the west today, total public expenditures constitute some 35–50 percent of the GNP, of which direct public 'resource-use' (public investment plus public consumption) is often of the magnitude of 20–30 percent of the GNP, whereas public transfer payments (including social security payments) usually constitute some 15–20 percent of the GNP.

Another important factor behind the changing role of the national state is that the policy targets have become increasingly differentiated. Governments are no longer satisfied with keeping a low *general* level of unemployment; they try to influence unemployment in *specific* sectors and regions and for *specific* types of employees such as married women, handicapped, elderly people, teen-agers, racial minorities, *etc*. We can also see how governments not only try to influence the vertical distribution of income, *i.e.* the distribution between different income brackets (the 'size distribution' of income), but also the distribution among specific socioeconomic groups – small farmers, people in declining rural areas, employees in specific industries, *etc*.

These more ambitious and disaggregated *targets* have often meant that available policy instruments are no longer appropriate; it has become increasingly necessary to have more differentiated and selective policy instruments.

Besides these changes in targets and instruments in politics, there may also be some 'immanent' tendencies in the economic system creating more need for interventionist policies. One example are the increased inflationary tendencies, which have induced more detailed governmental intervention in price formations, through price and wage control – 'incomes policy'. Another example is the rather permanent tendency toward balance-of-payments problems in a number of countries; this tendency has, of course, been a consequence of the system of fixed exchange rates which is, in fact, a disequilibrium system for the balance of payments, as the price for foreign exchange

THE CHANGING ROLE OF THE NATIONAL STATE

is then removed as an equilibrating mechanism. The increased scale of investment decisions in many industries, with repercussions on the entire economy, is another example of a factor which may have created demands for more central planning in various countries. Moreover, the increased expansion of public services in fields such as education, health and infrastructure rather automatically gives the central authorities a stronger say in the economy, though we now also see the emergence of ambitions by people in local communities in several countries to attain more 'local control'. Finally – and this is potentially important – the emergence of new environmental disturbances, and thereby connected emphasis on environment policy, means that a number of new important selective policy targets is introduced, as environment policy by its nature has to be rather differentiated for regions, types of disturbances and branches.

Personally, I also believe that the increased centralization and concentration of the powers of mass media, such as television, have increased the tendency of *specific* and *concrete* problems being highlighted, problems which politicians believe are necessary to deal with immediately by way of new laws, administrative regulation, or subsidies. Mass media can easily dramatize specific and concrete problems, which are easy noted by journalists and easy to show to the general public – a polluting factory, a poor farmer, an unemployed elderly worker in a declining area, *etc.* – whereas general, and more abstract problems, which often can be solved by rather *general* policies, are much more difficult to understand and transmit by mass media.

While opinion formation in earlier periods was rather slow, due to several decentralized channels of transmission of opinions, with an indirect effect on policy often by way of general elections, we seem to have obtained a society in recent years where politicians regard it as necessary to act directly, from case to case, after interventions of powerful mass media that reach practically the whole population immediately. In this situation, there are strong temptations for politicians to take improvised steps, from case to case, resulting in selective interventions on an *ad hoc* basis.

ASSAR LINDBECK

DEFENSE MECHANISM BY THE NATIONAL STATE

Thus, at the same time as national governments have raised their ambitions to direct the details of the domestic economies, international forces have made both many targets and several policy instruments less susceptible to domestic national manipulation than earlier. Many new problems can be fruitfully seen in the perspective of these increased domestic policy ambitions in combination with the weakening of the power of the national state relative to the ever stronger international forces. 'People' demand more and more of the national state, at the same time as the national state is losing much of its autonomy because of the internationalization process. This may be an important explanation for the apparent increased dissatisfaction in many countries with the performance of the national governments.

The problems are particularly acute for the LDCs. Many of them are now in the process of trying to build up their national states, *i. e.* to achieve political integration internally, at the same time as the world economic system tends to be more internationalized. Thus, whereas the political consolidation of the national states in the presently developed societies during the nineteenth century was well in harmony with the economic integration of the various local markets that occurred at that time, the LDCs of today try to achieve a political consolidation on a national level in a situation where markets and firms tend to 'explode' over the borders of the national state.

It would be a vast exaggeration, and even a misunderstanding, to talk about a 'death struggle' of the national state in the wake of the ever stronger international forces. But we can probably say that some 'defense mechanisms' of the national states have been released, when a number of problems have proved to be increasingly difficult to handle by previously existing instruments on the level of the individual national state. Such defense mechanisms show up in the form of a number of new policy tools, designed to prevent undesirable domestic developments and to restore some of the lost autonomy of the national state. It is, in this context, quite proper to talk about a 'new mercantilistic policy', as a number of countries have introduced strongly selective subsidies of production, investment, employment,

THE CHANGING ROLE OF THE NATIONAL STATE

research and development; public supply of capital; credit priorities; selective fees for imports and selective subsidies of exports; the tying of foreign aid to domestic exports; and increased protectionism in government purchases [11]. We can also see how product standards for environmental protection are, in fact, sometimes used for protectionist purposes in various countries. All this means also a tendency to a more centralistic economic system – at the same time as many citizens start to demand more decentralization, regional self-determination, and 'grass root participation'.

PROBLEMS WITH NEW POLICY TENDENCIES

The new mercantilist tendencies can be seen *both* in declining industries, where we might talk about 'defensive' measures, such as in textiles, *and* in research-intensive industries where we might talk about 'offensive' measures, such as in computers, atomic energy, electronics, and aircraft industries.

In certain cases, the selective measures might be seen as attempts to *improve* the information and incentive content of the price system from the point of view of economic efficiency. Examples of this are taxes on environmental disturbances, *general* subsidies on the use of labor in unemployment areas, *general* taxes on employment in overheated areas, *general* wage subsidies to elderly and handicapped people, who would otherwise, at the prevailing wage rate, be unemployed, *etc.*

However, to a large extent, the new mercantilistic policy is just a new shape of the old *protectionism*, as tariffs and import regulations have largely been removed as policy instruments from national governments by way of international agreements. When nations feel the pinch of increased international competition in some sectors, they introduce new protectionist measures which are not prohibited by international agreements, or which are difficult to control by authorities in other countries. For instance, strongly selective subsidies in the context of location policy, industrial policy or environmental policy are often used for clear protectionist purposes; the 'new mercantilism' is therefore in reality largely a new form of protectionism.

There is, of course, an obvious risk of serious distortions of the

37

ASSAR LINDBECK

allocation of resources, when the number and size of selective subsidies and taxes are spread throughout the system. Moreover, the
possibilities of individual firms prolonging mistakes are vastly increased when governments start guaranteeing their profitability by
subsidies. The French-British Concorde project is an obvious example
among many. And the working load for governments will increase
enormously when they have to administer and make decisions on
selective subsidies and interventions.

But the 'most important' effect, for society at large, is perhaps that
the power distribution may change in a rather complicated way. It
may, to begin with, be tempting to argue that there will be a concentration of power to centrally placed politicians and public officials within the nations. This is probably a correct hypothesis, even
if the new mercantilism, in contrast to the old one, perhaps does not
have, as its *main* goal, the increasing of the powers of the representatives of the national state. However, at the same time, entrepreneurs,
particularly in large firms, obtain a new means of competition: bargaining and dealing with public officials and politicians in order to
receive subsidies and various other kinds of discriminatory favors.
If these tendencies go on very far, *we might wind up in an economic system
where good contacts with government officials and politicians become more important for successful operations by firms than the ability of the management
to pursue efficient production, innovations and marketing.* I think this is in
fact what has already happened in a number of less developed
countries.

This could create a situation, paradoxically enough, where *both*
a number of politicians and administrators, and a number of managers of large firms, would have increased possibilities of acting, at
the cost of small firm managers and those with a limited ability or
willingness to bargain and make deals with public authorities. Politicians and administrators can easily make deals with a few big managers of large firms, but hardly with thousands of small businessmen.
I do not know how far the development has gone in this direction;
there are very few, if any, systematic empirical studies. However, in
some countries I think the development has progressed considerably
in recent years.

How to judge a development along these lines is, of course, a question of rather subjective values, *i.e.* about the desired role in the

THE CHANGING ROLE OF THE NATIONAL STATE

economic system of the government. Hence, everyone has considerable leeway to make his own evaluations. On the one hand, some
people may argue that it is 'good' that publicly appointed politicians
get more power relative to business leaders, in fact in particular
relative to those who are not able or willing to make selective bargains
and deals with government officials. On the other hand, some people
may regret that part of the pluralism in our society tends to get lost
when managers of large corporations, public officials and politicians
all become so involved in each others' business that it in practice
will be very difficult, if not impossible, to say who has really the
responsibility when something goes wrong. The risks for corruption
will also be considerable – as illustrated not only in several LDCs,
but also in some developed countries (such as the NIXON administration). If leaders of labor market organizations also become closely
involved in these deals, the threat to the pluralism is even larger, as
we then may wind up in a 'coalition' between leading politicians,
top public administrators, 'big' businessmen and top leaders of labor
market organizations. A 'corporate state' would partly replace the
traditional 'liberal state', which was based on the notion that the
state *mainly* establishes *the general rules* which the actions of various
private agents and organizations have to obey, rather than trying to
enter a coalition with these various agents. The tendency to 'joint
ventures' between governments and firms in two or more countries
may even make some of these coalitions 'international' in character;
it is interesting to see how some people start to talk about 'trans-
ideological corporations', consisting of an amalgamation of private
firms and governments from different countries. (The establishment
of such firms, based on cooperations between firms and governments
in capitalist and socialist countries has been advocated by, for instance, S. PISAR [14].)

If these tendencies go on for a long time we might, instead of a
'mixed economy' with a private sector *alongside* a public one, get
what the Swedish economist ERIK LUNDBERG has called a 'mixture
economy' with an unclear division of labor and responsibility between managers, politicians, public administrators, and labor union
leaders [13]. Those who are particularly suspicious about this 'new
coalition' might even fear a situation where well-informed people
no longer find it in their interest to criticize various evils in society.

39

ASSAR LINDBECK

A business manager who is dependent on public grants, subsidies, licenses, or favors in public purchases, will hardly be expected to criticize politicians and officials upon whose decisions he continuously depends. Similarly, politicians and public officials will find it natural to maintain good relations with the managers of the big firms, with whom they have to deal continuously.

Thus, a general collaboration easily emerges between managers, politicians, public officials, and possibly also labor union leaders, where only those who are willing to risk their careers, or those who are so young so that they do not understand that they risk their careers, will protest and criticize. Instead of a pluralistic society, we may arrive at a 'dualistic' society with, on the one hand, insiders, 'the establishment', who keep together, and, on the other hand, alienated 'outsiders' who have difficulties in obtaining proper information for an effective critique of society.

However, it is important to keep the 'proportions' in the discussion straight, particularly in a historical perspective. First of all, I have been talking here about *tendencies* rather than a completed development. Secondly, in modern times (from the industrial revolution) there have probably always been selective and highly discriminatory interventions in investment and production decisions by government officials, as well as bargaining and coalitions between governments and large firms. The building of the railway system during the late 19th and early 20th centuries is probably a good example of this. It is, in fact, rather difficult to compare the degree of selective interventions in production and investment decisions during periods that are far apart in time. What seems to be obvious, however, is that the fifties and early sixties witnessed a reduction in detailed, selective and highly discriminatory interventions and that the late sixties and early seventies have been characterized by an increase in such interventions.

NEW RULES OF CONDUCT?

There are, perhaps, many good reasons for the increased interventionist policies which we see today in many countries – *both* to adjust to the stronger international forces that hit the national economies

THE CHANGING ROLE OF THE NATIONAL STATE

today, market forces as well as the challenge to nations by large and internationally operating organizations, *and* to make it possible to reach the more ambitious and detailed policy targets that are characteristic for many governments. A question worth asking, though, is whether it is possible to satisfy the new policy ambitions with a minimum of new protectionism and a minimum of concentration of powers to the individual politicians and administrators representing the national government, and in some cases, 'associated' leaders of large corporations and powerful labor unions.

For instance, maybe it is possible to establish some *concrete rules of conduct* so that national governments can avoid the gravest risks of protectionism and concentration of power. More specifically, rules such as the following might be considered, some of them perhaps to be decided by individual nations themselves (such as rules 1 to 4 below) others to be agreed upon by nations (such as rules 5 and 6 below).

First of all, to avoid a serious deformation of the price system, the following rule is perhaps worth considering:

Rule 1: Make the intervention where the original distortion is, and avoid making the measure more selective than is necessary for its primary purpose.

For instance, attempts to increase employment in a declining area could be met by a *general* subsidy of labor cost in that area, rather than picking out some specific firm which would then be given selective subsidies with immediate protectionist implications and centralization of economic decision-making. And environmental disturbances could be fought, as much as possible, by fees (effluence charges) and *general* rules about maximum emissions and minimum safety.

Secondly, to fight low investment incentives and unemployment in a world of stiffer international competition, without using highly selective and centralistic policies, the following two rules may be worth considering:

Rule 2: If the general level of profits are squeezed in the national economy, devalue the exchange rate, or try general fiscal and monetary policy stimulation of investment, rather than selective subsidies to specific branches and firms.

Rule 3: Develop programs for domestic 'adjustment policies', such

41

ASSAR LINDBECK

as labor market policies and mobility increasing programs, as well as a system of income compensation within and between countries, and/or admit greater flexibility in wage relations so that the employee himself can choose between, on the one hand, money income, and, on the other hand, working conditions and geographical location. If subsidies of production are introduced in a declining sector, create some guarantee that they become *temporary* and that they do not result in expanded capacity in the sector.

To economize with the scarce administrative and political capacity in a country, and to avoid permanently increasing bureaucratization of human life, it would be most important that governments accept the following idea:

Rule 4: Concentrate on really *important* interventions designed to correct huge market failures, and try systematically to abolish some of the enormous number of government interventions that have accumulated over the decades, sometimes designed to solve rather trivial problems, and at other times being in fact 'counterproductive' relative to their purpose.

Moreover, to avoid protectionist measure for balance-of-payments reasons, the following rule may be of some use:

Rule 5: Admit greater flexibility in exchange rates, and develop better functioning international capital and credit markets, also between governments and central banks of various countries.

In the same way as markets for commodities, factors and capital help coordinate decentralized decision-making *within* nations, better functioning markets for foreign exchange and capital could to some extent help to coordinate 'decentralized' political decision-making by nations in a highly interdependent world economy.

However, perhaps the greatest challenge to the national state in our time is that many important problems cannot any longer be efficiently solved on the level of national states. Circumstances make it more and more necessary for the individual national state to co-operate with other states and with international organizations. In addition to international agreements on the international monetary system, and the systems of tariffs and import regulations, it may be useful to adhere also to the following well known advice:

Rule 6: Try to establish agreements between governments on principles for acceptable and non-acceptable economic policy measures –

42

THE CHANGING ROLE OF THE NATIONAL STATE

a kind of international code of conduct as a complement to the GATT rules – and try to develop systems for cooperation between governments also in fields such as stabilization policy, environmental protection, and the rules of the operations of multinational firms.

In fact, contemporary attempts by governments to form new international or regional authorities above the level of national states – *i.e.* attempts to internationalize the political system – can, of course, be seen largely as a response to the internationalization of the economic system. However, an important point here is that the grouping of nations in such a cooperation should not necessarily be the same for *all* questions. For instance, geographical closeness may be the crucial factor in grouping countries for cooperation about many environmental problems and infrastructure investment; similarity in economic structure may be an important factor in creating a system with a well-functioning monetary relation, whereas agreements about tariffs and trade relations certainly have to include countries of all types participating in international trade, if we are anxious to avoid trade wars and a general anarchy in international trade relations.

Whereas *Rule 6* – increased *international coordination* of national policies – implies an attempt to bring the political system of the world more in line with the more and more internationalized economic system, *Rules 1 to 4* – dealing with general economic policy, internal adjustments and compensation mechanisms – are attempts to make *national* policies more efficient by reducing the various disadvantages connected with the economic internationalization process. *Rule 5*, finally, is an attempt to create automatic adjustment mechanisms between the national states, in order to retain a considerable national autonomy of economic policy, without having to accept either a retreat in the internationalization process or more centralist and interventionist policies within the various countries.

In establishing concrete rules of conduct of this type, it might be possible to prevent, to some extent, a regression into protectionism and into subsidies of inefficient production. It might then also be possible to keep, to a considerable extent, the autonomy of individual firms and labor organizations, and hence a continued division of labor between the state, firms and labor unions. This would also mean that we could to some extent prevent an increasingly cen-

ASSAR LINDBECK

tralistic society, and also prevent a closer and closer coalition between managers of large corporations, public officials, politicians and top labor union leaders – and hence keep a fairly pluralistic society, rather than having a continuing development towards a more and more centralistic and 'monolithic', corporativistic state.

BIBLIOGRAPHY

[1] BALDWIN ROBERT E.: *Nontariff Distortions of International Trade*, Washington, D.C., The Brookings Institution, 1970.
[2] COLEMAN D.C. (Ed.): *Revisions in Mercantilism*, London, Methuen & Co. Ltd., 1969.
[3] COOPER RICHARD N.: *The Economics of Interdependence*, New York, McGraw-Hill, 1968.
[4] DEUTSCH KARL W. and MERRITT RICHARD L.: *Nationalism and National Development. An Interdisciplinary Bibliography*, Cambridge, Mass., The MIT Press, 1970.
[5] DUNNING J. (Ed.): *Economic Analysis and the Multinational Enterprise*, London, Allen & Unwin (forthcoming).
[6] HAYES C.J.H.: *Nationalism: A Religion*, New York, Macmillan, 1960.
[7] HECKSCHER E.: *Mercantilism*, London, Allen & Unwin, 1955.
[8] LERCHE C.O., Jr. and SAID A.A.: *Concepts of International Politics*, Englewood Cliffs, N.J., Prentice-Hall, 1970.
[9] MOHR H.J.: *The Idea of Nationalism*, New York, Macmillan, 1944, 1961.
[10] MOHR H.J.: *Nationalism: Its Meaning and History*, Princeton, Van Nostrand, 1955.
[11] LINDBECK A.: *The National State in an Internationalized World Economy*, Rio de Janeiro, Conjunto, Universitário Candido Mendes, 1973. (Also in Seminar Paper No. 26, Institute for International Economic Studies, University of Stockholm, Sweden.)
[12] LINDBECK A.: 'Possible Future International Conflicts in a Growing World Economy', in: M. MAROIS (Ed.), *Towards a Plan of Actions for Mankind*, Amsterdam-New York, North-Holland, 1974.
[13] LUNDBERG E.: Panel discussion, *Veckans Affärer*, No. 39, 1971, p. 23.
[14] PISAR S.: 'Global Ends and National Means. Present State and Future Perspective', Nobel Symposium 29, *Man, Environment, and Resources*, Stockholm, September 16–20, 1974.
[15] SHAFER B.C.: *Nationalism, Myth and Reality*, New York, Harcourt, Brace and Co., 1955.
[16] SHAFER B.C.: *Faces of Nationalism*, New York, Harcourt Brace Jovanovich, Inc., 1972.
[17] UNESCO: 'Mercantilism', in: *Dictionary of the Social Sciences*, New York, Macmillan, 1964, pp. 423–424.

[2]

Journal of Public Economics 28 (1985) 309–328. North-Holland

REDISTRIBUTION POLICY AND THE EXPANSION OF THE PUBLIC SECTOR

Assar LINDBECK*

Institute for International Economic Studies, University of Stockholm, S-106 91 Stockholm, Sweden

During the first part of this century, life-cycle and insurance-type considerations seem to have dominated redistribution policy, in particular when we look at the consequences for the expansion of public spending. By contrast, during recent decades, 'fragmented horizontal redistributions' between various minority groups have probably been the most important mechanisms. The self-interest of different groups of the electorate seems to have provided the most powerful motive behind these various policies, although welfare altruism and what in this paper are called considerations of 'consequential externalities' have probably been important motives behind redistribution in favor of the poor.

1. Introduction

The purpose of this paper is to explore the role of redistribution policy in the expansion of the public sector, as defined by expenditures and revenues of public budgets. The importance of this particular explanation of the expansion of the public sector is already suggested by the fact that the bulk of public spending today does not consist of collective goods and infrastructure expenditures, but rather of transfer payments, social security benefits and the subsidization or public provision of different types of non-collective, i.e. 'private', services to households; that is, expenditures with obvious redistributional consequences. Thus, what has to be explained is the emergence and expansion of a 'redistribution state'.

The exposition is organized around four types of asserted *targets* of redistribution policy:

(1) broad horizontal redistributions, i.e. redistributions among broad socioeconomic groups (or classes), regardless of the place of both the beneficiaries and the benefactors in the vertical (size) distribution of income and wealth;

(2) life-cycle and insurance-type redistributions for given individuals;

(3) vertical redistributions, explicitly designed to modify the size distribution of income, wealth or economic welfare; and

*Professor of International Economics, and Director of the Institute for International Economic Studies, University of Stockholm. I am grateful for comments on an earlier draft from Lars Anell, James Buchanan, Lars Calmfors, Thorvaldur Gylfason, Leif Lewin, George Stigler, Jörgen W. Weibull, Björn Wittrock and two anonymous referees.

(4) fragmented horizontal redistributions among a great number of minority groups of citizens in a society with a highly differentiated socioeconomic structure.

Since the last-mentioned target seems to have dominated redistribution policies in recent decades, particular effort will be made to understand redistribution of that type.

Different phases of redistribution policy will in this paper be identified as shifts over time in the emphasis not only of these different targets but also of various *instruments* of redistribution policy. The distinction between such phases will be further clarified by an analysis also of the *motives* of redistribution policy – here classified into three broad categories.[1] One is the use of the coercive authority of the state, by various agents, to further their own economic interest, with or without envy towards others – 'the narrow self-interest motive'. A second motive, 'welfare altruism', reflects positive attitudes towards the living standards of beneficiaries who are less affluent than those who bring about the redistributions. More specifically, the living standards of less affluent people enter the individual preference function with positive partial derivatives – in contrast to the case of envy, where the living standards of more affluent people enter the individual preference function with negative partial derivatives. Welfare altruism is often connected with what will be called, for lack of a better name, 'welfare ideology'.

While the second motive (like envy) reflects externalities between the preference functions of different individuals, i.e. 'dependent preferences', the third motive to be considered is based on the expected consequences for society at large of alternative distributions of income. For instance, poverty and/or inequality may result in seedy neighborhoods, miserable looking people and perhaps political instability. Redistribution policies based on such considerations will be said to reflect 'attitudes towards consequential externalities' of redistribution policy. Even though the last two mentioned motives – welfare altruism and the attitudes towards consequential externalities – could, of course, be regarded as expressions of a *broad* self-interest of the individual [see Thurow (1971), Hochman and Rogers (1969)], a differentiation between the three motives is a useful device to highlight important distinctions in redistribution policy.

The actual operation of all three motives is assumed to depend on both the living standard and political power of various agents in society. Such factors will be lumped together under the heading *driving forces*, or proximate circumstances, which in turn are strongly related to the socioeconomic structure and the political constitution. These driving forces are often, in turn, influenced by redistribution policy itself, which then feeds back on some of the conditions that initiate the policy. To the extent that these driving

---

[1]This classification of motives is broadly similar to the classification in Tullock (1983).

forces are explained by more 'fundamental' factors in this paper, reference will be made in particular to technological and demographic conditions, which will be lumped together here under the term *background factors*.

The distinctions in the paper between targets, instruments, motives, driving forces and background factors of redistribution policy, are schematically summarized in fig. 1.

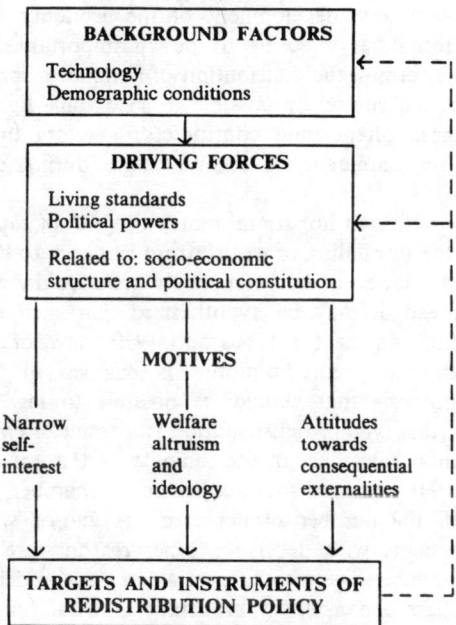

Fig. 1. Analytical structure of redistribution policy.

2. Broad horizontal redistributions

2.1. Labor and capital income shares

Perhaps the most obvious example of 'broad horizontal redistributions' is changes in the distribution of national income between labor income and capital income. Even though the classical economists were interested in just this breakdown of national income, conscious policies to influence it hardly existed before the emergence of macroeconomic growth and stabilization policies after the Second World War. It is tempting to hypothesize that leftist governments, as a reflection of both ideology and the short-term self-interest of their voters, usually try to increase the labor income share of national income, while, on the other hand, rightist governments try to boost the capital income share. However, this is clearly too simple a generalization. Governments of all colors often try to protect the capital income share for the purpose of keeping up capacity utilization, employment and capital formation, by for instance putting brakes on real wage rates by way of 'incomes policies' or devaluations. Thus, consideration of the medium- and long-term macroeconomic development of the economy – an example of consequential externalities – seems to be an important additional factor behind policies concerning the distribution of national income between labor and capital. Indeed, it should be possible to shed some light on the relative importance of these often quite contradictory factors by comparing the development of the capital–labor income share during different political regimes.

In the category of 'broad horizontal redistributions' of capital income, may also be included the reshuffling of wealth from creditors to debtors by way of inflation, when the latter is not completely reflected in after-tax nominal interest rates. Indeed, it may be hypothesized that such redistributions of wealth, via inflation, during the 1960s and 1970s have often been of much greater magnitude than redistributions via changes in tax and transfer systems – a hypothesis that should be possible to test. It is not clear, however, whether this type of redistribution is a result of conscious policy or simply an accidental side-effect of the inability of the government to avoid (higher) inflation. However, in societies where the number of net debtors is much larger than the number of net creditors and/or where the gainers (including governments with debt), for other reasons, are more influential politically than the losers, we may suspect an element of deliberate policy, in the sense that a less expansionary monetary or fiscal policy, and possibly also a slower expansion of public spending, would have been pursued if redistributions via inflation had gone in the opposite direction.

2.2. Agricultural protectionism, rent control and support of home-owners

It is also reasonable to regard *agricultural protectionism*, when it started at the end of the nineteenth century in Europe, as an example of broad horizontal redistribution policies, due to the fact that the farming community at that time usually made up more than half the population. The main 'immediate' driving force behind these policy actions seems to have been the drastic fall in the living standards of the farming population in Europe, due to the terms-of-trade deterioration for European agriculture, which was generated by the increased supply of inexpensive agricultural products from overseas markets. This in turn was a consequence of the drastic improvement in transportation technology over long distances (railways in America and steamships at sea).

It is my hypothesis that the protectionist response of governments to these events was considerably strengthened by the growth in the political power of farmers which occurred at about the same time, and which increased the political leverage of farmers' self-interest. These increased powers were in turn due to the widening of the franchise to include medium-sized and small wealth holders, which often made farmers a strong, often in fact the dominating, political force in Western European parliaments at that time. It should be possible to test this hypothesis by comparing the magnitude of the protectionist response in countries in which the farm populations had differing degrees of influence over the political process.

In a short- and medium-term perspective, when the basic factors of production in agriculture – labor, land and other types of real capital – are largely trapped within the sector, the 'specific factor model' of foreign trade theory predicts that the owners of *all* basic factors in agriculture will gain from a tariff increase [Brock and Magee (1979)], though in a more long-term perspective, land, being the least mobile factor, probably gains the most. Considering that the farmer's family itself often provides the bulk of all three types of factors, it is easy to understand that tariffs were regarded as an adequate tool for the transfer of income to the farm families.[2]

However, another explanation for choosing tariffs as the main policy instrument might be 'fiscal illusion', in the sense that support via tariffs is perhaps less visible than is support via subsidies that are financed by taxes. The tariff may also be presented as a guarantee for a 'just price', rather than as a 'handout' from the public purse. Indeed, there are some empirical studies that suggest that the opposition to 'hidden' taxes, like price increases via tariffs, is smaller than to highly visible ones [Wilinsky (1975)]. An additional reason why tariffs, rather than subsidies, were chosen is simply the limited administrative possibilities in the 1870s and 1880s for collecting the taxes that would be needed from the rest of the population to finance the subsidies – mainly because of the large relative size of the non-market sector in the economy, the great number of small firms and the primitive administrative technologies in the tax collecting system at that time.

Rent control, designed to prevent redistribution of income from tenants to landlords, is another example of broad horizontal redistribution policies in the sense that the policy attempts to favor a large fraction of the population, regardless of the place of the beneficiaries in the vertical distribution of income. It is interesting that rent control, in contrast to agricultural protectionism, has aimed at favoring consumers at the expense of producers (factor owners). In the context of the narrow self-interest principle, the most

---

[2]In the context of a Heckscher–Ohlin model with perfect factor mobility between sectors, which is perhaps relevant in a very long-term perspective, the predicted effect of higher tariffs for a given sector is instead that the price will increase for the factor that is used intensively in the protected sector (regardless of which sectors the factor operates in).

likely explanation is perhaps that the interest of producers is politically much weaker in a capital-intensive sector, like housing, than in a more labor-intensive sector like agriculture (at least when agricultural protectionism started). Metaphorically speaking, voting power among producers follows the factor labor rather than the factor capital. (The situation may occasionally be different in some less developed countries, where capital owners might dominate the voting patterns of their employees, particularly in the countryside.)

However, welfare altruism and ideology – or the political culture if we like – should not be ruled out as additional explanations for the different direction of the income support in agriculture and housing. For while in agriculture the factor owners have often been regarded as poor manual workers, worthy of support, the dominant factor owners in the sector of apartment houses are probably often regarded as rich capitalists or rentiers.

Both agricultural protectionism and rent control often seem to have been initiated to prevent sudden large *drops* in the income or wealth of the groups under consideration. To the extent that such policy responses have also been supported by groups other than the immediate beneficiaries, the policy could perhaps be regarded partly as a reflection of 'conservative social welfare functions', i.e. the notion that a large *reduction* in income, and not just a low level of income, motivates supporting policy actions.[3]

Home owners are certainly another politically influential group, today often encompassing a majority of the population. Since this group consists of individuals who are both consumers and producers, without association to rich capitalists, it is hardly surprising that politicians in many countries have been quite generous with income support to this group.

Agricultural protectionism, rent control, and tax concessions to home-owners all indicate that a group which benefits from redistribution policy does not necessarily have to be well organized, or indeed organized at all, in a democratic state. My hypothesis is that it is enough (1) that the group is easy to identify and reach by the politicians, and (2) that the individual members of the group can easily identify the political parties and/or individual politicians who support the benefits.

Broad horizontal redistributions as discussed above have rather limited consequences for the size and rate of expansion of public budgets, as redistributions of these types usually rely on tariffs, price and wage regulations, exchange rate policies and tax concessions, rather than on public spending (though increased tariff revenues may stimulate public spending). Of course, all such policies have to be administered, implying that they contribute, to some extent, to expand the number of public employees.

---

[3]For empirical evidence of the importance for redistribution policy of the attitudes towards reductions in previously existing real incomes, see Caves (1976).

3. Life-cycle and insurance-type redistributions

In contrast to the farmers, the employees in the expanding urban sectors in the late nineteenth and early twentieth century often did not have efficient life-cycle and income-insurance systems by way of income-sharing within multi-generation family households (though relatives and friends have, of course, traditionally been important for the economic security of the individual in the urban sectors as well). Thus, the industrialization and urbanization process created demands for new types of intertemporal redistribution systems. In particular, the government was increasingly asked to function as a mixed (compulsory) credit institute and insurance company by establishing public old-age pensions and sick, disability and unemployment insurance systems – hence bringing about redistributions of income over the life-cycle of the individual. We may also hypothesize that the rise of these demands was intensified by a tendency of the demand for economic security to increase at a greater rate than income and by the fact that many people prefer to base their economic security on 'impersonal', automatic entitlements rather than on discretionary private transfers from relatives and friends, e.g. transfers that create personal dependency on other individuals.

It is interesting to note that these types of reforms gained momentum just at about the time – around the turn of the century – when workers emerged as an important political force in society, as a combined result of ongoing industrialization and the move towards the general franchise. Thus, as earlier in the case of the push for agricultural protectionism by farmers, workers could use their increased political power to serve their self-interest.

However, workers' self-interest was most likely not the only motive behind these reforms. The systems helped to remove income risks for other groups as well. Besides the narrow self-interest of various groups, both 'welfare altruism' and 'consequential externalities' may also have played a part in the build-up of the social security systems. Indeed, social security reforms often started, though in modest forms, before workers became a dominant political force in society, as illustrated for instance by Bismarck's social policies.

A standard explanation for making life-cycle redistributions via political decisions, instead of relying on voluntary private credit markets, is the absence of perfect (or even well-functioning) capital markets for consumption loans, in particular due to the difficulties of using labor and human capital as collateral. There are also lots of conceivable explanations why the insurance against income risks has not been left mainly to private insurance markets. One is the asserted tendency to adverse selection, according to which high-risk people rather than low-risk people would choose to insure themselves, thus making the insurance market thin and the premiums high. However, it would seem that this explanation is in some conflict with the empirical observation that it is high- and median-income earners with modest income risks, rather than the high-risk, low-income groups that tended to join voluntary insurance systems. Neither is reference to moral hazard, due to the possibility for the insured individual to influence the outcome himself, an entirely convincing explanation, since this problem is not necessarily easier to solve in the context of public than private insurance.

The possibilities of keeping down the costs of acquisition of new members to the insurance system is a more clear-cut argument for compulsory systems, though this advantage has to be weighed against the risks of unnecessarily high administration costs due to the lack of competition, as well as the limited freedom of choice of the individual in compulsory systems.

Personally, I would, however, suggest that the main reason for the popularity of compulsory systems is that some people otherwise could choose to be without efficient insurance coverage either because of short-sightedness or because they expect to be helped in distress situations by discretionary transfers from the rest of the population. Hence, the main explanations for compulsory insurance systems, according to this reasoning, are 'paternalistic altruism' and a desire to avoid a free-rider problem (the latter basically an externality argument). An additional explanation might be a desire of political decision-makers to avoid the discrimination (on actuarial grounds) between different categories of insurance-holders as is done in private insurance systems, in response to individual differences with respect to risk. The reason for trying to avoid this may be both self-interest of potentially discriminated groups and (altruistic) concern for the distribution of life-time wealth. However, it remains to be explained why politicians and voters have chosen social security systems rather than discretionary tax-financed transfers. One reason may be that the first-mentioned method might create a greater (subjective) assurance among individuals that incomes will in fact materialize in periods without full and efficient work. Thus, by borrowing ideas from ordinary (private) actuarial insurance systems, social security systems may help create stronger property rights – entitlements – in the national wealth than would have been achieved by discretionary tax/transfer systems. However, the contrast should not be exaggerated: parliaments can, and actually do, make discretionary changes from time to time in the relationship between fees and benefits in social security systems, hence creating considerable deviations from both expected and actuarially calculated benefits. Although the individual, in the case of social security systems, would not have to be concerned with the risks of the returns on private pension and insurance funds, he would instead be exposed to macroeconomic risks and policy risks. For instance, he has to make uncertain forecasts about the ability and willingness of future generations to provide pension benefits via the public sector. And such forecasts have to rely, in a crucial way, on expectations about future phenomena like the macroeconomic growth rate, the demographic composition of the population and the propensity of various agents to exploit the potential benefits of various social security systems (such as the propensity to take early retirement) – as well as political powers and preferences in general in the future. It is not obvious that such things are easier to forecast than the real return on private pension funds.

Empirical studies of the motives and arguments of the advocates of social security systems could possibly shed some light on the relative importance of the various motives discussed above.

It is clear that the expansion of the social security systems, which today are dominant features of the modern welfare state, constitutes the most important single factor behind the expansion of public spending in the form of transfers during this century. Indeed, such systems today usually account for about a third of total public spending, and for as much as about fifteen percent of GDP in most OECD countries (OECD statistics). Though social security spending does not by itself imply the direct use of economic resources by the government, some administrative activities have to be built up, in particular in the case of the unemployment and sick insurance systems, where controls are required to limit the amount of cheating with benefits and fees.

4. Vertical redistribution policy

Horizontal, life-cycle and insurance-type redistributions of income, as discussed above, all have de facto effects on the vertical (size) distribution as well – not only in a yearly, but also in a lifetime perspective. When looking at policies that are *explicitly* designed to influence the vertical distribution of income, by contrast, it is useful to distinguish between three schematic strategies.

4.1. Strategy 1

One strategy would be to try to raise the incomes of a minority of people that are for long periods at the bottom of the size distribution of factor income. Transfer payments and the subsidization or public provision of specific goods and services to low-income groups are obvious instruments of such a strategy. The emergence of policies according to this strategy, which harks back to the charity of the church and to the old poor laws, can hardly be explained by the self-interest of the *beneficiaries*, as they have often exerted very little political power, particularly before the arrival of the general franchise. Moreover, if the beneficiaries themselves had designed the policies, we would have expected these benefits to have been given as cash income, rather than as selective support of specific goods and services (like food stamps, public provision of housing, education, etc.), since cash payments would be the most valuable type of support in terms of subjective individual utility maximization [Hochman and Rogers (1977)].

A more realistic hypothesis is therefore probably that the *benfactors* among middle- and high-income groups pursue redistribution in favor of the poor due to altruism and consideration for consequential externalities. As the benefactors seem to strive for a more even distribution of certain specific types of services, i.e. what Richard Musgrave calls 'merit goods', rather than a more even distribution of money income [Musgrave (1959), Tobin (1970)], we may in this context talk about 'altruistic paternalism'. Such ambitions may, often in combination with 'socialist' ideologies, also be important explanations for the tendency to shift over not only the financing and provision, but often also the *production* of certain types of services from private markets to the public sector. Indeed, such shifts of the production of services from the private to the public sector constitute an important explanation for the expansion of the public service sector during recent decades, in particular in Northern Europe.

An additional explanation for why governments provide specific services rather than cash incomes to low-income groups might simply be that the benefactors want to prevent, as much as possible, a reduction on the work effort of the beneficiaries. By providing *non-marketable* services to the poor, they will be forced to work in order to be able to buy other types of goods and services for which the marginal utility otherwise would be much above the marginal utility of the publicly provided services.

As low-income groups learn about this bias in favor of selective subsidies and transfers in kind to the poor, we would expect the latter, too, to emphasize such redistribution techniques for tactical reasons, as the total amount of benefits is thus enhanced.

As noted by many observers [e.g. Varian (1980)], transfer systems and progressive taxes may also, like social security, fulfill a role as income insurance systems; people with fluctuating incomes at all income levels have some narrow self-interest in such systems. However, the shifts in economic fortunes over the life-cycle of individuals are probably not strong enough for this explanation for progressive tax-transfer systems to carry much weight, particularly in societies with well-developed private and social insurance systems.

4.2. Strategy 2

Another strategy of vertical redistribution policy would be to cut very high incomes, for instance, by strongly progressive taxes or by the expropriation of property. As the income sum of top income earners, such as people in the highest percentile group, constitutes a rather modest fraction of the total income in most developed countries, it is natural to assume that envy, rather than the possibility of increasing the incomes for the rest of the population, dominates the self-interest motive in this case. However, a special type of fiscal illusion may also play a part in vertical redistribution policies of this type, as poor and middle-class advocates of such policies may mistakenly believe that taxes on the very rich could finance large transfers to the rest of the population. Of course, a majority may also believe (rightly or wrongly) that social and political stability is enhanced by cutting top incomes and wealth holdings – another example of 'consequential externalities'.

4.3. Strategy 3

Finally, a third strategy of vertical income redistribution policy is to reduce income differentials between people within the middle-income brackets – a phase of vertical income redistribution policy that seems to have become important in some of the most egalitarian welfare states in Western Europe in the late 1960s and early 1970s. For this strategy, progressive taxation *within* the middle-income brackets is an obvious tool. Reference to the median-voter theory, as applied to redistribution policy issues, may help explain the emergence of this strategy – at least to the extent that the policy consists of redistributions from people above to people below median income. However, there is also a *specific* explanation for this type of policy. In order to flatten out so-called 'poverty traps', and related drastic disincentive effects on the poor, many governments have felt compelled to extend income-dependent transfers into middle-income brackets, which has increased the progressivity of the tax/transfer system within these brackets.

As an empirical support of the self-interest hypothesis of vertical redistributions, roughly along the lines of the median-voter hypothesis, it is relevant to note that progressive tax and transfer programs emerged at about the same time as the general franchise was introduced. However, how shall we then explain the only *gradually* increasing ambitions over time to equalize the vertical distribution of income, rather than just a once-and-for-all increase in the progressivity of the tax/transfer system immediately after dramatic widenings of the franchise? One explanation may be that the mobilization of new voters is time-consuming and costly. It is also conceivable that the costs of such mobilization have been falling over time due to the emergence and expansion of cheap communication systems like mass media.

However, a good positive theory of redistribution policy has to explain not only why vertical redistributions occur, but also why these redistributions do not go even further, for instance, to 'the bitter end' of total equalization of yearly or lifetime incomes. To explain this, the median-voter theorem is often modified by the assumption that the deciding majority avoids creating so strong disincentive effects on productive effort that aggregate output in society is reduced so much that citizens below the median would also lose income [Stigler (1970), Meltzer and Richard (1981)]. Thus, these modified median-voter models assume an awareness among voters of a trade-off between efficiency and equalization.

Moreover, the uncertainty about future positions – the 'veil of ignorance' regarding future individual positions under which the tax rules are established to some extent – may be a reason not only for high-income groups to support social security systems and progressive tax/transfer systems, as mentioned above, but also for low-income groups to accept some income differentials, even aside from considerations of disincentive effects, provided they believe that they have a good chance of reaching above-median income positions in the future. Perhaps uncertainties of this type are in fact an important reason for the apparent popularity of the entitlement principle also among low-income groups, in the sense that individuals are regarded as 'entitled' to their factor return; [for empirical support for the popularity of entitlement principles, see Hochman and Rogers, (1977)]. Thus, entitlement principles might be interpreted not only as an expression of 'abstract' ideology, but also, to some extent, as a reflection of the narrow self-interest of both the rich and the poor – in an uncertain world.

Finally, drastic equalizations of the size distribution of income may have been prevented simply by the fact that high-income groups have financial and other resources enabling them to influence public opinion in their own interest and to lobby directly among politicians. Indeed, in many countries high-income groups seem to be highly over-represented in parliament and in the higher levels of the public administration.

5. Fragmented horizontal redistributions

Conflicts over the horizontal distribution of income during the post Second World War period have been strongly colored by the gradual replacement of the earlier rigid class society by pluralistic democracies with a large number of interest groups, some of which are organized, others not. As a result, horizontal redistribution policies have become much more 'fragmented' than during earlier periods.

The basic feature of fragmented horizontal redistribution policies, as analyzed below, is that the benefits are specific, whereas the taxes to finance them are more general. Politicians are, therefore, able to 'buy votes' from each interest group, separately, on the implicit or explicit assumption of the potential beneficiaries, that the accompanying tax increases are mainly paid for by others. While a given group of beneficiaries gets the entire *marginal* benefit itself, it pays only the *average* tax increase for all groups in society. For instance, assuming 100 equally large groups of voters in society, defined by various socio-economic variables, each group believes that it has to pay only 1 percent of the value of their additional benefits.

As long as the expected gain in votes from a group of beneficiaries is larger than the expected loss of votes among the rest of the population, new specific benefits will be offered by politicians. This theory is based on the assumption that large per capita benefits that are *concentrated* within a minority, buys more votes than the votes that are lost from the majority which is hit by diffused and therefore small per capita tax increases. A 'non-linearity' of the influence of benefits and taxes on individual voting behavior thus is assumed, which may be rationalized by some kind of 'recognition threshold' among voters. The theory may be strengthened by the assumption, that the (unavoidable) *uncertainly* about the future of the redistribution game creates strong temptations among voters to accept offers of 'safe benefits now', rather than hoping that a refusal to vote for such offers today would induce others to abstain from accepting similar offers in the future.

Schematically speaking, the *players* in the 'game' outlined above are political parties, and/or individual politicians, competing for votes – for the sake of power or economic benefits for themselves, or for the purpose of changing society in conformity with their ideologies (or perhaps most likely a combination of these ambitions). The *strategies* of the players involve buying votes by offering specific, highly concentrated and easily recognizable benefits, financed by general and widely diffused taxes. The players may understand that, in the long-run, most groups in society will lose on the game, at least after a certain point, when the excess burden (including the administration costs) becomes high. But the game may nevertheless go on, since a refusal by one political party to continue may be a sure way of losing (or never obtaining) political power.

If these considerations reflect a realistic picture of the real world, it is natural that there is always a strong pressure for increased public spending. People may prefer a simultaneous reduction of the benefits and the taxes for everybody, but as this is difficult (or costly) to bring about, because of the high costs of forming large coalitions, they instead opt for larger benefits for themselves. Thus, a 'prisoner's dilemma' situation is asserted to exist. This dilemma is heightened by the *recursive and incremental* nature of the process, which contributes to make the prisoner's dilemma difficult to overcome.

Moreover, as we all simultaneously belong to several different interest groups with 'overlapping membership', we are susceptible to offers from politicians in the context of our different roles in society in different instances: sometimes as consumers of a certain product or leisure activity; on other occasions as members of families with certain demographic character-istics; as employees in a specific production sector; as residents of a certain geographical region, etc. This may be the case even if we realize that in the end (ex post), we pay the entire bill ourselves. This shortsightedness of voters, due to the recursive nature of the process and the uncertainty about future redistributive political decisions, then interacts with the shortsightedness of the votebuying politicians – the latter phenomenon most likely accentuated by the limited period for which politicians hold power.

A characteristic of the theory outlined here is that the process may take place without the interest groups necessarily being organized, as politicians may buy votes directly from individual voters. However, lobbying and propaganda by organizations are, nevertheless, likely to be more important for the process described here than for the earlier discussed process of 'broad horizontal redistributions', where, as was seen above, organized interest groups were not a typical feature.[4] Indeed, we may hypothesize that organizations which were initially formed to raise the incomes and economic security of their members, at a later stage of their development, also try to achieve redistributions of income, wealth and economic power to *the functionaries* of the organizations – just as is often asserted for the behavior of self-serving public bureaucracies.

Even though the self-interest of members of interest groups, and their functionaries, is assumed to be the basic motive behind the actions discussed here, it is likely that various organizations in the real world feel a strong temptation to dress their demands in altruistic and ideological terms. Indeed, to 'prove' the asserted altruistic and ideological character of the organization, apparently altruistic actions may actually be taken occasionally.

Which types of interest groups are the most (and least) efficient ones in this redistributional process? In other words, who is likely to win and lose in the redistributional battle via the political process? We may, for instance, hypothesize that groups with low costs (per member) of organization and propaganda in the political sphere are particularly successful in this endeavor. Homogeneity of interest, and the existence of an organization for other reasons, would be expected to keep down such costs, obvious examples being producers' organizations, labor unions and various groups with common 'leisure activities' (such as sports or outdoor life). We would also expect one-issue groups, such as farmers, to be more effective in achieving political favors than many-issue groups. This may be a reason why the income support to farmers has survived the drastic decline of the farm population during the post Second World War period. However, this specific phenomenon may also reflect the fact that the costs to the general taxpayer of financing additional benefits falls as the group of beneficiaries becomes smaller over time – regardless of whether it is the self-interest of the beneficiaries, or welfare altruism and ideology among the benefactors, that is the motive behind the redistribution in question. According to these considerations, we would expect that both large and small groups of voters would be able to get subsidies – the large ones because of their voting powers, the small ones because of their homogeneity.

---

[4]Tullock (1971) as well as Buchanan and Tullock (1965) have emphasized the importance of competition among organized groups engaged in lobbying as well as 'log rolling'. Similar ideas, though with a Marxist-inspired capital–labor dichotomy rather than a fragmented pluralist competition, have been developed by Foley (1978).

The statement above, namely that benefits are usually more specific than taxes, has so far not been explained. One explanation may be that while benefits, such as transfers in cash or in kind, are tied to different types of households, or socio-economic groups, taxes, by their construction, usually refer to *production activities*, which makes the apparent consequences for the distribution of income among households quite diffuse. Moreover, perhaps people regard discrimination between household groups as more acceptable in the case of benefits than in the case of taxes. For instance, the idea of 'horizontal equity', i.e. the idea of treating people with similar income levels in the same way, may have a stronger appeal in the context of the tax system than in the case of the transfer system.

However, a good theory should also be able to explain the *exceptions* to its proposition. For instance, how do we explain highly selective 'tax loopholes', such as so-called 'tax expenditures', in particular for taxation of property incomes of various types?[5] Perhaps the answer is that the details of property taxation, due to their complexities, are understood and recognized only by the property owners themselves, but not by the rest of the electorate. As a consequence, the former group can be 'bought' with selective tax concessions without losing the support of the latter group. Asymmetric information would then be the explanation for this exception to the asserted rule.

It remains to determine the *speed* of the recursive process of redistribution and public sector expansion described above. It may be reasonable to assume that the speed is set mainly by two factors. The first one is a 'political credibility constraint': if politicians promise 'too much' during a given period of time, their promises will not be taken seriously by the electorate. Politicians are afraid of promising 'pies in the sky', which then explains the recursiveness of the process. The second factor is increasing unpopularity of taxes, partly because these will damage the national economy (with negative consequences for both current and future generations) and partly because high marginal tax rates make it difficult for the individual to influence his/her own economic situation by individual efforts.

Even though no *limit* has so far been assumed, or defined, for the process of public spending expansion, the possibility should not, of course, be ruled out that the process could stop, or even be reversed, precisely because of the same factors that have been assumed to influence the speed of the process, i.e. 'political credibility constraints' and increasing unpopularity of taxes.

However, in ideological discussions, another type of limit is often assumed to exist. It is often believed that conflicts over the distribution of income are likely to decrease when the distribution is strongly equalized, as then both envy and assertions of unfairness would be expected to recede. However,

[5]Alt (1983) attempts to explain 'tax expenditures' as a way for tax legislators to exploit the uncertainty connected with the incidence of taxation.

such an outcome is certainly not the only possibility. Indeed, a case can be made for an opposite view. First, conscious attempts by public authorities to redistribute income focuses political discussion and conflicts on distributional issues rather than on other issues. Secondly, the possibility for individuals to raise their incomes by way of productive effort tends to decrease due to higher marginal tax rates. Both factors would be expected to stimulate demand for income redistribution via the political process. Moreover – though this is a more speculative point – people are mainly likely to feel envy towards those who have only *slightly* higher incomes than themselves, because such incomes would be regarded as within reach, in contrast to the incomes of the very rich. On the basis of that hypothesis, the more equal the distribution of income is made, the more pronounced would be the conflicts over the remaining inequalities, as most people would then have more individuals than before to make relevant comparisons with; for instance, this seems to be the view of de Tocqueville (1848).

However, as it may take many decades, or even centuries, to reach conceivable limits for the expansion of public sector spending and redistributions, it is important not only to try to explain such limits (for instance in the form of a stationary equilibrium for fixed exogenous parameters), but also to explain *the dynamic process* by which such a limit (if it exists) is reached. This is exactly what has been attempted in this paper.

A main difficulty in reaching a limit, or a reversal, of the process is, in the context of our analysis, just the asserted specificity of the benefits relative to the taxes: each group expects to gain very little by the tax cuts that would be made possible by accepting reduced benefits for the group itself. Presumably governments would have to provide large *packages* of benefit reductions for a substantial fraction of the electorate to make the tax cuts attractive enough, and hence to break the earlier mentioned prisoner's dilemma situation. However, such a 'package approach' will also presumably be strongly resisted by those who mainly get their incomes from the public sector, including *both* tax-financed public sector employees *and* those who live mainly on public transfers. This point is of particular importance if a *majority* of the electorate belongs to these groups (such as in Sweden from about 1985, where 26 percent of the electorate are tax-financed public sector employees, and 28 percent of people live mainly on transfers; statistics from SIFO, Swedish Institute for Opinion Polls).

The theory outlined here is clearly consistent with two important characteristics of contemporary expansions of public spending. One is the 'incrementalism' (gradualism) of the observed expansion, which may be predicted from our theory, due to both the recursive nature of the process and to the assumed 'speed limits'. A second feature is that the gross transfers are much larger than the net transfers, which means that the theory is consistent with the observation of large 'cross hauling' (or 'churning') of benefits and costs among various groups of voters in the real world.

If ever higher tax rates, as would be expected, become increasingly unpopular over time, one obvious option for politicians is to try to shift the cost of public spending to future generations by way of higher *budget deficits* – an obvious application of the median-voter theory if applied to a multigenerational model. The social security system, too, may of course, be used as a means of such transfers at the expense of future generations. Indeed, most social security systems in the real world seem, when introduced, to have given heavy over-compensation to those who dominated voting when the systems were introduced, which most likely facilitated their introduction in the first place.

Another way for politicians to continue redistributions, in spite of ever more resistance to higher taxes, is to shift to *non-budget methods* in redistribution policy, for instance by way of price controls and other regulations, as such action may not require tax increases. Legally imposed systems of job sharing, in particular in cases of high unemployment, is another conceivable method.

Increased reliance on the redistribution of *items other* than income and consumption (without consequences for the size of public expenditures) is another likely response to increased unpopularity of high tax rates. Obvious examples are redistributions of 'power' by way of legislation leading to increased participation in decision-making by employees in low and middle positions in various hierarchies, as well as improved working and environmental conditions for low-income groups (financed by firms rather than the government). Indeed, the broadening of the type of 'goods' that are the object of redistribution policy, also outside the public budgets, is a typical feature of contemporary trends. Thus, not only higher evaluation of environmental qualities and of 'participation' in decision-making at work, but also of the difficulties of politicians to offer people additional favors by way of further expansions of public spending, may be important explanations for recent experiments with environmental policies and (legally imposed) reforms of the rules concerning decision-making in various hieriarchies.

This paper is not the place to formalize the theory that has just been outlined. It should be emphasized, however, that there is no compelling reason to model a process of an expansion of public spending as a series of static equilibria positions at different values of a set of exogenous variables, or even as a dynamic sequence of equilibria, representing the outcome of repeated games [as in Kramer (1977)]. For instance, it has turned out to be difficult to prove the existence of a unique and stable voting equilibrium, except under extremely restrictive assumptions, such as with one single decision-variable and single-peaked preferences among voters [Atkinson and Stiglitz (1980, lecture 10) and Hamada (1973)]. This is a defence of treating (in this paper) the expansion of the public sector as a dynamic endogenous process, which may or may not have a limit, and which may or may not be reversed.

Obviously, the theory outlined here differs substantially from the dominating theory today about the process of income redistribution, i.e. the median-voter theory [see, for instance, Roberts (1977) and Meltzer and Richard (1981)]. First, while the median-voter theory predicts that, in fact, half the population, ranked along one variable (the income level), is favored at the expense of the other half, our theory implies that politicians 'buy votes' from different minority groups that are defined by socio-economic variables rather than income. Second, while the median-voter theory assumes *one* policy instrument of redistribution policy (like a constant marginal tax rate), the theory outlined here assumes a great number of different policy instruments. In this sense our model is more similar to various *pressure group models*, such as those developed formally by Auman and Kurz (1977) and, in particular, Becker (1983).

It may be illuminating, finally, to compare the (non-formal) analysis here with Becker's (formalized) model. Three basic differences may then be worth pointing out.

(1) While Becker's analysis emphasizes *net* redistributions, the present analysis attempts to explain the expansion of gross redistributions, which is clearly the crucial issue when trying to explain the expansion of total public spending.

(2) While in Becker's analysis, interest groups are assumed to be organized, this is not necessarily so in the present analysis, as politicians are assumed to be able to buy votes directly from voters without *necessarily* the existence of organized lobbying on their part.

(3) While the *size* of public spending in Becker's model, as in the median-voter theory, is determined as a static equilibrium position (in Becker's model defined as a situation where for each organization the marginal lobbying costs equal the marginal benefits of lobbying), the present analysis implies a disequilibrium process, the *speed* of which is determined by characteristics of political competition.

6. Concluding remarks

It has been argued in this paper that self-interest has provided the most powerful *motive* behind redistribution policy, though welfare altruism and considerations regarding consequential externalities have probably been important for welfare policies favoring impoverished minorities. Clearly, the self-interest motive may result not only in attempted redistributions from others, but also in life-cycle redistributions and those connected with insurance principles. As a special case of the narrow self-interest motive we may also mention the support among producers of redistributions to others on the expectation of obtaining more bouyant markets for their own products as a side-effect. Obvious examples are the support among farmers of food stamps programs, and among public employees of various public services.

As to types of *targets* of redistribution policy, it would seem that while during the first five or six decades of this century life-cycle and insurance-type aspects were the most important, when we try to explain the rate of expansion of public spending, 'fragmented horizontal redistributions' between various minority groups have been the most important target during the last few decades. While the first types of redistribution mainly expanded transfer payments, the second type has stimulated the expansion of public consumption as well by a liberal public provision of 'private goods', in particular of various types of services to households.

An attempt has also been made in the paper to understand the shifts over time between the various targets of redistribution policy. For instance, whereas broad horizontal redistributions to farmers, when they started in Europe in the late nineteenth century, seem to have been initiated by terms-of-trade deteriorations for agriculture (due to technological developments) and the spread of the franchise to large groups of farmers, the later shift to life-cycle and insurance-type redistributions seem to have been initiated mainly by urbanization and the emergence of a general franchise. The latter was also, most likely, an important factor behind the increased importance during this century of vertical redistributions, broadly along the lines of the median-voter theorem.

The recent shift to *fragmented* horizontal redistributions has, by contrast, been seen mainly as a consequence of the emergence of a highly diversified socio-economic structure, with falling information costs between voters and politicians receding class loyalty in voting and related fierce political competition. As a consequence, the original 'welfare state', designed mainly to provide basic economic security, has gradually developed into a free-for-all competition for favors from the state, with 'every politician trying to buy votes from everybody'.

The analysis in the paper also asserts, in fact, that it is misleading to regard redistribution policy in a country as deliberately and systematically executed by some social planner, like a unified group of politicians or a political party. Redistributions via the state have rather been seen as *an unplanned end result of a great number of separate uncoordinated policy actions*, though the actions are, of course, 'intentional' on the micro-economic level of the various agents in the private and public sector – a point which has been emphasized in this paper by the attempt to identify various *motives* behind redistribution policy.

It has been (implicitly) assumed in the paper that the various targets, instruments, motives, driving forces and background factors operate in all types of (non-totalitarian) political systems. However, at least part of the explanation for differences in the rate of expansion of public spending in different countries can probably be found in differences in the political decision rules, in the sense that different political constitutions and mechanisms 'filter' the same type of social and economic forces behind the redistribution process quite differently [see, for example, Romer and Rosenthal (1979), Kasper (1971) and Lindbeck (1985)]. This important issue should be a fertile ground for future joint research efforts by economists and political scientists.

References

Alt, J.E., 1983, The evolution of tax structures, Public Choice 41, 181–215.

Atkinson, A.B. and J.E. Stiglitz, 1980, Lectures on public economics (McGraw-Hill, Maidenhead).

Aumann, R.J. and M. Kurz, 1977, Power and taxes, Econometrica 45, 1137–1161.

Becker, G.S., 1983, A theory of competition among pressure groups for influence, Quarterly Journal of Economics 48, 371–400.

Brock, W.A. and S. Magee, 1979, The economics of special interest politics: The case of the tariff, American Economic Review, Papers and Proceedings, May, 246–250.

Buchanan, J.M. and G. Tullock, 1965, The calculus of concent, (University of Michigan Press, Ann Arbor).

Caves, R.E., 1976, Economic models of political choice: Canada's tariff, Canadian Journal of Economics 9, 278–300.

Foley, D.K., 1978, State expenditure from a Marxist perspective, Journal of Public Economics 9, 221–238.

Hamada, K., 1973, A simple majority rule on the distribution of income, Journal of Economic Theory 6, 243–264.

Hochman, H. and J. Rogers, 1969, Pareto optimal redistributions, American Economic Review 59, 542–557.

Hochman, H. and J. Rogers, 1977, The simple politics of distributional preferences, in: F.T. Juster, ed., Distribution of economic well-being, (Ballinger Publishing, Cambridge, MA).

Kasper, H., 1971, On political competition, economic policy, and income maintenance programs, Public Choice 10, 1–19.

Kramer, G.H., 1977, A dynamic model of political equilibrium, Journal of Economic Theory 16, 310–334.

Lindbeck, A., 1985, What is wrong with the European economies?, The World Economy, June, 153–170.

Meltzer, A. and S.F. Richard, 1981, A rational theory of the size of government, Journal of Political Economy 89, 914–927.

Musgrave, R., 1959, The theory of public finance (McGraw–Hill, New York).

Roberts, K.W.S., 1977, Voting over income tax schedules, Journal of Public Economics 8, 329–340.

Romer, T. and H. Rosenthal, 1979, The elusive median voter, Journal of Public Economics 12, 143–170.

Stigler, G.J., 1970, Director's law of public income redistribution, Journal of Law and Economics, April, 1–10.

Thurow, L., 1971, The income distribution as a pure public good, Quarterly Journal of Economics 85, 327–336.

Tobin, J., 1970, On limiting the domain of equality, Journal of Law and Economics, 263–277.

de Tocqueville, A. Democracy in America, edited by J.P. Mayer. New York: Anchor Books. 1969. (Original edition in 1848.)

Tullock, G., 1971, The charity of the uncharitable, Western Economic Journal 9, 379–392.

Tullock, G., 1983, Economics of income redistribution (Kluwer–Nijhoff Publishing, Boston).

Varian, H.R., 1980, Redistributive taxation as social insurance, Journal of Public Economics 14, 49–68.

Wilinsky, H.L., 1975, The welfare state and equality: Structural and idelogical roots of public expenditures, (University of California Press, Berkeley).

PART II

CONSEQUENCES OF THE WELFARE STATE

[3]

European Economic Review 21 (1983) 227–256. North-Holland

INTERPRETING INCOME DISTRIBUTIONS
IN A WELFARE STATE

The Case of Sweden

A. LINDBECK*

University of Stockholm, S-106 91 Stockholm, Sweden

Received August 1982, final version received November 1982

It is shown in this paper that the distribution of purchasing power, and hence probably also 'economic well-being', in a Welfare State like Sweden is not tightly connected with the contribution of households in the production system. Moreover, economic inequality is drastically exaggerated when income statistics are not adjusted for differences in working time and in the time-profile of income over life. However, it is also shown that some important inequalities are not removed even by the very ambitious tax and Welfare State system in Sweden, and that some new inequalities are in fact introduced. The paper also tries to highlight the wide wedges which in an 'advanced' Welfare State are necessarily driven between factor costs for firms and factor rewards for households. All this holds in particular for annual income.

1. Introduction

To understand well the determinants of the distribution of income, including how it is affected by public policy, we would need an empirically formulated general equilibrium model, where factor income and disposable income are simultaneously determined for various groups of citizens. It is quite clear, however, that reliable models of that type do not exist today. For instance, it is well known how arbitrary the assumptions are that have to be made in such models about the shifting and incidence of taxes and government expenditure programs.

Until much more reliable models of that type have been constructed — if in fact these will ever be achieved — we have to settle for quite primitive substitutes. The most usual substitute is to make *comparisons* of various types of distributions — such as the distribution of factor income versus disposable income, of annual income versus lifetime income, of incomes of people with different profession and education, of total household income versus household income adjusted for factors like the length of working time and the size and composition of households, etc.

*I am grateful to Felix Nordström for research assistance. Mats Haglund has helped to revise the data.

Such a 'substitute' research strategy will be tried in the present paper as well, dealing with the income distribution in Sweden. More specifically, it is hoped that some light will be shed on four main questions:

First, a comparison of the distributions of factor income and disposable income shows how much information the first type of distribution gives about the latter in a modern Welfare State, such as Sweden. This issue is of interest mainly because public discussions often, implicitly or explicitly, assume that the distribution of factor incomes in fact gives useful information also about the distribution of disposable income.

Second, a study like the present one reveals the size of the marginal wedges that have been driven between factor costs for firms and factor rewards for households — for work, saving, asset choice, investment in human capital, etc. This is important information if we are interested in the disincentive effects, or the distortions, that are caused by tax and transfer payment programs. However, no systematic attempt is made in this paper to pin down such effects [see instead Lindbeck (1981a, c)].

Third, a comparison of various distributions may shed some light on the mechanisms by which disposable income is distributed. In fact, already a comparison of the distributions of factor income and disposable income gives some hint about the *ambitions* of governments to intervene, by way of taxes and transfer payments, in the formation of income in society. Moreover, a description of the distribution of different components of income, and hence a study of the different 'sources' of income for various income groups, give some hints about the forces behind the distribution of income, such as the relative importance of market processes and political processes. The explicit or implicit assumption behind this particular interpretation of comparisons of income distributions is either that the direct impact of government tax and transfer payment programs dominates over the indirect effects, *or* that a study of the direct impact is at least a useful starting point for a discussion of the effects of such policies on the distribution of disposable income. Moreover, by adjusting income for differences in working time, age, and size and composition of households, the importance of these factors for the distribution of 'income standards' of households is indicated. And by comparing lifetime incomes of people with different levels of education and profession, some information is provided about the return to education and to the choice of career.

Fourth, if the study is extended to components of income that are not adequately — if at all — covered by traditional presentations of income statistics, we may learn not only about the limitations of such statistics, but also about various ways in which households try to 'compensate' themselves for losses in disposable income due to government redistribution policies.

In other words, admitting that the present study *compares* distributions, rather than explicitly analyzes the total *effects* of various tax and transfer programs, the paper nevertheless provides useful knowledge for 'interpreting' — i.e., understanding and evaluating — distributions of income.

As in all studies of this kind, it is of course necessary to face the problem of the definition of income. Ideally, we may want to adhere to the traditional theoretical concept of income, i.e., the maximum consumption that is possible without reducing real net wealth. In reality, what we can hope for is only a rough approximation of this ideal. In the present paper, for instance, the focus is on an income concept that consists of the sum of the following components:

$$\underbrace{\text{recorded factor income} + \text{transfer payments} - \text{taxes}}_{\text{recorded disposable income}} . \tag{1}$$

However, at the end of the paper also a brief discussion is pursued on the importance of a few other income components, though quantifications at the present time are difficult to make: public consumption; consumption on the basis of home production; and income from illegal activities, including tax evasion and cheating with benefits from the government. Calculations are also attempted to include in the analysis real capital gains on assets and loans (to the extent that these are not included in the statistics on factor income). An attempt is also made to calculate income gains from legal tax avoidance (mainly from 'smart' deductions for income tax purposes).

Leisure time is not explicitly included as a component of income, though consideration to the length of working time is taken at various instances.

Much of the information in this paper is based on the Swedish Income Distribution Survey of 1979, which is a yearly survey consisting of interviews (in 1979 with 9,600 households) and data collected from various public registers, including tax returns. When other data sources are used it has often been necessary to change over to somewhat different income concepts than the 'basic' concepts of the study, i.e., factor income and disposable income.[1]

2. Annual income

Let us start with the distribution of annual income. In a brilliant exposition, *A Parade of Dwarfs (and a Few Giants)*, Jan Penn (1971) once asked us to visualize the distribution of income as a parade of people, each one assigned a 'height' proportional to the size of his income rather than to

---

[1]For a description of the various concepts and data sources that are used in this study, as well as some weaknesses of these, see the appendices in Lindbeck (1981b).

his tallness in centimeters. Fig. 1 may be regarded as a simplified version of Penn's imaginary parade of people, the parade being approximated by average incomes of various percentile income groups.[2] The figure shows three different concepts of annual household income — factor income per household, disposable income per household and disposable income per consumer unit of household.[3] (The Swedish exchange rate in 1979 was, as the average for the year, 4.29 Skr. per US dollar.)

The figure shows how the profiles of the distributions are drastically squeezed — with a regression towards the mean — when we move from the distribution of factor income to the distribution of disposable income and to the distribution of disposable income per consumer unit. For instance, whereas the *ratio* between the factor incomes of the 100th percentile group and the 2nd decile group is approximately 112 to 1, the corresponding ratio for disposable income is 7 to 1, and for disposable income per consumer unit 5 to 1.[4]

In fact, while the households in the lowest 30 percent of the distribution of factor income receive about 2 percent of the total (factor) income sum, the corresponding shares for the lowest 30 percent in the distribution of disposable income, and disposable income per consumer unit, are 13 and 18 percent, respectively. Thus, in this simple mechanical sense, a shift from the distribution of factor income to disposable income and disposable income per consumer unit 'raises' the share of the bottom 30 percent by 11 and 16 percentage points. Moreover, whereas the households in the highest decile of the factor income distribution receive 30 percent of the total (factor) income sum, the corresponding shares in the distributions of disposable incomes and disposable income per consumer unit are 22 and 18 percent, respectively.[5]

If we want to highlight the role of taxes and transfer payments as 'direct

[2] By the *i*th percentile groups is meant households between the $(i-1)$th and the *i*th percentiles.

[3] *Households* consist of 1 adult or 2 adults living together, married or unmarried, with or without children under 18 years old. *Factor income* is the sum of wages and salaries, entrepreneurial income, income from capital, imputed income from owner-occupied houses and incomes from 'temporary business activity' (i.e., mainly realized capital gains). Payroll taxes, i.e., taxes on wages and salaries, are not included in wages and salaries. *Disposable income* is factor income minus all direct taxes on households plus all direct transfer payments from various levels of government. *Consumer units* are defined by the following weights: 1 adult = 1.0 consumer unit, 2 adults = 1.8, children 16–17 years = 0.6, children 10–15 years = 0.45, and children 0–9 years = 0.3.

[4] Factor incomes are zero or negative for the first 8 percentiles, which makes ratios with factor incomes of these percentiles useless.

[5] It is interesting to note that the difference between mean income and median income is about the same in the distribution of disposable income as in the distribution of factor income. If we believe in conventional 'positive' public choice models of political behavior [e.g., Roberts (1977)] the tendencies, i.e., the political incentives, to income redistributions by governments are stimulated by the size of the difference between mean income and median income. Then the incentive to further redistributions of income in Sweden would in fact be quite as high on the basis of the rather even distribution of disposable income as on the basis of the uneven distribution of factor income!

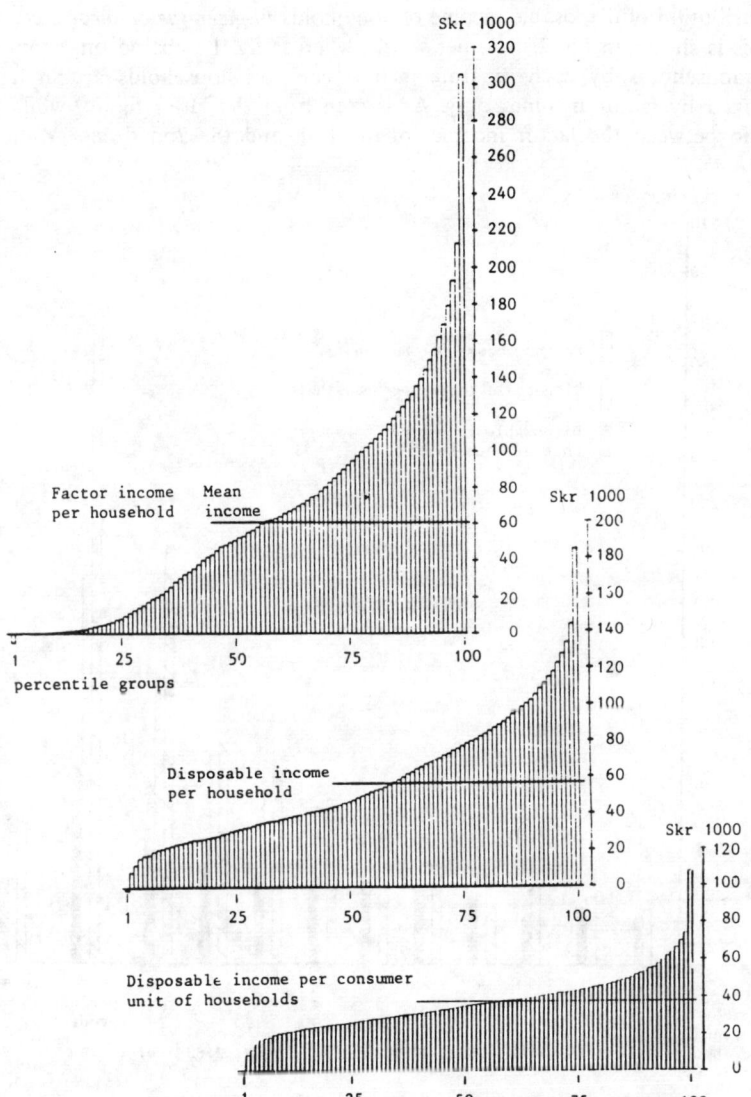

Fig. 1. Average incomes of percentile groups of households in Sweden, 1979 (percentile groups ordered by each concept of income used). *Source*: National Central Bureau of Statistics: Income Distribution Survey in 1979.

equalizers' of income for *given* households, it is useful to look instead at the distribution of disposable income of households *in given factor income classes*. This is shown in fig. 2. In other words, whereas fig. 1 is based on a ranking of households by each separate income concept, households are in fig. 2 ranked by factor incomes only. As is seen from the latter figure, while the ratio between the factor incomes of the 10th and the 2nd decile groups is

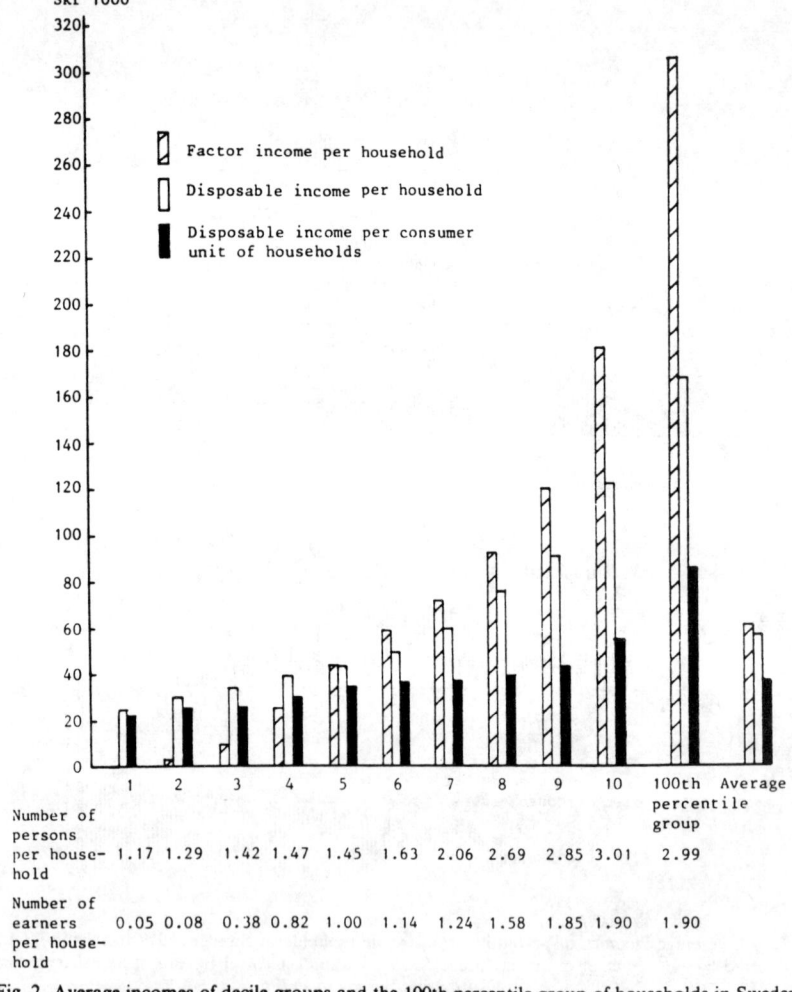

Fig. 2. **Average incomes of decile groups and the 100th percentile group of households in Sweden, 1979 (groups ordered by factor income per household).** *Source*: National Central Bureau of Statistics: Income Distribution Survey in 1979.

approximately 66 to 1, the ratio between the disposable incomes of the same factor decile groups is about 4.0 to 1. For disposable income per consumer unit it is approximately 2.2 to 1. Thus, the variation in 'income standards' is rather limited between individuals living in households with dramatically different factor incomes — when looking at average figures for factor income decile groups.

The observation that the distribution of disposable income *per consumer unit* of the various factor income classes is more even than the distribution of *total* disposable income of households reflects, of course, the fact that the number of family members, and consumer units, rises broadly by factor incomes (see the penultimate line in fig. 2).[6] One reason is that the three lowest deciles mainly consist of non-earning single persons, in fact mainly pensioners and students; another reason is that the number of children rises rapidly approximately from the 6th to the 8th decile group. In fact, while in poor countries family size often falls with income, the opposite relation tends to be the case in rich and advanced Welfare States.

3. The importance of working time

An important reason for the unevenness of the overall factor income distribution is that a large percentage of employees work part time — in Sweden approximately 18 percent of the men and 59 percent of the women (in 1979). Thus, whereas the Gini coefficient for factor incomes of all households is 0.50, of economically active households[7] 0.33, and of individual employees 0.26, it is as low as 0.17 for the earnings of full-time employees.[8]

The importance of working time for the distribution of annual income may be further clarified by looking at income *per working hour* of households with head of working age in various factor income groups. A schematic calculation is presented in fig. 3. This calculation is built on the assumption that a man-year of labor is 1,800 hours, and that persons working part time on the average work 60 percent of full time. According to the figure, factor income per hour rises, though not dramatically, with factor income decile group. Disposable income per hour rises too, but only modestly. However, the most interesting information provided by fig. 3 is the *fall* in disposable income per consumer unit per hour up to the 8th decile group, and the very

[6]The shift from total disposable income to disposable income per consumer unit in fig. 1 appears to equalize the distribution less than does the same kind of shift in fig. 2. The reason is of course that whereas in fig. 2 we compare incomes of people in various factor income decile groups, we compare different types of distributions in fig. 1 — the factor income distribution, the distribution of disposable income, and the distribution of disposable income per consumer unit. In other words, there is a considerable dispersion of disposable income *within* the various factor income deciles of fig. 2, and this dispersion is explicitly brought out in fig. 1.

[7]Constituting 93 percent of all households with heads in the age group 20–64.

[8]Employees with entrepreneurial income are not included in the figures for individual employees, covering the age group 20–60.

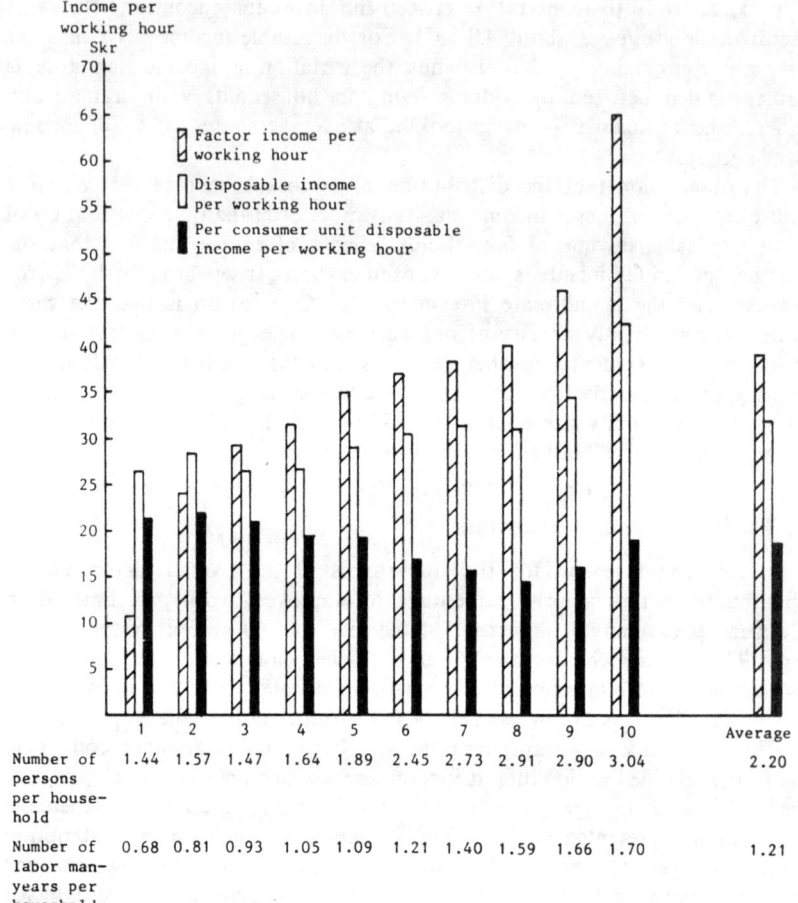

Fig. 3. Average income per working hour of decile groups of economically active households with head 20–64 years old in Sweden, 1979 (groups ordered by factor income per household). *Source*: Schematic calculations based on data from National Central Bureau of Statistics: Income Distribution Survey in 1979, and assumptions presented in the text.

modest recovery in the two highest decile groups. This pattern is in stark contrast to fig. 2 over annual (unadjusted) factor and disposable incomes, illustrating the exaggerated picture of economic inequality that is provided by income statistics that are not adjusted for working time. As people usually *voluntarily* seem to choose part-time rather than full-time work in Sweden [Arbetslivscentrum (1981)], income differences due to differences in working time should presumably as a rule not be interpreted as a sign of 'inequality'; they rather seem to reflect a labor–leisure (or home–work) choice.

4. Age and life-cycle aspects

Another important reason for the unevenness of the factor income distribution of households is, of course, that people of non-working age, such as pensioners and students, constitute a substantial part of the total population of households. Roughly speaking, two thirds of the households in the lowest third of the distribution have heads of non-working age (above 65 or below 20), which means very few income earners in the lowest decile groups (see bottom line of fig. 2). The importance of age for the distribution of income is evident already by looking at average incomes of households with heads in different age groups:

Age of head	Factor income 1000 Skr.	Disp. income 1000 Skr.
–24	40.4	33.9
25–44	86.2	71.8
45–64	83.5	69.7
65–	8.7	35.3
All	60.5	57.1

All this indicates, of course, the importance of looking at life-time aspects of income, particularly as the *combined* effects of progressive taxation and differences in life-time income profiles may be considerable. For instance, fig. 4 shows life income profiles (derived from cross-section data for 1980) of male civil servants with *different duration of education.* Obviously a comparison of yearly salaries at the age of, e.g., 45–64 gives a strongly exaggerated picture of the dispersion of life-time salaries, in particular before tax.

The issue is further clarified in fig. 5a. For instance, whereas the ratio of before-tax salaries at age 45–49 for the highest and lowest education groups is about 1.7 to 1, the corresponding ratio is 1.3 to 1 when looking instead at the capital value of life-time before-tax incomes, including pensions; the income stream is then discounted by a (real) interest rate of 2 (see fig. 5a). The ratio is less than 1.1 to 1 for discounted life incomes after tax for all three of the higher education groups. In fact, the return to education seems to be approximately 3–4 percent for the three higher education groups (relative to the lowest one) — in the case of civil servants (in 1980).[9]

The economic reward for higher education is somewhat greater for some specific professional groups (see fig. 5b). The ratio, for instance, of the average salary of a master of business administration and a skilled worker (represented by a welder) is 2.7 to 1 (in 1981) at age 45, while the corresponding ratio is about 1.3 to 1 if we look instead at the capital value

[9]At 3–4 percent interest rate discount, the capital values of disposable life income are about the same for education groups A, B and C as for D. It should be stressed, however, that all calculations of this type are approximations.

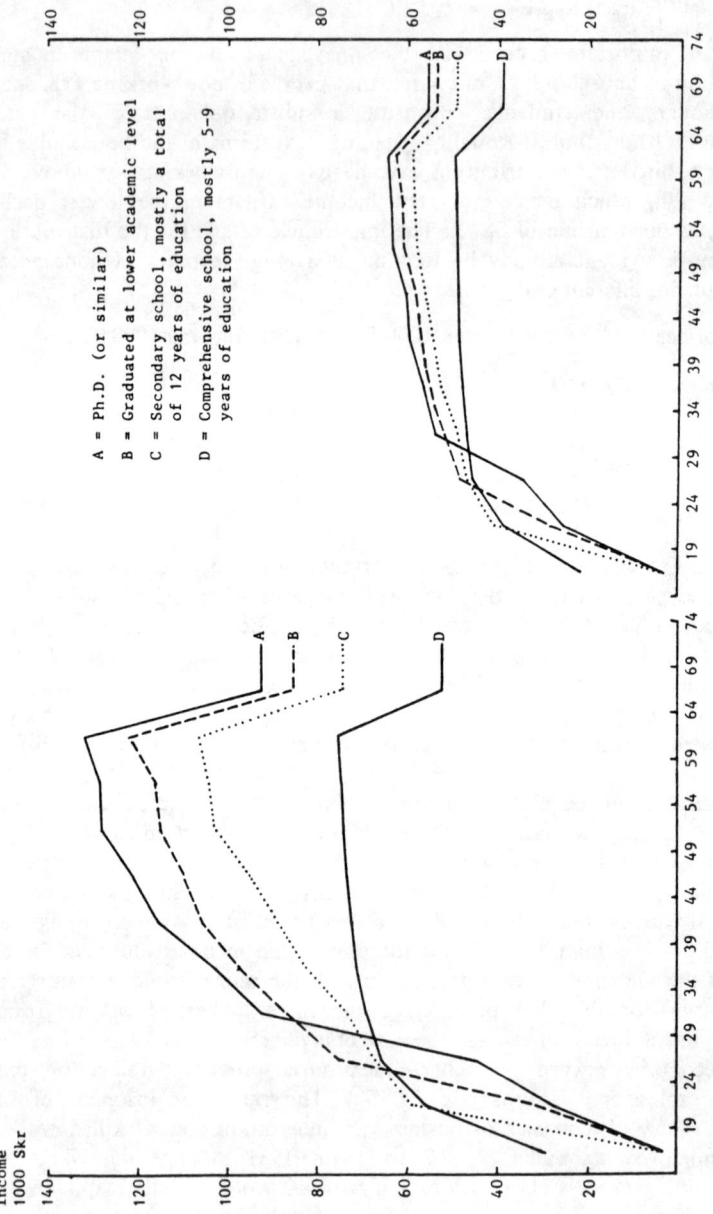

Fig. 4. Yearly income before and after tax for male civil servants with different levels of education in Sweden, 1980 (ordered by age groups). See fig. 5a. For a somewhat similar analysis for 1971, see Gustafsson (1976). *Source:* National Central Bureau of Statistics plus own assumptions and calculations.

A = Ph.D. (or similar)

B = Graduated at lower academic level

C = Secondary school, mostly a total of 12 years of education

D = Comprehensive school, mostly 5–9 years of education

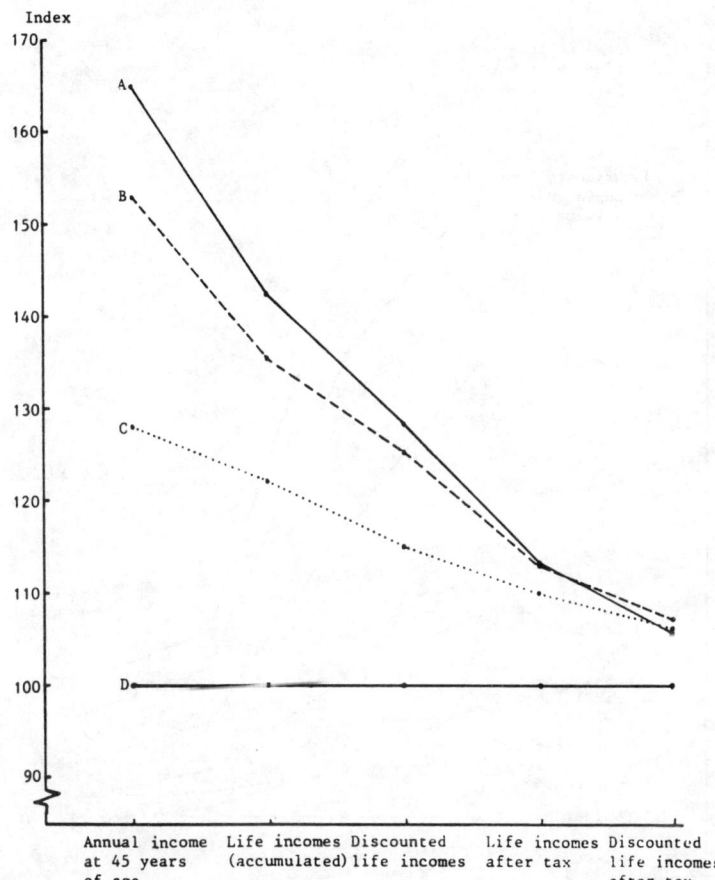

Fig. 5a. Income dispersion with alternative definitions of income for male civil servants with different levels of education in Sweden, 1980, according to fig. 4. To the official salary statistics have been added student grants and assumed income earned during holidays. The incomes of levels A and B have been adjusted to account for the receiving and the repayment of student loans. Levels A, age 24–29, has been assigned a taxable education grant comparable to half-time work in the public sector for that age and education group. At the age 19–20, eight months of military service has been assumed for all levels. Estimated expected pensions (at the age of 18) have been included. *Source*: National Central Bureau of Statistics plus own assumptions and calculations.

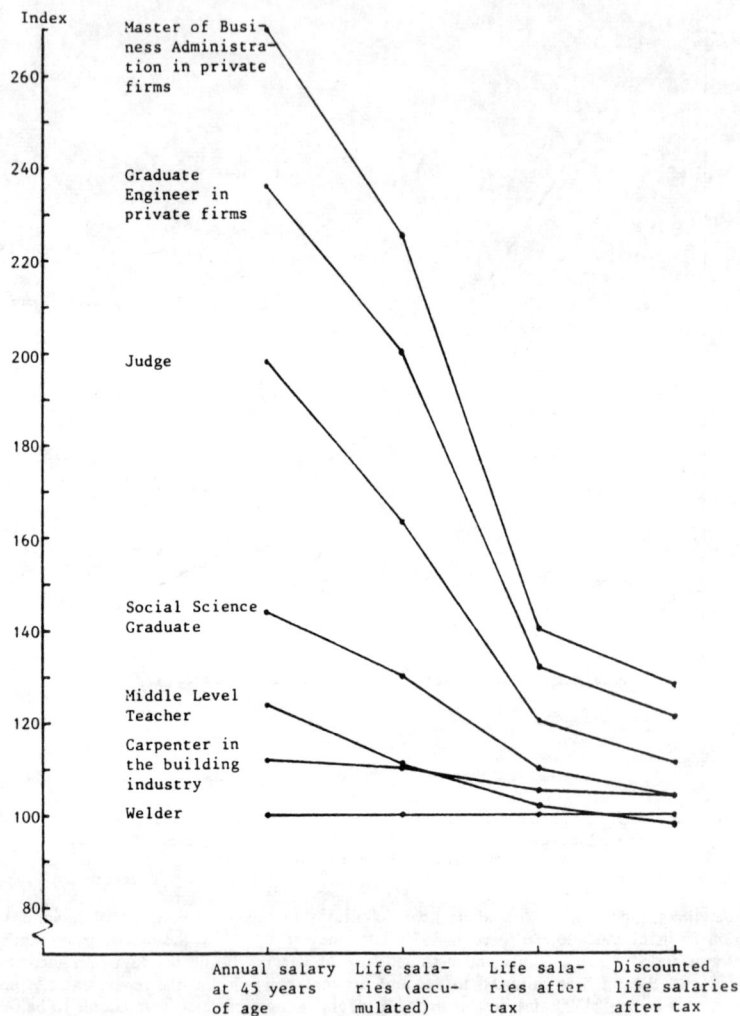

Fig. 5b. Salary dispersion with alternative definitions of income for males with different occupation in Sweden, 1981. *Source*: Swedish Confederation of Professional Associations.

of 'net' discounted after-tax life income. The last mentioned type of ratio is 1.2 to 1 for a graduate engineer and 1.1 to 1 for a judge.

Thus, even if the economic return to higher education *in general* seems to be only approximately 3–4 percent (for male public employees), it is somewhat higher for some *special* careers. For instance, for masters of business administration it is 7.3 percent and for judges it is 4.3 percent (according to calculations based on data behind fig. 5b after some statistical modifications to ensure compatibility).

5. Sources of income

The relative roles of market processes and political processes for the distribution of disposable income are further clarified if we look at *the sources* of incomes in various income classes.

Fig. 6 illustrates how large a fraction of disposable income in the various factor income classes (all decile groups plus the highest percentile group) is obtained from different sources. The three lowest decile groups obviously live on transfer payments, while from decile groups number 5 and upwards wages and salaries predominate completely as a source of disposable income. In fact, wages and salaries constitute about 89 percent of disposable income of the household sector as a whole. (The reason why wages and salaries in the highest decile groups are much larger than disposable income is, of course, that direct taxes — in the figure included in the concept 'transfers paid' — are much larger than transfers received.)

It is also of interest to note that property and entrepreneurial income, except for the two lowest decile groups, play about the same (modest) role in all factor income decile groups. Moreover, imputed income from owner-occupied houses is the predominant type of property and entrepreneurial income for more than half of the factor decile groups (see lower panel of fig. 6).[10] Thus, if a more equal overall distribution of property and entrepreneurial income is desired, the most important asset to redistribute is owner-occupied houses — except mainly for the very lowest deciles, where capital income[11] is more important, and the very highest *percentiles* where

[10]The official calculations by the National Central Bureau of Statistics (SCB) of imputed income of home ownership have been replaced by more realistic figures in this study. More specifically, the calculations by SCB imply that a low interest rate (about 3 percent) is multiplied by the assessed value of the house (for tax purposes), from which actual interest costs are deducted — 'the taxation method'. In the present study, by contrast, the houses have been assessed realistic market values, from which actual mortgage debt has been deducted. The remaining net wealth is then multiplied by an assumed interest rate, equal to interest rates on time deposits in banks. (While with the 'taxation method' the imputed income of home ownership was *minus* Skr. 8.3 billion in 1977, it was according to the calculation methods used in this paper *plus* Skr. 16 billion.

[11]Capital income consists of net earnings on financial assets.

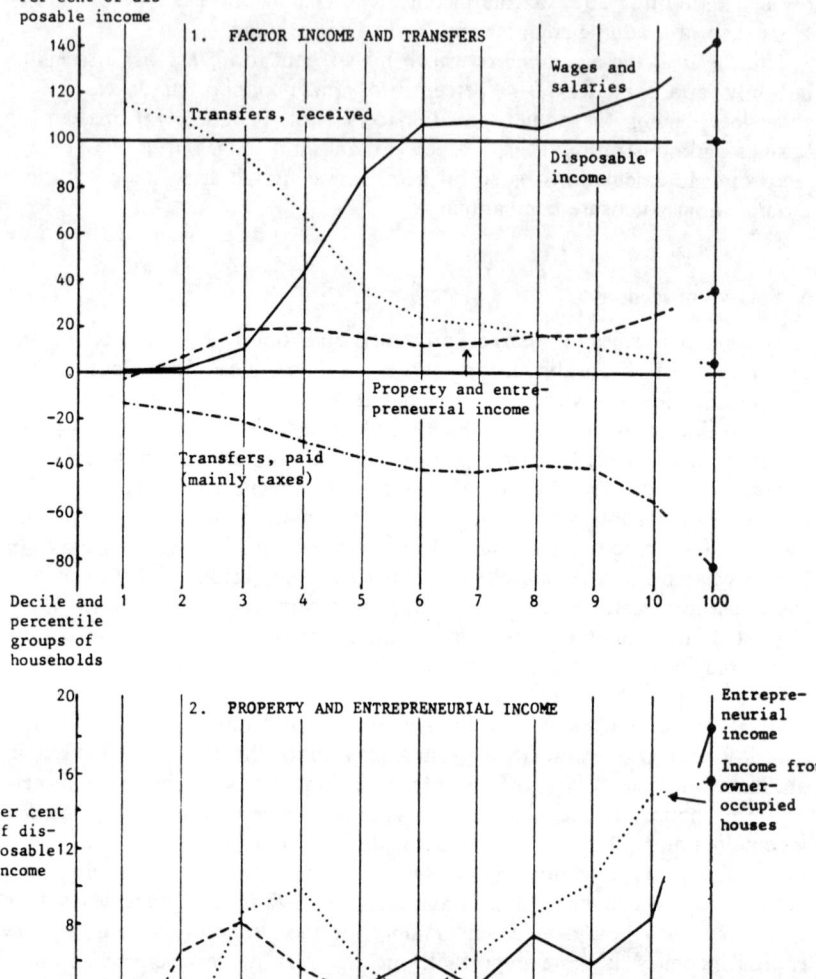

Fig. 6. Sources of incomes of households in Sweden, 1979 (decile groups and the 100th percentile group ranked according to factor income); disposable income = 100. *Source*: National Central Bureau of Statistics: Income Distribution Survey in 1979.

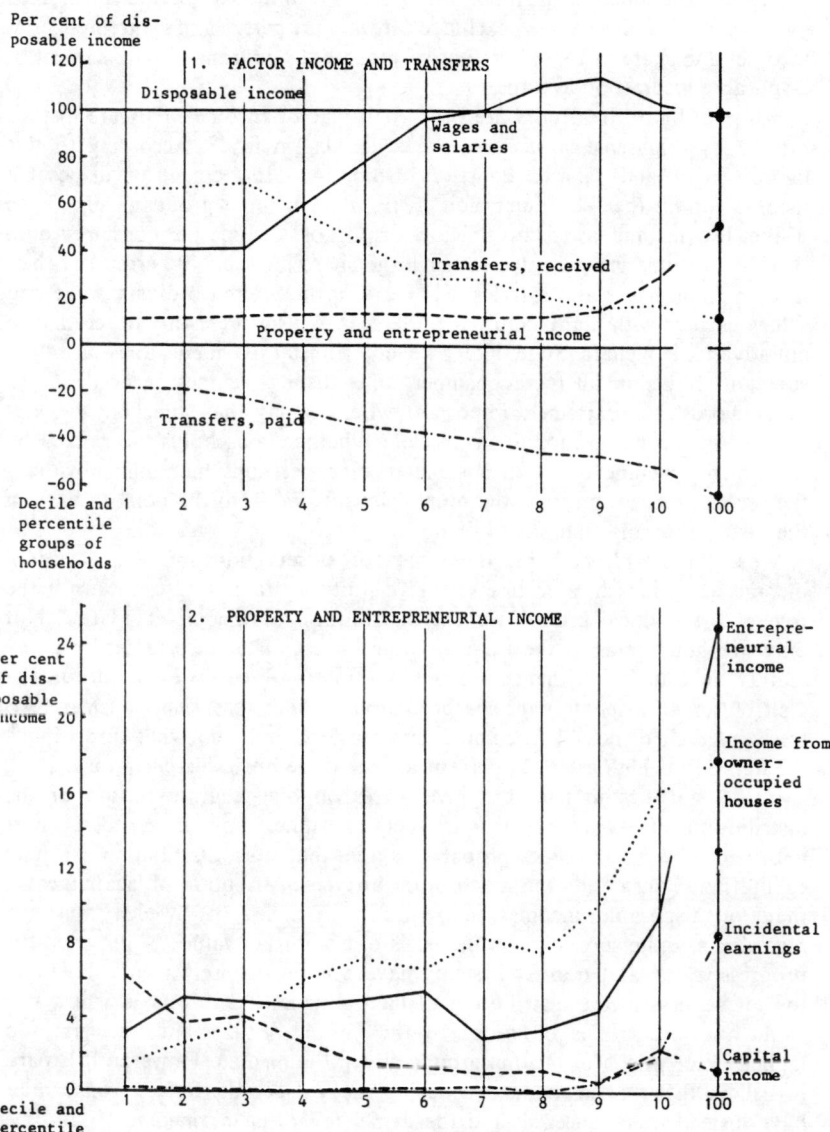

Fig. 7. Sources of incomes of households in Sweden, 1979 (decile groups and the 100th percentile group ranked according to per consumer unit disposable income); disposable income = 100. *Source*: National Central Bureau of Statistics: Income Distribution Survey in 1979.

entrepreneurial income is more important. If imputed (net) income from owner-occupied houses is excluded from 'property and entrepreneurial income', the share of the latter type of income drops from 15 to 7 percent of disposable income, on average.

While in fig. 6 the deciles are ordered by factor incomes, they are instead ranked by *disposable income per consumer unit* in fig. 7. According to this figure wages and salaries constitute some 40–115 percent of disposable income for *all* (per consumer unit disposable) income groups. Thus, if we define 'low income' as (relatively) low disposable income per consumer unit, then low-income groups get a rather large share (at least 40 percent) of their income from wages and salaries. They are, in fact, often ordinary wage and salary earners with many family members. It is also interesting to see that in an advanced Welfare State like Sweden, transfer payments play a rather substantial role in all (per consumer unit) disposable income deciles.[12] In other words, it is extremely important when we say that somebody belongs to the low-income groups to make clear whether households are ranked by total factor income or by disposable income per consumer unit; obviously the second concept must be the more relevant one from the point of view of the distribution of standards of living.

Most important, perhaps, these various observations on the source of income in various income brackets give quite a dramatic illustration of the role of the political process for the distribution of 'income standards'. Not only are households in the three or four lowest *factor income* deciles living mainly on transfer payments. Households in the three lowest deciles in the distribution of *disposable income per consumer unit* receive as much as two thirds of their disposable income from transfers; and somewhat surprisingly, the figure is as high as 16–20 percent for the three highest decile groups.

If the statistics in figs. 1–7 give a reasonably accurate picture of the distribution of disposable income per consumer unit in Sweden, most informed observers would probably agree that this distribution is quite egalitarian. Considering the much more uneven distribution of factor income than of disposable income, redistribution policies in Sweden must be regarded as quite successful on the basis of egalitarian values — provided the progressive tax and transfer systems have not by themselves contributed to the unevenness of the distribution of factor income. One way in which this could have occurred is, of course, by the shifting of taxes and transfers onto higher factor prices for income groups above the median. However, it is hard to believe that this has happened during the last decade. Relative wage rates have instead been squeezed; and the dispersion of factor income of full-time

---

[12]In fact, available statistics show that when households are ranked according to disposable income, pensions are rather evenly spread over all the deciles, with an emphasis on decile groups 1–8. Government grants and lending to students are also spread rather evenly over the various disposable income classes, with some emphasis on decile groups 1–7.

employees as well as factor incomes per hour of work of households have gone down.

6. Marginal wedges

However, a snake lurks in every paradise: It is impossible to equalize incomes drastically by tax–transfer programs without reducing the return to individual effort. More specifically, the wide difference between the distributions of factor incomes and disposable incomes implies very high marginal tax and transfer rates, i.e., very wide marginal wedges between factor costs for firms and factor rewards for households, which is bound to create disincentive effects. For instance, a rather 'typical' full-time worker in manufacturing, or a middle-income white-collar employee, had in 1979 a marginal *income tax* rate of 55–63 percent, in contrast to about 45–50 percent ten years earlier; just above the 99th percentile, the rate reached the maximum level, i.e., 87 percent in 1979.

A comprehensive picture of the marginal wedges between factor costs and factor rewards requires, of course, consideration of *both* marginal tax rates for all types of taxes, *and* marginal transfer rates in the connection with income-dependent transfers. An attempt to give such a picture is reported in fig. 8, which is constructed on the basis of detailed data on tax rates and transfer rates in different income brackets. It depicts the marginal tax *cum* transfer rates, defined as the sum of the explicit marginal income tax rate *and* the implicit tax rate of the most important income-dependent transfers, namely rent subsidies and subsidized day nursery fees; this will be called 'net' tax rates below. The rates refer to various levels of gross household income (approximately the same as income assessed for tax purposes) of married people (or couples living together), both parents gainfully employed and with income distributed approximately in the proportions 2/3 and 1/3, respectively, both before and after an income change; the family is assumed to have two children under 16 years of age.[13] (These calculations have been made by Irène Andersson.)

The dotted curve in the upper part of the figure depicts the marginal net tax rates when income increases by Skr. 1,000 (approx. $230). The reason for the steep peaks here and there is simply that the tax and transfer functions are discontinuous, with discrete jumps in the marginal tax rates and with discrete reductions in transfer payments when income reaches certain levels. The solid curve depicts the marginal net tax rates when income increases by Skr. 5,000 (approx. $1,160); in this case the path of the marginal rates is

---

[13]The curves show the marginal effects at different income levels *after* the income increase for the family. One spouse is assumed to work full time, the other $\frac{3}{4}$ time with earnings per hour $\frac{3}{4}$ of the hourly earnings of the full-time employed spouse. 'Normal' deductions are assumed.

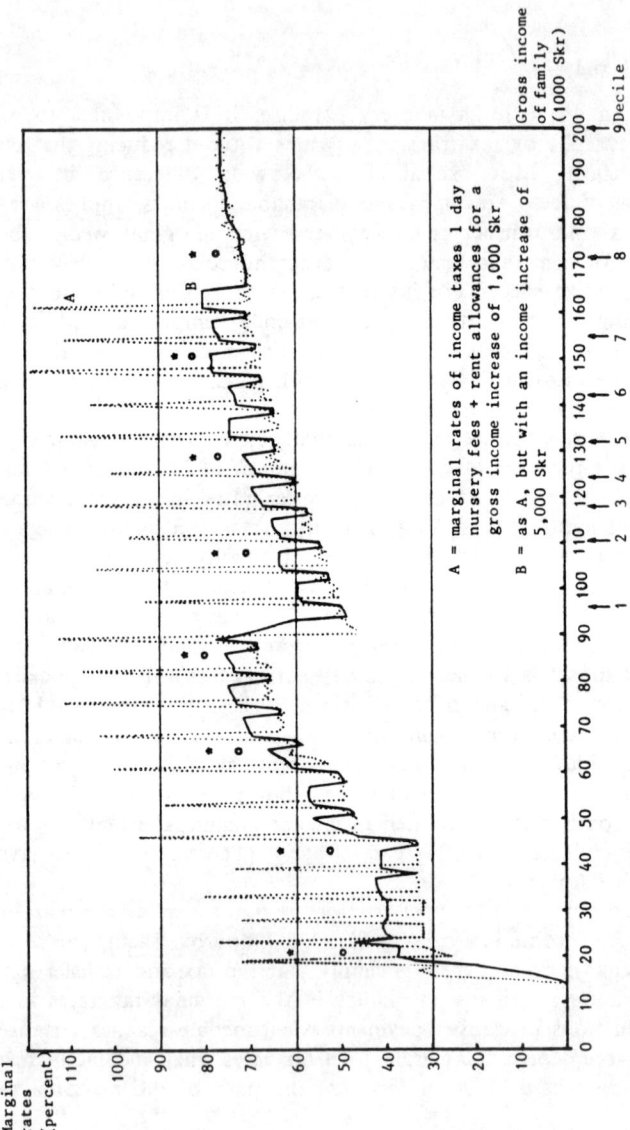

Fig. 8. Sum of marginal rates of income taxes, day nursery fees and rent allowances at different family income for 'hypothetical' families in Sweden, 1979. The deciles are approximative and refer to non-house owning households with children, one person working full time and one long part time (50–89 percent time). *Source*: Calculations, made by Irène Andersson at the University of Gothenburg, which are based on the rules of the tax and benefit system. (Asterisks, circles and deciles are added by the author.)

evened out considerably. However, it is — in Sweden as well as in other Welfare States — easy to give examples of *special* groups of households that are hit by marginal rates considerably in excess of 100 percent, when consideration is taken to *all* types of income-dependent transfers (and not just, as in fig. 8, of the two most important ones).

The reason why the marginal rates do not rise more rapidly by income above the median is that there are fewer income–dependent transfers to lose at medium and high incomes than at low incomes, which 'counteracts' the increased marginal rates of the income tax system. In fact, above approximately the 8th decile, most income-dependent transfers have already been lost, implying that the marginal rates from there on are determined by the income tax rates only.

If consumption taxes too are included (by reducing the figures on real disposable income by some 20 percent), the marginal tax rates are as denoted by the circles in fig. 8, i.e., about 60–80 percent for most decile groups, when incomes change by Skr. 5,000.[14] Thus, the ratio, on the margin, between what the firm pays and what the employee gets after all taxes and transfers, is approximately 3 or 4 to 1 for most employees, though it exceeds 6 to 1 for an employee in the 99th decile (with an income of Skr. 150,000 and a marginal tax rate of 85 percent). In the case of income changes of Skr. 1,000 'total' marginal rates even as high as 110–120 percent occur, as can be seen by adding the marginal consumption tax rates to the dotted curve in fig. 8.

Market price distortions due to monopoly, monopsony, monopolistic competition, oligopoly, etc. — which have worried economic theorists so much for such a long time — are usually insignificant as compared to these *policy-implemented* factor price distortions. Whereas the former often seem to create a wedge between price and marginal costs of some 5 or 10 percent, the marginal wedges between wage costs for firms and the returns to the individual are, as we have seen, often about 200 percent and occasionally more than 500 percent. I think that economists who continue to argue for more public intervention in the economy with reference to distortions between costs and prices due to 'spontaneous market imperfections' have reason to reexamine their position on the basis of this observation.

If also payroll taxes are included (by blowing up the factor income figures by some 30 percent), the marginal net tax rates would be even higher, as illustrated by the values with asterisks in the figure. However, such a calculation would be an exaggeration of the marginal rates, as the social

[14]There are also indirect subsidies (to goods and services) which reduce prices, hence functioning as 'negative indirect taxes' on consumer goods. (The most important ones are subsidies to agricultural products and to interest payments on housing.) These have been deducted from the indirect taxes when the 20 percent figure has been calculated — as a rough approximation. There are also payrolls, of about 4 percent, which are implemented by way of bargaining agreements; these fees are not included here.

security benefits to some extent are automatically raised for the individual when his payroll contribution goes up in connection with increased factor supply. Particularly in the sick insurance and pension systems there are elements of an actuarial connection between fees and benefits, which means that these fees should not be fully regarded as taxes and hence as *wedges* between factor income and disposable income. People might at least partly regard them as *prices* for such insurance.

It should be observed that these marginal rates refer to changes in family income when income increases in the same proportion for both spouses. If the income increase occurs for the spouse with the larger income, considerably higher marginal rates would result, while considerably lower marginal rates would result if income is increased for the other spouse — as taxes are assessed on the income of the *individual* (in contrast to the transfers which are assessed on *family income*).

While the *statutory* 'net' tax rates in fig. 8 are the relevant rates when discussing the (dis)incentive effects of the tax and transfer system, it may also be of interest to investigate how the relation between taxes and transfers, on the one hand, and factor incomes of households on the other, differs between various factor income groups in the *actual* size distribution of income. For that purpose fig. 9 is calculated on the basis of the information of factor income and disposable income in fig. 2. The average 'net' income tax rate is calculated simply by dividing factor income *minus* disposable income with factor income, while the marginal 'net' income tax rate is calculated by dividing the difference in 'net' taxes paid between two consecutive factor income decile groups with the difference in the factor incomes. It should of course be remembered that fig. 9, in contrast to fig. 8, depicts the *combined* effects of changes in factor income and various other variables, including changes in the size, composition and labor force participation of families as well as the distribution of income on various individuals *within* the family. This is the rationale for the term 'mongrel' net tax rates in fig. 9.

Some of the most striking features of fig. 9 are (1) that the *average* 'net' income tax is negative up until the medium, reflecting a system of pronounced 'negative income taxation'; (2) that it rises monotonically, though rather slowly in medium income brackets (deciles 7–9); (3) that the *marginal* 'net' income tax rate reaches a local peak in deciles 3–5; and (4) that the 'net' marginal income tax rates are quite low for deciles 6–7. It should then be observed that while fig. 8 depicts a special subgroup of households, with heads that are participating in the labor market, fig. 9 covers *all* households. Moreover, while in fig. 8 the denominator consists of gross income, it consists of factor income in fig. 9. If gross income had been used in fig. 9 as well, the marginal net rates had been higher, though to a varying extent at different income levels. (The average net tax rate curve would have been flatter, and higher, than in fig. 9 above the 7th decile group.)

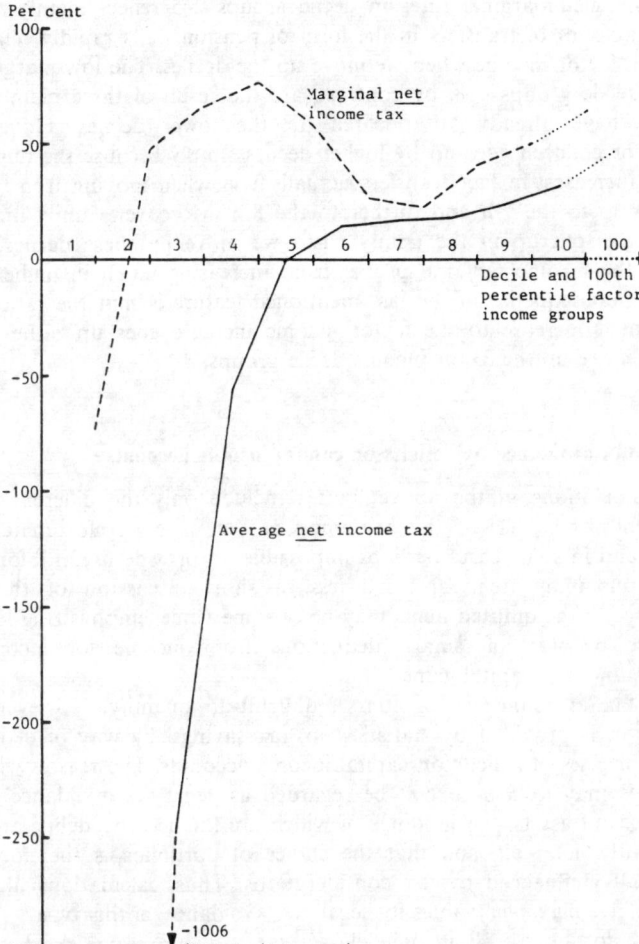

Fig. 9 'Implicit' actual 'mongrel' net income taxes for households in various factor income groups in Sweden, 1979. In the first decile group average net tax is not defined, since factor income is negative. *Source*: National Central Bureau of Statistics: Income Distribution Survey in 1979.

If the 'median-income theory' of redistribution policy [Roberts (1977)] is interpreted as a hypothesis that a democratic state tends to redistribute income from people above the median to people below the median, fig. 9 is quite consistent with that theory, in the sense that only people above the median income are 'net' tax-payers.

The high net marginal rates in decile groups 2–5 reflect mainly the fact that the amount of transfers in the form of pensions falls rapidly relative to the rise in factor income when we move up the deciles. The low marginal net rates in decile groups 6–8, by contrast, are the result of three main factors. Pensions have already 'disappeared' in the lower deciles. Government support for children goes up by higher deciles simply because the number of children increases; in fact transfers actually rise when moving from the 6th decile group to the 7th and further to the 8th. Moreover, family income is increasingly split up in the family when we move up these deciles, which prevents the income tax rate proper from increasing much in higher decile groups. A consequence of the last mentioned feature is that the ratio of the tax payment increase to the factor income increase goes up rather slowly when we move up the factor income decile groups.[15]

7. Legal tax avoidance by deficits on capital income accounts

The calculations in the above figures include only the different income components of eq. (1) at the beginning of the paper. Unfortunately it is difficult, and in some cases perhaps impossible, to provide useful information on the remaining items. Nevertheless, a short discussion of the likely importance of the omitted items may be of some value, emphasizing legal tax avoidance by way of 'smart' deductions from income for income tax purposes, and real capital gains.

Legal tax avoidance is, of course, difficult to quantify. However, some information is provided by statistics on 'tax savings' by way of deductions for tax purposes of deficits on capital income accounts. The reason why such deductions may *to some extent* be regarded as 'legal tax avoidance' is that many types of assets, the holdings of which are financed by debts, are taxed very slightly, if at all, and that the choice of portfolios is therefore often dramatically influenced by tax considerations. Thus, calculations like these probably give *maximum* values for legal 'tax avoidance' of this type.

Though for nearly all income classes tax reductions due to deficits on capital accounts are quite small relative to aggregate gross income, they are about 7–9 percent of gross income in the *very* highest income classes (the top of the highest percentile group), i.e., about 30–50 percent of the *disposable* income of that group of 'super-high' income earners (see fig. 10).

The size of deficits on real estate (due to deductible interest on mortgages) is somewhat higher, relative to gross income for most income groups (fig. 11). From about the 8th decile and upwards, the tax reduction is about 3–6 percent of gross income, i.e., some 6–18 percent of disposable income.

---

[15]For additional information, see fig. 13 in the appendix, where the 'net' marginal income tax rate is subdivided into a 'proper' marginal tax rate and a transfer payment rate.

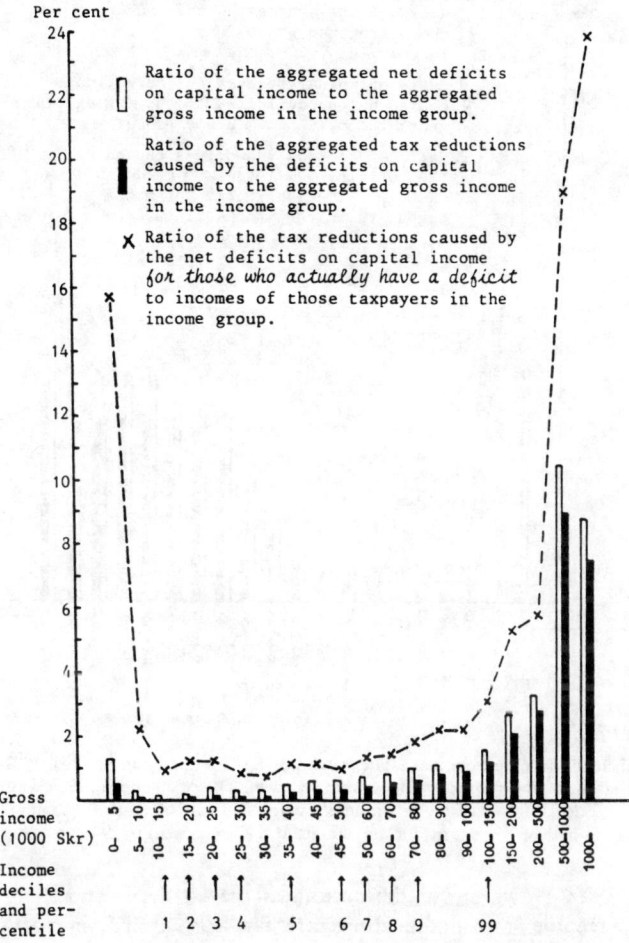

Fig. 10. Deficits on capital income in Sweden, 1977, according to taxation statistics and tax reductions caused by them. The calculations are very approximate. *Source*: Own calculations based on National Central Bureau of Statistics: Sample survey of income tax returns for individuals at the assessment in 1978.

To summarize, even though 'tax savings' by way of 'smart' deductions, in connection with taxed-induced asset choice, no doubt are important for *specific individuals* in various income brackets (see the broken curves in figs. 10 and 11, showing the tax savings for those *who actually have deficits*), the neglect of this factor in the previously presented figures does not seem to imply any *major* distortion of the statistics on factor income for entire

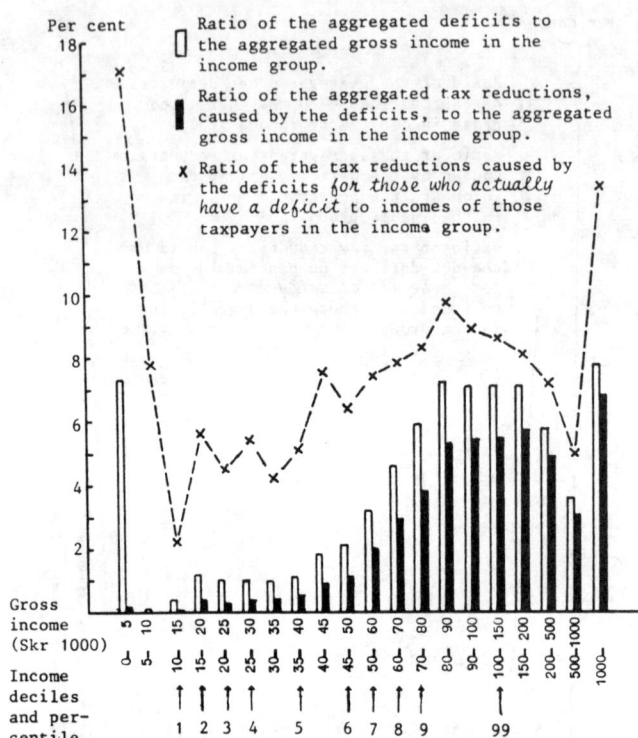

Fig. 11 Deficits on income from real estate, excluding farm property, in Sweden, 1977, according to taxation statistics and tax reductions caused by them. The calculations are very approximate. *Source*: Own calculations based on National Central Bureau of Statistics: Sample survey of income tax returns for individuals at the assessment in 1978.

income deciles. However, for the bottom of the 1st decile and the top of the highest percentile, the modifications are far from trivial, in particular for those who actually have deficits on their capital income accounts.

8. Real capital gains

Accrued real capital gains too are difficult to calculate in a reliable way for various income groups. For instance, to achieve a calculation that is reasonably 'representative' for real yearly capital gains during the second half of the seventies, this study uses figures for the *average* annual rate of change in prices of assets and consumer goods during the period 1975–1980, rather than the price changes in 1979. The results are summarized in fig. 12. Statistically recorded *realized* capital incomes have been removed from the

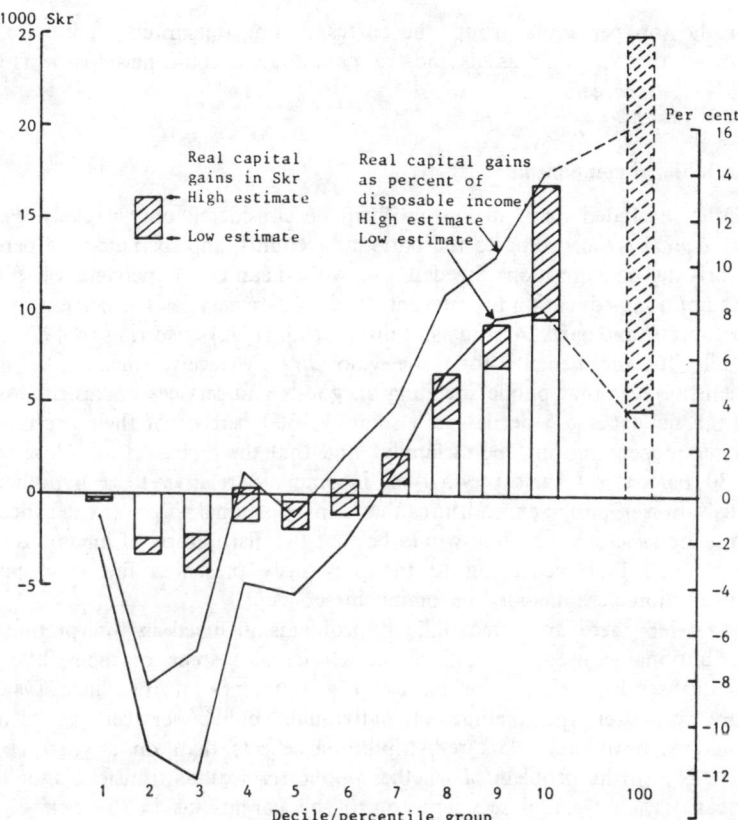

Fig. 12. Real capital gains (left-scaled) and real capital gains as percent of disposable income (right-scaled) of decile groups and the 100th percentile group of households in Sweden, 1979 (groups ordered by factor income per household). *Source*: Lindbeck (1981b) and Nordström (1982).

income figures, to avoid, 'double counting'; however, for all income groups except the very highest one this adjustment is quite minor.

The real capital gains rise roughly, as percent of disposable income, by factor income class, from negative values in the three lowest decile groups to about 8–14 percent in the 10th decile group.

To summarize the attempted *modifications* of the picture given in figs. 1–7, it would seem that for groups a little above the median factor income (such as the 7–8th deciles), *disposable* income should perhaps, as a *maximum* calculation, be raised by some 10–12 percent for 'tax savings' due to deficits on capital accounts, including debt on home ownership, and by slightly less for real capital gains — i.e., a *maximum* of some 20–25 percent altogether.

For the top percentile group, the corresponding (maximum) figure for the sum of 'tax savings' on assets and real capital gains could perhaps be as high as about 75 percent.

9. Additional components

Other excluded items in figs. 1–7 can be considered only vaguely. *Public consumption* is, according to the national accounts, approximately 55 percent of private consumption Sweden — with health (24 percent of public consumption), education (21 percent), and welfare services (16 percent) as the most important parts. A study [Franzén et al. (1975)] referring to 1970 tried to allocate the benefits to those who *directly* receive them. The main conclusion was that public spending on goods and services makes the lowest pre-tax net income[16] deciles gain some 30–300 percent of their pre-tax net income (depending on type of family), and that the highest deciles lose some 10–30 percent (of their pre-tax net income) — relative to a hypothetical distribution of public expenditures that is proportional to pre-tax net income. Thus, the *general* conclusion would be that the distribution of income is even more equal than according to the previously presented figures if public consumption were included in the income concept.

However, there are some difficult problems involved in interpreting the distributional consequences of public services, as some of them, like free hospital services, simply reflect *ex post* outcomes of insurance systems. Moreover, over the lifetime of individuals public services, as transfer payments, have much less redistributional effects than on a yearly basis. There is also the problem of whether public services, as transfers, should be allocated to the actual recipients or to the parents (as in the case of free education) or to their children (as in the case of subsidized old-age care), who are relieved from helping their parents financially.

It is also quite clear that some items of public consumption create new types of inequalities between families, in particular *within* income classes. An obvious example is the subsidized day care centers for children, a service that is strictly rationed. Those who are lucky enough to get their children into these centers obtain services that cost the public authorities about Skr. 30,000 (about $7,000) per child per annum, i.e., an amount of money that is difficult to obtain (after taxes) by increased, ordinary work.

Moreover, studies of time budgets for Sweden [Ingelstam (1980)] suggest that various types of *home-work* (with the preparing of food, cleaning, laundry, work with children, maintenance and travelling predominating) comprise about the same number of hours as work in the market. However, there is hardly any evidence from the limited statistics that is available that

---

[16]This concept is quite close to taxable income.

the number of hours of home work differs much between households with 'high' income (more than Skr. 70,000) and households with lower income.[17] Thus, if we evaluate the return on hours of work at home by the after-tax real wage rates (an equality that may be interpreted as an equilibrium condition for the household), the inclusion of do-it-yourself work in disposable household income would probably not change very much the conclusion of the above analysis. (Labor is combined with more capital, in the form of durable consumer goods, the higher is disposable money income.[18] This is an indication that an assumption about rising labor productivity of work in the home with after-tax income may be reasonable.)

Incomes from *economic crimes*, too, including cheating with taxes and public benefits, may of course bias the official figures on (factor as well as disposable) incomes. Though the consequences for the size distribution of income is not known[19] there are obvious reasons to assume that small businessmen and self-employed have greater opportunities than most other groups to cheat with taxes. However, it is also likely that employees cheat more than self-employed with various kinds of public transfers, like unemployment and social insurance benefits.

10. Concluding remarks

(1) The most striking conclusion from this study is perhaps that purchasing power, and hence probably also 'economic well-being', in a Welfare State like Sweden, is not tightly connected with the contributions of households in the official production system — in particular when looking at yearly income. Factor income — the first component of the schematic definition of income in eq. (1) — no longer seems to dominate over the other component. In fact, information about the distribution of yearly factor income is quite useless even as a rough indicator of the distribution of disposable income per consumer unit, and hence also of the 'need' for further redistributions of income by way of policy actions.

(2) It is obvious that economic inequality is drastically exaggerated when income data is not adjusted for differences in *working time*, provided that the length of working time reflects 'free' (unconstrained) choices; this holds for

[17]Mail inquiry by the Swedish Government Consumer Protection Board, 1979. Also a study for Norway indicates that the number of hours of home production differs very little between income classes; Tid nyttet til egenarbeid, Statistisk Sentralbyrå 1975.

[18]The value of purchases of 'household machines' is about twice as high in middle factor income deciles as in the lowest deciles and about three times as high in the top decile.

[19]Vogel (1970) did not find in his questionnaire study for the late sixties any significant difference in the frequence of (admitted) tax cheating between different income groups, while a questionnaire study by SIFO in 1980 (En nation av fifflare) suggests that the frequency of tax cheating increases by income. However, neither study tells us in which income classes the *value* of tax cheating is highest — absolutely or relative to income.

factor income as well as disposable income. In fact, disposable income per consumer unit *per hour of work* falls rather than rises by factor income of households.

(3) It is equally clear that figures for yearly income considerably exaggerates *lifetime* income differences — in particular of course in the case of factor incomes when age groups over 65 are included in the statistics. For instance, the capital value of life-income does not seem to vary much between various levels of education, except for *specific* professions like masters of business administration, graduate engineers, etc.

(4) Though it is possible to make the connection between factor contributions and 'income standards' quite tenuous, by way of taxes and transfers, it is obvious that some inequalities between families are *not* removed by such policy actions — in particular between families with many members relative to the number of income earners. In fact, families with many children tend to be pronounced low-income groups in terms of disposable income per consumer unit.

(5) Moreover, some 'new' types of inequalities have been introduced by the tax and welfare state reforms. For instance, if the length of working time, as it seems, reflects a voluntary choice, progressive taxation of annual income redistributes income from people with a relatively low to people with a relatively high valuation of leisure. Another example is the creation of inequalities due to the non-symmetries in the taxation of different types of assets in an inflationary economy, and therewith connected 'smart' asset transactions of individuals. The most important example is probably differences in disposable income between households with owner-occupied houses and high debt, on the one hand, and tenants with money in fixed interest bearing financial assets on the other — in particular when inflation rises without full adjustment of after-tax interest rates. It is also clear that some new types of inequalities are created by the different degrees of willingness and ability of people to shift from conventional income to capital gains. Both types of adjustment seem to favor high income groups relative to others, though the main effects seem to arise between people *within* the various income classes.

Other types of 'tax and Welfare-State created' inequalities arise between those who happen to get and those who do not get rationed public services of various kinds, such as free higher education in schools with limited entry, subsidized loans for owner-occupied houses, and the access to subsidized old-age care centers for parents or subsidized day-care centers for children. To some extent, the distribution of such benefits looks like a 'public service lottery', with the dice loaded in a very complicated way — with favorable treatment sometimes of 'disadvantaged' groups like unmarried mothers, but also of people with great ability to argue, and 'good contacts' with public administrators. A different type of 'tax and Welfare-State created' inequality is of course income gains connected with illegal tax evasion and economic crimes in general — for which the incomes are tax-free!

Thus, while the tax-transfer system has removed much of the income inequalities that are related to *productive effort*, including not only work but also investment in human and physical assets, some of the losers in various income classes have been able to compensate themselves in various ways — such as by exploiting asymmetries in the tax system, in particular in connection with asset transactions and capital gains connected with price changes, probably also through illegal tax evasion. The other side of the coin is that some of the groups which have gained on the tax-transfer system, particularly pensioners living in rented apartments and with assets in bank deposits and bonds, have lost part of their income gains due to capital losses on the asset side.

Thus, we would expect that a considerable part of the differences in income standards today are connected with differences in demographic variables, success in 'jumping' queues for rationed public services, 'smart' asset transactions, real capital gains due to speculation in inflation, various types of dishonest activities, etc., rather than with differences in productive effort. The problem, then, for those who want to increase their income, or even become rich, in a Welfare State like Sweden is *not* that it is impossible, but rather that it is difficult to achieve by way of honest and productive effort.

(6) The paper has, finally, demonstrated the wide *marginal wedges* that are necessarily driven between factor costs for firms and factor rewards for households when disposable income is redistributed drastically, relative to factor incomes, by tax-transfer policies. It would be surprising if, in a long-run perspective, the emerging 'distortions' and 'disincentives' for effort and the allocation of resources did not have considerable effects on economic efficiency. [For attempts to analyze such effects, see Lindbeck (1981a,c).] It is no doubt the risks of consequences like these that have made the Swedish parliament decide to reduce the marginal income tax rates gradually over the years 1983–1985.

References

Arbetslivscentrum, 1981, Deltidsanställningens orsaker, Vol. 1 (Deltidsanställdas Levnads-förhållanden, Stockholm)

Franzén, T., H. Lövgren and I. Rosenberg, 1975, Redistributional effects of taxes and public expenditures in Sweden, Swedish Journal of Economics 1, 31–55.

Gustafsson, S., 1976, Lönebildning och lönestruktur inom den statliga sektorn (Industriens Utredningsinstitut, Stockholm).

Ingelstam, L., 1980, Arbetets värde och tidens bruk (Liber Förlag. Stockholm).

Konsumentverket, 1979. Konsument 79 (Tidsbudgetundersökning. Stockholm).

Lindbeck, A., 1981a, Work disincentives in the Welfare State, Nationalökonomische Gesellschaft lecture no. 79–80 (Manz, Vienna). Also as Reprint no. 176 (Institute for International Economic Studies, University of Stockholm, Stockholm).

256   A. Lindbeck, Income distributions in a welfare state

Lindbeck, A., 1981b, The distribution of factor income versus disposable income in a Welfare
    State: The case of Sweden. Seminar paper no. 171 (Institute for International Economic
    Studies, University of Stockholm, Stockholm).
Lindbeck, A., 1981c, Disincentive problems in developed countries, Lecture at the conference on
    growth and entrepreneurship (International Chamber of Commerce, Manila). Also as Reprint
    no. 171 (Institute for International Economic Studies, University of Stockholm, Stockholm).
Lindbeck, A., 1982, Tax effects versus budget effects on labor supply, Economic Inquiry, Oct.
Nordström, F., 1982, Hushållens förmögenheter och reala kapitalvinster 1979 (Economics
    Department, University of Stockholm, Stockholm) unpublished.
Roberts, K.W.S., 1977, Voting over income tax schedules, Journal of Public Economics 8, 329–
    340.
SIFO, 1980, En nation av fifflare (Stockholm).
Statistisk Sentralbyrå, 1975, Tid nyttet till egenarbied (Olso).
Vogel, J., 1970, Aspirationer, möjligheter och skattemoral. En rättssociologisk undersökning av
    deklaranter, SOU 25. (Betänkandet avgivet av Skattestraffslagsutredningen, Stockholm).
    Summarized in: J. Vogel, 1974, Taxation and public opinion in Sweden: An interpretation of
    recent survey data, National Tax Journal, 499–513.

Appendix

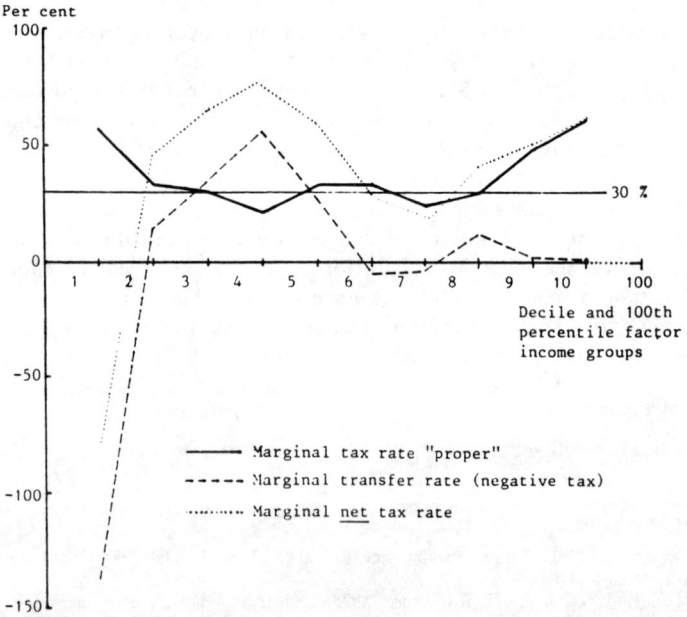

Fig. 13. Components of 'mongrel' actual net marginal tax rates. The curves would be higher up
on the scale if the denominator had been gross income or income assessed for tax purposes
rather than factor income. Source: National Central Bureau of Statistics: Income Distribution
Survey in 1979.

[4]

DISINCENTIVE PROBLEMS IN DEVELOPED COUNTRIES

Assar Lindbeck

In combination with economic growth, the build-up of elaborate welfare state systems in the developed countries during this century has helped improve the economic security of ordinary men and women. Reforms have evened out income over the life-cycle of the individual by income transfers from periods of productive employment to periods of unemployment, sickness and old age. There has also been a dramatic increase in the availability of low-priced services in such fields as schooling, medical care and old age care. In several countries, welfare state programmes have helped wipe out economic misery among citizens with various physical, psychological and cultural handicaps and have produced a more equal distribution of economic well-being among the rest of the population. Most well-informed observers with humanitarian values today agree that the development of the welfare state represents, up to a point, a considerable achievement of modern civilization.

It is also likely that some welfare state reforms have helped to increase the **efficiency** of the economy. One obvious example is the stimulation of investment in human capital through publicly-financed education, health care and improved nutrition of the poor. A more speculative point is that the greater equalization of living standards may have increased the loyalty to society of otherwise seriously disadvantaged citizens, thus reducing the risk of disruption of political and economic processes.

Apprehension about welfare state

However, there is considerable apprehension that welfare state policy — with respect to social security systems, transfer payments,[1] public services and, in particular, the

---

I am grateful for valuable comments to a draft of this paper from June Flanders, S.O. Lodin, and Martin Wassell.

1 Money paid by the government for no productive activity to people in need, such as the old, the sick, or the unemployed.

financing of these programmes — may in the long run undermine the structure of economic incentives in our societies. Similar concern is felt about the likely disincentive effects of the numerous laws, regulations, taxes and subsidies affecting firms which have been introduced over the years for reasons similar to those underlying the build-up of the welfare state: to enhance the income and economic security of social groups and individuals. There is also considerable doubt whether public services are produced in the most efficient ways possible and whether their delivery allows the individual enough freedom of choice. Some people even argue that, as a result of all this, both the general living standard and the desired content of welfare reform may be undermined in the long run.

What is a disincentive?

Before trying to identify the various types of disincentive effects of government policies in the developed countries, it is important to be clear about the terms "incentives" and "disincentives". A well-functioning incentive clearly does not mean one that makes people work, save and invest as much as possible. Rather, there should be a certain correspondence between the social return and the return to the individual on productive effort.

Suppose, for example, that a person produces additional output worth $10 by one more hour of work. If he is rewarded for that extra hour by just this amount, we way say that there is a perfect correspondence between the private and social returns on his work effort (assuming no additional effects on society). By contrast, if he is allowed to keep only $5 or perhaps even $1 — for instance, because of an income tax — there is a substantial deviation between the private and the social return. The income tax reduces the reward for additional work, making leisure cheaper as measured by income forgone, even though the firm has to pay the pre-tax rate. This is called in economic jargon a "substitution effect" in favour of leisure, i.e. against work, implying a deviation between the private and social returns from work. It is this deviation which we mean, or should mean, when we speak of inappropriate incentives for work effort and hence of a distortion of the choice between leisure and income.

Similarly, suppose that the reward to the individual for additional saving is smaller than the contribution to society as a whole of increased investment — for instance, because of a tax on interest income. There is then a substitution effect against saving, and hence a distortion of the choice between consumption today and consumption tomorrow.

Suppose further that income from a specific type of production or investment is taxed at a much higher rate than income from other types, so that the return to the individual becomes much lower on some of these activities than on others, as compared to the returns to society as a whole. This would mean a substitution effect on, and a corresponding distortion of, production decisions or asset choices, and hence a disincentive effect on the allocation of factors of production and asset holdings in the economy.

More generally, what is meant by a disincentive is a wedge between the social and private returns on individual activity — due, for instance, to the insertion of a tax at the margin between the cost to firms of using various factors of production and the reward to the owners of those factors.

However, because a tax increase also imposes on the individual a loss in disposable income, it has in addition what are called "income effects" against consumption, saving and leisure; the individual can afford less of all these things. Conversely, the recipients of transfer payments and free or subsidized services can afford more consumption, saving and leisure; they experience positive income effects.

Substitution effects

This paper will concentrate on the substitution effect, i.e. the fall in the reward for additional productive effort, and ignore the income effect. The reason is that the disincentives, i.e. the distortions, as defined here, are tied to the substitution effect rather than to the income effect since only the former influences the return to additional effort.[2]

In discussing disincentive effects, it is not enough to look at just **income** tax rates. **Indirect** taxes on consumer goods are also relevant. The same holds for transfer payments which are automatically reduced when the income of an individual rises — so-called "income-dependent transfers". Moreover, some payroll taxes function in fact as taxes on labor income to the extent that the expected social security benefits to the individual do not automatically adjust fully to higher social security payments by the individual. This

---

2 A. Lindbeck: "Work Disincentives in the Welfare State". Seminar Paper No. 164 (Stockholm. Institute for International Economic Studies. 1980).

means that disincentive problems are also usually connected with some component of the social insurance system, such as old age pensions, sickness insurance, and unemployment insurance.[3]

Obviously, all these explicit and implicit marginal tax rates should be considered when the disincentive effects of public policies are being examined. Then the "marginal tax rates" of typical full-time employees in northwest Europe are often seen to be not 30-50%, as for income tax alone, but in some countries as high as 60-80% and, occasionally, even higher. Similarly, all types of regulations of and subsidies to firms should in principle be considered, for a complete picture of the incentive and disincentive effects of public policy on production.

Work effort and the labor market

Considerable attempts have been made in various countries to measure empirically the disincentive effects on labor supply of taxes and welfare state programmes. Unfortunately, this has proved to be an exceedingly difficult task. However, the **types** of disincentive effects on work effort are quite well known.

Taxes

Higher marginal tax (and transfer) rates create incentives to shift not only from work to leisure but also to do-it-yourself work and the barter of goods and services — as well as to opt for a slower pace of work ("on-the-job leisure") when pay is connected to effort. There is also a decline in the reward for work associated with special "disutilities" (such as physical and psychological strain), as well as, if the tax system is progressive, for investment in human capital. In particular, we would expect high marginal tax rates to induce people to choose jobs that give "income" (or rather utility) in kind, which is usually tax free, rather than income in money terms. We would also expect some students to be induced to choose easy and enjoyable subjects rather than difficult ones which subsequently enable them to earn high pre-tax

---

3 See, for instance, A. Lindbeck, *op. cit.*, and S. Danzinger, R. Haveman and R. Plotnick: "How Income Transfer Programs Affect Work, Savings, and Income Distribution: A Critical Review", mimeo, forthcoming in *The Journal of Economic Literature*.

money incomes; in other words, students would increasingly choose consumption-oriented rather than investment-oriented studies.

Taxes also imply a fall in the financial reward for the trouble of changing job and geographical location in response to higher pre-tax pay — at the same time as the need for such mobility has increased in many countries because of several factors: new types of international competition, drastically altered cost relations between different sectors of production, and frequently also minimum wage legislation and policies designed to narrow pay differentials whose effect is to reduce employment opportunities in weak production sectors and for low-skill labor.

Legislation

Recent legislation on job security, redundancy payments and seniority rights has similar effects, often rendering labor a fixed cost for firms over a considerable period of time. Not only do such laws make the engagement of employees a heavy investment for firms, but the system of "last in first out" is tantamount to a tax on labor mobility since people forgo seniority rights like firm-specific pensions, when they change employer. In other words, both the interest of firms in hiring people rather than buying machines and the willingness of employees to shift jobs have been reduced by these new arrangements. As a result, there tend to be more "mismatches" in the labor market, with a simultaneous increase in both vacancies and unemployment and a negative effect on economic growth.

Some of the new laws may, up to a point, be regarded as rational responses to information costs and to the absence of appropriate insurance systems. A indication that this interpretation makes sense is that employers and employees often make formal or informal labor contracts with similar provisions on a completely voluntary basis. However, the result is still a deterioration in the functioning of the labor market. Moreover, it is quite conceivable that legislation in this field has gone much further than can be explained on such grounds — at least in some countries.

Social insurance systems

The effect of social insurance systems on the supply of labor is a more complex issue still. It is even difficult to know what a "disincentive effect" should mean in this context. One conceivable definition is the substitution effects which ensue when individual insurance contributions exceed the actuarial value of expected benefits connected with a change in individual work effort. That is what I mean by a "disincentive effect" in this context. "Standard analysis" predicts that both pension and sickness insurance systems will have a negative substitution effect on hours worked during an individual's lifetime, while the unemployment insurance system will cause longer periods of "search unemployment" — provided the systems have the above-mentioned property. However, there may be some counteracting effects. For instance, it is often argued that some people, such as housewives, enter the labor market from a desire to become participants in various social security systems.[4]

Individual and collective responses to incentive effects

In a highly organized society, it is difficult for the individual himself to choose the number of hours he wishes to work. It is often argued that the practical possibilities are limited to variations in overtime and "moonlighting". In a long-run perspective, however, the institutional obstacles too may be influenced by the incentive effect on individuals of taxation and welfare state programmes. We would, for instance, expect an increased interest in part-time work to induce employers to reorganize work routines to accommodate it.

We would also expect both bargaining (between unions and employers) and legislation about working hours and various types of benefit systems to respond to changes in the incentive content of taxation and welfare state programmes. For example, the recent drastic expansion in some countries of various employee "rights" to paid vacation and absence from work because of studies, family illness, small children, etc. may well be seen in part as a response, through legislation and the collective bargaining system, to reduced incentives to work. In other words, the effects on individual behavior operate through collective bargaining and the political decision-making process, as well as via individual actions in the market. An important consequence of all these reforms is that temporary absenteeism from work becomes both easier and less expensive for the individual than in the past.

---

4 S. Danziger, R. Haveman and R. Plotnick, *op. cit.*

Women and the labor market

Existing empirical studies of a number of countries do not indicate dramatic substitution effects stemming from welfare state and tax policies on the total number of hours of work supplied in the labor market by men, though the effects for married women seem to be much more pronounced.[5] But other factors have at the same time given a strong encouragement to married women to supply more labor in the open market. Obvious examples are technological developments that have contributed to the rationalization of household work, and probably also the emergence of a preference for smaller families and of new attitudes in general towards the role of women in society.

The trend for married women to join the labor force has been accentuated by several welfare state programmes, in particular the expansion of personal social services for children, the old and the sick. Since these types of public service assume responsibilities traditionally borne by the household, they have induced married women to shift from housework to labor market activities — sometimes to working in precisely those public institutions that have taken over personal services from the household. In the latter case, women simply shift from taking care of their own children and elderly parents to taking care of the relatives of other families.

Overall disincentive effects

For all the reasons discussed, the most pronounced disincentive effects on the labor market of taxation and welfare state programmes are probably not the tendency for the total number of working hours to fall, but rather:

• a general reduction in the flexibility and mobility of labor among different jobs and different regions;

• an increase in temporary, and often unpredictable, absenteeism from work which complicates the operations of individual firms and institutions, small ones especially;

5 O. Ashenfelter, "Using Estimates of Income and Substitution Parameters to Predict the Work Incentive Effects of the Negative Income Tax: A Brief Exposition and Partial Survey", mimeo, Princeton University, November 1970; G.C. Cain and H.W. Watts (eds.), "Income Maintenance and Labor Supply", Institute for Research on Poverty Monograph Series (New York, Academic Press, 1973); L. Godfrey, *Theoretical and Empirical Aspects of the Effects of Taxation on the Supply of Labour*, OECD, 1975; IFS (Institute for Fiscal Studies), *The Structure and Reform of Direct Taxation*, Allen and Unwin, 1978; Royal Commission on Taxation, Ottawa, Canada, 1967; and A. Lindbeck, *op. cit.*

• a tendency to choose jobs which yield income (or utility) in kind — often tax-free — rather than income in money terms;

• a tendency among students to opt for easy and enjoyable subjects rather than complex ones that may subsequently permit high pre-tax earnings; and

• a reduced interest in striving for promotion and higher skills — accentuated by a trend, particularly in the public sector, to employ, fire and promote employees according to seniority rather than competence (a criterion often urged strongly by labor unions).

Admittedly, these judgements about the importance of various kinds of effects in the labor market are heuristic, based on scattered empirical information, rather than conclusions that can be supported by systematic and non-controversial scholarly evidence.

Saving and asset choice

In a hypothetical non-inflationary economy with modest marginal tax rates, and with the returns on all assets taxed uniformly, the disincentive effect against saving and the holding of certain types of asset might not be very large. However, this is not the world in which we live today. The actual situation is largely one of high inflation, a nominalist income tax system which is blind to inflation, high marginal income tax rates, and very different treatment of different types of assets. As a consequence, strong discriminatory effects often occur, creating a disincentive against both saving and the holding of certain types of asset.

More specifically, taxes on income in kind from the holding of durable consumer goods and collectors' items are often very low, if they exist at all (though some countries levy taxes on the notional income from owner-occupied houses). Moreover, there are usually no taxes on the real capital gains the debtor derives from inflation and often only rather low capital gains taxes, if any, on houses, durable consumer goods and collectors' items. As a result, the combination of high income tax rates and inflation systematically siphons away funds from bank savings, private bonds, and shares to owner-occupied houses, durable consumer goods and antiques. Moreover, when interest is tax deductible, households become quite insensitive to interest rates in their demand for consumer credit.

Forcing interest rates up

To curtail borrowing by households, the government often has then to force interest rates so high that private investment in producer goods, mainly by firms, is severely restricted. It is not difficult to understand that the supply of risk capital to firms tends to dry up under such circumstances. Thus, high marginal tax rates in an inflationary economy of this type may create very strong disincentive effects not only against saving but also against credit flows that finance the purchase of producer capital goods.

Moreover, since the low rate of return on shares tends to depress share prices, there will be a strong tendency towards "take-over bids" in the capital market by both other firms and various capital market institutions with funds from, for instance, insurance payments, pension contributions, and retained earnings. The tax system may therefore contribute heavily towards a concentration of ownership and industrial structure that could not be defended on ordinary efficiency grounds.

Unstable tax rules

In several countries there is also a considerable instability in actual and expected tax rules, often resulting in violent fluctuations in the market value of assets. Consequently, accurate forecasts about tax rules for various assets are frequently much more important for successful portfolio management than accurate forecasts about "spontaneous" market developments. This means that speculation about the future behavior of politicians is often of much greater concern to portfolio managers than speculation about changes in the behavior of private agents.

Social security

We would also expect social security systems for sickness, unemployment and old age to have substitution effects on private savings. Since such systems often provide substitutes for private saving, "standard analysis" suggests that private savings are reduced as a result, though consideration of certain conceivable indirect effects may lead to more ambiguous conclusions.[6] It is probably fair to say that, on balance, available **empirical** studies do indicate some neg-

---

6 S. Danziger *et al.*, *op. cit.*

ative substitution effects.[7] However, it is difficult to judge the net effect of the social security system on the total (aggregate) saving of society as a whole. For this depends to a considerable extent both on how the system is organized in its details and on how it is financed. For instance, if it is financed by compulsory contributions that are much larger than the benefits, and hence considerable social security funds accumulate, it is even likely that the aggregate saving ratio for the economy as a whole may be positively influenced, for some time at least.

Production and investment

It is a truism, but an important one, that a private enterprise system can function reasonably well only if actual and expected profits exceed certain minimum levels. This requirement is particularly delicate for those sectors of the domestic economy that are exposed to foreign competition. Considering the important role of wages in national income, we may, as a rough approximation, say that a certain correspondence has to exist between the domestic nominal wage level and the exchange rate for given prices of products supplied by competitors in other countries. This requirement —often called "cost parity" (per unit of output) *vis-à-vis* other countries— is a necessary condition for a satisfactory rate of return on physical assets for firms in the sectors exposed to foreign competition. It is by now generally accepted that such a cost parity is necessary both for keeping down unemployment and for achieving a reasonably rapid growth of production and the stock of capital assets in the market-oriented part of the economy.

Cost parity

Thus, the really important and difficult question is how to bring about and sustain such cost parity, i.e., a reasonable level of profitability in the economy. Assuming a given rate of productivity increase, the issue for the sectors that are exposed to foreign competition is how to limit the inflationary bias of factor prices, particularly for labor, in the domestic

---

7 It is striking that, while households in a welfare state like Sweden save only some 3-4% of disposable income, the corresponding ratio in Japan, with little social security, is about 25%. It is far from obvious, however, how much of this difference can be explained by the difference between their social security systems.

economy relative to the outside world. This is certainly too large and too difficult a topic to be dealt with in detail here. I will limit myself to two crucial points.

1. Shift in responsibility for employment level

First, it is very difficult to hold back increases in factor prices sufficiently as long as individual employees, labor unions and employers believe that the government has the whole responsibility for the employment level in the country. For that creates confidence that the government will always "accommodate" any increase in factor prices and product prices not only through an expansion of aggregate monetary demand and an adjustment of the exchange rate, but also by selective subsidies to firms in trouble. The policy implication of this point is, in my judgement, that wage bargainers must assume a greater responsibility than today for the employment level in the domestic economy. In practice, it means that the government must declare itself unwilling to eliminate the unemployment consequences of pay rises higher than in competing nations. This is, in fact, exactly what has been tried in countries whose governments have announced a goal of adhering to a fixed exchange rate or, in countries with floating exchange rates, of adhering to a fixed rate of expansion of the money supply.

2. Increasing tolerance towards profits

Secondly, it might prove easier to limit the rate of increase in nominal wage rates if the interest in the return on physical assets was anchored more broadly in our societies than at present. Perhaps this could be brought about if the ownership of corporate shares was distributed much more widely among individual employees, a change which would probably require reforms to make investing in shares much more attractive to small wealth holders than it is today. A removal of the discriminatory tax treatment of shares is one obvious option; another might even be a temporary positive discrimination in favor of small shareholders. Another reform which might increase tolerance of profits would be the establishment of new types of capital market funds with a much broader recruitment of board members than is typical of existing capital market institutions.

Tariffs and subsidies

Of course, taxes, welfare state programmes and macro-economic policies which influence the rate of return on equity capital are not the only public measures that influence the production and investment incentives of firms in a fundamental way. Tariffs and subsidies which affect trade and the allocation of resources are other obvious examples.

In most highly developed countries, where tariffs are now so low and the tariff structure so even, the disincentive effects of tariff policy are probably a minor problem today. The most important exception relates perhaps to imports of mainly labor-intensive products from the developing countries. Moreover, the high tariffs against these countries are supported by various types of **quantitative** import restrictions, which have proliferated in the past decade in blatant violation not only of GATT principles but also of the interest of consumers in developed countries.

1. Industrial policy

However, a form of interference with international trade and the allocation of resources which is today even more important are the huge subsidies to industry that have e-merged, particularly during the last decade, under the title of "industrial policy".

The consequences of these new trends for the domestic economy are often quite drastic. The most obvious one is a less efficient allocation of resources and a more sluggish reponse of the allocation mechanism to changes in circumstances. However, a more profound effect is that corporate managers find a **substitute for competition** in the market: lobbying and bargaining for subsidies, often in co-operation with labor unions and local politicians.

2. New criteria for entrepreneurship

This means, in fact, that firms often rely on the transfer of resources from taxpayers, rather than trying to create new resources by way of efficient production. It is likely that, in a society where lobbying and bargaining for subsidies become an important part of what was earlier called "entrepre-neurship", the attitudes of business managers will change fundamentally over time— partly because they will be selected according to different criteria. As a consequence, the allocative efficiency and dynamism of the economy would be expected to decline even further, at least in the long run.

One reason why subsidies are most likely to have such effects is that they will be expected to be allocated systematically to declining industries and inefficient firms. For it is more rewarding for politicians in highly competitive political systems to save threatened jobs for known persons in existing firms than to try to create new jobs in often unknown firms for unknown persons. The pressure groups are usually much stronger for existing jobs than for new ones.

General consequences for society

An underlying assumption in this exposition has been that an economic system cannot function reasonably efficiently if the relation between effort and reward is drastically cut off — as has happened in some countries, particularly in northwest Europe, for rather large segments of the population and for firms. It has been argued that the main problem for economic efficiency is probably not that the number of hours of labur supplied by households is negatively influenced, but rather, that:

● people's ambition to acquire skills and be promoted is weakened;

● that the general functioning of the labor market deteriorates;

● that private financial saving is reduced; and

● that the supply of credit tends to be siphoned away from the purchase of producer goods by firms to the purchase of durable consumer goods and various types of non-productive investment. Another important effect is that asset-holders concentrate on asset transactions which are favorable only because of the combined effects of inflation and existing tax rules.

No more carrot, no more stick!

In addition, not only the rewards for success but also the penalties for failure in the production system have been generally reduced — both for households, through the elaborate social safety net and the system of transfer payments, and for firms, which are increasingly bailed out by government when they fail in the competitive race. For instance, bankruptcy today tends largely to have been abolished as a punishment for failure as subsidies and grants of equity capital, not only to publicly-owned firms but increasingly to private corporations also, remove from shareholders their traditional role in society of carrying the risk of default. In other words, both the carrot and the stick have been largely displaced from the production system!

However, in addition to these economic effects, there are some profound consequences for the general character of our society. Some of the most important general consequences may be summarized as follows.

Shift to the political arena

First, when falling profits and higher marginal tax rates reduce the return from ordinary market activities, relative to the resource transfers from taxpayers, both producers and consumers will increasingly turn to government to improve their economic situation. Competition for income among various groups of income earners will shift from the market to the political arena. It appears a good proposition to obtain extra benefits from government on the assumption that other groups pay the bulk of the cost. When employees, savers and firms increasingly shift from the positive-sum games of productive activity to what may look like zero-sum games of transfers, a slower growth rate of gross national product (GNP) is a predictable outcome, making the process in fact a negative-sum game for society as a whole. Another predictable result is a rapid expansion of public expenditure, and probably of public ownership also.

The family is weakened

Secondly, the role of the family is profoundly influenced by tax and welfare state reforms. Subsidies to students and transfers to the old induce children and their elderly parents to establish separate small households. The responsibility for personal service — caring for the young, the sick, and the old — tends to move outside the household to public institutions, while households, because of tax-induced shifts to do-it-yourself work and barter, devote increasing time to "non-personal" services — for instance, improving their own property by decorating, plumbing, gardening, etc. Thus, while the provision of personal **services to people** (one's own relatives) is socialized, the provision of **services to things** is transferred partly from markets to households, with rather drastic effects on the family unit and its role in society.

Loyalty to society is weakened

Thirdly, increased marginal tax rates necessarily mean higher financial rewards from criminal activities, including tax evasion, relative to other activities, since income from criminal activities is usually tax-free... Honesty becomes expensive. It was argued at the beginning of this paper that the welfare state reforms and the system of progressive taxation might by **themselves** improve the social fabric of society, in particular by deepening the loyalty to society of less advantaged citizens. On the other hand, because high marginal tax rates on productive effort also imply very high taxation of honesty, loyalty to society may be weakened — not only among those who are hurt by high tax rates, but also among those who notice that others are cheating or being excessively "smart" with tax-motivated transactions.

Profitability of cheating

Black markets — "the underground economy" — are a striking result of the same forces.[8] It is well known that the scope for gainful activity of that type is particularly large for small firms which sell services directly to households or to other small firms. When tax evasion — of sales taxes, income taxes, social security contributions, etc. — starts to prevail in a sector, it will be reflected in output prices. Honest entrepreneurs then have only two options: to start cheating as well or leave the business. Since in the long run the return on cheating probably tends to fall to a level that corresponds to a normal return for risk-taking, the consequence of cheating is perhaps not so much a problem of the distribution of income as of the allocation of resources — and also, of course, a problem of ethics.

However, it would be a mistake to think that cheating is practised only by small businessmen and people with large asset holdings. Ordinary households cheat — and not only by buying black-market services, or engaging in barter, or evading taxes on moonlighting: there is also evidence of considerable cheating in the transfer and social security systems. It has been observed in some countries — such as the United States and Sweden — that people give false information not only about incomes but also about employment and family status in order to obtain welfare benefits from the government. For instance, a person engaged in "the underground economy" may at the same time be receiving unemployment benefits. Or a couple may forgo marriage and pretend they are not living together in order to obtain certain benefits for unmarried mothers.

Thus the problem with a high-tax, high-inflation society is not that it is impossible or even difficult for individuals to increase their income, or perhaps even to become rich, but that it is increasingly difficult to do so by way of **productive activity** in the "official" part of the economy. The exploitation of inflation and the peculiarities of the tax system, resource transfers from government, tax evasion and avoidance, and various other dishonest activities become a more promising road to a higher standard of living.

---

8 V. Tanzi, "Underground Economy Built on Illicit Pursuits is Growing Concern of Economic Policymakers", *IMF Survey*, February 4, 1980, pp. 34-37.

Actual importance of disincentives

There is great controversy among both politicians and economists about the quantitative importance of the disincentive effects and other problems associated with modern
welfare state reforms, tax policies, industrial policies, and
government regulations. My personal judgement is that the
disincentive effects discussed here were probably not very
serious when welfare state policy mainly took the form of:

• redistribution of income over the lifetime of individuals,
largely through the social security system;

• redistribution in favor of the poor; and

• increased supply of some basic social services like health
and education.

For in those days — reaching perhaps into the 1950s and
1960s — marginal tax rates, even in the most advanced
welfare states, were quite small for most people, often no
higher than 20-40% for ''normal'' income earners. Empirical
studies of the United States and the United Kingdom in the
1950s, 1960s and early 1970s do not on balance suggest
very dramatic disincentive effects on work, savings and
investment, though the results of the studies are no doubt
extremely shaky. Moreover, selective subsidies to firms and
governmental regulation of economic activity were not of
overwhelming importance in those days.

Increased risk today of disincentives

The risk of serious disincentive effects is much greater
today in some of the most advanced welfare states where
the marginal tax/transfer rates for ordinary income earners
often amount to 60-80% or more if both direct income taxes
and indirect taxes on consumption and social security payrolls are considered. The risk is accentuated if we also take
into account the reduction in transfers to low- and me-
dium-income groups when their earnings rise (the so-called
''poverty trap''). In other words, for marginal increases in
individual effort, the labor costs to firms are often five or
sometimes even 10 times as high as the marginal reward to
the individual. It is likely that such large wedges between
factor costs and factor rewards have considerable effects
not only on household choice in the use of time, but also on
the choice of firms between using labor or machines or
between categories of labor with different skills. The disincentive effects, particularly on savings and asset choice,
have been strongly reinforced by the dramatic increase in
inflation during the 1970s.

Redistribution within the middle class

Another important development is that additions to welfare state policies during the 1970s increasingly had the character of redistributions from the middle class to the middle class itself — or even from the right to the left pocket of given individuals. Examples are tax-financed increases in the subsidization of food, housing and dozens of activities that are not particularly related to low income, including subsidies to inefficient firms. Other examples are the various "rights", discussed earlier, to (often paid) absenteeism from work.

To a considerable extent, it is probably the growth of redistribution within the large middle class of the population during the 1970s which has pushed the "marginal tax bite" to problematic levels in some countries, particularly in northwest Europe. At the same time, government subsidies to ailing firms and direct regulation of economic activity have almost literally exploded. Most well-informed economists in Sweden, for instance, are by now quite convinced that the country entered the 1980s with very severe disincentive problems concerning work, saving, asset choice and entrepreneurship — and with the considerable risk of a drastic deterioration in the honesty of individual citizens, particularly in their relations with the public authorities. In other words, it is not the principle of the welfare state that is a problem, but rather its tendency in some countries to overshoot its limits.

Why financial rewards?

Or course, individuals in their work, saving and entrepreneurial activities are influenced by motives other than economic reward. The desire to do a good job, or interact with others, or build self-esteem, or enjoy either cooperation or competition, certainly play important roles as motives for individual behavior in the various dimensions discussed in this paper. However, I have assumed that entrepreneurship cannot be fully successful and vital without financial rewards, that such rewards play a very important role for some individuals and a non-negligible role for most and, particularly, that markets cannot function well without them.

Both theoretical analysis and empirical experience strongly suggest that it is difficult to replace financial rewards to any considerable extent by other kinds of reward. One reason is simply that, to a much larger extent than other rewards, financial rewards can be continuously varied and easily differentiated for millions of different activities. Another advantage is that they both measure productive effort and inform about socially productive activities in conformity with consumers' preferences.

In other words, both profits and factor prices (such as wage rates) fill the **triple role of measuring, informing and rewarding**. This combination is very difficult to bring about by other types of reward such as prestige, esteem, the pleasure of exercising power, or altruism. Most likely, it is this combination of properties which has made financial rewards so predominant in the world and which has also induced countries that had tried to play down their importance to reestablish them.

However, there is perhaps an even more fundamental reason. Since alternative kinds of reward have proved too weak, societies that have been unwilling to rely much on financial rewards have been forced to depend heavily on **commands** — not only to firms but to households as well. In such command-economy societies a dramatic centralization of decision-making has proved necessary, curtailing individual freedom in the economic field. Since economic freedom is a prerequisite for other types of freedom, the appeal of financial rewards, i.e. economic incentives, is very compelling for people with a high regard for individual liberty.

Ways out

What are the possibilities of breaking out from the present impasse?

1. First, in many countries it is potentially useful, not to say crucial, to improve the general incentives to invest in producer goods by raising the rate of return on physical investment by firms.

2. A second step would be to try to reverse the gradual increase of highly selective subsidies and grants to firms, as well as the expansion of non-tariff barriers to trade.

3. Reforming the taxation of assets is a third important task. If inflation remains high, it will probably be necessary not only to make the taxation of different types of asset more symmetrical, but also to shift to a system of **real taxation** — either within the framework of income taxation or by adopting an expenditure tax system. To tax the imputed income from various types of durable consumer goods and collectors' items could also, in principle, improve the allocative efficiency of the economy, particularly if households are permitted tax relief on interest payments on debt incurred for consumption purposes. In addition, a number of "positive" incentive policies could increase investment in productive capital and R & D (research and development) expenditure; among these are tax credits or accelerated depreciation. However, it is important to realize that measures like these cannot be an effective substitute for a general improvement in the level of profitability.

4. Fourthly, in some countries it is also very important to reduce the marginal tax/transfer rates on household income and consumption. Obviously, this presupposes other policy changes as well, such as:

• a reduction in public spending relative to GNP;

• an increased use of charging for public services to avoid their over-supply relative to people's willingness to pay for them;

• a shift to more reliance on "pure insurance" for some of the social security systems, so that an individual's social security contributions would be more like insurance premiums than taxes on income;

• higher efficiency within the public sector, for instance by exposing it to more competition;

• more reliance on fixed-sum, "as-of-right" benefits — for instance, child allowances and pensions to the handicapped and old people — rather than income-dependent transfers.

Of course, a reduction of income redistribution, at least within the broad group of middle-income earners, would also facilitate a reduction of marginal tax rates and hence an improvement in the structure of economic incentives.

Clearly, several of these potential reforms would raise strong ideological objections and provoke considerable resistance from various pressure groups. In particular, some of the reforms may severely conflict with a widely-accepted objective of rendering more equal the distribution of income, wealth and economic well-being. Thus, what is worth striving for and what can be achieved in terms of practical politics are certainly open to some doubt in a great number of countries. The real challenge is how to restore efficient incentives to productive activity without jeopardizing the social achievements of the modern welfare state. It is a task which would probably be simplified if both the labor movement and various opposition and minority groups could be better integrated than at present in the political and economic processes of society.

[5]

Consequences of the Advanced
Welfare State

Assar Lindbeck

HAT are the basic problems, economic as well as non-economic, of the modern welfare state? Before trying to answer that question it is necessary to decide what is meant by the term 'welfare state'. In this article the term is reserved for the array of publicly-financed social-security systems, transfers and subsidies and for the public provision or subsidization of personal services such as health, education, old-age care and child care.[1] By 'welfare state spending' I therefore mean various types of public spending programmes apart from those related to the 'classical' role of the government to enforce contracts, to provide collective goods, to take care of various externalities in the production system (such as environmental disturbances) and to supply physical infrastructure. Regulations and macro-economic 'stabilization policies' will not be covered, although the arguments and, in some cases possibly, also the motives for such policies are similar to those for the types of public spending programmes which are analyzed in the article.

The discussion relates to the most 'advanced' welfare states in North-western Europe where public spending today is some 50 to 65 per cent of gross national product (GNP) and where foreign trade is a large fraction (25 to 50 per cent) of GNP. Only incidental references, mainly for comparison, will be made to the more limited welfare-state system, or perhaps even 'pre-welfare' situation, in the United States where public spending amounts to no more than about 33 per cent of GNP (in spite of a defence budget of some 7 per cent of GNP). Indeed, as will be shown, the 'welfare state problems' in North-western Europe and the United States are quite different.

ACHIEVEMENTS OF THE WELFARE STATE

Before turning to various problems in connection with the welfare state, it is important to record some of its main achievements. These may be divided into four categories.

ASSAR LINDBECK: Professor of International Economics, and Director of the Institute for International Economic Studies, University of Stockholm, Sweden.

19

One important achievement is certainly to have mitigated, or even eliminated, destitution among people with extremely low life income. Most probably, concern for 'social morality' and, indeed, altruism are important driving forces behind this achievement. But it is certainly also believed that many citizens enjoy a society without poverty around them (which is basically an externality argument) and, too, that social stability and human relations are enhanced by the mitigation of poverty. It is obvious that the elaborate, highly 'general' welfare-state systems in the most advanced welfare states of North-western Europe have been much more successful in this endeavour than has been the less elaborate, but hardly less complex, 'selective' welfare-state system in the United States.[2] This can be seen, for example, by comparing national statistics on poverty, infant mortality and child mortality, where the achievements in the United States are rather mediocre given the high per-capita income of that country.[3] Indeed, one does not have to look at statistics to discover poverty in the United States. It is enough to walk the streets and follow the mass media. Many areas of housing in the United States are more reminiscent of a developing country than a highly developed country. This is probably a combined effect of poverty and the high cost of decent housing. As long as there is demand for slum housing, there will be a supply of it.

A second, and related, contribution of some of the most advanced welfare states is to have evened out (life-time) wealth among households in general — not only *ex post* (that is, when looking at actual outcomes), which occurs automatically in all insurance systems, but also *ex ante* (that is, when considering expected incomes of individuals). Income-dependent transfers and the wealth-redistributional elements of the social-security system, as well as in some countries progressive taxation, are important factors behind these results. Of course, it is a question about subjective values whether this should be regarded as a positive or negative contribution.

A third achievement of the modern welfare state has been to raise productivity in the national economy by inducing investment in human capital, in particular by the subsidization of services such as education and health care, for which, at least until recently, the social return seems to have been higher than the return on alternative investments. One motive behind these subsidies is probably the desire to make corrections for the assumed lack of information among some citizens, especially low-income groups, about the private return on such investment. In other words, there is probably an element of 'paternalistic altruism' behind these measures. Such subsidies, however, may also represent an attempt to correct for imperfections in either capital markets or insurance markets. It is also widely believed that investment in human capital creates positive externalities. What is more, many governments have been anxious to achieve a more equal distribution among citizens of such investment than of purchasing power in general. This approach has turned the services mentioned above into what the American economist Richard Musgrave has called 'merit goods'.[4]

A fourth achievement of the modern welfare state, and probably the most important one for the electorate in general, has been to help individuals to reduce economic uncertainty and to even out consumption over the life cycle. Since this effect has probably been most pronounced for individuals who would not manage that by themselves, through private saving or private insurance, there is probably a strong element of paternalistic altruism behind these policies as well. Although this economic certainty has mainly been achieved through social-security systems, progressive income taxes and income-dependent transfers have somewhat similar effects. In fact, even a majority of citizens may have gained from the introduction of social-security systems, for such systems may be regarded as a method of preventing some people from taking 'free rides' on the altruism of others: compulsory social-security fees imply that individuals cannot escape from contributing to their own economic security in situations like old age, bad health or unemployment. [5]

All this means that quite large fractions of the population may in fact have gained from the introduction of social-security systems — a gain that is accentuated by the very low administrative costs of such systems as compared with individual private insurance schemes. These gains, however, have partly occurred at the expense of the freedom of individuals to design their saving and insurance according to their particular needs and preferences.

The four achievements of the modern welfare state discussed above — the mitigation of destitution, the overall equalization of (life-time) wealth, investment in human capital, and the reduction of economic uncertainty and the evening out of consumption over the life cycle — indicate that the social and economic achievements of the modern welfare state are both far-reaching and impressive. Indeed, I would go so far as to regard the welfare state as a triumph for modern civilization.

LIMITS OF THE WELFARE STATE

Notwithstanding these major achievements of the modern welfare state, it is reasonable to argue that the marginal contributions of welfare-state spending gradually fall as the level of spending increases — assuming that the most beneficial reforms tend to be made early in the development of welfare states. At the same time, it is known that the marginal costs of welfare-state policies tend to rise as the size of the programmes increases. This is due to various types of distortions in relative prices and, therefore, in economic information and economic incentives, resulting in particular from the accompanying tax increases.

This suggests that it is reasonable to speak of a limit for welfare-state policies when the marginal costs start to exceed the marginal benefits. It is important, however, to realize that these costs include not only (i) various 'economic consequences', as conventionally defined, but also various types of non-economic effects, such as (ii) the consequences for the role of the family in society, (iii) negative effects on the freedom of choice of individuals and (iv) regrettable implications for the relations between the individual and the state. The discussion below starts with the economic consequences since these are the basis for some of the most important non-economic effects.

ECONOMIC CONSEQUENCES

It is useful to distinguish between three main types of economic consequences associated with welfare-state policies: administrative costs, 'dead-weight costs' and macro-economic consequences. While the nature of the administrative costs is straightforward, it is necessary to dwell somewhat on the dead-weight costs and the macro-economic consequences.

Dead-weight Costs

Dead-weight costs are created by policy-induced changes in relative prices or, more specifically, by the wedges that are driven by government policies between the production costs of firms and the net returns to individuals on additional productive effort, hence generating deviations between social and private returns on individual effort.

The types of dead-weight costs that have been studied by economists are mainly those associated with the allocative distortions of the choice of hours of work, saving and the composition of assets. When discussing such costs, it is important to emphasize the many channels through which they arise — and hence the pervasiveness of such costs — rather than a single cost. For instance, when analyzing the dead-weight costs on work, it is important to remember that marginal tax rates on labour income create disincentive effects (so-called 'substitution effects') not only (i) against hours of work in the regular labour market but also (ii) against the intensity of work (that is, in favour of 'on-the-job leisure') if life-time income is related to work effort and (iii) against investment in human capital if taxation is progressive (and the after-tax discount rate does not fall much). In addition, marginal tax rates on labour income create incentives in favour of (i) the pursuit of do-it-yourself work, (ii) production for barter, (iii) the choice of occupation with relatively large non-pecuniary benefits and (iv) the search for tax loopholes ('tax avoidance').

There was a strong tendency in the empirical literature of public finance during the 1950s and 1960s to minimize these costs. Recent empirical studies, however, suggest much stronger effects and, indeed, quite high economic costs, particularly on the margin in most advanced welfare states. One reason is that marginal tax rates in some welfare states have been much higher in the late 1970s and early

1980s than they were twenty or thirty years ago (although the 'tax reform' movement of the 1980s has recently resulted in reduced marginal tax rates in some West European countries, hence not only in the United States). Indeed, the marginal costs of tax wedges, in the context of simple economic models of the allocation of resources, are basically proportional to the initial tax rate. Moreover, the early studies usually only examined the effects of isolated tax changes, even though it is the combined increase in public spending and taxation that has budgetary implications for the development of welfare states. In other words, the early studies tended to forget that the positive 'income effects' on labour supply of higher taxes (that is, the attempt by the household to compensate, by way of more work, for the tax-induced fall in disposable income) are mitigated, or in some cases even cancelled, by the negative income effects of the accompanying increases in public spending.[6] It is also well known today that the early studies did not treat the progressiveness of the tax system in an analytically satisfactory way which resulted in an under-estimation of the dead-weight costs of increased income taxes.[7]

In fact, there are even more fundamental reasons why the early studies under-estimated, and many contemporary studies still under-estimate, the dead-weight costs of welfare-state programmes and the associated taxation. In particular, many effects are transmitted via collective decisions and institutional adjustments, not just via adjustments by individuals. This means that part of the effects on working hours may be considerably delayed.[8] Such effects via collective decisions and institutional adjustments may not be fully reflected in statistical studies of the relationship between tax rates and working hours of individuals (such as studies using information from different population groups). For example, the number of working hours is often regulated in collective bargaining agreements or by government regulations which create obstacles to adjustments by individuals. But after some time (which may be one or several decades), when labour-union members and voters discover that high marginal tax rates have made the loss of income from reduced working hours small, union leaders will feel pressured to bargain for shorter working hours instead of for higher wages; and politicians will be tempted to legislate shorter working hours, longer vacations and more possibilities for the individual to stay away from work for various reasons.

For instance, in several countries in North-western Europe there is not only a strong tendency among labour unions to bargain for a shorter working week and work sharing. There has also been accumulating legislation with generous provisions for the individual to stay away from work with a very small loss in after-tax income, even no loss at all. Important examples are very liberal rules for sick leave and maternity leave and the permission to stay at home to take care of sick children as well as to be absent from work in order to visit one's children in day-care centres or schools. (Such legislation has recently been passed in, for instance,

Sweden.) Tax-induced collective decisions of these types may very well be an important reason why the number of working hours has fallen so much recently in North-western Europe, where the marginal tax rates have been relatively high for long periods — as compared with the United States, Japan and Switzerland, where the marginal tax rates are, and have for a long time been, much lower. Some support for this hypothesis is provided by the fact that there is a strong negative relationship in cross-country data between hours of work per person and marginal tax rates.[9] It would be hazardous, though, to regard this evidence as conclusive, for differences between countries in hours of work may depend on many other, poorly understood factors, some of which may be 'spuriously' correlated with marginal tax rates.

It is likely, however, that not only collective decisions, through bargaining or new legislation, but also individual decisions, made on the basis of existing legislation, are delayed due to customary behaviour patterns of individuals. Working habits are partly a cultural phenomenon and economic incentives may influence them mainly in a long-term perspective, especially perhaps when a new generation enters the labour market. Moreover, changes in working habits are probably strongly influenced by many factors other than economic incentives. For instance, it strikes me, as a casual observer of the services sector in the United States, notably retailing and public services (such as mail), that the intensity of work and the quality of service have fallen dramatically in that sector since my first visit to the United States some three decades ago. Increased tax rates and income-dependent transfers can hardly explain this change, for the increases have most likely been too small during the period since World War II to account for the pronounced fall in the quality of services that seems to have taken place. It is perhaps tempting to refer to negative income effects on work intensity of economic growth — that is, increased demand for on-the-job leisure when disposable income rises over time. Given, however, that disposable income has increased quite slowly in the United States during the last two decades, this is probably not an important explanation either. A more promising explanation is that the service industries have experienced a negative selection of employees associated with the increased demand for educated labour in other parts of the economy. Moreover, the possibility cannot be ruled out that there are also various poorly understood social, cultural and attitudinal changes. (This point is, of course, an admittance of the limitation of the powers of rigorous economic analysis to clarify such phenomena.)

Space does not allow a summary of the vast literature on the dead-weight costs of taxes and public spending programmes in various countries. But it may be useful to report some results concerning the marginal costs of extending or contracting public spending programmes and related taxation. Marginal costs are particularly important because the issue of the limits to the welfare state is not a question of whether the welfare state should be abolished, but whether it should be expanded or contracted from the existing levels.

When discussing problems and limits of welfare-state policies, it is particularly interesting to look at the most advanced welfare states. The best available studies for the most advanced welfare state of all, Sweden, suggest that the distortions in the allocation of labour between the (taxed) market sector and the (untaxed) household sector are quite costly. The studies indicate that the 'marginal costs of public funds' are as high as $3 to $7 per additional tax dollar collected in the form of progressive income taxes to finance money transfers to households.[10] The economic meaning is that tax-transfer programmes of this type should be implemented only if the spending which they finance is considered to be worth three to seven times more than the income which is taken away from households in the form of tax payments. If these calculations are applied to increases in the marginal tax rates from the late 1960s to the early 1980s in Sweden, it is found that the figures are equivalent to a reduction of the yearly rate of GNP growth by about one percentage point — that is, nearly half of the actual drop in GNP growth.

It is easy to see how such costs of marginal tax rates arise. Suppose that individuals allocate their labour hours to get the same after-tax return (monetary and non-monetary) from work in the taxed and untaxed sectors (the latter covering leisure, do-it-yourself work and earnings in the 'underground' economy). Let us further assume that the marginal return in the untaxed sector is $10 per hour of work and that the marginal tax rate is 75 per cent, which is the actual figure for full-time employees in Sweden when all types of taxes on labour income are included. This means that people will choose to work in the taxed sector only up to the point where the marginal product of labour is $40 — because then they will get the same private after-tax return in both sectors, namely $10. This means that every hour, on the margin, that is shifted from the untaxed sector to the taxed sector would increase output by $30. But the marginal tax wedges prevent just such a reallocation. Here lies the dead-weight cost of the marginal tax rates. To estimate the total costs for the economy as a whole, one would also have to estimate the number of hours of labour that have been reallocated in this way due to the tax increases, which is a question of the response of working hours to the change in taxes and public spending programmes.

Such studies cover only one of the earlier-mentioned channels through which the tax system distorts the labour market, namely the reallocation of working hours and capital between the market sector and the household sector (including leisure) due to distortions in the reward to labour. It is likely that the sum of all the distortions in the labour market is much larger, for there is no good reason to assume that the various distortions usually cancel out, or even mitigate, one another. For instance, the disincentive (substitution) effects against the intensity of work and against the acquisition of skills certainly would be expected to add to the efficiency losses that are related to the reallocation of working hours between the market sector and the household sector.

By contrast, the marginal tax rates in the United States, which are typically 25 to 40 per cent, create considerably smaller dead-weight costs. Usual estimates of the marginal costs of public funds in the United States, due to distortions in the allocation of labour, are around $1.5 (including administrative costs). [11]

Rigorous formal analysis, however, is not the only way of acquiring an understanding of the real world. People walking through life with open eyes — and such people do exist — can give numerous examples of adjustments in the work effort of individuals due to high marginal tax rates. Physicians and dentists paint their houses and operate their boats rather than operate on patients who then may have to wait for years for important treatment. Professionals and craftsmen barter services rather than exchange them for money. Some people abstain from promotion, especially if such promotion requires longer working hours or geographical moves. Unskilled workers abstain from acquiring extra skills because of the low after-tax returns. Highly skilled people with an international labour market move abroad while some unskilled foreigners are induced to immigrate due to the generous welfare benefits. Unfortunately, most of these adjustments, and many others, are difficult, perhaps impossible, to quantify in reliable ways by scientific methods. It is important, however, not to draw the conclusion that, for this reason, such adjustments either do not exist or are necessarily unimportant. Formal scientific methods are not the only way to discover and understand social phenomena. Careful observation of everyday life should not be under-estimated as a complementary way of acquiring knowledge about important processes and mechanisms in society.

In general, marginal tax rates operate much like tariffs on market transactions, giving rise to various types of autarkic economic behaviour. It is surprising, therefore, that some economists and politicians who worry about the dead-weight cost of tariffs, and hence pledge against tariff increases, are much less concerned about the often much higher dead-weight cost of taxes. While tariffs create a distortion in relative prices by at most 10 to 30 per cent in developed countries today, marginal tax rates of two thirds or three quarters create distortions in relative prices between the taxed sector and the non-taxed sector of the economy by 200 per cent and 300 per cent, respectively. This comparison is highly relevant because the type of distortion is the same in both cases. Tariffs and taxes discriminate in the same way against trade: in the first case, in favour of production in the national economy rather than international trade; and in the second case, in favour of household production (including leisure) and various types of underground economic activities rather than exchange in the regular market.

In fact, the traditional model of international trade — with a production function for the domestic economy, a set of trade-possibility lines and a preference function — is well suited to analyze the effect of taxes on the allocation of time between household production, leisure and work in the open labour market.

Another important distortion relates to asset choice, in particular due to the interaction of strongly asymmetric tax rules for different types of assets, high marginal tax rates and inflation. Since different types of assets are taxed according to completely different principles in all countries, the real effective tax rates are sometimes as high as *plus* 200 per cent for some types of assets and as low as *minus* 200 per cent for other types during periods of high inflation.[12] If there is any principle at all behind these differences, it seems to be that consumption-oriented assets, like owner-occupied houses and durable consumer goods, are usually favoured as compared with bank deposits, shares and investment in producer goods. (This statement refers to the direct effects. Indirect effects, via induced changes in wealth and relative prices, are extremely difficult to calculate in a non-controversial way.)

The enormous asymmetries in the taxation of different types of assets also mean that 'smart' speculative financial transactions — those not having much (if any) contribution to the productive capacity of the economy — are often strongly favoured. This is probably because 'productive' investments are often, both technically and politically, particularly easy to tax (whether directly or indirectly through taxation of the returns on financial assets, including shares). As a result, it is often the 'wrong' people who become rich in high-tax societies, from the point of view of the contributions to economic efficiency. In other words, the problem with high-tax societies is not that it is impossible to become rich in them, but that it is difficult to do so through productive effort in the ordinary production system.

It may be tempting to argue that these distortions in asset choice have nothing to do with welfare-state policies since countries without elaborate welfare-state systems may also experience tax-induced financial speculation and the exploitation of tax loopholes. But there is a link because the higher the marginal tax rates in an economy, the stronger will be the leverage on the allocation of resources of the exploitation of various asymmetries. To give a trivial example, if the marginal income tax rate is 1 per cent, the consequences of various asymmetries in the taxation of capital income are trivial, while with marginal income tax rates of, say, 50 to 70 per cent for people who are important actors in asset markets, these tax asymmetries have a strong influence on asset choice.

Marginal income taxes create distortions (substitution effects) in favour of consumption at the expense of savings (as compared with both lump-sum taxes and consumption taxes), while the income effects operate in various directions for lenders, borrowers and recipients of the benefits that are financed by the taxes. In simple models of savings behaviour, social-security systems also create substitution effects against private saving, although more complex effects arise in more sophisticated models, with an endogenous retirement age and complementarity between saving and early retirement.[13] It is probably fair to say that at present we are not sure about the net effects of these various, partly counteracting, forces. For instance, it is not yet clear how various cross-country comparisons of saving and social security should be interpreted. Looking at extreme examples, however, it is significant that in Sweden, which has a particularly elaborate social-security system, household saving has been zero for a number of years, while in Japan, where the development of the social-security system is very incomplete, household saving is still about 20 per cent of the household's disposable income.

As in the case of the dead-weight costs of the taxation of labour, available quantitative studies of the effects of taxation on saving and asset choice have to be regarded as highly tentative. Even so, considerable costs would be expected in some high-tax societies of North-western Europe, where the leverage of various asymmetries in the taxation of capital income is much stronger than in the United States, when inflation is high (such as over 5 or 10 per cent a year). [14]

Macro-economic Consequences

The effects on labour supply, saving and asset choice, discussed above, are a natural basis for studies of various macro-economic consequences of welfare-state policies — that is, the consequences for GNP growth, unemployment and inflation. The most obvious consequence for the macro-economic performance is perhaps that the various distortions in the allocation of resources, discussed above, will result in a slow-down in the rate of (net) productivity growth. [15] Output growth, too, would be expected to fall if public saving is not increased enough to compensate for the fall in net productivity growth and private saving.

Moreover, to the extent that governments try to enhance short-term job and income security by means of subsidies to declining industries, one would expect losses in economic efficiency, especially if such support extends over long periods. Part of these losses is associated with the ensuing distortions in foreign trade. There are obvious tensions between the desire to maintain a liberal trade regime and the ambitions of governments to improve short-term job security. [16] It is still an open question whether this tension will be accommodated by retreats from the liberal trade regime or by lower ambitions to give individuals 'rights' to keep their jobs, for considerable periods of time — or whether a reconciliation between free trade and job security can be provided by a 'redefinition' of job security. Such a redefinition could cover the chances of getting new jobs in other industries and geographical regions, rather than the right to stay in declining industries and regions. These problems seem to have been more pronounced in the highly open economies of Western Europe than in the more 'closed' United States, although the over-valued exchange rate in the United States during the first half of the 1980s created similar tendencies as in Western Europe for demands for employment security in industries where jobs are threatened.

Since the rate of productivity growth in a country depends on so many different economic, political, technical and psychological factors, it is not possible to draw reliable conclusions on the effects of welfare-state policies, or distorted tax structures, on output and productivity growth simply by comparing levels of per-capita GNP or rates of output or productivity growth across countries. For instance, the possibility discussed earlier that the effects of high marginal tax rates are delayed is a general problem. It is not a problem specific to the labour market. It may take one or several decades before people are convinced that the introduction of a social-security system has reduced the need for private saving. And if new entrepreneurship and the expansion of small firms are barred by high tax rates, the 'full' effects on the rate of productivity growth for the national economy may take decades to emerge since the production of new firms, for a long time, constitutes a very small fraction of GNP and productivity growth. Indeed, the standard of living in a country at a given time depends largely on the *stock* of physical capital and human skills and therefore on economic incentives in past decades or even centuries.

The problem is rather similar to the consequences of the accumulation of ecological disturbances. Because of the long time-lags and the many factors involved, the effect may be discovered so late that serious damage has been done to the natural environment by the time that a general consensus is reached on the damage. The counter-actions may then be effective only after one or several decades. There may also be strong elements of 'irreversibilities'.

This raises the important question of how to deal with uncertainties over the effects of government policies. Some economists seem to argue that as long as the evidence is not more conclusive than today of severe costs associated with tax distortions, there is no strong case for reducing marginal tax rates.[17] By contrast, when we consider the negative side-effects of human activities on the natural environment or the side-effects of medicines, even extremely small risks of severe damage are usually regarded to be a sufficient reason to take action. Why isn't the same principle usually applied to the risks of severe damage of high tax rates on 'the economic and social environment'?

The consequences of welfare-state policies for stabilization-policy variables like the aggregate rate of unemployment and the rate of inflation are more difficult to analyze. Even so, unemployment-insurance systems would be expected to contribute to 'frictional unemployment', for the incentives to devote time to job search are increased. This effect, however, may well be counteracted, or even eliminated, by more effectively functioning systems of labour-market exchange, to which the public-sector labour-market exchange boards could perhaps contribute. It is also an interesting question whether increased costs of hiring and firing labour will increase or reduce unemployment. The most likely answer, in my view, is that such reforms will stabilize employment when there is a 'regular', mild and predictable business cycle — of the type that existed in the period 1950-73 — while unemployment will be 'stabilized' in a prolonged recession, with great uncertainty over the sustainability of an increase in the demand for goods and services and higher profitability of firms. The reason for this differential effect is that high hiring and firing costs create incentives to hoard labour during short-lived recessions in the context of regular and predictable cycles, while such costs make firms reluctant to hire labour during a business upswing in a deep and prolonged recession if firms are uncertain if they will need more labour in future years. This means that while 'job security' legislation that raised hiring and firing costs was probably favourable for aggregate employment in the early years after World War II, the opposite has probably been true since the mid-1970s.

It is important to add that open unemployment, at least for a while, may also be kept down by an expansion of public-sector employment as well as by policies that induce employees to leave the labour force. In Sweden, for example, it has proved possible to keep unemployment at a level of 3 to 4 per cent during the 1970s and 1980s, not only with the help of aggressive devaluations, which have reduced real wage rates drastically, but also by raising the share of public-sector employment by fifteen percentage points of the labour force since 1970 (from 20 to 35 per cent of the labour force) and by keeping, more or less permanently, 3 to 4 per cent of the labour force in public works and retraining programmes, as well as by giving 7 per cent of the labour force (between age 57 and 65) early retirement.

The consequences of welfare-state policies for the rate of inflation are also difficult to evaluate. It is often believed that increased taxes tend to increase the rate of cost inflation — so-called 'tax-shift inflation' — and some theoretical reasons can no doubt be given for this opinion.[18] The empirical evidence for tax-shift inflation, however, is not strong which suggests that the rate of inflation mainly depends on factors other than the cost-raising effects of higher taxes.

NON-ECONOMIC CONSEQUENCES

So much for the economic consequences of welfare-state policies. What about the non-economic consequences?

Changing Role of the Household

The dead-weight costs of welfare-state programmes and related taxes may be the most interesting aspects for an economist of the consequences of welfare-state spending. But other aspects probably attract greater interest among the general public. One such aspect is the consequences for the role of the family in society or, more specifically, the division of labour between households, markets and government. In particular, while the disincentive (substitution) effect of higher marginal tax rates shifts the production of certain services from the market sector to the household sector, for both men and women, publicly-provided services that are close substitutes for household work (and often also to market production) tend to shift the production of such services to the public sector. Household members, especially married women, will then be induced to increase their labour supply in the market, in particular through higher labour-force participation rates. Obvious examples, from an early stage of the welfare state, are education and health care. More recent examples are child care and old-age care which in some countries of North-western Europe, notably the Scandinavian countries, have largely been taken over by the public sector due to extremely large subsidies to publicly-provided care centres.

Generally speaking, while the services that have been shifted from markets to households, due to high marginal tax rates, largely relate to the maintenance of durable consumer goods, houses, gardens and so on — that is, the care of things — the services that have been shifted from households and markets to public authorities essentially relate to the care of persons. In other words, while households are induced to take care of things, the public sector increasingly provides personal services to household members. This means that many households are induced to act contrary to what has traditionally been regarded to be 'the comparative advantage' of the family, namely the care of other family members, especially children and elderly parents. In the advanced welfare states, it is not production firms in product markets that are nationalized, which was the old socialist dream, but rather households or, more precisely, the provision of personal services to family members. In addition, there is nationalization of a substantial part of the factor income of households via taxation.

Freedom of Choice

This brings us to the issue of the freedom of choice of the individual, of which there are two aspects.

The first aspect is simply the size of the budget set of the individual. The more resources you have, the greater is your freedom of choice, in the sense of the size of your economic option. It is clear that welfare-state policies, by redistributing income and wealth, redistribute the freedom of choice in this specific sense as well. To what extent this type of redistribution of freedom of choice is considered an advantage or disadvantage of the welfare state depends, of course, on how the redistribution of wealth itself is evaluated.

An analytically more challenging aspect is changes in the scope for individuals to influence their own lives by their own actions. For instance, everybody would probably agree that an individual who is exposed to a marginal tax rate of 100 per cent, by being 'trapped' into one level of income, has lost his freedom of choice between income and leisure. But the same argument holds when the marginal tax rate is 90, 80, 70 or 60 per cent, for such rates still make it very difficult, although not impossible, for individuals to change their standards of living by their own actions through honest market activities. Obviously this type of limitation on the freedom of choice is closely related to the dead-weight costs resulting from high marginal tax wedges.

Moreover, if government-service programmes are very large, the average tax rates, not just the marginal rates, will be very high. As a consequence, in order for a household to earn enough money income to buy the goods and services it needs from the market, all adult household members, or at least husband and wife, may have to work in the open market, even though one of them may have preferred to stay at home to look after the small children. The tendency of welfare-state policies to shift personal services away from the household will therefore be accentuated. In Sweden, for example, it is practically impossible for one adult family member to stay at home to look after the children, for the family's standard of living would then be extraordinarily low in terms of normal consumption goods. The reduction in the freedom of choice of the family is accentuated if government services are rationed and provided by public monopolies, in the sense that private alternatives are either prohibited by law or discriminated against so much by subsidies to public institutions that private alternatives cannot survive in the market.

All this means that the policy-induced effects on the family in the most advanced welfare states of North-western Europe are quite different from the asserted 'welfare-state' problems for families in the United States, which largely seem to be associated with the failure to remove poverty.

Relations between the Individual and the State

Another profound consequence of advanced welfare-state policies, with accompanying high tax rates, is that high marginal tax rates automatically imply a high return for cheating the government — not only by avoiding taxes for normal economic activities but also by conducting illegal transactions, such as fraud in the context of ordinary business activities, and by engaging in illegal 'business areas', such as theft or drug peddling.

Shifts of economic activities to the underground economy are often considered to be a source of economic inequality in society because some individuals, but not others, may avoid taxes on their incomes. But this may not be the chief problem of an underground economy. When tax evasion becomes significant in a certain part of the economy (such as in the case of many craftsmen and small family restaurants in several countries) competition and entry would be expected to drive down the rewards to the factors of production to what is normal for the 'corresponding' type and level of risk. Thus, in the long run, tax cheating in a particular activity is not so much a problem of the distribution of income but rather a problem of the allocation of resources, for activities where cheating is fairly easy will over-expand relative to other activities. Many people may also view underground economic activities as a problem of 'social morale'.

In general, it may be said that honesty becomes expensive in a high-tax society and, as a consequence, the supply of honesty will become scarce. This is a serious problem since honesty may be regarded as a very important collective good in society. Honesty is a collective good in the production sector since, if individuals trust each other, contracts can be simple, enforcement is inexpensive and, therefore, transaction costs are kept low. Honesty is probably also a collective good in the private lives of individuals, for honest relations with each other are presumably preferred to dishonest relations. [19]

This does not necessarily mean that one would expect high-tax societies to be less honest than societies with lower taxes. There may also be a reverse causation. Historically, honest societies may have been able to develop more advanced welfare states, with higher tax rates, than less honest societies — without running into serious cheating problems. There is a real risk though that high-tax welfare states will gradually depreciate their historically inherited 'capital stock' of honesty and it might then become difficult, or take a long time, to restore it.

As a consequence of reductions in honesty, the government may feel compelled to adopt a more and more elaborate control system to increase tax compliance, to fight illegal economic activities in general and to prevent individuals from giving misleading information in order to receive benefits for which they are not eligible. Moreover, as individuals try to avoid the consequences of laws and regulations, there is a continuous race between them and adjustments of the individual. As a result, one would expect the laws in society to change rapidly, possibly at an increasing rate, which implies that planning for the future will become extraordinarily difficult for the individual because there is no confidence in the stability of the rules of the game.

Another expected reaction of the government to the continuous adjustments of individual citizens is to make the laws and regulations so vague that the authorities can catch an individual who acts against the 'intent' of the laws, even though he does not formally violate any laws. This means that the borders of what the citizen can and cannot do become blurred. Political uncertainty may then replace, or add to, the market uncertainty which the welfare state was partly intended to mitigate.

FROM WELFARE STATE TO TRANSFER STATE

When considering the various problems of the modern welfare state — in terms of the economic consequences and the effects on the role of the family, the freedom of choice of the individual and the relations between the individual and the state — it is important to emphasize that these problems are not mainly the results of the attempt by the government to eliminate poverty and to provide the individual with basic economic security. That could certainly be achieved by public spending of much less than 50 per cent of GNP — that is, at levels that were typical for the welfare states of North-western Europe about two decades ago (including publicly-funded social-insurance systems).

Really serious problems did not emerge, in my judgment, until the 'welfare state' started to be transformed into a free-for-all 'transfer state' with policy-induced redistribution, in cash and kind, back and forth between practically all population groups. In other words, it is important to make a distinction between a 'welfare state', which existed in several countries of North-western Europe fifteen or twenty years ago, and a 'transfer state', with public spending of some 50 to 65 per cent of GNP, which has emerged recently in some countries. In my view, one of the basic problems facing the modern welfare state is how to prevent the traditional welfare state from developing into a generalized transfer state.

If such a development of the traditional welfare state into a generalized transfer state cannot be prevented, we are bound to encounter not only severe incentive problems but also redistributional conflicts among practically all population groups. Indeed, redistributional conflicts seem to be the dominant 'obsession' in several advanced welfare states of the North-west European type. In Sweden, for example, distributional conflicts are rampant, even though the inequalities in yearly disposable income of households, in particular on a per-capita (or consumption-unit) basis, are extremely small. [20]

Moreover, when the return to individual action in markets becomes minute, individuals would be expected to direct their aspiration for higher standards of living — both in absolute terms and relative to others — towards the political authorities rather than towards productive effort in traditional markets. Voters will 'ask' for more tax-free transfers and public consumption, in addition to increased leisure via collective bargaining and new legislation. This may speed up the expansion of the public sector even more, with the possibility that the tax rates will become even higher, creating even greater temptations for various population groups to ask for political favours at the expense of the taxpayer. [21]

This is a reason to be sceptical of the notion that social stability in society increases monotonically by reduced income differentials, even though during the early phases of the development of a welfare state, social and political conflict may indeed have been mitigated by what many people probably have regarded as increased 'social justice'.

Moreover, if a majority of the electorate, as a result of the process just described, either becomes employed by the public sector or mainly lives on public transfers and other public benefits, it may become extremely difficult to cut public spending, even if most politicians say privately that such cuts would be desirable. [22] This problem is accentuated if, as in for instance Sweden, members of parliament are mostly public-sector employees and employed representatives of various interest groups.

WAYS OUT

In principle, it is not difficult to identify what could be done to mitigate the welfare-state problems discussed above, either (i) by trying to reduce the costs of reaching given welfare-state ambitions or (ii) by lowering these ambitions. Some welfare-state problems could certainly be considerably mitigated by the first-mentioned strategy, in particular by various reforms designed to change the financing of the welfare state — that is, by 'tax reform' which has become a popular catchword in politics today. An obvious example is reforms directed at the rampant loopholes and asymmetries in the tax system, for such reforms may substantially reduce the allocative costs of public spending, without losses in the ambitions of the welfare state. Moreover, it would certainly be possible to increase the freedom of choice of the individual by limiting the role of public monopolies in the services sector, for instance by subsidizing consumption rather than insisting on the provision by public authorities of services to households. To give citizens vouchers for various types of services, by which individuals could purchase the services where they like, is one obvious possibility. It is nowadays also generally agreed that it would be possible to change the system of economic support to the poor, including single mothers, in order to mitigate the anti-work bias in the welfare state.

Another way of reducing the dead-weight costs of the welfare-state and tax system would be to shift from taxes to fees for the financing of both public services and social-security benefits, for the marginal tax wedge might then be considerably reduced. (For instance, suppose that the social-security system is 'actuarially fair' in the sense that the additional social-security fee, which has to be paid for an additional hour of work, also raises the expected benefit by the same amount. In that case there is, in principle, no marginal tax wedge in the social system.) It is clear, though, that such a reform might also have undesired redistributional consequences. The same would clearly be the case if the marginal tax rates in the high-income brackets were reduced or, more radically, if there was a shift from progressive income taxes to proportional consumption taxes. A basic efficiency argument for the last two types of tax reform is that they would mitigate the disincentive effects on work of highly trained and educated employees and would reduce the distortions in saving decisions and asset choice.

It is likely that the bulk of the disincentive problems associated with public spending in the United States could be removed by such reforms of taxes and welfare payments, without reductions in total public spending (as a fraction of GNP). But for countries in North-western Europe, where public spending is much higher than in the United States, existing disincentive problems could not probably be solved without reductions in aggregate public spending and without, probably, some 'retreats' in the ambitions of redistribution policy, at least among people above 'low-medium' income levels. The reason is that, in reality, it is difficult to find non-distorting taxes, or even non-distorting 'tax packages', except for cost-based fees on public services, for major reliance on 'lump-sum taxes' is ruled out on distributional grounds. In countries with public spending of some 50 to 65 per cent of GNP, it is therefore hardly possible to mitigate the problems discussed above — concerning economic efficiency, macro-economic performance, the role

of the family in society, the freedom of choice of the individual and the relationship between the individual and the state — without lowering total public
spending as a share of GNP. Theoretically, it would be possible to privatize many
of the public-sector services and, too, the social-security system (still keeping the
bulk of it compulsory), without much loss in the distribution ambitions. The same
is the case for much of the general subsidies of private consumer goods such as
housing. By contrast, transfer payments to the poor certainly cannot be drastically
reduced without a considerable retreat in the ambitions to alleviate poverty.

If the expansion of welfare-state spending cannot be stopped in time — and the
level of such spending (as a share of GNP) cannot be rolled back in some countries
— there is, in my judgment, a severe risk that other types of public spending will
instead have to be cut substantially. That may mean that the classical role of the
public sector — that is, to supply collective goods — may suffer seriously with
respect, for instance, to justice, defence, culture and research. Paradoxically, the
private sector might then be increasingly forced to take over the provision of
collective goods because the government devotes so much of its resources towards
stimulating and directing household consumption of private goods. [23]

More generally, while the family in an advanced welfare state may be forced to
act against its comparative advantage of providing personal services to household
members, the public sector may be pushed out of activities where it has its
comparative advantage — that is, to provide collective goods. In other words, it is
possible that the traditional role of the government to provide collective, rather
than private, goods will be reversed in high-tax societies, perhaps because it is
easier for politicians to acquire votes by offering various interest groups private
benefits than by promising collective goods, for which the interests of voters may
be more diffuse. Here, then, is another reason for trying to control the size of the
transfer state.

---

1. This article is based on a lecture to the Political Economy Group of Harvard University,
Cambridge, Massachusetts, in March 1987.

2. These two types of welfare-state systems are often, in the terminology of the British
sociologist Richard M. Titmuss, called the 'institutional redistribution model' and the 'residual
welfare model', respectively. See Richard M. Titmuss, *Income Distribution and Social Change*
(London: Allen & Unwin, 1962).

3. For instance, in 1984 just over 20 per cent of all children in the United States were reported as
living in a family with cash income, including government cash transfers, below the poverty line for
a family. (The poverty line for a family with four children, for instance, was $10,609 in that year.)
See David T. Ellwood, ' "Divide and Conquer" Responsible Security for America's Poor
Families', mimeograph, Kennedy School of Government, Harvard University, Cambridge,
Massachusetts, November 1986.

4. See Richard Musgrave, *The Theory of Public Finance* (New York: McGraw-Hill, 1959).

5. See James Buchanan, 'The Samaritan's Dilemma', in Edmund S. Phelps (ed.), *Altruism,
Mortality and Economic Theory* (New York: Russell Sage Foundation, 1975); Assar Lindbeck,
'Redistribution Policy and the Expansion of the Public Sector', *Journal of Public Economics*,

Amsterdam, December 1985; and Lindbeck and J.W. Weibull, *Strategic Interaction with Altruism: the Economics of Fait Accompli*, Seminar Paper No. 376 (Stockholm: Institute for International Economic Studies, University of Stockholm, 1987).

6. See Lindbeck, 'Tax Effects versus Budget Effects on Labor Supply', *Economic Inquiry*, Long Beach, California, October 1982.

7. See J.A. Housman, 'How Taxes Affect Economic Behavior', in Henry J. Aaron and Joseph A. Pechman (eds), *How Taxes Affect Economic Behavior* (Washington: Brookings Institution, 1981).

8. For a fuller discussion, see Lindbeck, 'Work Incentives in a Welfare State', *Nationalökonomische Gesellschaft Lectures 1979-80* (Vienna: Manz, 1981).

9. See Ingemar Hansson and Charles E. Stuart, 'Labour Supply Estimation Using Cross-country Data', Department of Economics, University of Lund, 1985, pp. 115-30.

10. Hansson, 'Marginal Cost of Public Funds for Different Tax Instruments and Government Expenditures', *Scandinavian Journal of Economics*, Stockholm, Vol. 86, No. 2, 1984.

11. See E.N. Browning, 'The Marginal Costs of Public Funds', *Journal of Political Economy*, Chicago, March-April 1976; and J.B. Shoven, 'Applied General Equilibrium Tax Modelling', *IMF Staff Papers*, Washington, June 1983.

12. For calculations for the United States, see Dale Jorgenson, 'Capital Taxation and Welfare', *Scandinavian Journal of Economics*, Vol. 88, No. 2, 1986. For calculations for Sweden, see Gunnar du Rietz *et al.*, *Skatterna ett Samhällsproblem?* (Stockholm: Riksbankens Jubileumsfond, 1986).

13. See Martin Feldstein, 'Social Security, Induced Retirement and Aggregate Capital Accumulation', *Journal of Political Economy*, September-October 1974.

14. For a survey of empirical studies in this field, see Hansson, 'An Evaluation of the Evidence on the Impact of Taxation on Capital Formation', paper presented at the 41st Congress of the International Institute of Public Finance held in Madrid, Spain, August 1985.
Some studies for the United States, in particular various quantitative general equilibrium simulations in Jorgenson, *loc. cit.*, also report very high dead-weight costs for capital income taxes.

15. See Lindbeck, 'The Recent Slowdown of Productivity Growth', *Economic Journal*, Cambridge, March 1983.

16. See Lindbeck, 'Economic Dependence and Interdependence in the Industrialized World', in *From Marshall Plan to Global Interdependence* (Paris: OECD Secretariat, 1978) pp. 59-86.

17. Gary T. Burtles, of the Brookings Institution in Washington, and Robert H. Haveman, of the University of Wisconsin, seem to be very close to this position. See their article 'Taxes and Transfers: How Much Economic Loss?', *Challenge*, White Plains, New York, March-April 1987.

18. See Lindbeck, 'Budget Expansion and Cost Inflation', *American Economic Review*, Papers and Proceedings, Menasha, Wisconsin, May 1983, pp. 285-90.

19. For a detailed analysis of this issue, see Lindbeck, 'Individual Freedom and Welfare State Policy', mimeograph, Institute for International Economic Studies, University of Stockholm, 1987.

20. See Lindbeck, 'Interpreting Income Distributions in the Welfare State', *European Economic Review*, Amsterdam, Vol. 22, No. 2, 1983.

21. See Lindbeck, 'Redistribution Policy and the Expansion of the Public Sector', *loc. cit.*

22. By counting the number of voters in Sweden who today are either publicly employed or get the bulk of their income from public transfer programmes, it is found that more than half the electorate (approximately 55 per cent) is in this specific sense 'living on' the public budget.

23. See Lindbeck, 'Redistribution Policy and the Expansion of the Public Sector', *loc. cit.*

[6]

WORK DISINCENTIVES IN THE WELFARE STATE*

Assar Lindbeck

There is no precise and generally accepted definition of the term The Welfare State. Some people use it as a catchword for all types of public arrangements and policies that are thought of as enhancing the well-being of individuals. However, in this paper the term will be reserved for the collection of public transfers, social insurance systems, and subsidies of certain important goods and services, such as education and health – as well as their financing.

Most well-informed observers today probably agree that the Welfare State has been extraordinarily successful in enhancing economic security, in redistributing incomes and, perhaps in particular, in helping to wipe out economic misery among disadvantaged groups in our societies. It is also quite likely that the Welfare State programs have contributed to making the Western economic system – largely based on markets, competition and private ownership – more acceptable to the general public. Perhaps these programs have even "saved" the system from being rejected by a majority of citizens. Personally, I would in fact go as far as to regard the construction of the Welfare State system as a major achievement of modern civilization.

---

* I want to acknowledge competent research assistance by Felix Nordström in the preparation of this paper. I am also grateful for useful comments by Bengt-Christer Ysander, as well as by the audience of the Annual Meeting of the Austrian Economic Association.

28   A. LINDBECK

However, as we know, anxieties and warnings have
been plentiful over the years that Welfare State programs,
and in particular the taxes and fees that are required to finance them, will sooner or later create severe problems of
efficiency due to disincentives for work, saving, asset
choice and entrepreneurship. It is, I think, important that
also ardent friends of the Welfare State idea take these
anxieties and warnings seriously.

In this lecture, only disincentives for *work* will be considered – not because other types of incentive problems are
less important, but because of the need for some kind of limitation of the topics to be discussed. However, before ap-
proaching this topic it is important to specify what is
meant by the term "work disincentive". Obviously, every-
thing that does not stimulate households to work as long
and as hard as possible should not be regarded as a "work
disincentive": there is of course no reason to strive for economic arrangements that maximize hours and intensity of
work. Instead, I shall by the term "work disincentives"
simply mean *wedges* between the social and the private returns on work effort, and therewith-connected violations
of the conventional requirements (marginal conditions) for
an optimal use of time of individuals, such as equality of
the subjective marginal rate of substitution of households
and the marginal rate of transformation in production between "leisure" (in the sense of recreation time) and consumption.

When looking at the scholarly literature on public finance it is probably fair to say that the prevailing view
during the post-war period has been that serious disincentives for work have *not* arisen so far.[1] In *theoretical* ana-

---

See for instance Barlow 1967; Godfrey 1975; Stern 1976a; Meade,
IFS 1978; Musgrave 1978; Rosen 1979.

lyses, this view has largely been based on standard microeconomic theory of households, according to which the effects on labor supply of isolated reductions in the after-tax wage rate are ambiguous, as a positive income effect on work counteracts the negative substitution effect.[2] In *empirical* studies the assertion has been based on information which indicates, on balance, that the income effects are at least of the same size as the substitution effects, though the category of married women seems to be an exception.[3]

However, these assertions of the absence of major disincentive effects of taxation on work may be questioned on several grounds. *Firstly*, many of the empirical studies in this field have been made in countries where, and at a time when, the marginal tax and transfer rates were much lower than they are today in the most advanced Welfare States, such as in the countries of North-Western Europe. This point is rather important as the magnitude of the disincentive effects, measured for instance by the size of the "excess burden", increases more than in proportion to the marginal tax rate – in fact by the *square* of the per unit tax according to conventional formulas of the "excess burden" (Harberger 1964). (As an illustration, let us assume that an initial income tax rate of 20 percent is raised by ten percentage points, i. e. to 30 percent. Then the income retention ratio (the ratio of after-tax income to pretax income) falls by 12.5 percent. By contrast, it falls by as much as 50 percent in the case of a ten percentage point increase of a tax rate that is initially 80 percent.)

This holds for stochastic models, using the expected utility approach as well. See Block and Heineke 1973.

See, for instance, surveys of various empirical studies in The Royal Commission on Taxation 1967; Barlow 1967; Cain and Watts (eds.) 1973; Godfrey 1975; Stern 1976a; Beenstock 1979; Axelsson, Jacobsson and Lövgren 1979; IFS 1978; and Nordström 1980d.

30   A. LINDBECK

A *second* objection is that the effects on economic behavior may be considerably delayed due to lags in the transmission of information about the tax and benefit systems, and about the opportunities to adjust to these.

A *third* and perhaps more fundamental objection to most studies in this field is that they concentrate on individual adjustments in the context of given institutional constraints, rather than including changes in institutional conditions as parts of the adjustments to changes in the incentive system. In particular, the disincentive effects on work may become far more apparent if *both* bargaining between unions and employers' associations, *and* part of the process of political decision-making, are seen as endogenous variables that adjust to new incentives for citizens.

A *fourth* objection to prevailing views in the literature on public finance is that statements on these issues are usually – except mainly for some studies of the social insurance systems – based on analyses of the consequences of *isolated* tax changes, whereas a consistent analysis has to be built on simultaneous increases in taxes and public spending. For instance, it is necessary to consider that the positive income effects on labor supply of a tax increase tend, for the average citizen, to be counteracted by a negative income effect of the spending programs that are financed by the tax increase (see Lindbeck 1980 and Stuart 1980).

In other words, the more the citizens evaluate the higher public spending that is financed by a tax increase, the less likely it is that there will be a positive *net* income effect on labor supply of a combined tax and expenditure increase – and the more likely is that labor supply will fall, due to the influence of the negative substitution effect.

Due to conceivable income redistribution effects of combined tax and spending programs, there may of course be considerable net income effects on *specific subgroups* of the population. For instance, for people who do not feel fully compensated for the tax increase by the higher public spending, there will be a positive net income effect on labor supply, while for those who feel more than fully compensated there will be a negative net income effect.

A *fifth,* and even more fundamental objection to the traditional position of much of the literature in this field is that the income effects, even when they *do* occur, are not really relevant when we are concerned with disincentive problems. For there is no inefficiency, or "distortion", involved in the fact that some people may react to changes in (lump-sum) income by adjusting not only consumption and saving but also leisure and other non-market uses of time. Thus, a study that is concerned with the effects on economic incentives, i. e. with deviations between private and social returns, should be confined to *the substitution effect*; in other words, such a study should refer to the shape of the compensated rather than the uncompensated supply curve for work effort. More concretely, the emergence of disincentive effects on work does not depend on the "positive economics issue" of whether work effort falls or rises in response to some government action, but rather, as indicated earlier, on the "welfare economics issue" of whether deviations are created, or raised, between the social and private return on (marginal) work effort. (It is another matter that the government might choose a size or composition of public spending that does not correspond to individual preferences, which may be regarded as a distortion of the entire process of political decision-making, and hence of the allocation of resources in society.)

There are some exceptions of this principle, however. For instance, if a certain minimum amount of work is necessary for the survival of a nation (such as during a war), the supply of labor becomes crucial for a welfare-theoretic point of view, even aside from "distorting" substitution effects on work effort; we might say that aggregate labor supply is a *collective good* in this case. Moreover, the work of *specific* persons may create *externalities* for others – such as the work by scientists and artists – which makes the work effort of such persons important to others from a welfare-theoretic point of view. In both cases, it would be relevant – from a welfare-theoretic point of view – to consider the income effect, and not just the substitution effect, on labor supply.

A *sixth* objection, finally, against assertions that the disincentive effects on work of tax-financed welfare programs are weak is that such assertions are often based on a *too limited domain* of the studied effects. More specifically in the academic literature there has been heavy concentration on the issue of the effects on *hours* of work in the market, as compared to leisure (in the sense of recreation time). Only recently, perhaps largely inspired by the general political discussion, have economists started to consider more thoroughly a broader spectrum of conceivable disincentive effects on work of tax and Welfare State programs.

It is the ambition of this lecture to avoid, as much as possible, these various limitations and pitfalls of earlier discussions of the disincentive effects on work. For that reason my discussion will refer to *the substitution effects of parallel increases in taxes and benefits* – rather than the sum of the income and substitution effects of isolated tax changes. Moreover, an attempt is made to consider not only individual adjustments of households with given institutional rules and constraints, but also adjustments over time in these very rules and constraints because of pressure from individuals in their roles as citizens and members of labor market organizations. Moreover, rather than restrict the discussion to the effects on hours of work in the market, I will deal with a broad spectrum of effects on households' use of time – in fact nine types of effect. They will be classified here as the effects on (1) the choice between income and leisure (in the sense of recreation); (2) the pursuit of do-it-yourself work; (3) production for barter; (4) the choice of intensity and dexterity (quality) of work; (5) the choice of occupation; (6) the investment in human capital; (7) the choice by the individual of geographical location; (8) the search for tax loopholes (legal tax avoidance); and (9) the engagement in illegal activities, including illegal tax evasion and cheating with public benefits.[4]

This broad approach implies, of course, that the traditional dichotomy of time into working time and leisure time is in fact replaced by a division of time into a great number of different uses. The reason for the broadness of my discussion – and therewith-connected risks of shallowness in the exposition – is that a main point of the lecture is to demonstrate the *wide* repercussions of the incentive effects on work of Welfare State programs. At the end of the paper, the perspective will be even further broadened by looking at some general consequences for the role of the individual in society.

Ideally, we should probably analyze all these various types of effect on work *simultaneously*. We may then assume that the individual adjusts his behavior so as to make the value to himself the same, on the margin, for all conceivable uses of time and energy, adequately adjusted for risk – i. e. a situation with the same "net marginal benefit", pecuniary plus non-pecuniary in all pursuits. Unfortunately, such a simultaneous analysis is outside the range of what is analytically feasible. Instead I am, with a few exceptions, simply going to analyze each of the nine types of effect, mentioned above, one by one. We should neverthe-

---

[4]   The reason for not referring to the so-called Laffer-curve is that this concept easily leads us into a sidetrack from the point of view of the issue of economic incentives. After all, hardly anyone has suggested a social welfare function in the form of the maximization of tax revenues.

34 A. LINDBECK

less try to keep the fundamental simultaneity of the various issues (or at least many of them) at the back of our minds; for a more formal analysis of many of the theoretical issues in this paper, see Lindbeck 1980.

Moreover, when making welfare-theoretic statements about "distortions" and "disincentives" it is, of course, important to consider the possibility that the Welfare State-induced wedges, in some cases, may directly or indirectly counteract some of the wedges that exist for other reasons, though there is hardly any presumption that higher marginal tax and transfer rates would as a rule, or even often, have this *simple* second-best implication.

Of course, the fact that the lecture is concerned with *economic incentives* does not imply a denial that there are many other motives behind work effort – such as a desire to do a good job per se, a desire to enjoy social interaction with others, an attempt to avoid the monotony of "doing nothing", an ambition to boost one's self-respect, status or power, as well as adherence to formal and informal social control ("supervision"), etc. My defense for not studying these aspects too is simply that the *topic* in this paper is the effects on economic incentives to work of certain specified fiscal reforms and actions.

However, it is, of course, important to try to avoid, as much as possible, the temptation of arguing that some observed phenomenon in the real world on which Welfare State and related tax policies are likely to have effects is only, mainly or even substantially caused by these policies, rather than by some other developments in society, such as economic growth, inflation, technological developments, minimum wage legislation, wage bargaining, changes in preferences – or perhaps a reduction in "social discipline" in society, for instance because of a fall in the authority of managers, foremen, public administrators, politicians, or even parents.

A fundamental problem in the analysis in this paper is how to specify a reasonable norm of comparison ("bench mark") for the study. Clearly, economics – or any other social science for that matter – does not provide adequate tools for analyzing the consequences of *having* a Welfare State rather than *not having* it. To visualize what society would be today without *any* Welfare State provisions at all is certainly to strain the imagination unduly. What can perhaps be done with some success – and in fact will be attempted here – is to seek the effects of existing tax and benefit rates, as compared to a situation where these rates would have been *somewhat lower*. This is the reason for choosing the title "Work disincentives *in* (rather than *of*) the Welfare State". In fact, even a limited ambition like this raises formidable problems.

It is also important to remember that the emergence of disincentive effects of public policies does not *necessarily* mean that there is something "wrong" with the policies. Economic reforms and policies should not be evaluated on the basis of efficiency considerations alone; equity considerations, for instance, have to be given their weight too, which makes a second-best trade-off between efficiency and equity unavoidable. As we know, the analytical properties of this kind of trade-off have been thoroughly investigated in the literature on "optimum taxation".

The paper is designed as a survey of the *problems* rather than of the literature in the field of work incentives, though references to the literature will be rather liberal. It is also important to remember that the discussion in the paper particularly refers to the *the most advanced Welfare States*, such as the Scandinavian countries and Holland, with the most generous benefits and the highest marginal tax and transfer rates. For less advanced Welfare States, the discussion is of interest mainly as a hint of conceivable implications of following the lead of the most advanced ones. In

36   A. LINDBECK

this sense, the study may be regarded as a model-experiment rather than a study of a "typical" developed nation of today, even though, when considering the size of various elasticities, I will draw on empirical studies in many different countries in Europe and North America.

(1) The income–leisure choice

It is quite conceivable that shifts away from work in the open labor market largely take the form of shifts to other forms of activities than "leisure", in the sense of recreation time (or idleness). I am therefore anxious to avoid a one-sided emphasis on the traditional income-leisure choice. However, it is nevertheless convenient to start with that very issue, before other uses of time are looked at.

Adhering to the meaning of the term disincentive, as defined above, the only disincentive on working time (in the regular market) of higher income or consumption taxes designed to finance expanded income-independent transfers (such as children's allowances and certain transfers to the handicapped) is the negative substitution effect of the higher marginal tax rate itself. If instead higher taxes are designed to finance expanded income-dependent (means-tested) transfers, there would of course be an additional negative substitution effect on working time of the *implicit* marginal tax rates of the higher income-dependent transfer payments. The latter case has, as we know, been extensively discussed in the literature on "poverty traps" and negative income taxation.[5]

---

[5]   In this case, both the income and the substitution effect are negative on hours of work; see for instance Boskin 1967; Green 1968; Kesselman 1969.

Alternatively, higher income taxes may of course finance either subsidies of private goods or the free (or subsidized) provision of rationed public goods. There may then, in addition to the negative substitution effect on hours of work of the higher marginal tax rate, also be a cross-substitution effect on labor supply – which would be negative if leisure is a complement to (or income a substitute for) the subsidized or the "provided" good, but positive if leisure is a substitute for (or income a complement to) that good. However, it is hardly reasonable to say that such cross-substitution effects, due to complementarity or substitutability with leisure (or income), constitute disincentive effects, i. e. distortions of the allocation of resources – except in the special case when the subsidy of the private good, or the free (or inexpensive) provision of the public good, should itself be regarded as such a distortion.

When turning our interest to conceivable "disincentive effects" of various *social insurance programs*, it is important to realize that the rules differ considerably between countries, which makes it extremely difficult to make *general* statements in this field. It is, of course, also important to resist the temptation to regard *all* increases in leisure time due to social insurance systems as disincentive effects. After all, a basic idea behind the unemployment insurance system is to allow the unemployed a chance to search and choose without economic hardship; and the rationale for the sick and pension insurance systems is to make it possible for people to abstain from work when they are not well enough for it! What can, however, be regarded as a "disincentive problem" is the extent to which the fees and benefits are not connected in an "actuarially" calculated way; see Lindbeck 1980. This could happen either because the benefits do not rise in "proportion" (i. e. in an actuarially "fair" way) by the higher fees that hit the individual when he raises his income by greater effort; *or* because the ben-

38   A. LINDBECK

efits are reduced by higher income without a corresponding (i. e. an actuarially "fair") reduction in the fees. It is
then important to realize that I am here talking about the
expected value of the benefits, rather then the (ex post) actually received benefits.

Elements of these three types of "distortion" probably
exist in all countries – though in different ways and to different degrees. For instance, the theory of job search suggests that subsidized benefits of a general *unemployment
insurance system* – i. e. benefits in addition to "actuarially"
calculated insurance benefits for the individual – do create
substitution effects in favor of greater frequency and
longer duration periods of unemployment, as higher unemployment benefits reduce the search costs in the labor
market (Lippman and McCall 1976). Indeed, empirical
studies do indicate a statistically significant effect of this
type.[6] However, the issue is complicated by several circumstances. First of all, the systems that exist in reality often
have incomplete coverage, and the benefits usually have limited duration, implying that it is often short-term rather
than long-term unemployment that is "subsidized".[7] Moreover, when making normative statements about such subsidies, the point could possibly be made that some subsidization of unemployment insurance for the individual can

---

[6]   See, for instance, surveys by Hamermesh 1977; Grubel and Walker
      (eds.) 1978; and Nordström 1980a. However, in Sweden, no such ef-
      fects have been established (Björklund 1978; Stahl 1979), perhaps
      because the mirror image of variations in employment in Sweden
      nowadays is usually variations in the number of people in public
      works, public retraining programs and early retirement, rather than
      open unemployment.
      Moreover, Feldstein (1978) concludes from his studies of the behav-
      ior of firms that the unemployment insurance system of the U.S.
      creates incentives for firms to undertake layoffs of employees to a
      larger extent than would otherwise occur.

[7]   See for instance Burdett (1979).

perhaps be motivated, on efficiency grounds, as a modification of the consequences of imperfectly functioning credit markets; i. e. there is a conceivable second-best defence for at least *part* of this subsidization.

In principle, one would also expect a negative substitution effect on hours of work of publicly subsidized *sick insurance benefits*, though there are considerable differences among countries for this system as well. Unfortunately, there is very little empirical research on this issue.[8]

The effects on hours of work of subsidized *public pension schemes* is, for most countries, an even more difficult issue, particularly perhaps because of rather complex substitutions *between periods* of the labor supply of individuals. For instance, if the size of the pension is reduced by higher factor incomes of the pensioner – due to a so-called "earnings test" – there will not only be a sustitution effect away from market work by the elderly, but also a substitution of hours of work before retirement for hours of work after retirement (Burkhauser and Turner 1978); the latter effect will counteract the negative substitution effects on hours of work before retirement of *the financing* of the pension system – to the extent that people do not regard the taxes and fees that finance future pensions as "actuarial" prices for the individual of the pension insurances.[9]

---

[8] However, one study for the U.K. (Doherty 1979) indicates that absenteeism has indeed been stimulated by more generous sick benefits. It is also of interest to note that absenteeism due to sickness in Sweden has increased considerably and rather immediately after every liberalization of the sick-benefit system during the postwar period – from about twelve sick days per year in the early fifties to about 22 sick days per year in the late seventies for the average employee; see also Lindbeck (1981).

[9] For a useful survey of studies of the effects on labor supply of the pension system in the U.S., see Campbell and Campbell 1976; Boskin 1977; Clark, Kreps and Sprengler 1978. For studies exploiting cross-country data, see Gordon 1963; Peckman, Aaron and Taussig

40   A. LINDBECK

Moreover, in some countries early retirements may be subsidized, or deferment of retirement may be "taxed" (in the
sense of not giving "fair" benefits relative to the sum of the
fees and the deferments of the benefits). However, the
whole issue is complicated by the fact that special features
of the pension systems in individual countries can either
strengthen or counteract these effects for *specific age
groups* ; for instance in the US there seems to be an implicit subsidy of old employees to work.[10]

Another important aspect of the social security systems
is that they may provide *practical outlets* for people to cut
down their working time *both* in conformity with individual preferences (at undistorted rewards for work effort),
and in response to disincentives for work that have been
created by other types of policies, such as the general tax
and transfer systems – in a society where institutional obstacles of various kinds prevent people from making individual adjustments of hours of work in more ordinary
ways. In other words, some Welfare State reforms – even
when not creating disincentives to work in themselves –
may remove some of the institutional obstacles that have
both prevented people from adjusting their behavior to individual preferences (at undistorted rewards) *and* prevented disincentives that are created by other policies from
influencing factual behavior.

Generous benefits during absenteeism from work for
studies, child care and the care of sick relatives may create
similar outlets. In fact, if people are allowed by law to stay

---

1968; and Feldstein 1974. Gallaway (1971) has analyzed cross-section data from various states in the U.S. For a summary of some of
this literature, see Nordström 1980b.

[10] It has recently been argued that in the U.S. the rules of the public
pension insurance system give a net *positive* incentive to work for
individuals in the age group 62–64; see Blinder, Gordon and Wise
1980.

at home a certain number of days per year for reasons like these – particularly if this can be done without much loss of income – it is quite likely that a considerable number of citizens (at least after a while) would start to regard absenteeism of this type as a *right* to subsidized absence from work in the market that should be exploited.

A likely consequence of all this is that the frequency and length of absenteeism due to asserted need for early pension, sickness, the care of children or sick relatives, and studies, tend after a time to approach the maximum allowed limits simply as methods of increasing "leisure" and other types of non-market time, in particular for employees with rigidly institutionalized hours of work and with very little career possibilities in their work. That would mean, in fact, that *the definition* by the individual of states and activities like old age, sickness, the need for the care of children or relatives, and studies becomes an *endogenous variable* that adjusts to the overall incentive systems in society.

If instead of subsidizing absentees from work in the regular market, we would just like to give people a chance to adjust freely, i. e. without severe institutional obstacles, to individual preferences at undistorted rewards, one conceivable approach might of course simply be instead to allow the individual more *flexibility* of hours of work – without any subsidy elements.

It is important to realize that considerable effects on the supply of hours of work may arise not only by way of individual action, but by collective action as well. For instance, strong substitution effects in favor of leisure would in the long run be expected to create pressure on both labor unions and governments to try to implement, by way of bargaining and legislation, a shorter working week, longer vacation, earlier retirement age, and perhaps also more generous rules for the right of employees to be absent from

42   A. LINDBECK

work, without much loss of income, for the reasons mentioned above.[11] In other words, the new legislation just
mentioned that gives individuals increased rights to stay at
home and to retire earlier may to some extent be regarded
as *the effect* of previously implemented tax and Welfare
State policies. This means, of course, that the effects of
taxes on work may in fact be much stronger than the effects that are calculated only on the basis of individual adjustments in the context of *given* institutions. It would
seem that most (all?) studies of elasticities of the supply of
labor with respect to wage rates and tax rates are based
only on such individual adjustments; this means, most
likely, that they *underestimate* the long-run effects on
hours of work.

A substantial part of the Welfare State reforms, and
therewith-connected tax policies, has of course been motivated by equity considerations, which is the background
for "the optimum tax" literature with its attempt to derive
theorems and tax formulae that define the best possible
trade-off between efficiency and equity – usually in the
context of utilitarian social welfare functions.[12] However,
this literature only takes care of rather limited aspects of

---

[11] Charles Stuart (1979) asserts in an econometric study that the de-
      sired working week of those presently fully employed in Sweden is
      not 40 hours, as the actual *formal* working week may indicate, but
      rather, due to institutional rigidities, 30 hours a week. Incidentally,
      this is very close to the number of hours which workers in the
      engineering industry *in fact* seem to work in Sweden; see pp. 47–48.

[12] See for instance Mirrlees 1971; Sheshinski 1972; Feldstein 1973 and
      1976; Cooter and Helpman 1974; Sadka 1976; Stern 1976; Seade
      1977; and Brito and Oakland 1977.
      The few *general* normative conclusions in that literature are (a) that
      low-income groups should get net transfers from the authorities;
      (b) that the marginal tax rates should be between zero and unity;
      and that the marginal tax rates should be *lower* (c) the more equal is
      the distribution of income-earning capacity among individuals,

the distribution issue, by neglecting not only "entitlement principles" – i. e. the notion that the individual may feel that he is entitled to the fruits of his own efforts – but also envy, altruism and egalitarianism as a goal *per se*.[13] More important perhaps, it is not possible to derive many practically useful conclusions about the optimum tax schedules – for instance whether they should be progressive or regressive – even within the narrowly defined aspect of the models of optimal taxation without *quantitatively* specified assumptions about parameters concerning the preferences between income and leisure, the distribution of income-earning capacity and the attitudes of society towards inequality – all of these parameters being extremely difficult to estimate empirically.

(2) Do-it-yourself work; (3) Barter

There are many reasons for increased *do-it-yourself work* – shorter statutory working week (for reasons other than higher tax rates), increased relative prices of services bought in markets, and new, simple and efficient tools for

---

(d) the larger is the (compensated) elasticity of substitution between income and leisure, (e) the smaller is public spending on goods and services, and (f) the higher is the tolerance in society of inequality.

A case is also made in this literature for reducing the *marginal* tax rate for the highest income earner to zero, as then he would no longer experience any distortion of the choice between income and leisure, at the same time as nobody else would be hurt.

[13] While the adherence to "entitlement principles" makes a case for *lower* marginal rates than those inferred by the optimum tax literature, envy by the poor of the rich, altruism by the rich for the poor, and a general quest for egalitarianism as a goal *per se* , i. e. independently of utilitarianism, make cases for *higher* rates; see Feldstein 1976.

do-it-yourself work.[14] Nevertheless, it is unquestionable
that tax and Welfare State programs, too, create substitution effects in favor of do-it-yourself work in the form of
the production of services in the house, in the garden and
on various durable consumers' goods. Such effects would
be expected to be particularly strong when governments
subsidize goods and services that are complements to recreation, such as recreation equipment and recreation services, or when leisure largely takes the form of home production of the *non-subsidized* goods (for which the relative
price is then increased), as the subsidy would then stimulate home production, rather than purchases on the market, of the non-subsidized goods; see Lindbeck 1980, p.19.

The negative substitution effects of higher marginal tax
rates in favor of do-it-yourself work may fruitfully be compared with the tendency of Welfare State policies to let
public institutions take over the care of intimate personal
services – of the children, the old and the sick. Thus it
would seem that a strong *joint effect* of the Welfare State
buildup *and* its financing is that the household sector is
stimulated to take care of the servicing of *things*, while
public institutitons increasingly take care of *intimate personal services* like the care of children, old people, the sick
and the disabled. In other words, intimate personal services are increasingly socialized whereas the servicing of
things is increasingly being transferred from markets to the
household sector – in spite of the fact that homes have traditionally been regarded as the "natural" institution just
for intimate personal services. The market economy will
shrink on both counts, though increased subsidies and/or
public provision of education and child, old age and sick

---

[14] For a useful discussion of the concept of do-it-yourself work, see
Skolka 1976 and Hill 1979. For theoretical models with a simultaneous analysis of leisure, home work and work in the market, see Gronau 1977; and Atkinson and Stern 1979.

care have also the effect of stimulating females, who have traditionally been doing these types of services in the homes, to increase *their* supply of labor in the open labor market (Lindbeck 1980) – though often in fact by working in just the public institutions that have taken over intimate personal services from households. (It is also well known that factors outside tax and Welfare State policies have stimulated married women to increased work in the open market. Obvious examples are technological developments that have contributed to the rationalization of household work and probably also the emergence of preferences for smaller families and new attitudes in general towards the role of women in society.)

When considering *barter* activities, it is a commonplace that not only skilled and semi-skilled personnel – such as manual craftsmen like maintenance and building workers and academic professionals like lawyers, accountants, consultants and dentists – engage in such activities; firms are also engaged in considerable barter activities with their employees, in the form of fringe benefits of various types, such as subsidized meals, nice offices, subsidized travelling, vacation-oriented conferences and various kinds of country-club activities. In fact, the personnel management of firms have today to devote considerable time to bargaining with their employees, often individually, over other elements than the money wage rate in the "benefit vector" that constitute the compensation for labor services rendered. In spite of the increased transaction costs of such barter activities, relative to the exchange of money, it is obvious that both the employees and the firms often gain from shifting to relatively more non-monetary elements in these "benefit vectors" in response to higher marginal tax rates, as these elements are often both tax-free (or only modestly taxed) for the employee and, like wages, deductable costs for the firm.

The existence of substitution effects in favor of do-it-yourself work and barter does of course not necessarily mean that these activities are more important today than 25 years ago. What these substitution effects mean is only that activities like these are nowadays more than earlier influenced by tax considerations, rather than by the comparative advantage of barter and do-it-yourself work relative to market activities and to the old habit of engaging in "goodwill-oriented" exchange of services among friends.

It is even conceivable that the previous long-term trend of an increased relative importance of the money exchange economy, relative to barter and do-it-yourself work, may in the future slow down or even be reversed in the advanced Welfare States, at least for men, with a subsequent reduction in the division of labor for this part of the labor force, and therewith-connected losses in economic efficiency. The reason why I confine this statement to men is, of course, that strong trends in society operate in favor of labor force participation of married women.

There are by now a number of empirical studies, particularly in the US, that shed some light on the quantitative importance of the substitution effect on hours of work of higher tax/transfer rates. These studies should in principle cover the *sum* of the substitution effects in favor of leisure, do-it-yourself work and barter activities. In the case of men, and perhaps also unmarried women, an (average) elasticity for the substitution effect on hours of work (with respect to the after-tax wage rate) of *the general order* of 0.1–0.2 would seem to be a reasonable assumption on the basis of the best available studies.[15] That would mean that a rise in the marginal tax/transfer rate from, say, 20 per cent to 70 per cent would have a negative substitution ef-

---

[15] See, for instance, surveys of various studies in Kosters 1966; Ashenfelter 1970; Hall 1973; Cain and Watts 1973; and Stern 1976a.

fect on the supply of hours of work for this group of about 2.5–5 hours per week, assuming the length of the original working week to be 40 hours. I believe that most people would *not* regard this effect as drastic. It should then be remembered, however, that the main effects on hours of work very well might occur by way of induced changes in institutional arrangements, rather than by way of individual adjustments in the context of *given* institutions.

For married women, by contrast, an elasticity of the substitution effect of about unity is not an unrealistic figure according to available empirical studies, implying in the example above a reduction in working time of 25 hours per week, i. e. a reduction down to less than half-time work. It is therefore quite likely that the present tax/transfer system in many North-West European countries has a rather dramatic disincentive effect on hours of work in the open market by married women, by contrast to men. One conceivable way of mitigating this effect is, of course, to shift over from a system of joint assessment of incomes of husband and wife to individual assessment, implying that the income of the wife would no longer be "added" to the income of the husband.[16] I am, of course, aware that such a shift may be criticized on other grounds.

Additional *indications* of the quantitative importance of incentive effects on work in the open labor market could perhaps be obtained by looking at some time series in a rather "advanced" Welfare State like Sweden. We may then note that the labor force participation rates for adult men have fallen only moderately – from 85 percent in the early sixties to 78 percent in the early seventies (National

---

[16] Assume, for instance, that the marginal tax/transfer rate for married women is reduced from 0.7 to 0.3. By applying the earlier mentioned elasticity (of unity) for the substitution effect, this effect would expand hours of work by about 13 hours per week for a person who initially worked 10 hours.

Central Bureau of Statistics); and for females they have increased. However, working hours per person have gone
down quite considerably – not only by reductions in the
statutory number of hours per week for the fully employed, and by way of an expansion of part-time work,
mainly for women, but also by a liberal use among some
employees of the opportunities for absenteeism. For instance, while 8 percent of men were absent from work
(during certain survey weeks) in the early sixties, the figure
had increased to 14 percent in the late seventies. For
women, the corresponding increase is from 10.5 percent to
18 percent, and for women with children under 7 years of
age it is from about 14 to 28 percent.

Studies for specific sectors show even higher figures. In
the case of hospitals, for instance, absentee figures of 25
percent were found in 1980; (preliminary figures from
Landstingsförbundet). And the number of days of absenteeism in 1979 in the engineering industry was 66 per year
in Sweden, as compared to an average of 45 days for
Western Europe as a whole. The difference is nearly entirely accounted for by reasons other than "vacation";
such non-vacation absenteeism accounted in Sweden for
41 days per year, while for other countries the figure varied
from 11 days (in Great Britain) to 30 (in Norway). As a
consequence, the number of working hours per week (av-
eraged over the year) of full-time employees in the
engineering industry was 29 in Sweden as compared to 32–
35 for most other countries in Western Europe. (Figures
from Studier av Svenska Verkstadsföreningen, Stockholm
1980.) Unfortunately there are no reliable studies that tell
us to what extent these phenomena are a result of tax and
Welfare State policies. However, they are at least consistent with rather widely held views in Sweden that these
policies have in recent years induced people to cut down
the number of working hours per year.

WORK DISINCENTIVES IN THE WELFARE STATE   49

(4) Intensity and dexterity (quality) of work; (5) Choice of job

Heuristically, we may treat a lower *intensity of work* in the same way, in principle, as increased "leisure" – i. e. as "leisure at work" rather than "leisure at home" – with a negative substitution effect on intensity of work of higher marginal tax/transfer rates, Unfortunately, there is very little useful empirical knowledge about this issue.[17] There may, of course, also be negative substitution effects on the *dexterity (quality) of work.* At first glance, the latter effect may appear to be a more tricky issue analytically than the effects on hours or intensity of work, as high-quality work *per se* may give personal satisfaction – in addition to the extra income that is often connected with a higher quality of work. However, the issue is analytically really not greatly different from the issue of hours (or intensity) of work, as many individuals may very well, up to a point, regard also hours of work (and possibly also intensity of work) as a utility rather than a disutility. For what is required for the traditional income-leisure-choice model to make sense is not that any amount of work is a disutility, but rather that the individual on the margin locally (in the neighborhood of the optimum point) evaluates work *per se* less highly than leisure – hence that there is locally a *net* marginal disutility of work as compared to leisure (see for instance Layard–Walters 1967, pp.308–10). It is perhaps reasonable to assume, in a similar way, that the individual (locally), on the margin, evaluates the satisfaction from achieving a higher quality of work *per se* less highly than a relaxed attitude to the effort that is required for high-dex-

---

[17] However, a study by Stafford and Duncan (1977) indicates that intensity of work is positively related to education and age, which are both positively correlated with wage rates.

50   A. LINDBECK

terity work. For only then can we argue – in a parallel
fashion to the income-leisure model – that the individual
makes a trade-off between income and effort, and hence
that higher income (locally) can be regarded as a compensation for the greater work effort that is needed to improve
the quality of work, and that there is then a negative substitution effect of higher marginal tax/transfer rates on quality of work.[18]

Our next concern is the effects on *the choice of job* .
One obvious difference in principle between the effects on
hours of work (in or outside the labor market), intensity
and quality of work on the one hand and the effects on the
choice of job on the other is that while in the former cases
increased monetary compensation is required for the loss
of leisure (in the sense of recreation time), a switch from
one type of job to another would require compensation
only for the *difference* in the utility (or disutility) of two
different jobs.[19] We might hypothesize that the latter would

---

[18] There may of course also be a (non-distorting) income effect on intensity and quality of work – the sign depending on whether people
feel less than fully compensated, or overcompensated, by the increase in public expenditures that has been made possible by higher
taxes.

In the case where the motive behind higher quality of work is a desire to get promotion rather than personal satisfaction from a high
quality of work *per se* , that case can perhaps most conveniently be
analyzed as an intertemporal aspect of the choice of job, with elements of investment in human capital or goodwill.

[19] Moreover, while the choice of the length of working time, intensity
of work and quality of work can reasonably be regarded as *marginal* decisions, the choice of type of work (as well as migration decisions) is usually (except mainly for "moonlighting" and home work)
a discrete non-marginal decision; mathematically speaking the
choice-set is not convex. Hence when studying the choice of job the
relevant issue is usually not the return on one additional hour of
work but rather the difference in total income (and other consequences) of *alternative* jobs.

require less compensation than the former, at least in a long-run perspective when the labor force has had a chance to adjust its skills via new entrants in the labor force, particularly in the case of youth and married women; see Lindbeck 1980.

One important factor that determines the consequences for the choice of job of higher taxes and public spending programs is whether it is the absolute wage *differences* that matter, or whether it is instead the relative wage *ratios* . In the former case, we conclude that both proportional and progressive taxes (and tranfers) create negative substitution effects on jobs that are connected with greater disutilities than other jobs. If, by contrast, it is relative wage rates that matter, only progressive taxes have such effects. There are, of course, also well-known substitution effects of tax increases on the choice of job because of *asymmetries* in the tax treatment of benefits and costs of different types of jobs – taxes on money income creating substitution effects in favor of jobs with relatively large income in kind or psychic income, and progressive taxes inducing people to choose jobs with stable money income over time; assuming that most people are risk-averse there will also be a substitution effect in favor of jobs which are connected with relatively low risks of various types (Goode 1949).[20]

---

[20] We do not worry here about the income effect on risk-taking – the sign of which depends on the third derivative of the preference function with respect to income.

(6) Investment in human capital; (7) Location and mobility of labor

In the simplest type of deterministic human capital model where all the costs of human capital investment are earnings foregone, a uniform proportional income tax does not have any substitution effect against such investment as all costs and benefits are reduced in proportion (Boskin 1975); a progressive tax, by contrast, has such an effect, creating a conflict between equity and efficiency of investment in human capital.[21]

Unfortunately the "optimum tax" models do not give much practically useful information about the best way of handling this conflict, without quite specific quantitative assumptions.[22] It has been shown by Hamada (1974), however, that with a combination of income taxes and education subsidies approximately any desired degree of income equality can be achieved in that kind of model without loss of efficiency in the allocation of resources to investment in human capital. There are, however, some severe limitations of the realism of that statement. Firstly, it is difficult to subsidize *all* types of education, such as various types of home studies and vocational on-the-job train-

---

[21]   For an indication of the sensitivity of human capital investment decisions to the rate of return on these, see for instance Willis and Rosen 1978. For considerations of the importance, in principle, of these effects on risk and capacity utilization of human capital, see Eaton and Rosen 1979.

[22]   See for instance Fair 1971; Sheshinski 1972; and Atkinson 1973.
In addition to the relevant conclusions mentioned above, in connection with "the labor supply version" of the optimum tax literature, the most important general results in the optimum tax literature concerning the "education model" seem to be that the marginal income tax rate should be *lower* (a) the more equal the distribution of "innate" ability; and (b) the lower the economic return on education to the individual.

ing. Secondly, we would expect that a combination of high
income tax rates and education subsidies would create a
substitution effect in favor of education with a relatively
large element of "private consumption", such as easy and
elementary studies of the humanities and the social
sciences, like literature, art and sociology, at the expense of
advanced studies of hard topics, such as mathematics, the
natural sciences and technology. This hypothesis is, of
course, simply an example of the point that increased taxes
on money incomes create substitution effects in favor of
activities with high psychic income – both during and after
the period of schooling. It is in fact interesting to note that
there has recently, in several countries, been a strong increase in the relative enrollment of college students to elementary studies of easy "consumption-loaded" topics, relative to advanced studies of hard "investment-loaded"
ones.

It is, however, also important to recognize that Welfare
State programs that make poor people better able to afford
nutritious food, housing, education and health care most
likely will increase the ability of these groups to work. This
then is an important example of the fact that public redistribution may *stimulate* investment in human capital
among some people even if the policies may have the opposite effects on other groups. It is particularly likely that
redistributional reforms had this favorable effect on poor
people during the first decades of the Welfare State policies, when a main ambition was to remove poverty, rather
than to redistribute income within the large groups of
"middle-income" earners. It is less likely that the recent expansion of redistribution policies has had such effects in
the most advanced Welfare States.

There may of course be substitution effects on the
choice by labor of *geographical location* as well: against
locations that are regarded as less pleasant than others –

54   A. LINDBECK

though if it is *relative* rather than absolute after-tax wage
differences that matter, only progressive (but not proportional) tax transfer rates have such effects within an area
with a uniform tax/transfer system.

We would also expect a negative substitution effect
against the *mobility* of labor within an area (such as a nation) with a uniform tax/transfer system, as there would be
a fall in the monetary compensation of undertaking the
disadvantage that many people seem to attach to *changing*
geographical location. (Similar effects may of course arise
when pre-tax wage differentials are reduced by way of bargaining or minimum wage legislation.) This reduction in
the economic compensation for geographical mobility has
taken place, in many countries, at the same time as at least
three factors seem to have increased the obstacles for families to move geographically, which in turn would be expected to increase the size of the compensation that people
would *require* to move: increased participation in the labor market by married women, increased home-owner-
ship, and a greater number of school years for children
(though the rise in the number of families *without* children
in some countries has the opposite effect).

A likely consequence of all this is a deterioration in the
flexibility and short-term allocative efficiency of the labor
market, and probably also a deterioration of the short-term
Phillips curve trade-off. We would also expect that reduced labor mobility hits the employment possibilities of
different groups of citizens with quite different severity.
For when the currently employed become less willing to
shift to vacant positions, those who are unemployed, as
well as the new entrants in the labor market, if they do not
happen to "fit" into existing vacant positions, will experience increased difficulties in finding jobs. By contrast, in a
more flexible labor market these groups would be able to
replace those presently employed when some of the latter

Work Disincentives in the Welfare State 55

are induced to move over to job areas with vacancies. Thus when the process of continuous replacements and substitutions in the labor market is slowed down by squeezed after-tax wage differentials, the unemployed and the new entrants will experience a reduced probability of finding appropriate jobs.

However, while higher tax rates, designed to finance the welfare programs of an individual nation, would be expected to create substitution effects against labor mobility within the nation, we would at the same time expect that *international migration* would be stimulated when tax rates and Welfare State programs are expanded in one nation relative to others – *ceteris paribus* for other factors that influence migration decisions. More specifically, poor people would be expected to be pulled into the most advanced Welfare States by their relatively high welfare payments, while high-income groups would be expected to be pushed out of such countries (a variant of the "brain drain problem"). This two-way effect illustrates, again, the importance of considering taxes and public spending programs simultaneously.

In fact, empirical studies of labor mobility between states in the U.S. seem to confirm the hypothesis of a two-way mobility of this type, though the effects on migration between nation states would be expected to be considerably smaller.[23] In the latter case it is probably also more important to look at the expected *long-term* ("permanent") change in the economic *and* social situation of the individual, implying that changes in the *expected* tax and public expenditure programs over a great number of future years

---

[23] For surveys of the empirical literature in this field, see Greenwood 1975. See also studies by Mincer 1978; and Cebula 1979.

To get a flavor of the complexity of the causes and consequences of international migration, see various papers in Bhagwati (ed.) 1976 and Bhagwati 1979 (mimeo).

56   A. LINDBECK

have to be considered. (However, "guest workers" are
probably an exception, as they often choose temporary migration.)

When considering the brain drain problem, it may be
hypothesized that the national autonomy of income equalization policies is greater in a country with a rather "national culture" (including the language), and with a relatively high average income; both factors would tend to
keep down the size of the elasticity of substitution between
living at home and abroad for high income groups, and
hence create a "leeway" for national redistribution policies. On both counts England is, of course, in a particularly difficult position (though England, as we know, has
been able to regain certain types of skilled employees from
countries with even lower average income and with cultural ties to the U.K.).

It has been shown, however, that a combination of *three*
policy instruments – a national income tax, an educational
subsidy and a home-country tax (surcharge) on incomes of
emigrants – could in principle bring about approximately
any desired degree of equality without distorting the choice
of either investment in human capital or the international
geographical location of labor (Hamada 1977; Bhagwati
and Hamada 1980). However, such a policy mix has of
course the same kind of limitation as the previously-dis-
cussed policy mix of progressive taxation and education
subsidy (pp. 52, f.). Moreover, a policy package that is optimal in a model with three "target variables" only (equity,
migration and investment in human capital) may, of
course, be quite inoptimal, or even unfeasible, in models
with a greater number of target variables – such as hours
of work, do-it-yourself work, barter, intensity of work,
choice of job, tax avoidance, tax evasion, economic crimes,
etc. And if governments in nations with relatively generous
welfare payments would instead want to limit the inflow of

low–income groups, quite different policies would become
of course necessary (such as immigration restrictions and/
or limitations on the availability of welfare programs for
recent immigrants).

(8) Legal tax avoidance; (9) illegal economic activities

The previously-discussed shifts to leisure, do-it-yourself
work and barter may be regarded as rather "innocent"
forms of legal *tax avoidance*. However, there will of course
also be a substitution effect in favor of less innocent forms,
such as tax-induced deductions from gross income of expenditures that yield utility to the individual himself and
shifts to types of work where such deductions are relatively
easy. Beside the resulting deterioration in the efficiency of
the allocation of resources, there will, of course, at least in
a short-term perspective, also emerge new types of inequalities in society, as the ability and willingness to manipulate
the tax system, and to hire competent tax experts, probably
differ strongly among individuals. (The search for and exploitation of loopholes are, as we know, intensive also in
connection with asset transactions; however, that important issue is outside the scope of the paper.)

Substitution effects in favor of illegal *tax evasion* is
probably an even more spectacular effect of high marginal
tax/transfer rates.[24] An important aspect of this issue is
that when tax cheating starts to dominate in a sector, such
as for many types of services sold to housholds, and when
the product prices therefore become influenced in a funda-

---

[24] The microeconomic theory of tax avoidance and tax evasion is discussed in for instance Allingham and Sandmo 1972; Srinivasan
1973; Weiss 1976; Gottlieb 1979; Isachsen and Strom 1980 and
1980a; Marchon 1979; Pencavel 1979.

mental way by the cheating, almost everybody in that sector has to choose either to give up the competition or to start cheating himself. In other words, tax cheating may become a necessary requirement for the survival of individuals and firms in certain sectors of our economies, such as in the restaurant business and in the sales of many other services, perhaps in particular by small firms, to households. An interesting consequence is that the often-predicted increase in relative prices of services will be mitigated in many cases. Thus, the "Baumol Law" of the fading away of private (non-subsidized) services from the market, because of a slow rate of productivity increase, may not materialize for a number of services where tax cheating is relatively easy, and hence becomes an alternative to a transfer of the supply of services to the household sector or the public sector.

It is also worth noting that while the previously mentioned substitution effects of higher tax rates against risk-taking, and against activities where incomes fluctuate considerably, tend to favor salaried employment in general, relative to entrepreneurial activity, the opportunities for legal tax avoidance and illegal tax evasion probably work in favor of both employers and employees in small firms – often in fact family firms.

However, even though tax evasion may be difficult to pursue for people employed by the government and by large corporations, these groups too may often be able *to cheat with public benefits,* for instance by giving misleading information about marital status in connection with subsidies for housing and child care, by combining unemployment benefits with work in the irregular market, by receiving transfers for faked subsidized activities, as well as by the earlier-mentioned exploitation of the benefit rules concerning for instance the absence from work for sickness, the care of children and other relatives, adult education, etc.

The substitution effects in favor of (illegal) tax evasion and (illegal) exploitation of public benefits are of course only two examples of a more general problem: a substitution effect in favor of *all types of economic crimes* , including forgery, theft, gambling, drug peddling, prostitution, etc. After all, incomes from criminal activities are systematically tax free in all countries – except for the "stochastic" type of taxation that is implied in the punishment of discovered crimes! However, when an initially increased return on crime, relative to other activities, pulls more people into crime, we would expect that, in a long-run perspective, the return will be brought down to what is a "normal" rate of return on risk-taking. Thus, in a long-run perspective, the substitution effect in favor of illegal economic activities is probably *mainly* a problem of the allocation of resources rather than the distribution of income. However, to the extent that a large number of people have inhibitions against engaging in criminal activities, or against shifting to jobs where dishonesty pays best, the return on such activities may also in a rather long-run perspective be higher than the normal compensation for risk taking.

More fundamentally then, higher taxation necessarily means *higher taxation also of honesty* . As honesty may be regarded as a scarce resource, a reduced availability of honesty due to high taxation is not a comfortable thought. More generally, we could perhaps regard honesty as a *collective good* in society – both for consumers and producers. It is a collective consumers' good in the sense that people probably enjoy a society characterized by honesty. And it is a collective producers' good, in the sense that honesty keeps down the transaction and law-enforcement costs in society. Thus, very high marginal taxation of honesty, and a therewith-connected drift towards a less honest society, may result in considerable welfare losses for citizens in general – directly or indirectly.

All of this, of course, does not mean that the most advanced Welfare States today are necessarily plagued with more dishonest economic behavior than other countries. Perhaps even the opposite is the case, as many of the most advanced Welfare States *traditionally* have been rather honest and disciplined countries with considerable confidence among the citizens in public authorities. It is probably also important to resist the temptation of interpreting a parallel rise over time in taxation and economic crimes as evidence of a *dominating* causal connection. The expansion of several types of economic crimes has probably many other explanations, such as a fall in informal social control in connection with urbanization and international mobility of labor, economic regulations and unemployment. What the tax-induced substitution effects in favor of economic crimes and dishonesty do mean, however, is that we would expect a gradual rise in tax cheating and other economic crimes in these societies *ceteris paribus* for other circumstances that influence such activities.

Some conclusions

Unfortunately we do not know much at the present time about the *quantitative* importance of the various above-mentioned effects of the buildup of "high-tax" Welfare States. In fact, I have a suspicion that existing analytical tools in the social sciences are much too blunt to catch the complicated, multi-facetted and possibly delayed effects. For instance, different rather reasonable studies of the size of the substitution effects on hours of work give rather different results depending both on the choice of data base and the theoretical specification of the model, such as the inclusion or exclusion of wealth variables in the labor supply function (see for instance Cain and Watts 1973). More-over, useful studies of the effects of taxes and Welfare State programs on the intensity and quality of work and on the choice of job hardly exist. There is perhaps more in-formation on the effects on investment in human capital and migration, though there seem to be fewer studies on the determinants of migration between nations than within nations. Systematic empirical knowledge of the quantita-tive effects on do-it-yourself work, barter, (legal) tax avoid-ance, (illegal) tax evasion and other criminal activities scarcely exist at all, though there have been some attempts to find macro-indicators of the size of the "irregular mar-ket sector", with estimates ranging from about 5 to 30 per-cent of GNP.[25]

This means that the assessment of the quantitative importance of effects like these is still to a considerable ex-tent an issue of personal judgement, in spite of much em-pirical research in recent years. My personal judgement, for what it is worth, is that the effects in a country like Sweden *recently* , in particular during the seventies, have tended to become quantitatively quite important – not only on hours of work (largely because of high absentee-ism) but also on do-it-yourself work, tax avoidance, tax evasion and other types of economic crimes (in addition to probably very substantial distortions of the asset markets, which, however, are not discussed here).

For even if each separate one of the previously-dis-cussed disincentive effects of each individual policy meas-ure, would be rather modest in the short run, *the sum of all the effects of all policy measures may nevertheless be sub-stantial in the long run* . A basic reason why the disincen-

---

[25] For surveys of empirical studies of the "irregular" sector, see for in-stance McDaniel 1973; Feige 1979 and 1979a; Tanzi 1980; Deloro-zoy 1980; Nordström 1980c; and Macafee 1980.

tive effects, according to most of the literature in public finance, look rather innocent is probably just that each separate study tends to concentrate on the effects of one single
policy measure on one variable at a time. Moreover, and
as emphasized above, consideration is usually not taken of
the possibility that in a long-run perspective, the *institutional* obstacles that in the short run constrain individual
adjustment may be removed in response to changes in economic incentives.

I would also hypothesize, at least tentatively, that the
various disincentive problems that have been discussed
here were probably not very serious as long as budget policies mainly took the form of (1) redistributions of income
over the life-time of individuals, largely in fact by way of
social security systems; (2) redistributions in favor of the
poor; and (3) increased supply of some basic social services. For in those days – reaching into the fifties or sixties
– the marginal tax and transfer rates were, also in the most
advanced Welfare States at that time, quite small for most
people, often in fact not higher than 30–40 percent for
"normal" income earners. The risk of serious disincentive
effects is probably much greater now when in some of the
most "advanced" Welfare States the marginal tax/transfer
rates of highly educated people are some 80–90 percent,
particularly if payroll taxes and other indirect taxes are included – and many low and medium income earners are
exposed to nearly as high marginal rates; for statistical
information on this issue for Sweden, see Lindbeck
1981.

In fact, it would seem that Welfare State policies during
the seventies increasingly have the character of redistributions *from the middle class to the middle class itself* – or
even "from the right to the left pocket" of given individuals in the large middle class – in addition to redistributions
from the rich to the poor. Examples of such policies are

tax-financed increases in the subsidization of food, housing and dozens of activities that are not particularly related to low incomes, including in fact subsidies to inefficient firms.[26] Tentatively, I would therefore hypothesize that it is the expanding public redistribution *within* the large "middle class" of the population during the seventies in particular – approximately among people in the fourth to the ninth deciles of the size distribution of factor income – that has pushed the "marginal tax bite" to problematic levels in some countries of North-West Europe; for some information on conditions in Sweden, see Lindbeck 1981.

A rather challenging question is why so many countries – with quite different magnitudes of the disincentives for work – start to be worried at about the same time. Is it because of an international transmission of ideas, or is it because the increase in inflation that has occurred in the countries has accentuated the distortions of a tax system that is nominalistic in nature, i. e. is constructed for a world with constant prices? On that matter we can only speculate at the present time.

While the effects on the allocation of resources would be expected to be stronger in the long run than in the short run, the reverse would be expected for the incidence, i. e. the effects on *the distribution of income* . The reason is, of course, that various types of long–run reallocations of resources tend to mitigate the effects on the distribution of income – in the case of planned as well as unplanned redistributions. Another important point concerning incidence that is brought out by the paper is that "free rider" problems are not really, as usually asserted in the theory of public finance, solved by compulsory public provision of

---

[26] For instance, A.Selden (1980) asserts, on the basis of his calculations, that about half of the transfers in the U.K. are returned to the same income groups who pay the taxes to finance them.

64   A. LINDBECK

collective goods, as people may remove themselves from
the tax base by way of shifts to do-it-yourself work, barter,
(legal) tax avoidance, (illegal) tax evasion and other types
of economic crimes; see also Fisher 1980.

Taking a long historical point of view, the industrial
countries of the West have largely built up their affluence
on the basis of an economic system within which the individual has been able to improve upon his own economic
situation through his own efforts. In other words, in addition to the natural ambition of many of us to do a good
job *per se* , people have been motivated by material rewards. Put in another way, there was for a long time a reasonably good conformity between private and social rates
of return on individual actions. For instance, according to
the economic historians Douglass North and Robert Thomas (1973), a strengthening of the system of "property
rights", such as the abolishment of feudalism – at the end
of the medieval period and at the beginning of the Renais-
sance – were basic prerequisites for the subsequent successful economic development, as the economic returns to individual efforts increasingly went to those who made the
productive contributions, rather than to others, such as feudal lords.

The new wedges which have recently been driven between the social and the private rates of return on individual efforts imply that individuals already in average income brackets now often have to give up the bulk of the
return to additional effort – not to feudal lords but to public authorities, which then redistribute the funds back to
the citizens in the form of public consumption and transfer
payments (sometimes in fact in ways that accentuate the
disincentive effects of the taxes).

Thus, a society has (again) been created where it is difficult for the individual to influence his own economic situation by way of "productive" work.

The crucial question is, of course, if an economic system can function in a reasonably efficient way when the link between effort and benefit – and hence between production and consumption – has been cut off in this drastic way. I have my doubts. A counter argument which is sometimes heard is that the countries with the highest marginal tax/transfer rates belong to the group of the very richest countries in the world. Unfortunately, this does not indicate that the long-run disincentive effects are negligible, or even that they are modest. For the accumulation of physical and human capital, as well as technological and organizational know-how, which is the basis for the present affluence of these nations, took place *long before* the establishment of the present incentive system, which is not older than about a decade. To disperse several hundreds of years of accumulation of stocks of capital and knowledge will probably take some time – at least perhaps a few decades.

A wider perspective

The discussion so far has been limited mainly to disincentive effects with given *attitudes* (preferences) of individuals. However, in the long run there may of course be important consequences for this variable as well. Three types of conceivable effects on attitudes to work may be particularly worth considering. First, it is possible that better health and education of poor people will boost not only their ability to work but also their attitude towards work. Secondly, however, subsidies to people who are in principle able to work, but choose not to do so because of the subsidies/taxes, might develop less favorable attitudes towards work – an often-asserted risk of having people "liv-

66   A. LINDBECK

ing on the dole".[27] It would be presumptuous to assert that
we know the net effect of these counteracting forces. We
might, thirdly, also speculate that new generations of income earners will exploit the tax and benefit system more
thoroughly than earlier generations – partly because they
develop their attitudes under a system of more generous
rules for social support and of stronger incentives to cheat,
partly because the respect for law may fall when honest
persons see others earning on dishonesty.[28] (In Sweden,
young people nowadays talk about work in the irregular
market as "working stainless" – taxes being regarded as
"stain", rather than necessary sacrifices for public benefits!)

Moreover in a society where individuals cannot easily
increase their income, or accumulate private wealth, substantially on the basis of incomes earned by ordinary
work, we would expect the individual to turn increasingly
to the *zero-sum games of transferring incomes* from others
– perhaps in particular by speculation in asset markets and
by political actions, but also by activities like gambling and
economic crimes – rather than by the *positive-sum games
of producing incomes* through work, capital accumulation
or productive risk-taking. In other words, the problem of
the present high-tax Welfare States is probably *not* that it is

---

[27] Gunnar Myrdal (1962) has expressed this view (at the same time as
he has argued for increased specific public expenditures in kind to
boost the health, the nutrition and the education of the poor).

[28] However, the latter point is complicated by the *possibility* that "dissatisfaction" over taxes may be smaller among people who are
"born into" a high-tax society – and hence have never experienced a
situation in which individuals were allowed to keep the bulk of additional money earnings – and that the attitudes to work *might* be
positively influenced by this (assumed) smaller dissatisfaction.
(G.Schmölders (1970) has argued that the more negative the attitudes of the individual are to the tax system, the greater is the probability that he will engage in tax evasion.)

impossible, or perhaps even difficult, to increase income and to accumulate personal wealth, but rather that it is difficult to do so by way of socially productive behavior.

It is probably not the role of the economist to speculate about conceivable consequences of these developments for the psychological well-being of individuals. However, it is often argued in the scholarly literature in psychology that "psychological security" is enhanced if it is possible for the individual to influence his own situation by his own effort in a predictable way (Seligman 1975; Magnusson 1980). If this is true, the attempts by politicians to equalize incomes by way of tax and social security programs, for the purpose of increasing the security and autonomy of people, may, paradoxically – if the policies are pursued above certain limits – in fact *reduce* the subjective "feeling" of security and autonomy of the individual, by hampering the ability of the individual to influence his own economic situation substantially and in a predictable way. This effect of the high-tax society may be accentuated if the tax and benefit rules not only imply high marginal rates, but if in addition these rules are highly unstable (which seems to be the case in many countries).

We may also hypothesize that the authorities will react to the ever-increasing exploitation of legal and illegal tax loopholes, as well as to the expansion of illegal economic activities in general, by more and more detailed and interventionist legislation and control of the economic lives of individual citizens – in a similar way as reduced work incentives are likely to induce the management of firms to increase their supervision of employees. As a result, individuals will have to gain more and more skills in finding *new* ways of adjusting. In fact, we might wind up in a vicious circle of the search for loopholes and other adjustment methods by individuals and ever tighter government supervision and control over individual behavior. There is

68   A. LINDBECK

an obvious possibility that the end result will be a dramatic
reduction in the privacy and autonomy of individuals and
hence an ever more narrow domain of individual decision
making.

It is not easy to see speedy ways out of these problems.
One possibility to reduce the disincentive effects of high
marginal rates might be to try to *hide* the taxes as much as
possible from the citizens. For instance, it is often believed
that increased reliance on consumption taxes would reduce the distortions of the choice between work in the
open labor market and other activities, including "leisure",
as decisions to work may not be completely connected
with decisions to spend, which means that "tax illusions"
may exist in labor supply behavior due to different degrees
of visibility (or perceptibility) of different taxes.[29] Admittedly, this is a speculative point, and if we indulge in further speculation about tax illusions we might perhaps also
argue that there is the possibility of an element of "protest
behavior" against *visible* taxes, and that this protest could
perhaps be weakened by hiding some of the taxes from the
citizens; Lindbeck 1980. It would indeed seem that suggestions to shift from direct income taxes to indirect consumption taxes are partly motivated by such ambitions to
exploit tax illusions and protest behavior of these types.

---

[29] As suggested by for instance Charles Stuart (1980), maybe the concept of "hidden" tax increases should be widened to include other
types of tax increases as well, such as automatic tax-rate increases
due to growth and inflation in the context of a progressive tax
schedule, the "inflation tax" on money balances, and budget deficits
that transfer the burden of taxation to future generations. There is
indeed some evidence (Wilensky 1976) that it is the reliance on *visible* taxes rather than the factual tax burden that is the best explanation of tax revolts.
However, an international cross-sectional study by H.G.Petersen
(1980) suggests that the "imperceptibility" of indirect taxes tends to
disappear with increasing rates.

However, the ambition to hide taxes is, of course, connected with severe problems from the point of view of both the allocation of resources and the democratic process. After all, in the case of private goods, governments are increasingly, as a part of consumer protection policies, introducing legislation for the purpose of making it *easier* for the consumer to see the full costs of "ordinary" private products. It would then be somewhat paradoxical if in the case of public services the politicians went in the opposite direction by trying to hide the costs from the citizens.

Thus, let us assume that the government is neither willing nor able to hide from the citizens how much they pay for public services, social security benefits and transfer payments. What then could be done to reduce the disincentive effects on work? Neglecting political difficulties, obvious possibilities are of course: (1) a lowering of the ambition to redistribute incomes, in particular perhaps among people above the levels of the low-income brackets; (2) a reduction in the share of public spending on goods and services relative to GNP, implying in fact the privatizing of some public services, possibly in combination with "voucher systems" to retain the distributional ambitions of government policies in this field; (3) increased reliance on fees for public services; (4) a tighter connection between contributions and benefits in the social security system so that the contributions are, more than now, seen as actuarially calculated *prices* for insurance services; (5) administrative techniques to increase efficiency in the public sector, for instance by allowing competing private services; and (6) a removal of unnecessarily distorting *forms* of taxes and transfers, for instance by switching to a system with "real taxation" and possibly also to expenditure taxes, which would have the advantage of taxing not only consumption that is financed by capital gains but also money increases that are earned by illegal

70   A. LINDBECK

activities. As we know, there have also been suggestions to mitigate the substitution effects in favor of "leisure", in the form of recreation time, by (7) taxes on close complements to such leisure, for instance by way of higher indirect taxes on owner-occupied houses, travelling and sports equipment. The often-suggested idea of (8) taxing "full income", i. e. in fact hourly earnings, would help to solve *one* of the above-mentioned incentive problems, namely the effects on *hours of work* (to the extent that these can be determined in a reasonably unambiguous way, which is however a quite hopeless task for many people, particuarly perhaps for the self-employed).

Obviously, reforms of these types would be politically difficult to make. Not only do they often come into conflict with factual or conceived consequences for the distribution of economic welfare. Cuts in public spending also easily come into conflict with basic forces of the democratic political process, as the benefits of public spending (like protectionism) are usually *specific* for various population groups, whereas the benefits of tax reductions (like freer trade) are rather *vaguely* spread over most categories of citizens. The opposition among public employees to expenditure cuts, too, is well documented.

Perhaps large packages of reduced expenditures and taxes would be a way out of this impasse. Another alternative might be to start with a decision for a large across-the-board reduction in taxes, hence making later across-the-board reductions in public spending inevitable ("the California method"). However, to pursue a discussion on such strategies would be to plunge into a different topic than the one dealt with in this lecture.

REFERENCES

M.G. Allingham and A. Sandmo. "Income Tax Evasion: A Theoretical Analysis", *Journal of Public Economics 1* (1972), pp.323–338.

O. Ashenfelter. *Using Estimates of Income and Substitution Parameters to Predict the Work Incentive Effects of the Negative Income Tax: A Brief Exposition and Partial Survey*, mimeo, Princeton University, November 1970.

A.B. Atkinson. How Progressive Should Income Tax Be?, in M. Parkin with A.R. Nobay (eds.): *Essays in Modern Economics*, Longman, London 1973.

– and N.H. Stern. *On Labor Supply and Commodity Demands*, Social Science Research Council Programme, Taxation, Incentives and the Distribution of Income, no.1, 1979.

R. Axelsson, R. Jacobsson and K-G. Löfgren. *Utbudet av arbetskraft i ekonomisk teori och empiri*, mimeo, University of Umea, 1979.

R. Barlow. *The Effects of Income Taxation on Work Choices*, Studies of the Royal Commission on Taxation no.4, Ottawa 1967.

M. Beenstock. "Taxation and Incentives in the UK", *Lloyd's Bank Review*, October 1979.

J.N. Bhagwati. *The Economic Analysis of International Migration*, mimeo, Nordic Council of Ministers, Oslo 1979.

– and K. Hamada. *Tax Policy in the Presence of Emigration*, mimeo, The MIT Press, September 1980.

– (ed.). *The Brain Drain and Taxation II: Theory and Empirical Analysis*, North–Holland, Amsterdam 1976.

A.Björklund. "On the Duration of Unemployment in Sweden, 1965–76", *Scandinavian Journal of Economics 80* (1978), pp.421–439.

A. Blinder, R. Gordon and D. Wise. *Reconsidering the Work Disincentive Effects of Social Security*, National Bureau of Economic Research, Working Paper no.562, 1980.

M.K. Block and J.M. Heineke. "The Allocation of Effort under Uncertainty: The Case of Risk-averse Behavior", *Journal of Political Economy 81* (1973), pp.376–385.

M.J. Boskin. "The Negative Income Tax and the Supply of Work Effort", *National Tax Journal 20* (1967), pp.353–367.

M. Boskin. *Notes on the Tax Treatment of Human Capital*, mimeo, National Bureau of Economic Research, 1975.

–. "Social Security and Retirement Decisions", *Economic Inquiry 15* (1977), January, pp.1–25.

D.L. Brito and W.H. Oakland."Some Properties of the Optimal Income Tax", *International Economic Review 18* (1977), pp.407–423.

72 A. LINDBECK

K. Burdett. "Unemployment Insurance Payments as a Search Subsidy: A Theoretical Analysis", *Economic Inquiry 17* (1979), pp.333–393.

R. Burkhauser and J. Turner. "A Time-Series Analysis on Social Security and Its Effect on the Market Work of Men at Younger Ages", *Journal of Political Economy 86* (1978), pp.701–715.

G.G. Cain and H.W. Watts (eds.). *Income Maintenance and Labor Supply*, Institute for Research on Poverty Monograph Series, Academic Press, New York 1973.

C. Campbell and R. Campbell. "Conflicting Views on the Effects of Old-Age and Survivors Insurance on Retirement", *Economic Inquiry 14* (1976), pp.369–388.

R.J. Cebula. "A Survey of the Literature on the Migration-Impact of State and Local Government Policies", *Public Finance 34* (1979), pp.69–84.

R. Clark, J. Kreps, and J. Spengler. "Economics of Aging: A Survey", *Journal of Economic Literature 16* (1978), pp.930–939.

R. Cooter and E. Helpman. "Optimal Income Taxation for Transfer Payments under Different Social Welfare Criteria", *The Quarterly Journal of Economics 88* (1974), pp.656–670

R. Delorozoy. *Le Travail Clandestin*, Assemble Permanente des Chambres de Commerce et d'Industrie, mimeo, April 1980.

N.A. Doherty. "National Insurance and Absence from Work", *Economic Journal 89* (1979), pp.50–65.

J. Eaton and H.R. Rosen. *Taxation, Human Capital, and Uncertainty*, Industrial Relations Section Paper no.117, Princeton University, 1979.

R.C. Fair. "The Optimal Distribution of Income", *The Quarterly Journal of Economics 85* (1971), pp.551–579.

E.L. Feige. "How Big Is the Irregular Economy?", *Challenge 22* (1979), pp.5–13.

–. *The Irregular Economy: Its Size and Macroeconomic Implications*, mimeo, Social Systems Research Institute, University of Wisconsin–Madison, 1979a.

M. Feldstein. "On the Optimal Progressivity of the Income Tax", *Journal of Public Economics 2* (1973), pp.357–376.

–. *Social Security and Private Capital Accumulation: International Evidence in an Extended Life-Cycle Model*, Discussion Paper, Harvard Institute of Economic Research, 1974.

–. "On the Theory of Tax Reform", *Journal of Public Economics 6* (1976), pp.77–104.

–. "The Effect of Unemployment Insurance on Temporary Layoff Unemployment", *American Economic Review 68* (1978), pp.834–846.

M. Fisher. *An Australian Perspective on Taxation* , mimeo, The Fraser Institute, Vancouver, 1980.

L. Gallaway. *Manpower Economics* , Irvin: Homewood, IL, 1971.

L. Godfrey. *Theoretical and Empirical Aspects of the Effects of Taxation on the Supply of Labour* , OECD 1975.

R. Goode. "The Income Tax and the Supply of Labor", *Journal of Political Economy 57* (1949), pp.428–437.

M.S. Gordon. Income Security Programs and the Prosperity to Retire, in R.H. Williams, C. Tibbitts and W. Donahue (eds.): *Processes of Aging, II* , Prentice Hall, New York 1963, pp.436–458.

D. Gottlieb. *Tax Evasion and the Optimal Rate of Detection* , Research Report no.119, The Hebrew University of Jerusalem, 1979.

C. Green. "Negative Taxes and Monetary Incentives to Work: The Static Theory", *The Journal of Human Resources 3* (1968), pp.280–299.

M.J. Greenwood. "Research on Internal Migration in the United States: A Survey", *Journal of Economic Literature 13* (1975), pp.397–433.

R. Gronau. "Leisure, Home Production and Work – The Theory of the Allocation of Time Revisited", *Journal of Political Economy* , 1977.

H.G. Grubel and M.A. Walker (eds.). *Unemployment Insurance: Global Evidence of its Effects on Unemployment* , The Fraser Institute, 1978.

R.E. Hall. Wages, Income, and Hours of Work in the U.S. Labor Force, in G.G. Cain and H.W. Watts (eds.): *Income Maintenance and Labor Supply* , Rand McNally College Pub.Co., Chicago 1973.

K. Hamada. "Income Taxation and Educational Subsidy", *Journal of Public Economics 3* (1974), pp.145–158.

K. Hamada. Taxing the Brain Drain: A Global Point of View, in J.N. Bhagwati (ed.), *The New International Economic Order: The North-South Debate* , The MIT Press, 1977.

D.S. Hamermesh. *Jobless Pay and the Economy* , The John Hopkins University Press, Baltimore 1977.

A.C. Harberger. Taxation, Resource Allocation, and Welfare, in *The Role of Direct and Indirect Taxes in the Federal Revenue System* , National Bureau of Economic Research and Brookings Institution, Princeton University Press, Princeton 1964.

T.P. Hill. "Do-it-yourself and GDP", *The Review of Income and Wealth 25* (1979), pp.31–39.

A.J. Isachsen and S. Strom. "The Hidden Economy: The Labor Market and Tax Evasion", *Scandinavian Journal of Economics 82* (1980), pp.304–311.

–. *Den Skjulte Okonomi og det Svarte Arbeidsmarked* , mimeo, University of Oslo, 1980a.

74 A. LINDBECK

J. Kesselman. "Labor-Supply Effects of Income, Income-Work, and Wage Subsidies", *Journal of Human Resources 4* (1969), p.275–292.

M.H. Kosters. *Income and Substitution Effects in a Family Labor Supply Model*, University of Chicago, P–3339, 1966.

P.R.G. Layard and A.A. Walters. *Microeconomic Theory* , McGraw-Hill, New York 1978.

A. Lindbeck. *Tax Effects versus Budget Effects on Labor Supply* , Seminar Paper no.148 (*revised* Dec. 1980), Institute for International Economic Studies, Stockholm 1980.

–. *The Distribution of Factor Income vs Disposable Income in a Welfare State: The Case of Sweden* , Seminar Paper no.171, Institute for International Economic Studies 1981.

S. Lippman and J. McCall. "The Economics of Job Search: A Survey", *Economic Inquiry 14* (1976), pp.347–368.

K. Macafee. *A Glimpse of the Hidden Economy in the National Accounts* , Economic Trends, no.316, 1980.

D. Magnusson. "Inlärd hjälplöshet – välfärd på gott och ont", *Skandinaviska Enskilda Banken Kvartalsskrift* , no.3–4 (1980), pp.63–69.

M.N. Marchon. "Tax Avoidance, Progressivity, and Work Effort", *Public Finance 34* (1979), pp.452–462.

P.R. McDaniel. "Tax Shelters and Tax Policy", *National Tax Journal 26* (1973), pp.353–388.

J.E. Meade. *Introduction, in Taxation and Incentives* , The Institute for Fiscal Studies, pp.1–3.

J.E. Meade, IFS (Institute for Fiscal Studies). *The Structure and Reform of Direct Taxation* , Report of a Committee chaired by Professor J.E. Meade, Allen and Unwin, London 1978.

J. Mincer. "Family Migration Decisions", *Journal of Political Economy 86* (1978), pp.749–773.

J.A. Mirrlees. "An Exploration in the Theory of Optimum Income Taxation ", *Review of Economic Studies 38* (1971), pp.175–208.

R.A. Musgrave. *The Future of Fiscal Policy. A Reassessment, Prof. Dr.Gaston Eyskens Lectures* , Leuven University Press, 1978.

G. Myrdal. *Challenge to Affluence* , Parthenon, New York 1962.

F. Nordström. *Arbetslöshetsersättning och dess inverkan på arbetslöshet och sysselsättning, empiriska erfarenheter från senare ar;* artikelreferat, del 1,del 2 (1980a). *Pensionsförmåner och de äldres arbetsutbud* , en översikt (1980b). *Dolda sektorn, skattefusk, attityder till skatter mm* , en översikt (1980c). *Skattertryck, marginalskatter och incitamentseffekter* , artikelreferat (1980d). Mimeos, Institute for International Economic Studies, University of Stockholm.

D.C. North and R.P. Thomas. *The Rise of the Western World* , Cambridge University Press, 1973.

J. Pechman, H. Aaron and M. Taussig. *Social Security Perspectives for Reform* , Brookings Institution, Washington DC, 1968.

J.H. Pencavel. "A Note on Income Tax Evasion, Labor Supply, and Nonlinear Tax Schedules", *Journal of Public Economics 12* (1979), pp.115–124.

H.G. Petersen. *Taxes, Tax Systems and Economic Growth – A Survey of Recent Developments* , mimeo, Kiel Institute of World Economics, 1980.

H.S. Rosen. *What is Labor Supply and Do Taxes Affect It?*, Working Paper no.411, National Bureau of Economic Research, 1979.

Royal Commission on Taxation, Ottawa, Canada, 1967.

E. Sadka. "On Income Distribution, Incentive Effects and Optimal Income Taxation", *Review of Economic Studies 43* (1976), pp.261–267.

G. Schmölders. "Survey Research in Public Finance – A Behavior Approach to Fiscal Theory", *Public Finance* , 1970. pp.300–306.

J.K. Seade. "On the Shape of Optimal Tax Schedules", *Journal of Public Economics 7* (1977), pp.203–235.

A. Selden: *United Kingdom,* mimeo, The Fraser Institute, Vancouver 1980.

M. Seligman. *Helplessness: On Depression, Development, and Death* , W.H. Freeman, San Francisco 1975.

E. Sheshinski. "The Optimal Linear Income-tax". *The Review of Economic Studies 39* (1972), pp.297–302.

J.V. Skolka. *Long-term Effects of Unbalanced Labor Productivity Growth on the Way to a Self-sevice Society* , in: L. Solari and J.N. du Pasquier (eds.), *Private and Enlarged Consumption: Essays in Methodology and Empiricical Analysis* , North Holland, Amsterdam, 1976.

T.N. Srinivasan. "Tax Evasion: A Model", *Journal of Public Economics 2* (1973), pp.339–346.

F. Stafford and G. Duncan. *The Use of Time and Technology by Households in the United States* , mimeo, University of Michigan, 1977.

N.H. Stern. "On the Specification of Models of Optimum Income Taxation", *Journal of Public Economics 6* (1976), pp.123–162.

–. *Taxation and Labour Supply – A Partial Survey,* in *Taxation and Incentives* , The Institute for Fiscal Studies. 1976a.

C. Stuart. *Swedish Tax Rates, Labor Supply and Tax Revenues* , Department of Economics, University of Lund, 1979:64, 1979.

–. *The Swedish Tax System – What Can We Learn from it?* University of Lund, mimeo, 1980.

76   A. LINDBECK

I. Stahl. *Unemployment Insurance: The Swedish Case* , Reprint Series no.20, Department of Economics, University of Lund, 1979.

V. Tanzi. "Underground Economy Built on Illicit Pursuits is Growing Concern of Economic Policymakers ", *IMF Survey* , February 4, 1980, pp.34–37.

L. Weiss. "The Desirability of Cheating Incentives and Randomness in the Optimal Income Tax", *Journal of Political Economy 84* (1976), pp.1343–1352.

H.L. Wilensky. *The "New Corporatism", Centralization, and the Welfare State* , Sage Publications, Beverly Hills, 1976.

R. Willis and S. Rosen. *Education and Self-Selection* , mimeo, University of Chicago, 1978.

[7]

TAX EFFECTS VERSUS BUDGET EFFECTS
ON LABOR SUPPLY

ASSAR LINDBECK*

This paper analyzes the effects on labor supply of parallel changes in taxes and public spending of various types. A number of important recent developments in the labor supply behavior of households are highlighted by such a study of various types of "budget effects," rather than isolated "tax effects." This comes out in particular when considering cross substitution effects on labor supply of changes in public spending on goods and services or of the subsidization of goods and services provided by private markets. Moreover, the income effects of tax changes are often mitigated, or possibly even removed, by the income effects of the accompanying expenditure changes.

The government budget constraint implies that when, for instance, a certain tax is increased, some other taxes have to be lowered, government transfers or expenditures on goods and services to be increased or less government bonds or money to be issued. Of course, to respect the government budget constraint does not necessarily require an assumption about balanced budgets, or even parallel changes in taxes and government spending. However, several scholars have over the years pointed out *the practical importance* of studying just such cases. Early examples are classical scholars of public finance like Knut Wicksell and Antonio de Vito De Marco.[1] The same view has been expressed in connection to contemporary analyses of the effects of budget policies on the distribution of income, for instance by studying what Richard Musgrave (1959, 213-15) has baptized "balance-budget incidence" and "differential tax incidence" (the latter when one tax is substituted for another).[2]

However, this view has spread very reluctantly and incompletely to the literature on the consequences of higher tax rates for the supply of labor, and the related issue of the "incentive effects" of taxes on work. One exception is some studies during the late seventies of the consequences of social security systems for retirement decisions, where the combined effects of pension fees and pension benefits have been analyzed in the context of a

---

*Institute for International Economic Studies, University of Stockholm. I am grateful for comments on an earlier draft by the members of the graduate economics seminar at Simon Fraser University, Burnaby, B.C., Canada, as well as by William Baumol, Peter Lloyd, Agnar Sandmo, Lars Svensson, Gordon Winston, and an anonymous referee.

1. See Buchanan (1960, pp. 30-41).

2. See for instance Buchanan (1960, Chapters VI and VII), Shoup (1969, Chapter 1), Musgrave-Musgrave (1976), and Browning-Browning (1979), as well as A. C. Harberger (1962) and the empirical incide ce literature inspired by that paper.

473

life cycle model of household decision-making (Feldstein 1977; Sheshinski 1978; and Hu 1979). Other exceptions are the studies of "negative income taxation"[3] and the literature on optimum taxation, where in fact the effects of combined changes in income tax rates and transfer payments are studied. However, in neither case is there much, if any, concern for the consequences for labor supply of parallel variations in taxes and government subsidies or spending on goods and services.[4]

Against this background, the present paper tries to show the usefulness of studying systematically the effects on labor supply of *various combinations* of higher tax rates and higher public spending. In other words, this is a study of "budget effects" rather than "tax effects" on the supply of labor. Indeed it would seem that such studies of a parallel expansion of taxes and expenditures (though not necessarily with a balanced budget), rather than of isolated changes in tax rates, is the relevant approach when we ask what are the consequences for labor supply of moving to "high-tax societies." For the aggregate of employees or citizens, and hence the average employee or the average citizen (except in very special cases) "get back" at least part of a tax increase in one form or another — by way of increased public spending or reductions in other taxes (or possibly by the tax increase preventing a rise in the general price level). By constrast, in most of the literature in this field, the effects of changes in general income taxes, and in the context of one-period models also general consumption taxes, are analyzed in the same way as are the effects of isolated changes in real wage rates, with mutually counteracting income and substitution effects.[5]

Among the many different types of "combined" tax and expenditure changes, this paper concentrates on *four*. More specifically, a tax increase is assumed alternatively to finance:

(1) transfer payments;
(2) indirect subsidization of ordinary (private) goods, supplied in equilibrating markets;
(3) the provision of ordinary (private) goods, in contrast to collective goods, that are delivered by public authorities at regulated prices on markets characterized by excess demand and with the goods being rationed to households; *and*

---

3. See for instance the surveys in Boskin (1967) and Green (1968).

4. Typically, the optimum tax literature assumes that the government considers alternative distributions of a fixed value of net revenues (taxes minus transfers) for the government, or of taxes that bring about a fixed ratio between total private consumption and total output at a given level of the production of public services. See for instance Mirrlees (1971), Sheshinski (1972). Feldstein (1973), Stern (1976b). Atkinson and Stiglitz (1980, Chapters 13-14).

5. A typical formulation in the literature is this: "If the income effect of a rise in the real wage rate outweighs the substitution effect, with the result that work effort declines, then it would be reasonable to conclude that the income effect of a proportional income tax, which would be equivalent to a fall in the real wage rate, would likewise outweigh the substitution effect, so that work effort would increase" Barlow (1963, pp. 27-28). Among recent examples of similar formulations. see for instance Cain-Watts (1973, pp. 3-4), Godfrey (1975, p. 11), Meade (1978), Stern (1976) and Thurow (1980) — and in fact most exposition on the consequences of high-tax rates for labor supply.

(4) the provision of collective goods, for which there are no market prices.

The traditional approach to analyzing the effects on labor supply of *isolated* tax changes will then appear as a special case which is relevant only under very specific circumstances.

To highlight the main points of the paper, the simplest possible analytical framework will be used — a preference-theoretic analysis of the choice between "leisure" and the consumption of two commodities by an individual agent. Even though the paper formally deals only with the supply of hours of work, the general principles of the analysis apply to several other dimensions of labor supply as well, such as intensity of work; see Lindbeck (1982).

To simplify matters, simultaneity of decision-making by different households, and by different members of the same household, is not considered; and Becker-type specifications of "consumption technologies" of households (*i.e.*, the production of utility-generating entities by way of inputs of goods and time) are not attempted. The analysis will be pursued in the context of direct rather than indirect preference functions, the main reason being that I want to give formal and intuitive explanations of how the conclusions depend on the properties of the original (direct) preference function.

It should be emphasized that the paper, like most other studies of incentive effects on the willingness to work, is concerned only with a partial study of *the (ex ante) supply* of labor (in fact hours of work). A study of "total" effects on the number of *hours actually worked (ex post)* would require a macroeconomic general equilibrium model where also the production side, including labor demand, is specified.[6]

A partial study of labor supply is of course only a modest, though necessary, first step to such a study of the total general equilibrium effects. However, the paper contains the message that also a partial study of fiscal policy effects on one single behavior function, e.g. the labor supply function, has to rely on a logical and realistic definition of *the macroeconomic context* of the experiment that underlies the study. In other words, it is important that the macroeconomic foundations of partial and microeconomic experiments be specified. Thus, there is a "dual" to the need of specifying the microeconomic foundations of macroeconomics.[7]

---

6. Some attempts have been made in the literature to analyze the consequences of social security systems for retirement decisions in the context of general equilibrium (growth) models, where also the requirement of balanced budgets is incorporated (Hu, 1979). Kotlikoff and Summers (1979) have in a similar context analyzed the consequences of income-compensated labor income taxes on simultaneous decisions on retirement and investment in human capital. Moreover, some authors, such as Shoven and Whalley (1977), have experimented with algorithms in the tradition of Scarf to compute general equilibrium effects on both product and factor markets of various types of parameter changes, granting the government budget restriction.

7. The reason for talking about "partial effects on labor supply," or simply "labor supply effects," rather than "partial equilibrium effects," is that the latter expression gives an association to the interaction between demand and supply in a small market. I am instead referring to the effects on the supply side only, though for a large market, in fact for the entire labor market or considerable parts of it.

I. THE MODEL

Let the following notations be introduced:

T = available time; N = labor time; $L = T - N$ = leisure time; W^* = nominal wage rate; $X = tW^*N - A$ = tax function; $W = W^*(1 - t)$ = after tax wage rate; p_i = product prices; q_i = product quantities.

Without loss of generality, I will assume that $W^* = 1$, and hence that $W = (1 - t)$.

Assume that the behavior of an individual can be analyzed in the context of the maximization of the preference function

$$(1) \qquad\qquad U = f(q_1, q_2, L),$$

subject to the budget constraint

$$(2) \qquad\qquad (1 - t)N + A = p_1 q_1 + p_2 q_2.$$

The first-order necessary conditions for maximum are

$$(3) \quad \begin{cases} R^{21}(q_1, q_2, T - N) = p_1/p_2 \\[1mm] R^{32}(q_1, q_2, T - N) = p_2/(1 - t) \\[1mm] (1 - t)N + A - p_1 q_1 - p_2 q_2 = 0, \end{cases}$$

where $R^{21} \equiv \dfrac{f_1}{f_2} \equiv -\dfrac{dq_2}{dq_1}$ and $R^{32} \equiv \dfrac{f_2}{f_3} \equiv -\dfrac{dL}{dq_2}$, R^{ij} being the marginal rate of substitution of good i for good j.[8]

The second-order sufficient conditions for maximum are then

$$(4) \qquad\qquad D = \begin{vmatrix} R_1^{21} & R_2^{21} & -R_3^{21} \\[1mm] R_1^{32} & R_2^{32} & -R_3^{32} \\[1mm] -p_1 & -p_2 & (1 - t) \end{vmatrix} > 0.$$

8. The reason for working with the *ratios* of the f's (i.e. R^{ij}), rather than them separately in the subsequent analysis, is that I want to analyze changes in the marginal evaluation of the various arguments in the preference function without having to assume cardinality.

It is assumed that the functions of the model have all the necessary mathematical properties to guarantee a unique and economically meaningful interior solution when the budget restriction is equation (2).[9]

Differentiation of equations (3) gives the solution

$$
(5) \quad dN = \frac{\left(\frac{1}{p_2} dp_1 - \frac{p_1}{p_2^2} dp_2 \right) D_{13} + \left(\frac{1}{(1-t)} dp_2 + \frac{p_2}{(1-t)^2} dt \right) D_{23}}{D}
$$

$$
+ \frac{(Ndt - dA + q_1 dp_1 + q_2 dp_2) D_{33}}{D} \quad ,
$$

where D_{ij} denotes the cofactor of the ijth element of the determinant D, and where

$$
D_{13} = (-p_2 R_1^{32} + p_1 R_2^{32}), \qquad D_{23} = -(-p_2 R_1^{21} + p_1 R_2^{21}),
$$

$$
D_{33} = (R_1^{21} R_2^{32} - R_2^{21} R_1^{32}).
$$

II. APPLICATIONS

It is time to apply the model.

Case 1. In the case of an increase in the income-tax rate (t) for the purpose of financing higher *income-independent, i.e.* lump-sum, transfers (A), equation (5) simplifies to the Slutsky equation,

$$
(6) \qquad dN = \left(\underbrace{\frac{p_2}{(1-t)^2} \frac{D_{23}}{D}}_{\substack{\text{subst.} \\ \text{effect} \\ \text{of } dt \\ -}} + \underbrace{\frac{ND_{33}}{D}}_{\substack{\text{income} \\ \text{effect} \\ \text{of } dt \\ +}} \right) dt - \underbrace{\frac{D_{33}}{D} dA}_{\substack{\text{income} \\ \text{effect} \\ \text{of } dA \\ -}},
$$

assuming $dp_1 = dp_2 = 0$.

---

9. A reason for neglecting corner solutions is that the analysis refers to averages of aggregates of individuals, like the "representative" employee, pensioner, low-income earner, etc. Another reason is that the goods in the preference function are composites of many goods and that (almost) all individuals would be expected to buy positive amounts of some component of each composite good.

The reason for obtaining one rather than two second-order sufficient condition is that the number of first-order equations in (3) has been kept down by one as a result of using the ratios R" rather than the separate partial f_i.

The second order sufficient conditions for maximum guarantee that the substitution effect of dt on N is negative.[10] The income effects of dt and dA are *assumed* to be positive and negative respectively by the argument that leisure is most likely a "normal good."[11]

The simplest, and in fact rather trivial, application of equation (6) is when the lump-sum transfers are paid out to the same individual who pays the tax, implying that the negative substitution effect on labor supply of dt is accentuated by the negative income effect of dA but counteracted by the positive income effect of dt. In the *special* case when utility is constant $(dU = 0)$, there is of course an "unchallenged" negative substitution effect of dt on labor supply.[12]

A more interesting experiment is when the combined rise in t and A has redistributional consequences. For instance, if the income tax increase is confined to "ordinary" employees, and the transfers consist of payments to "pensioners," there would, in the context of our one-period analysis, be a positive income effect on labor supply of the "representative employee" (counteracting the negative substitution effect), and a negative income effect on labor supply of the "representative pensioner." (Rigorously, we may assume that all active employees among themselves are identical and that all pensioners are, too, among themselves.) If we could (as an approximation) ignore the income effect on labor supply of pensioners, we would be back to the "traditional" case of an isolated income-tax increase for employees — with ambiguous net effects.[13]

The case just discussed, with a simultaneous increase in t and A, may alternatively be interpreted as an expansion of *negatively income-dependent* transfers to low-income groups, *i.e.* transfers that fall when income goes up (means test transfers). Assuming that other groups of citi-

10. In terms of the notations used above, a sufficient condition for the substitution effect to be negative is that $R_1^{21} < 0$, $R_2^{21} > 0$, *i.e.* that the marginal evaluation of q_2 relative to q_1 rises by higher q_1 and falls by higher q_2.

11. Formally this requires that the cofactor $D_{11} > 0$. A sufficient condition for this to be the case is that not only are $R_1^{21} < 0$, $R_2^{21} > 0$, but also are R_1^{12}, $R_2^{12} < 0$. The latter two expressions imply that the marginal evaluation of leisure (relative to commodity 2) rises by higher consumption of each of the commodities. Intuitively speaking, we may say that leisure and consumption then are complements *in the context of the preference function*, what is here called "Edgeworth-complements"; see Edgeworth (1923, p. 119).

The difference between the concepts of "Edgeworth substitutes (complements)" and "Hicks substitutes (complements)" is highlighted by the fact that while in a two goods model (with the preference function $F(q_1, q_2)$) the goods are *necessarily* Hicks-substitutes, they have to be Edgeworth-complements (defined as F_{12}, $F_{21} > 0$ in the case of cardinality and R_1^{21}, $R_2^{21} < 0$ in the case of ordinality) to assure that the goods are "normal." This is easily shown by deriving Slutsky equations for the two-goods case and developing the determinants of these equations.

12. In terms of calculus, when utility is constant $(dU = 0)$, $Ndt = dA$, and hence money income is constant at the initial N.

13. Moving outside the formal model, the issue is further complicated by the possibility that without the budget changes under consideration, employees may instead have made (higher) *voluntary* transfers to their parents; and that would (when comparing the alternative with and without the discussed budget changes) have reduced the asserted income effect of the budget changes on the supply of labor of both groups.

zens are called upon to finance the net transfers to low-income groups by an income tax, labor supply of low-income groups would unambiguously fall, by mutually reinforcing income and substitution effects, while the effects on labor supply of the other groups are theoretically ambiguous.[14]

If "leisure" takes the form of the production of goods or services within the household, we would expect leisure and purchases of consumer goods to be stronger Hicks-substitutes than when leisure is just "recreation time" (consumption time). Then the negative substitution effect on labor supply would be expected to be stronger. This is probably an explanation why married women, who frequently shift from market work to home production, according to available empirical studies show stronger substitution effects of changes in after-tax real wage rates on hours of work in the market than do men and unmarried women; see Mincer, 1962.[15] A more general formulation of the same idea is perhaps that the effects on *type of job* of a change in after-tax wage differentials between two different types of work (hence not only between labor-market activity and home production) would be expected to be stronger than the effects of after-tax wage rate changes on "recreation time" (consumption time) — as different jobs are very close substitutes to each other as methods of providing resources for consumption.

However, while the substitution effect of dt would be expected to be stronger for married women than for other groups, the income effect would be expected to be weaker, as the size of that effect is proportional to the number of hours of work in the market (N), and married females usually work fewer hours in the market than do other groups. A negative *net* effect of an *isolated* tax increase is therefore a more reasonable assumption for (a group of) married women than for (a group of) other employees.

A variation of case 1 is that the size of the transfer payments is *positively* rather than negatively dependent on earned income, making t negative. A non-trivial version is a social security system where the taxes ("fees") and the benefits refer to different periods. For instance, assume heuristically an ordinary two-period model of household behavior with the fees paid in the first period, while the benefits are received in the second. Let us also assume that there is a perfect capital market, where the individual is able and willing to borrow freely. Then if the capital value of the expected benefits of working one more hour is smaller (greater) than

14. This case has been extensively discussed in the literature on "negative income taxation" and "poverty traps," though the tax increase for other groups has often been neglected. See for instance Boskin (1967), and Green (1968).

The conclusions above concerning tax financed transfers to low-income groups should perhaps be modified in the context of a long-run perspective, with endogenous (positive or negative) changes in productivity or in preferences for leisure due to the transfer program. See for instance Boskin (1967), Conlisk (1968), Cain-Watts (1973), and Myrdal (1962, pp. 40 f).

15. For many purposes an *explicit* disaggregation of leisure into these two components is useful. See the excellent article on that issue by R. Gronau (1977). (As Gronau points out, the Becker and Lancaster type models do *not* include home production of goods that are substitutes for market goods; these models assume "consumption technologies" rather than ordinary production activities.)

the capital value of the fees on that hour of work, there is a negative (positive) substitution effect against work in general (*i.e.* in both periods). Moreover, the higher fees in the first period also create a substitution effect that shifts work from the first to the second period. If there is also an "income test" on the benefits in the sense that the size of the benefits are reduced by higher earned income in the second period, as is sometimes the case for pensions, there is an additional substitution effect against work in general (for which the return declines), as well as a substitution effect that shifts work from the second to the first period. If there are income effects as well depends, of course, on how the capital value of life income is affected by these various changes, *i.e.* on the relative size of the changes in the capital value of the fees and the benefits.

Social security systems in the real world are, of course, even more complex than this — and so are probably also the behavior patterns of individuals.[16]

It may be noted that the pure substitution effect, derived by assuming $dU = 0$, or equivalently $Ndt - dA = 0$, differs from the effects when keeping the budget balanced. This may be shown analytically most easily if all individuals are assumed to be identical so that we may write the *per-capita* balanced budget requirement $tN - A = 0$, with $tdN + Ndt - dA = 0$ for changes in the parameters t and A. With p_1 and p_2 constant, the labor supply function may be written (a) $N = F(t, A)$. By assuming that the budget is always balanced, regardless of the value of t, A becomes a function of t, implying that the *(per-capita)* budget balance may be written (b) $A(t) = t \cdot F(t, A(t))$. By differentiating (a) and (b), and by proper substitution, we then obtain

(6a)
$$\frac{dN}{dt} = \frac{\left.\frac{\delta F}{\delta t}\right|_{\bar{u}}}{1 - t \cdot \frac{\delta F}{\delta A}},$$

where dN/dt is the balanced budget effect of a change in t, and

---

16. For instance, many pension systems allow individual variations in retirement age, with the benefit adjusted according to more or less complex schedules. Population growth and productivity change are other variables that are highly relevant for the functioning of the social security system. Factors like these are analyzed in different versions of life cycle models, though often with the rather restrictive assumption that labor supply is fixed in the first period. Usually, the time of retirement is an endogenous variable in these models. See for instance Feldstein (1974), (1977), Sheshinski (1978), and Hu (1979).

$$\frac{\delta F}{\delta t}\bigg|_{\bar{u}} \quad \text{the pure substitution effect.}[17]$$

Assuming $\delta F/\delta A < 0$ (leisure being a normal good) the balanced budget effect is negative, like the pure substitution effect, but numerically smaller than the latter. The intuitive explanation is that when the negative substitution effect on N reduces tax revenues by tdN, the government has to reduce A to keep the budget balanced, which partly counteracts the fall in N (leisure being a normal good). We may notice that a combined increase in t and A, keeping the budget balanced, may be interpreted as a shift to a more progressive income tax for the person in question (with the average tax rate kept constant).

Case 2. If instead the tax increase is designed to finance higher indirect subsidization of *one* of the commodities, say q_1,[18] the effects on labor supply are, according to equation (5), defined by

(7)

$$dN = \left(\frac{D_{13}}{p_2 D} + q_1 \frac{D_{33}}{D}\right) dp_1 + \left(\frac{p_2 D_{23}}{(1-t)^2 D} + N \frac{D_{33}}{D}\right) dt =$$

cross subst. effect of dp_1 ?	cross income effect of p_1 +	subst. effect of dt −	income effect of dt +

$$= \frac{p_2}{(1-t)D}\left(-\frac{D_{23}}{(1-t)}dW + \frac{(1-t)D_{13}}{p_2^2}dp_1\right) + \frac{D_{33}}{D}\left(q_1 dp + Ndt\right).$$

| subst. effects | income effects |

17. Follows from the following manipulations:

$$\frac{dN}{dt} = \frac{\delta F}{\delta t} + \frac{\delta F}{\delta A}\cdot\frac{dA}{dt} \quad \text{from (a). If } \frac{dA}{dt} \text{ is replaced by } \frac{dA}{dt} = N + t\frac{dN}{dt}$$

from (b), we get

(c)
$$\frac{dN}{dt} = \underbrace{\frac{\delta F}{\delta t} + N\frac{\delta F}{\delta A} + t\frac{\delta F}{\delta A}\cdot\frac{dN}{dt}}_{\delta F/\delta t\,|\,\bar{u}}.$$

18. If the subsidy is instead *general*, the net substitution effect on labor supply is negative, positive or zero depending on whether the relative fall in the price level is smaller than, greater than or equal to the relative fall in the after-tax wage rate. (The sign of the net income effect may, of course, be determined by the authorities by appropriate variations in A.)

Of course in the *special* case when $dU = 0$, only the two substitution effects operate.[19] (A selective *tax* on q_i can be analyzed symetrically, *i.e.* as a *rise* in p_i.)

To come further in the analysis, it is necessary to take a close look at the cross substitution effect of dp_1. The positive substitution effect in favor of the commodity for which the price has fallen accentuates the negative substitution effect on labor supply of dt if leisure and the subsidized commodity are Hicks-complements (requiring $D_{13} > 0$), but counteract the substitution effect of dt if they are Hicks-substitutes (requiring $D_{13} < 0$). It is easy to show that L and q_1 have a stronger tendency to be Hicks-complements the closer an Edgeworth-complement to L is q_1 as compared to q_2.[20]

Applying the model to the real world, a subsidy to recreational equipment and recreational services, which most likely are Hicks-complements to leisure (in the form of recreation time), would be expected to create a negative cross-substitution effect on labor supply in the open market. A similar effect will arise when leisure largely takes the form of home production of the non-subsidized good (for which the relative market price has risen). These are cases when the combined tax-subsidy increase would be expected to result in a particularly strong flight to do-it-yourself work at the expense of labor in the open market.

A positive cross-substitution effect on labor supply, by contrast, implying that the subsidized good is a Hicks-substitute to leisure, would be expected to occur if leisure largely takes the form of home production of *the subsidized* good (or a close substitute to it). This is likely to happen in the case of subsidies to services such as education and the care of children, the old and the sick. It is therefore quite likely that the heavy subsidization of several services like these in many countries during recent decades has contributed to *raising* the supply of labor in the open market — in fact mainly for married women — counteracting the negative substitution effect of the higher tax rates that have been required to finance these reforms. This is most likely one of the reasons why the labor supply of married women, particularly in highly "advanced" welfare states, has increased strongly in recent decades in spite of higher tax rates.

Case 3. A third case is a tax increase that finances the public provision of an "ordinary" (non-collective) good at a fixed price, below the market equilibrium price, and the good therefore is rationed (formally or informally). Such a good is in this paper simply called a "publicly-provided good"; in most developed countries this is the dominating type of public spending on goods and services.

---

19. In terms of calculus, "the real monetary resources" of the household are then constant at the initial value of N, in the sense that $Ndt + q_1 dp_1 = 0$, for $dp_2 = dA = 0$.

20. *I.e.* the more the marginal evaluation of leisure (relative to q_2) rises due to an increase in q_1 as compared to the case of an increase in q_2 (*i.e.* the greater numerically is R_1^{12} relative to R_2^{12}).

Assuming, in the context of our model, that good number 1 is such a publicly provided good, both p_1 and q_1 are exogenous for the household.

For $dp_1 = dp_2 = dA = 0$, we then get the Slutsky equation

(8)

$$ dN = \left(- \frac{R_1^{32} p_2}{D^*} + \frac{p_1 R_2^{32}}{D^*} \right) dq_1 + \left(\frac{p_2^2}{(1-t)^2 D^*} + \frac{N R_2^{32}}{D^*} \right) dt, $$

direct	money	subst.	income
dq_1	income	effect	effect
effect	dq_1 eff.	of dt	of dt
?	+	−	+

(4a) $$ D^* = \begin{vmatrix} R_2^{32} - R_3^{32} \\ -p_2 \ (1-t) \end{vmatrix} = R_2^{32} \cdot (1-t) - R_3^{32} \cdot p_2 < 0. $$

The new feature of equation (8), as compared to the Slutsky equations in the previous cases, is of course the effects on labor supply of the exogenous change in q_1. In the context of equation (8) this effect is subdivided into two — one "money income effect" and one "direct effect." The source of the money income effect is that higher q_1 draws money income from the individual (by the amount $p_1 dq_1$), generating an "ordinary" positive money income effect on N, as L is assumed to be a normal good (by the assumption $R_2^{32} < 0$). Similarly, a change in p_1 at fixed q_1 would operate like a lump-sum change in income. The sign of the direct effect of dq_1 by contrast is, of course, ambiguous.[21]

The *direct dq_1-effect* is not a "pure" substitution effect. It includes also an imputed income-effect component, as higher q_1 means higher imputed income of the individual, which by itself should have a negative income effect on N. Thus, there are really two opposing income effects of higher q_1 — one positive money income effect and one negative imputed income effect — in addition to the pure substitution effect of dq_1. The change in *net* income is then the "savings" in expenditures by higher imputed income *minus* the loss in money income, due to higher q_1 — in addition to the income effect of the increase in the tax rate.

It can be shown that the "net" income effect of dq_1 is negative on labor supply iff $R^{21} \equiv -(dq_2/dq_1) > p_1/p_2$, *i.e.* iff the marginal evaluation of q_1 relative to q_2, $(-dq_2/dq_1)$, is higher than the price ratio p_1/p_2.[22] The

21. If q_1 and L are Edgeworth-complements — in the sense that the marginal evaluation of L rises by higher q_1 ($R_1^{32} < 0$) — the sign of the direct dq_1-effect is negative (and positive in the reverse situation).

22. The "net" income effect of dq_1 can be derived by first calculating the substitution effect of dq_1 and thereafter subtracting this effect from the effect of dq_1 according to equation (8): see Lindbeck (1980).

meaning of this condition is that the individual at the existing relative price between q_1 and q_2 would like to consume more of the rationed good (q_1), *i.e.* that the physical constraint of the consumption of q_1 is *binding*.[23] Intuitively speaking, when the employee gets more of a rationed good that he evaluates higher than its price, on the margin, he feels richer, which creates a negative net income effect on labor supply. In the opposite case the net income effect of $d\bar{q}_1$ on labor supply is positive.

Whether the pure substitution effect of dq_1 is negative or positive depends of course on the type of public good we are talking about. It is likely to be zero or negative *either* if the good provided by the government is a complement to leisure in the form of "recreation time," such as in the case of recreational facilities, *or* if the good is difficult to produce by the household itself, as the public good then would *not* be expected to be a substitute for leisure in the form of home production.

By contrast, obvious examples when positive cross-substitution effects on labor supply will emerge are publicly provided services that are close substitutes to home production, like education, and the care of children, the sick and the old. If the publicly provided and the home-produced goods are close enough substitutes, the substitution effects of dq_1 and dt may in fact approximately cancel. If also the mutually opposing income effects of dq_1 and dt happen to cancel approximately we get a situation of (nearly) "complete offset." Of course, if the substitutability of the publicly provided and the home-produced goods are extremely good substitutes, it is not unlikely that labor supply in the market will in fact increase substantially as a result of a *combined* increase in taxes and the provision of the public good, at least in the case of *married women*. (A similar effect may emerge, as was seen in the context of "case 2," if these types of services are instead subsidized on equilibrating markets.)

It is worth noting, when applying this analysis to real world issues, that while tax increases by themselves tend to shift "services of things" from the market to the household (by way of the substitution effect in favor of home production), "personal services" like the care of the very young, the sick and the old, tend, because of the welfare state programs, to be removed from households to public institutions, *i.e.* to be collectivized. Due to the traditional division of labor within households, men will then be induced, by the tax increases, to shift from market work to home work, while married women will be induced to move their work in the opposite direction because of the cross substitution effect of the increased public provision

---

23. This conclusion is closely related to a theorem in the general theory of rationing, according to which an increased provision of a rationed good generates an income effect on the household, the size of which is determined by "the difference between the virtual and the actual price of the rationed good"; see Neary and Roberts (1980, pp. 29-35). (The concept of a "virtual price" corresponds in the above analysis to the marginal rate of substitution, R^{21}.) However, Neary and Roberts do not point out that their income effect may be subdivided into two parts with different signs — by way of a fall in "money income" and an increase in "imputed income" (as defined above).

and subsidization of services that are close substitutes to traditional home work by women. The combined effects may be a profound change in the role of the households in society.

Case 4. A somewhat different situation emerges if the tax increase is used to finance the provision of a collective good. *i.e.* a good that cannot be marketed and for which there is then no market price. Thus. analytically case 4 is a special version of case 3, for $p_1 = 0$, implying that q_1 and p_1 do not enter the budget equation of the individual. Geometrically, the projected budget line in the $q_2 - L$ plane is unaffected by *ceteris paribus*-variations in q_1 by contrast to case 3. Variations. therefore. in the amount of the "provided" good do not *ceteris paribus*. influence the individual's command over marketable goods and leisure.[24]

The only change, in principle, of the *formal* analysis of the above case with a non-collective public good is that the positive term $p_1 R_2^{12}/D^*$ in equation (8) now drops out as people do not lose monetary command over q_2 and L when q_1 rises. Thus, even the *theoretical* possibility of a positive income effect on labor supply of dq_1 disappears.[25]

However, there is another difference too between the effect of the provision of a non-collective and a collective publicly provided good *(i.e.* in addition to the disappearance of the "money-income effect" in the latter case). For it may be argued that the substitutability between "leisure" and the publicly provided good is probably smaller in the case of a collective good (like defense and law and order) than in the case of a non-collective, rationed publicly provided good (like education and the care of children, the old and the sick): home production of substitutes is usually much more difficult in the former case. As a consequence, the direct dq_1-effect — expressed by the first term in the parenthesis in equation (8) — is in reality likely to be negative in the case of a collective good, hence strengthening rather than weakening the negative substitution effect on labor supply of the tax rate increase itself.

All this means that a negative *net* effect on labor supply would be a more realistic assumption in the case of a tax-financed provision of a collective good than of an "ordinary" (rationed) non-collective publicly provided good; only the income effect of the tax increase would be expected to work in the opposite direction in the former case.

24. Scitovsky (1952, pp. 90-92) has argued that an income tax financed expansion of free public services (with constant utility) — *always* tends to diminish labor supply as the positive income effect of the tax increase would be eliminated by the negative income effect of higher income when the provision of public services increases. Obviously, as Scitovsky did assume that *money income* was constant his analysis is relevant for what has in this paper been called "case 1." *i.e.* a tax-financed increase in income-independent money transfers rather than public goods. Gordon Winston, by contrast, has pursued a geometric analysis that is in principle *consistent* with the analysis of our "case 4" with utility kept constant.

25. Of course, if the money income that is available for consumption (of q_2 and L) is kept constant, or if $q_1 \cdot p_1$ rather than q_1 is kept constant in case 3, the effects on labor supply are in *principle* the same whether we talk about a (rationed) non-collective publicly provided good or a collective good — *ceteris paribus* for the cross-substitution effects.

Of course in reality public provision of rationed goods — whether ordinary goods or collective goods — often has redistributional consequences. For instance, we may want to look at the case where the public good is provided to low-income groups only, while the accompanying tax increase has its initial impact on the rest of the population. We can then be sure that the labor supply of the low-income groups falls only if the public good is neutral or a complement to leisure (as then the net income effect lowers labor supply[26] and the substitution effect is zero or negative). For those who pay the tax increase, there is of course the usual negative substitution effect and the positive income effect of the tax increase.

III. CONCLUDING REMARKS

The considerations in this paper are of rather *general* relevance when income effects on microeconomic behavior are analyzed. For instance, it is well known that while the substitution effect on savings of an interest rate increase is unambiguously positive, the income effect is of opposite signs for lenders and borrowers, with the sign of the net income effect uncertain. Opposing income effects on consumption (and saving) is an essential aspect also in the case when a real wage increase that is *not* accompanied by a productivity increase occurs. For instance, if a real wage increase occurs at the expense of real capital income, a negative income effect on consumption by way of reduced capital income would counteract the positive income effects on consumption of higher employee income. Thus, the analysis in this paper is an application of a rather general principle requiring a realistic specification of *the macroeconomic foundations* of microeconomic and partial analysis — when studying averages of large groups of agents, such as "the representative income earner."

When applying these principles to the classical issue of the effects of taxation on the supply of labor of "the representative employee," we may heuristically say that the higher people value the public expenditures that are financed by a tax increase, the stronger are the tendencies for labor supply to *fall*. For then the positive income effect on labor supply of the tax increase will be considerably mitigated, or even eliminated, leaving the negative substitution effect in command. Of course, this general statement has, as we have seen, to be modified to the extent public expenditures are substitutes or complements to leisure.

Many more cases may of course be worth studying. A rather special case occurs if the increased public spending consists simply of deadweight administration without any benefits to individual citizens. In this case, where a tax increase, to quote Luigi Einaudi, is treated as a "hailstorm" (*"imposta grandine"*),[27] the analysis can be confined to the effects of an

---

26. Requiring in the case of a non-collective good that the physical constraint of the consumption of q_1 is binding; see pp. 11-12.

27. Quotation from J. Buchanan (1960, p. 39).

isolated tax increase, with its counteracting substitution and income effects. Thus, this rather special case seems in fact to have been implicitly used in the many studies when the effects of tax increases are analyzed as an *isolated* reduction in the after-tax real wage rate.[28]

It is finally worth noting that this paper has been confined to *positive economics*. If we shift to *normative economics*, in the sense of studying efficiency problems (*i.e.* incentive effects or the excess burden of taxes), we get, of course, an additional reason for concentrating on the substitution effects rather than the income effects, as efficiency (disincentive) effects, according to generally accepted welfare economic theory, are connected with the substitution effects of tax changes — rather than with the income effects or with the effects on labor supply due to the complementarity or substitutability between leisure on the one hand and public expenditures or subsidized commodities on the other. Thus, there seem to be two main reasons for emphasizing the substitution effects rather than the income effects when considering the consequences for broad aggregates of citizens (employees) of tax increases: (1) that the existence of income effects is *dubious* (often absent or at least small) when averages of large aggregates of employees are studied, and (2) that income effects are *not relevant* from the point of view of incentive and efficiency considerations. The importance of these two points is illustrated by the prevalent tendency in the literature to argue that a domination of the income effect over the substitution effect of an isolated tax increase is evidence that there are no disincentive effects on hours of work of existing tax rates.[29]

---

28. The notion of a "spite effect" (Musgrave, 1959, p. 240) against labor supply implies that a tax rate increase *per se* raises the (revealed) marginal evaluation of leisure relative to consumption. Formally the utility function, and hence also the marginal rates of substitution of leisure for consumption — R^{31} and R^{32} — includes t as a (fourth) argument, with R_t^{11}, $R_t^{12} < 0$. A recalculation of the analysis with this revised utility function means that, for instance, equation (6) would have to be replaced by

$$(6a) \qquad dN = \left(\frac{p_2 D_{21}}{(1-t)^2} - \frac{ND_{13}}{D} \right) dt - \frac{D_{11}}{D} dA - \frac{R_t^{12} D_{21}}{D} dt.$$

	subst.	income	income	"spite"
	effect	effect	effect	effect
	of dt	of dt	of dA	of dt
	−	+	−	−

where the spite effect has the expected sign. The possibility than an expansion of the government budget will have negative effects on labor supply then increases, of course, by the influence of the last term.

29. However, for expositions *not* making this incorrect inference, see Goode (1949), and more explicitly Layard-Walters (1978, pp. 82-83).

REFERENCES

Atkinson. A.B. and Stiglitz, J. E.. *Lectures on Public Economics*. McGraw-Hill, Maidenhead 1980.

Barlow. R.. "The Effects of Income Taxation on Work Choices." *Studies of the Royal Commission on Taxation*. No. 4, 1963.

Boskin. M. J.. "The Negative Income Tax and the Supply of Work Effort," *National Tax Journal*, Vol. XX. No. 4, 1967, 353-67.

Browning. E. K. and Browning. J. M.. *Public Finance and the Price System*. Macmillan, New York 1979.

Buchanan. J.. "*La scienza della finanze:* The Italian Tradition in Fiscal Theory." in *Fiscal Theory and Political Economy*. Chapter II. Chapel Hill Press, Durham 1960.

Burtless. G. and Hausman. J.. "The Effects of Taxation on Labor Supply." *Journal of Political Economy*. 1978. 86. 1103-30.

Cain. G. and Watts. H.. eds.. *Income Maintenance and Labor Supply*. Academic Press, London 1973.

Conlisk. J.. "Simple Dynamic Effects in Work-Leisure Choice: A Sceptical Comment on the Static Theory." *Journal of Human Resources*. 1968. 3.

Edgeworth. F. Y.. "The Pure Theory of Monopoly." *Papers Relating to Political Economy*. Section II, Macmillan & Co.. London 1925.

Feldstein. M.. "On the Optimum Progressivity of the Income Tax." *Journal of Public Economics*. 1973. 2. 357-76.

_____ . "Social Security and Private Savings: International Evidence in an Extended Life Cycle Model." in *The Economics of Public Services*. eds.. M. Feldstein and R. Inman. The Institute of Economic Affairs. 1977.

Godfrey. L.. *Theoretical and Empirical Aspects of the Effects of Taxation on the Supply of Labour*. OECD. Paris 1975.

Goode. R.. "The Income Tax and the Supply of Labor." *Journal of Political Economy*. October 1949, 428-37.

Green. C.. "Negative Taxes and Monetary Incentives to Work: The Static Theory." *The Journal of Human Resources*. III:3. 1968. 280-99.

Gronau. R.. "Leisure. Home Production. and Work — the Theory of the Allocation of Time Revisited." *Journal of Political Economy*. No. 6. 1977. 1099-1123.

Hall. R.. "Wages. Income. and Hours of Work in the U.S. Labor Force." in *Income Maintenance and Labor Supply*. eds.. G. Cain and H. Watts. Academic Press. London 1973.

Hansen. B.. *The Economic Theory of Fiscal Policy*. Allen and Unwin. London 1958.

Harberger. A.. "The Incidence of the Corporation Income Tax." *Journal of Political Economy*. 1962, 215-40.

Hicks, J. R.. *Value and Capital*. Clarendon Press. Oxford 1946.

Hu. S. C.. "Social Security. the Supply of Labor and Capital Accumulation." *American Economic Review*. 1979. 69. 274-83.

Kotlikoff. L. and Summers. L.. "Tax Incidence in a Life Cycle Growth Model with Variable Factor Supply." *Quarterly Journal of Economics*. 1979. 93. 705-18.

Layard. P. R. G. and Walters. A. A.. *Microeconomic Theory*. McGraw-Hill. Maidenhead. 1978.

Lindbeck. A.. "Tax Effects versus Budget Effects on Labor Supply." Seminar Paper No. 148. Institute for International Economic Studies. Stockholm 1980.

Lindbeck. A.. *Work Disincentives in the Welfare State*. NÖG Lectures 79-80. Austrian Economic Association. Manz. Vienna 1982.

Meade. J.. "The Characteristics of a Good Tax Structure." in *The Structure and Reform of Direct Taxation*. The Institute for Fiscal Studies. Chapter 2. Allen and Unwin. London 1978.

_____ . "Introduction." in *Taxation and Incentives*. The Institute for Fiscal Studies. London 1976.

Mincer. J.. "Labor Force Participation of Women." in *Aspects of Labor Economics*. ed., H. G. Lewis, National Bureau of Economic Research. New York 1962.

Mirrlees. J. A.. "An Exploration in the Theory of Optimum Income Taxation." *The Review of Economic Studies*. 1971. 175-208.

Musgrave. R. A.. *The Theory of Public Finance*. McGraw-Hill. New York 1959.

_____ and Musgrave, P. B.. *Public Finance in Theory and Practice*. 2nd ed.. McGraw-Hill. New York 1976.

Myrdal. G.. *Challenge to Affluence*. Pantheon. New York 1962.

Neary. J. P. and Roberts. K. W. S.. "The Theory of Household Behavior under Rationing." *European Economic Review*. 1980. *13*.

Scitovsky. T.. *Welfare and Competition*. Unwin University Books. London 1952.

Sheshinsky. E., "The Optimum Linear Income Tax." *Review of Economic Studies*. 1977. *39*. 297-302.

_____ . "A Model of Social Security and Retirement Decisions." *Journal of Public Economics*. 1978. *10*. 337-60.

Shoup, C. S.. *Public Finance*. Aldine Press. Chicago 1969.

Shoven, J. and Whalley. J.. "Equal Yield Tax Alternatives: General Equilibrium Computational Techniques," *Journal of Public Economics*. 1977. *8*. 211-24.

Stern, N., "Taxation and Labor Supply — A Partial Survey." in *Taxation and Incentives*. The Institute for Fiscal Studies. 1976a. 4-10.

_____ , "On the Specification of Models of Optimum Income Taxation." *Journal of Public Economics*. 1976b, *6*. 123-62.

Thurow, L., *The Zero-sum Society*. Penguin Books. Harmondsworth 1980.

Winston, T.. "Taxes, Leisure and Public Goods." *Economica*. 1965. 65-69.

[8]

RENT CONTROL AS AN INSTRUMENT OF HOUSING POLICY

ASSAR LINDBECK
The Stockholm School of Economics

I. INTRODUCTION

Two main problems are discussed in the present paper : (1) the usefulness of rent control as an instrument of housing policy, and hence the effects of such control, and (2) the possibilities of realizing the goals of housing policy by other methods, without rent control.

Whereas price control in most markets of the economy has usually been confined to periods of war, or immediately after wars, government control of rents tends in some countries to become a more or less permanent phenomenon. To some extent this may be explained by well-known, rather specific properties of the market for housing. Thus, reference is often made to the limited elasticity of supply of housing in the short run due to the smallness of annual production of new dwellings as compared to the existing stock of dwellings (partly because of the long durability of houses), the geographical immobility of dwellings and the high capital-output ratio of housing. It is also often believed that demand for housing is characterized by a combination of a rather high income elasticity and a low or moderate price elasticity (particularly with respect to the *number* of dwellings demanded).

All these factors, to the extent they are present, tend to make short-run equilibrium rents rather high (compared to the long-run equilibrium level) during periods of rapid economic growth and substantial shifts in the inter-regional distribution of population, with considerable income and capital gains by house-owners as a result. Undoubtedly, these circumstances are often regarded as arguments for rent control. Moreover, due to the limited availability of land with good location, prices tend to rise for such property when cities are expanding, with resultant continuous capital gains for the owners. However, in some countries, another reason for the reliance

53

The Economic Problems of Housing

on rent control is no doubt the limited consideration given in the design and implementation of housing policy to the importance of the price system for the functioning of the housing market.

II. A SIMPLE MARSHALLIAN MODEL

A simple Marshallian equilibrium model may, in spite of the drastic simplifications implied, serve as a frame of reference for the subsequent discussion. In diagram I below, the stock-supply of dwellings at a given moment is denoted by the vertical SS-line. (The problem of aggregation is neglected here.) DD is the (stock-) demand curve ; this is less elastic if the volume demanded is measured by the number of dwellings than if size and equipment-standard of dwellings are also included in the volume component. Let us further assume that rent happens to be r^1, and an equilibrium (at point a) therefore exists in the *housing market*.

The flow-supply curve for dwellings during a given period is assumed to be UU (measured from the SS-line). Thus, it is assumed that house-building is stimulated by higher rents.[1] Below r_1 incentives are created for disinvestment in housing. As UU passes through point a, equilibrium is assumed to prevail even in the *house-building* market, in the sense that no incentives exist to increase or reduce the stock of dwellings ; thus long-run, or stationary, equilibrium is assumed to prevail.

Suppose now that demand for housing increases, whether because of population increase, expansion in *per capita* income or changes in preferences of households, and that the new demand curve is $D'D'$ *Momentary equilibrium* is then at point b at rent r_2, whereas *short-run* (one-period) *equilibrium* is at point c at rent r_3. The position of the *long-run* (stationary) *equilibrium* depends on whether the housing market is a constant-cost industry or not. The presumption seems to be that it is an increasing-cost industry. The reason is that increased demand for housing raises rents, and hence land values, for the existing stock of houses with better location than new houses. (As house-building in long-run equilibrium equals reinvestment, it does not seem to be very important for the position of the long-run equilibrium position whether the house-*building* industry is a constant-cost or not.

---

[1] This assumption about a rising flow-supply curve for dwellings is consistent with several different market forms — not only pure competition but also, for instance, monopolistic competition if r is defined as the average rent in the market (or in a given submarket).

Lindbeck — *Rent Control and Housing Policy*

Cost conditions in the house-building industry, reflected in level and slope of the flow-supply curve, greatly influences the *speed* by which the long-run equilibrium is approached, however.) Hence, the long-run equilibrium position will presumably not be at point *d*, with the housing stock $S^n S^n$, but at a point along the $D'D'$-curve to the north-west of point *d*.

Let us, to begin with, assume that the dynamic properties of the market are such that rents start rising due to excess demand for housing, created by the assumed shift in the demand curve, and that a new short-term equilibrium in the housing market at the end of the period attained at point *c*, rent being r_3. At the beginning of the next period stock-supply is given by the $S'S'$-curve. The new flow-supply curve is U' (the part of the curve to the left of $S'S'$ is not shown in the diagram). The short-run equilibrium at the end of this period is at point *e* at rent r_4. The stock-supply and flow-supply curves in the next period are $S''S''$ and U'', respectively, and the process repeats itself until a new long-run equilibrium is attained.

The diagram illustrates *inter alia* the idea that momentary and

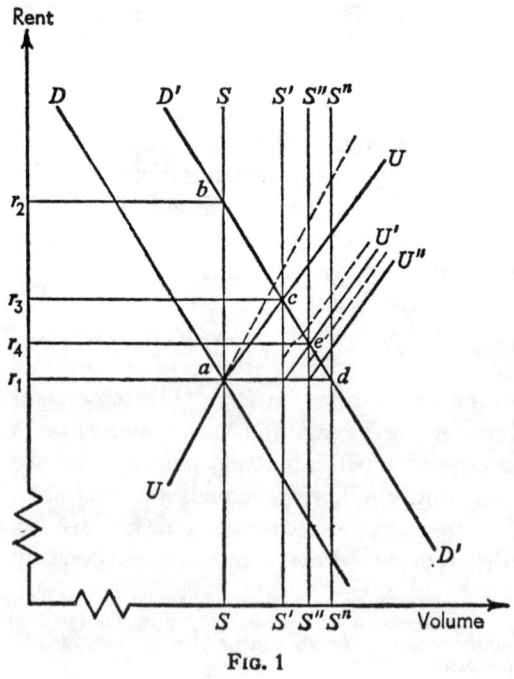

Fɪɢ. 1

55

The Economic Problems of Housing

short-run equilibrium rents can be rather high (compared to the long-run equilibrium rent) in a market of this type, and that the achievement of a new long-run equilibrium, *i.e.* equilibrium in both the housing market and the house-building market, may take rather a long time (each period may be thought of as, say, a year). During the approach to long-run equilibrium, 'excess profits' will be earned in house investment, and income and capital gains will accrue to owners of houses produced earlier, particularly houses with good location.

If prices of production factors are driven up by the increased building activity, the flow-supply curve in the first period might look something like the broken curve starting from point a instead of the curve UU, which means, of course, that the short-run equilibrium rent would be higher than r_3. Particularly if prices of production factors are sticky downwards, the flow-supply curves in later periods would also be higher than indicated by the curves U' and U'' ; this is indicated by the broken curves in the diagram. This would prolong the process of reaching a long-run equilibrium position. (Of course, productivity increases in house-building works in the opposite direction, by pushing down the flow-supply curves.)

However, as further shifts to the right of the demand curve would be expected to occur from time to time, the long-run equilibrium may, in this market as well as in others, be regarded mainly as a *hypothetical* position, in the direction of which the market is moving without ever fully reaching it. Due to stickiness of rents in the short run, even the momentary and short-run equilibrium positions may be regarded as hypothetical positions, giving only the direction in which the market is moving. In the meantime, temporary disequilibria may exist in the market, with excess demand (housing shortage) or excess supply (more than 'normal' vacancy rates) for housing.

When rent control is discussed below, it is assumed that rents are regulated by the authorities to below their short-run equilibrium levels in each period. It will be convenient to base the analysis of rent control on a comparison between the disequilibrium situation which is thereby created, and the hypothetical equilibrium situation in the market. Later, it will be considered whether it is reasonable to identify a market without rent control with an equilibrium market.

In spite of the special features of the housing market, the experiences of rent control are quite similar to those of price control in other markets — the creation of permanent excess demand (short-

Lindbeck — Rent Control and Housing Policy

ages), queues, limitations to consumer sovereignty, black and grey markets, limitations to incentives for producer efficiency, difficulties in finding criteria for distributing goods among consumers, etc. Actually, due to some special properties of the housing market, particularly the long life of dwellings, these problems are in some respects, as pointed out below, more severe than in many other markets.

III. THE OBJECTIVES OF RENT CONTROL

The effects of rent control depend, of course, on the control system. Instead of analysing a number of different systems, the present paper deals with the type of control used for two decades in Sweden, according to which rents cannot be raised without the approval of the authorities. However, it is hoped that the subsequent discussion will be relevant in the main for most control systems where rents are regulated below their equilibrium levels, so that excess demand for housing (housing shortage) prevails. The exposition will be illustrated with empirical data from the Swedish housing market during the period of rent control, mainly in footnotes.[1]

To evaluate the usefulness of rent control it is necessary to specify the motives for (retaining) such control under peace-time conditions. Even though the motives vary somewhat, the following seem to be of importance in several countries. It is obvious, however, that many of these arguments played very little, if any, rôle when rent control was originally introduced. Thus, many of them have been invented during the course of rent control, mainly as arguments for not *removing* rent control.

(1) To stimulate general housing demand in order to achieve a

---

[1] In the Swedish system, rents in houses built before the introduction of the control system are regulated on the basis of rents at the time when the control system was introduced (*i.e.* in 1942). In houses built later, rents are based on actual production costs, including schematically calculated costs on equity capital, and running costs.

Approval to increase rents is given by the authorities only as compensation for schematically calculated increases in running costs and interest rates on borrowed funds. Between 1939 and 1963 rents (excl. fuel and light) in the cost of living index have risen by 80 per cent while prices of consumer goods in general have risen by 170 per cent (including rents). At the same time average wage rates (per hour) for industrial workers, as well as *per capita* disposable income of the household sector, have risen by about 450 per cent.

Thus, real income in terms of housing has risen by 205 per cent while real income in terms of other commodities has risen by 105 per cent. All figures in the paper are, if not otherwise pointed out, from official Swedish Statistics.

The Economic Problems of Housing

high and rapidly increasing housing consumption of the population as a whole. (The general housing consumption goal.)

(2) To keep down rents of *new* houses in order to stabilize costs and volume of house construction. (The construction market stabilization goal.)

(3) To prevent a (considerable) redistribution of income and wealth from tenants to house-owners (the general income-distribution goal) and also to achieve a more equitable distribution of real income among tenants (the inter-tenant income distribution goal).

(4) To help low-income families, particularly such families with children, to compete in the housing market with other household categories. Thus, the authorities want to guarantee these families a larger fraction of total housing consumption than they would get in a market without rent control. (The housing consumption distribution goal.)

(5) To direct total demand for housing consumption in favour of large well-equipped dwellings. (The housing-demand composition goal.)

(6) To dampen tendencies to cost inflation. (The general anti-inflation goal.)

IV. THE GENERAL HOUSING CONSUMPTION GOAL

The idea that rent control could contribute to a higher general housing standard, often implied in defence of rent control, is paradoxical. As at a given point of time a country's general (average) level of housing consumption depends on the stock of existing dwellings, the level and structure of rents have no immediate effect on the general housing standard.[1] Hence, when the removal of rent control is often criticized, by the adherents of rent control, on the ground that this would reduce general housing consumption, a confusion is probably made between quantity of housing *demanded* (which undoubtedly would be reduced) and housing *consumption* (which for the population as a whole, approximately speaking, would not be immediately affected). *Or* it is not the immediate effects that are considered.

However, rent control results in an expansion of tenants' consump-

[1] Neglecting short-run variations in the vacancy rate and also neglecting rapid changes in the rate of conversions of apartments to other uses, such as offices.

Lindbeck — Rent Control and Housing Policy

tion of other commodities, for which supply more or less automatically adjusts to changes in demand. This phenomenon is due both to a conventional income effect and to a 'spill over' of unsatisfied demand in the housing market to other markets (assuming that not *all* unsatisfied demand for housing results in increased 'involuntary' saving). Thus, it is not the tenants' housing consumption which is stimulated by rent control but rather their consumption of other commodities.

On the macro level, the increased demand by tenants for consumer goods other than housing, due to rent control, is to some extent counteracted by reduced demand by house-owners. However, this reduction can be expected to be smaller than the expansion of demand by tenants, as a considerable fraction of changes in income of house-owners automatically goes to tax payments (in Sweden the marginal tax rate can be expected to be at least 50 per cent for private house-owners), and the marginal propensity to consume can hardly be expected to be higher for house-owners than for tenants (possibly the opposite).[1]

Thus, when rent control is said to be an appropriate means of increasing a country's general (average) housing consumption, it must be the effects after some time, hence via house-building, that are considered. However, the argument is still difficult to follow. If rent control keeps down rents below their 'free market' level not only in existing houses but also in new ones, rent control would, of course, have negative effects on house-building, assuming that this is positively related to the profitability of new houses.

As existing dwellings in a system with rent control, and hence with excess demand for housing, can be let out (at regulated rents) practically regardless of quality, the incentives, as well as the availability of liquid funds, for maintenance will, as is often pointed out, presumably be rather low. Hence the stock of dwellings can be expected to deteriorate (unless the control system is constructed so as to stimulate maintenance expenditures). Even via these effects rent control tends, in the long run, to have a negative influence on general housing standards.

The negative effects of rent control on general housing standards are, at least in principle, accentuated by the incentives created by rent control to demolish houses and use the land for something else, such as office buildings (if office rents are not efficiently controlled too) or possibly new apartment houses (if the rent control system keeps

[1] Wealth effects on consumption are neglected.

The Economic Problems of Housing

profitability lower in older houses than in new ones).[1] At the same time, it is probable that rents in some low-quality houses will be kept *up* (*i.e.* above their 'free market' levels) by the general excess demand for housing created by rent control. There will thus be less incentive to renew such houses. Thus, rent control could lead to renewals in the 'wrong' part of the housing market.

In some countries, where private investment in housing has fallen considerably during the period of rent control, house investment by non-profit organizations, such as public authorities and co-operatives, has instead expanded considerably.[2] Such shifts in the ownership of the stock of houses have important implications for the performance of housing policy. For instance, we cannot be so sure any longer that the volume of house-building is positively related to the profitability of new houses, as we have no generally accepted theory for the behaviour of co-operative and public enterprises in the housing market, particularly not for how they would behave in a market without rent control. Moreover, there are no guarantees that non-profit enterprises will adjust rents, particularly not in old houses, to the equilibrium rent structure.

To know how house investment by non-profit enterprises would be influenced by the removal of rent control, we have to know both their price and their investment behaviour. If they behave as private enterprises in both respects, they will of course expand housing investment if rent control is removed, provided this removal leads

[1] In Sweden the number of demolitions have (in 1965) induced the authorities to introduce regulations which prevent house-owners from pulling down old houses, if these, in the view of the authorities, include dwellings appropriate for housing purposes. After some time this will probably result in the houses deteriorating.

[2] In Sweden, which is an extreme example in this respect, the ratio between private, public, and co-operative housing investment, and in the long run also the distribution of the *stock* of dwellings between different kinds of owners, have changed drastically during the post-war, rent control period. While in 1939 88 per cent of all new dwellings in apartment houses (with more than two apartments) were private, and the private share in 1945 was still as high as 65 per cent, the figure in 1964 was only about 20 per cent. Of the 80 per cent of new dwellings which are now (1965) non-private about 43 per cent are co-operative and 57 per cent are owned by municipalities or other non-profit organizations. This drastic change has affected the structure of ownership of the stock of dwellings in Sweden. Since 1945 the private share of dwellings in apartment houses has fallen from 80 to about 50 per cent, which means that about 25 per cent of all dwellings (including residential houses) are now public or co-operative. (It can be pointed out that the rent control system is not the only factor behind these altered proportions. It has, since World War II, been a conscious policy of the government, as well as of many municipalities, to promote public and co-operative housing in Sweden. Some of the means have been more favourable credits for public and co-operative housing than for private housing, and favouring non-profit enterprises in town and city planning, for instance when municipalities decide who is allowed ready-planned land for building purposes.)

Lindbeck — Rent Control and Housing Policy

to higher rents not only in older houses but also in new ones. If, on the other hand, they keep rents unchanged even after the removal of rent control we can feel confident that they expand housing invest- ment only if they are stimulated in their investment behaviour by the size of excess demand for dwellings rather than by profitability. (If rents in private dwellings are raised, but rents are unchanged in non-profit enterprises, we would expect excess demand for dwellings in non-profit houses to rise at the same time as total excess demand would fall.) If non-profit enterprises keep rents unchanged but have an investment behaviour of the same type as private investors, one would expect their investment to be unaffected by the removal of rent control (at least for the time being). Only if they behave as private firms in their price policy, and thus raise rents, but react on excess demand rather than on profitability in their investment be- haviour, would a decline in their investment be expected as a result of the removal of rent control.

The notion that rent control contributes to increased housing con- sumption is sometimes developed along rather different lines. In- stead of arguing that rent control via high demand for housing automatically (hence via the market) creates high housing investment, it is asserted that the excess demand situation in the housing market ('housing shortage') creates political pressure on the authorities to stimulate house production (presumably at the expense of investment in other sectors of the economy). The idea is somewhat similar to the notion of unbalanced growth for underdeveloped countries, as formulated for instance by Hirschman, according to which the creation of bottlenecks by excess demand in particular sectors is an efficient way of persuading the authorities to expand investment in these sectors.

This argument is rather difficult to evaluate. One problem with the argument, as applied to rent control in highly developed countries, is that it is presumably the same authorities who decide, at top level, whether rent control is to be retained and how much to stimulate house construction. Thus, it is somewhat unclear *who* is supposed to put pressure on *whom*. And if the authorities really want to stimulate investment in housing, this can be done directly (for instance by subsidizing house production or consumption, or by easy credit).

Actually it is rather easy to turn the argument upside down : as demand for other types of consumer goods are stimulated by rent control, the authorities may, to prevent inflation, find it necessary to restrict rather than expand house-building, because this is a rather simple administrative method of reducing total demand in the

The Economic Problems of Housing

economy. Thus, it is not completely unlikely that the stimulus created by rent control to consumption in other markets, has actually induced the authorities to dampen rather than stimulate house-building. However, we are now in rather deep water, as it is difficult to construct a theory which explains the behaviour of governments.[1]

V. THE CONSTRUCTION-MARKET STABILIZATION GOAL

Another argument developed in favour of rent control is that the removal of such control, by raising rents in new houses, would disturb the stability of the market for house-building — via higher demand for production factors, possibly due to 'unrealistic' expectations among house-investors concerning the long-run equilibrium position of rents — with increases in production costs as a result.[2] Thus, it is often argued that it is 'desirable', from the point of view of market stability, to prevent a temporary excess demand situation from resulting in higher rents. In terms of our diagram, it is argued that the stability of the market can be improved by using rent control to prevent a shift in demand (or supply) from raising rents to r_2 or r_3. If for instance r_4 is expected by the authorities to be the long-run equilibrium level, it might be argued that it is 'desirable' not to accept a much higher rent increase than to r_4.

However, even if the basic assumptions behind this argument are accepted, it does not necessarily follow that (retaining) rent control is the only conceivable, or even the most efficient, method for achieving stability. An alternative method might be to combine the removal of rent control with restrictive measures of economic policy, such as higher interest rates on loans (in general or to housing).

The worries for the stability of the market, which imply that the removal of rent control would stimulate house-building, looks as an apparent contradiction to the earlier discussed argument that rent control is an appropriate means of stimulating higher general housing consumption. A possible reconciliation might be to argue that,

[1] If the argument that rent control is a powerful stimulus to high house-building is correct, we might expect that the fraction of resources devoted to this would be large during periods of rent control, as compared to other periods. It is therefore of some interest to note that total housing construction as a fraction of GNP, as well as of total gross investment, in Sweden has fallen since the end of the thirties and the first post-war years. (Rent control was introduced in 1942.) Whereas the relation of house investment to GNP was 7·4 per cent in 1938/39 and 8·8 per cent in 1946, it had fallen to 6·7 per cent in 1963. Housing construction as a percentage of total gross investment was 30·3, 30·9, and 21·4 per cent respectively in the same periods.

[2] By a disturbance of stability is here simply meant that the amplitude of fluctuations in house-building is increased.

Lindbeck — Rent Control and Housing Policy

because of downward stickiness of prices and wages, cost increases immediately after the removal of rent control would tend to be permanent. As a result, it may be argued, future house-building would be lower than if increases in production costs had been prevented by rent control. Thus, the argument would basically be an attempt to show that rent control promotes more house-building *in the future*. The argument suggests in fact that greater incentives for house-building today would be unfavourable to house-building tomorrow. (In terms of diagram I, it is thus assumed that rent control can prevent the flow-supply curves U, U', U'' from shifting upwards to the broken curves.) It remains to be explained, however, how house-investment can be stimulated when rents are controlled. In theory, it is quite conceivable, of course, that a rent policy which accepts some rent increases, though smaller than to r_3, could prevent the flow-supply curves from shifting upwards without holding back incentives to house-building very much. However, this would mean creating a more or less permanent excess demand for new dwellings.

It is important to note, however, that even if the assumptions behind the argument were granted, rent control may not be the most efficient remedy. Reductions in the profitability of housing investment by other economic policies, such as measures of monetary or fiscal policy, are alternatives.

Moreover, the 'once-and-for-all' increase in costs of production which in the absence of restrictive measures of economic policy might follow the removal of rent control, has to be compared with the *permanent* tendency for production costs to rise in a market with a permanent excess demand, due to the lack of market-resistance in such a situation against shiftings of cost increases on to prices.[1] This does not mean, of course, that (short-term or long-term) equilibrium in the market for dwellings is a *sufficient* condition for efficiency in the house-building industry. It might very well be that the market, due to the great number of small firms with small research expenditures, often is rather slow in increasing efficiency even when no permanent excess demand for housing exists.

---

[1] This would mean that the gains from technological development in a market with a permanent excess demand would tend to wind up in the hands of the owners of the production factors, such as landowners, construction workers, house builders and sellers of intermediary products to house construction.

It is possible, though difficult to prove, that the fairly rapid increase in building costs in Sweden during the post-war period, in spite of the availability of considerable technological improvements in house-building, to some extent ascribe to this tendency to a permanent excess demand for dwellings, and hence to the lack of market-resistance to cost increases.

The Economic Problems of Housing

VI. THE INCOME DISTRIBUTION GOAL

In the political debate about rent control, at least in Sweden, the reluctance to accept a redistribution of income and wealth from tenants to house-owners has been a major argument against the removal of rent control.[1] As low-income groups tend to devote a larger proportion of disposable income to housing than do higher-income groups, the gain in real income due to rent control is proportionately greater for the former than the latter. However, influencing the distribution of income by rent control is a rather clumsy procedure, as the gains in income will be rather stochastically distributed on people in various income brackets, particularly if rents vary considerably between houses built in different years, so that for instance tenants in older houses are favoured regardless of whether they are rich or poor. As in the Swedish system young families (often with small children) tend to be concentrated in rather new houses (as people are reluctant to leave their inexpensive apartments in older houses, due to the low rents in these), families with small children are generally at a disadvantage as compared to other tenants ; this seems to be against established goals in housing policy. Clearly, a more elegant method of favouring low income groups, and people with children, is to subsidize these particular groups (without using rent control), rather than keeping down rents for everybody living in houses built in certain years.[2]

VII. THE HOUSING CONSUMPTION DISTRIBUTION GOAL

To the extent that rent control affects the distribution of income in favour of low-income groups, housing demand also probably tends

[1] It would be interesting to know, of course, how large the income redistribution would be. As we know neither the size of excess demand nor the price elasticity of demand (in Sweden) it is however impossible to give a realistic forecast at present.

According to a rough estimate, an increase in rents by 25 per cent in private apartment houses in Sweden would lead to a redistribution of income from tenants to house-owners of about the same magnitude (about 400 million Swedish crowns) as a redistribution by one-half of a per cent of national income from employers to employees. See R. Bentzel, A. Lindbeck, I. Ståhl, *Bostadsbristen* (The housing shortage), Stockholm, 1963, pp. 86 87. As pointed out, however, at least 50 per cent of the income increase for house-owners would automatically go to the public sector in the form of taxes.

[2] Another important factor in considering the distributional effects of rent control is the effects on prices of residential houses. Even if prices on residential houses are free, rent control on apartments can have considerable effects. As excess demand for dwellings in rent-controlled apartment houses 'spills over' into the market for residential houses, prices for these tend to be pulled up. (A counteracting tendency may arise if tenants presently living in rent-controlled apartment houses have higher preferences for residential houses than do people presently living in residential houses.)

Lindbeck — Rent Control and Housing Policy

to be redistributed in favour of these groups. Whether this redistribution of housing *demand* between households in different income brackets also results in a corresponding redistribution of housing *consumption* will depend on how housing consumption is actually distributed in the rent-controlled market. It is therefore of interest to analyse the principles by which housing consumption is distributed in the regulated market.

The prevention of equilibrium in the housing market violates the sovereignty of the consumer in disposing of his income as he pleases. The marginal rate of substitution between housing and other commodities cannot be equated to the price ratios ; and the structure of rents of different apartments does not reflect the evaluations of these apartments by households.

These problems are particularly acute, of course, during a period of rapid inflation, as in this case a rent control system based on historical building costs results not only in low rents as compared to prices of other commodities but also in lower rents in older houses than in new (even after allowing for differences in quality). To some extent, these 'non-planned' distortions of the structure of rents may be removed by a more flexible system of rent control than has been implemented in most countries, such as by special price-index clauses on rents and possibly also by index-loans to house-building.

Whereas in a commodity market with equilibrium the distribution of the commodity between different households is determined by a general market mechanism — *i.e.* mainly by the distribution of income and wealth and by individual preferences — the commodity distribution in a market with price control and excess demand must take place according to some other principles.   In Sweden the following principles seem to predominate.

As the bulk of the dwellings available during a year consists of the existing stock, rather than of houses produced during the year, the main problem in the distribution of housing consumption concerns the stock of existing dwellings. In a system characterized by rent control and protection against eviction, the leading principle for the distribution of housing consumption during a given year is that those who already have contracts are in a preferential position compared to those with no apartment of their own, even though some people in the latter group may have a higher 'need' for the apartments in question in the sense that they are willing to pay a higher rent than some people in the former group (possibly without having a higher income).

The Economic Problems of Housing

It is not fully known how people without an apartment of their own can get one. One possibility is to join the queues organized by municipalities or co-operative organizations. The allotment principles in these queues are rather complicated and difficult to grasp. The dominating principle seems to be waiting time, presumably not because waiting time is regarded as a good measure of the 'need' for a dwelling but because of the difficulty of finding less arbitrary principles.[1] The most usual way of obtaining apartments in Sweden, however, seems to be via personal contacts, mainly contacts with relatives, friends, or the employer.[2] As in other markets where price control is exercised, grey and black markets have arisen, of course. In these markets wealth and borrowing capacity are important factors for the distribution of house consumption. A contract for an apartment becomes in the rent-controlled society an asset, which can be transformed into money or some other asset. A further way of obtaining an apartment is via the 'free', legal sectors of the housing market, *i.e.* primarily the market for residential houses.

Thus even if it is believed that the queue system, administered by municipalities, is the ideal (or least unfair) method of distributing housing consumption, it is quite clear that only a limited part of housing consumption in Sweden during a given year is distributed via this mechanism. This is mainly because the authorities do not ration the *stock* of dwellings, which would require rules for how many rooms or square feet every person is allowed to occupy. Obviously price control and rationing are much more complicated matters in a durable goods market than for perishable goods. In the latter case, commodities can in each period be distributed according to some

[1] Somewhat shorter waiting time is required for families with children, and in some places certain occupations, such as civil servants, physicians, nurses, construction workers, etc., have priorities. In many places, a quota is simply given to a firm which can then distribute the apartments mainly as it wishes.

The waiting time in the official queues in the city of Stockholm in January 1965 was about 8–10 years. In municipalities immediately outside the city of Stockholm the waiting time was about half of that in the city of Stockholm.

[2] According to an unpublished study for three Swedish towns, the most usual ways by which tenants had obtained their apartments was : via their employer (20–24 per cent), via exchange for some other apartment (2–18 per cent), via official or co-operative queues (14–29 per cent) or 'some other way' — mainly relatives, friends, advertisement, black markets, etc. (30–57 per cent). *Bostadsbyggnadsutredningen*.

A study for Stockholm among people just taking out marriage licences has given rather similar results : via the employer (17 per cent), via official or other queues (29 per cent), via relatives or friends (31 per cent), via advertisement or other ways (19 per cent). W. William-Olsson, *1000 brudpars hem*, Stockholm, 1965, p. 39. Some deficiencies in the sample make the figures in the latter study uncertain.

Both studies indicate that only a minority of the households obtain their apartments via the official queues.

Lindbeck — Rent Control and Housing Policy

socially accepted (or enforced) principle, and everybody can — neglecting the black market — be forced to pay the same price. In the case of durable goods, however, prices and consumption during a given period are mainly determined by how the commodities have been distributed in the past. Thus, unless the authorities also enforce rationing of commodities obtained earlier, it is quite impossible to achieve a distribution of consumption according to some socially determined principle. Whereas the general (average) housing standard is successively rising, a minority of the population is unable to get apartments of their own, even though the preferences for housing for many people in this group may be relatively high.[1] This is probably one of the most severe problems connected with rent control, particularly as a permanent phenomenon. Whereas the effects of rent control on house-building might be largely eliminated, the problems created on the consumption side, such as the problem of the distribution of housing consumption, are very difficult to solve.

In this complicated pattern for the distribution of housing consumption in the Swedish rent-controlled housing market, who gains and who loses, as compared to a market with equilibrium rents? Low income groups are favoured in the sense that their real income, and hence presumably their housing *demand*, is kept up relative to the demand by higher-income groups. However, this does not necessarily mean that their housing *consumption* is favoured. It is quite

---

[1] The following figures for people per 100 rooms, number of vacancies, and number of people in the official queues in Stockholm are instructive in this respect.

Year	Number of People per 100 Rooms	Number of Vacancies	Number of People in the Queue
1921	—	66	
1926	126	620	
1930	120	1,323	
1935	111	3,547	
1940	105	3,068	
1945	99	68	
1950	95	0	51,162
1955	89	0	94,130
1960	85	0	106,910
1963	—	0	122,600

Assuming that the average size of the family in the queue is 2·5 persons, the queue would represent about 315,000 people, *i.e.* about 40 per cent of the total population in the city of Stockholm. About 45 per cent of these are people living in Stockholm without an apartment of their own, about 8 per cent are living outside Stockholm and the rest (about 47 per cent) have an apartment of their own in Stockholm but want another (usually larger) one. In the first group about 37 per cent are households consisting of two or more people.

The Economic Problems of Housing

possible that low-income groups as a rule have less contacts with people who can help them get apartments — employers and 'influential' relatives and friends. Low-income groups are also in a rather weak position in the black and grey markets, as well as in the free market for villas, where wealth, liquidity, and borrowing capacity become important factors. Disfavoured in terms of housing cost are also lodgers in furnished rooms, where rents are in practice not controlled.

Favoured are undoubtedly older people with apartments from earlier on, whereas young people and people who have just moved geographically from one place to another are disfavoured. Taking all these factors together, it is very doubtful whether the present system of distributing housing consumption in a country such as Sweden — where only a fraction of housing consumption during a given year is distributed according to the principles of the public queues — can be said to favour low-income groups, and families with children, as compared with a system with equilibrium rents.

VIII. THE HOUSING-DEMAND COMPOSITION GOAL

Another problem with rent control is that there are no guarantees that the composition of production on different kinds of dwellings follows consumer preferences ; practically any type of dwelling can be let out, which means that there is very little market testing of new dwellings. For instance, we do not know if the heavy reliance on large apartment houses in Sweden after World War II — only about 20 per cent of production is in the form of residential houses — really corresponds to the preferences of households. (The picture is further complicated by the fact that home-owners are favoured, as compared to tenants in apartment houses, by the taxation system.)

However, the advocates of rent control have pointed out that the control system directs housing demand towards larger and better equipped apartments than would be the case if rents were higher. The question remains, however, as to what is gained by raising demand for higher and better dwellings in a market with excess demand (housing shortage). One conceivable argument for such a policy is that it is 'desirable' to direct the composition of housing demand in this way in order to obtain a composition of house-building which reflects the preferences of consumers in the future rather than

Lindbeck — Rent Control and Housing Policy

today. Thus, it seems to be assumed that house investors in a free market are short-sighted in the sense that they consider mainly the demand structure at present but forget to plan for the future composition of housing demand. The realism of this hypothesis concerning the behaviour of private investors is naturally very difficult to evaluate. Let us, however, for the sake of the discussion, *assume* that private investors behave in this way.

A change in demand in favour of larger and better equipped dwellings will presumably not arise suddenly but rather by a continuous process, whereby (in a market without rent control) profitability would tend to rise for large and better equipped apartments, so that production factors would be attracted over to the construction of such dwellings. Thus, it does not seem self-evident that, in a market without rent control, the market mechanism would be unable to adjust the stock of dwellings to slow changes in the structure of demand.

Let us assume, however, that it is 'desirable' to have another composition of housing production than automatically tends to arise in the market. Then a change in the composition of production today could be achieved by subsidizing production of, for instance, large and well-equipped apartments ; obviously the creation of excess demand for such apartments by rent control is not necessary.

IX. THE GENERAL ANTI-INFLATIONARY GOAL

When rent control was introduced during the war one main motive was to fight inflation. It can still be argued, of course, that a removal of rent control would create an impulse to cost inflation. Even if this impulse may not be greater than other such impulses that appear from time to time, it cannot be denied that a removal of rent control would have such effects.[1]

On the other hand, a removal of rent control would increase the saving ratio in the economy, as a large part of the income increase for house-owners would go to the public sector in the form of taxes. Thus, the removal of rent control would be rather similar to an increase in sales taxation (though restricted to one commodity : housing) and hence increase the economic scope for investment in

[1] As housing expenditure constitutes about 10 per cent of total consumer expenditures (excl. fuel and light) in Sweden, and as about half the stock of dwellings is in apartment houses, the immediate effect on costs of living of a 20 per cent increase in rents (excl. fuel and light) would be about 1 per cent.

The Economic Problems of Housing

the economy without running into demand inflation.[1]   Thus, the disadvantages of impulses for cost inflation of a removal of rent control has to be balanced against the smaller risks for demand inflation. The increased room for investment might be used, for instance, to boost house-building.

X. CAN HOUSING POLICY DO WITHOUT RENT CONTROL?

Several effects of rent control have been discussed in the previous sections.   There are, of course, others, such as restrictive effects on labour mobility (due to the housing shortage), with related losses in efficiency for the economy as a whole.   However, a major problem in this paper is whether the main objectives of rent control, as defined on page 57, can be reached with other policy measures (hence without rent control).   Some alternative policy measures have already been mentioned in the exposition above.   A more systematic account of such policy alternatives will be summarized below.

(1) The first goal was to try to achieve a more rapid increase in the general (average) level of housing consumption than 'automatically' tends to arise in the market.   As this goal can be accomplished only by stimulating house-building, appropriate measures are subsidies and/or easy credit for house-building, or possibly for housing demand (at least in new houses), whereas rent control is obviously of doubtful value in this case.

(2) The second goal, to stabilize the house-building market, can in principle be achieved by stabilization policy of the same kind as in other sectors of the economy, even though the problem might be more delicate for this market than for some others.   However, there is no reason to believe that stabilization of the market for house-building nowadays would fail as it did before World War II, *i.e.* before the start of modern stabilization policy.   By general monetary policy, specific credit actions for the housing market, investment taxation (or investment subsidies), possibly also physical controls, it should be possible to stabilize this market in the same way as other investment sectors in the economy, where stabilization policy in several European countries has been rather successful in recent decades.

[1] If there are sales taxes (or other indirect taxes) on other consumer goods, there will be a fall in consumer good tax revenues due to the fall in consumption of goods other than housing.   This tends to dampen the contractive effect on the economy of the rent increase.

Lindbeck — Rent Control and Housing Policy

(3) If the authorities want to prevent redistributions of income and wealth from tenants to house-owners (to a larger extent than is automatically achieved via existing marginal tax rates), higher property taxation, specific taxes on property in the form of houses, and sales taxes on housing expenditures are examples of adequate policy measures.   In a market with equilibrium rents, a sales tax on housing expenditure cannot be immediately shifted to tenants, as the supply curve momentarily is completely inelastic.   (Only by changes in the supplied volume can a tax be shifted forward.)   Even over a few years, the possibilities of shifting the tax on to tenants is rather limited, as flow-supply is small when compared with the existing stock of dwellings.

If the authorities are anxious to protect real income of some specific group among tenants, such as low-income families with children or elderly people, more progressive tax rates in income taxation, higher children's allowances, and higher old-age pensions are examples of adequate policy measures ; these are more direct ways than rent control of supporting exactly the groups which the authorities wish to help.

Non-profit enterprises may not raise rents on their own initiative in a market without rent control, which would prevent equilibrium in the housing market.   This phenomenon is an important one in a housing market such as the Swedish one, where about a quarter of all dwellings are public or co-operative.   Here the price policy of these enterprises becomes of the same importance as the rent control by the government.   If it is regarded as unfair that housing costs are raised only for people living in private apartment houses, a sales tax on housing consumption has obvious advantages, as thereby housing costs would be raised also for people living in public and co-operative houses, as well as in villas.   Due to price rigidities even in the private housing market, temporary shortages can be expected also for such dwellings even in the absence of rent control.   This phenomenon might be particularly relevant after a long period of rent control. If so, a housing tax could help to move rents towards equilibrium even in private houses.

(4) If the authorities do not accept the preferences of certain household groups, such as low-income families with children or elderly people, direct support of their housing demand, rather than general transfer payments, is an adequate measure.   Subsidies for housing consumption for these particular groups seem to be a more effective measure for these goals than does rent control — which keeps

D   71

The Economic Problems of Housing

down housing expenditures for all tenants — particularly as it is doubtful if low-income groups can compete effectively on a market with a permanent excess demand, created by rent control.

(5) If the authorities want to direct the composition of housing investment in favour of larger and better equipped dwellings than automatically tend to be built in the market, specific subsidies for the production or consumption of such apartments is a possible measure.

(6) The sixth goal was to dampen tendencies to general inflation. In principle, it may be argued that general inflation can be fought with measures other than rent control.   However, it is quite clear that the problem of how to fight cost inflation is not solved on the political level, even if in theory a number of appropriate techniques may be designed.   Therefore, it seems realistic to assume that some increase in the general price level is unavoidable when rent control is removed.   The authorities then have to evaluate this increase in the general price level against various disadvantages connected with rent control.

As in the case of practically all economic policy, the various measures have to be implemented interdependently rather than in isolation, as most measures have effects on several target variables at the same time.

PART III

BROADER ASPECTS OF THE WELFARE STATE

9

ASSAR LINDBECK

Limits to the Welfare State

The burgeoning public sector not only alters economic incentives and the distribution of income and wealth, but shifts the role of the family, restricts freedom of choice, and taxes honesty.

It is becoming abundantly clear that welfare states have limits, whether in terms of size or coverage, beyond which lies dangerous territory. Although the definition of such limits is open to debate, it is likely to include the following three factors: (1) induced inefficiencies in the economic system due to various disincentive effects on the allocation of resources and on productive effort in general; (2) "unpopular," and perhaps also partly unexpected, consequences for the role and freedom of choice of the household; and (3) unwanted implications for the relations between the individual citizen and the state.

The term "welfare state" I reserve for the collection of publicly organized social-security systems, transfers and subsidies, or the public financing and provision of such personal services as health, education, old-age care and child care. By this definition, the modern welfare state has obviously been highly successful both in enhancing economic security for the average citizen, and in helping wipe out economic misery among disadvantaged minority groups in our

ASSAR LINDBECK is Professor of International Economics and Director of the Institute for International Economic Studies at the University of Stockholm. He is the Chairman of the Committee of the Royal Swedish Academy of Science for the Prize in Economic Science in Memory of Alfred Nobel.

January-February 1986/Challenge   31

societies. In some countries it has even contributed significantly to a more egalitarian distribution of life-income and wealth.

My purpose here is to examine, using the three factors noted above, the negative effects that appear when welfare-state systems "go too far" and exceed their admittedly ill-defined limits. Such negative effects become noticeable when public spending reaches the levels observed today in some "advanced" welfare states in Western Europe. Examples will be taken from Sweden, perhaps the most advanced welfare state of all, where public spending (including transfer payments) today is about 65 percent of GNP, compared with about 45 percent in the United Kingdom and 33 percent in the United States (OECD statistics). As we shall see, however, a major difficulty in discussing these issues is that it is not obvious which features should be regarded as inherent to an advanced welfare state and which should rather be regarded as reflecting idiosyncrasies specific to certain countries.

Disincentive effects

Discussions about "disincentive effects" of welfare state policies, particularly their financing, often focus on potentially negative consequences for the aggregate supply of labor and saving. From the point of view of economic analysis, however, the issue of "disincentive effects" is not really a question of whether the aggregate supply of labor or saving falls or not. For instance, it is not appropriate to talk about a "disincentive" simply because policy-induced changes in incomes—so-called "income effects"—may influence the choice of leisure and consumption of private agents. (It is also often forgotten that the income effects of higher taxes are counteracted by the income effects of the higher benefits that those taxes financed.) In conformity with traditional economic theory, "disincentives" will instead arise if *wedges* are created, or widened, between the social and private return on the factors of production.

Assume, for the sake of argument, that the individual allocates his/her labor and capital endowments to realize the same after-tax returns (monetary or non-monetary) from all uses in both high-tax and low-tax sectors (the latter covering leisure, do-it-yourself work, earnings in the shadow economy, etc.). The above-mentioned "tax wedges," however, induce private agents to allocate too much of their resources to the latter sectors, where the marginal social returns (measured by the pre-tax returns) will be lower. The tax wedges, in other words, drain resources from high-tax to low-tax sectors, and act as a barrier to the raising of total output (goods plus leisure) that could in principle result from a reallocation of resources.

In technical jargon, the allocation of resources is "distorted" by *the substitution effects* that the tax wedges created, i.e., broadly speaking by the effects on demand and supply of tax-induced changes in the relative rewards of additional (marginal) factor supplies (with real income held constant). Moreover, it is important to include in the resource costs the administrative costs connected with welfare-state programs and tax collection.

In principle, nearly all types of economic behavior that have economic consequences may be influenced by such tax wedges. Indeed, it is the *pervasiveness* of the effects, rather than their impact on some specific economic action that is potentially important. However, the most obvious disincentive effects of marginal tax wedges could perhaps be summarized as follows: substitution effects in favor of (1) leisure (recreation) time, (2) lower intensity of work ("on-the-job leisure") if wages are tied to productive effort, (3) the pursuit of do-it-yourself work, (4) production for barter, (5) occupations with relatively large non-pecuniary benefits, and (6) the search for tax loopholes (legal tax avoidance).

If the tax system is progressive, and the after-tax discount rate does not fall (much) as a result of marginal tax increases, there is also a substitution effect (7) against investment in human capital—an effect which is, however, often strongly counteracted by government subsidies to education. There will also be a substitution effect (8) against labor mobility, induced by wage differentials, within a given tax-jurisdiction domain if there are some disadvantages (disutilities) connected with breaking away from relatives and friends.

Moreover, in an advanced welfare state, with a highly progressive tax/transfer system, (9) high-income earners will be stimulated to leave the country. As foreigners with lower skills, mainly from poor countries, are pulled in—if the latter type of migration is allowed by domestic immigration policy—the size and composition of the stock of human capital could be considerably changed over the long term.

To the extent that welfare-state programs are financed by taxes on income rather than on consumption, there will also be a substitution effect (10) against saving (due to the double taxation of saving implied in income tax systems). Moreover, as all tax systems in the real world are characterized by drastic asymmetries in the taxation of assets of various types, the effective real tax rates will, *in fact*, differ drastically between various types of assets, with distorting effects on (11) asset choice. This often arises from discrimination against investment in shares, bank saving and physical assets in the production sector, as opposed to investment in consumption-related fields like housing, durable consumer goods and various types of collector's items (for all of which the returns are usually taxed lightly, if at all). Inflation often strongly magnifies these effects in the context of a nominal (nonindexed) tax system and liberal rules for the deductibility of interest costs.

It is perhaps tempting to say that these consequences for asset choice are not really caused by the welfare-state system, but rather by the above-mentioned asymmetries and loopholes in the tax system. But such asymmetries and loopholes are to a considerable extent unavoidable, *partly* because of the technical difficulty or the high cost of removing them, and *partly* because of political and psychological factors (such as in the case of house owners and people receiving inflation gains due to the nominal nature of the tax system).

Given this fact, the higher the level of total public spending, and the greater the ambitions to redistribute income (hence the marginal tax rates), the stronger will be *the leverage* for individual agents to exploit such asymmetries and loopholes.

• *Effects on saving.* We are often told that we should not worry so much about the possibility of negative consequences for private saving, as it is possible, in principle, to compensate for such effects by increased public saving, either by way of increased public budget surpluses, or by way of sufficiently large "funding" of the social security systems. However, even though public saving may be a perfect substitute for private saving when we are concerned with the macroeconomic balance between saving and investment, the two types of saving are far from perfect substitutes in other respects. In particular, the availability of both decentralized equity capital and a decentralized supply of credit are crucial for a decentralized economic system.

This means that *the availability of decentralized private saving* increases the chances for the emergence of a society characterized by decentralized economic decision-making and entrepreneurship—and for pluralism in society and culture. Thus, the composition of saving between the private and the public sector are an important consequence of the effects of welfare-state policies.

When looking at various attempts to *quantify* the inefficiency costs of welfare-state programs and related taxation, particular importance should be attached to the "marginal costs of public funds," i.e., the *sum* of the higher tax payments and the efficiency costs ("excess burden") of wider tax wedges. The reason is, of course, that the politically interesting issue is whether public expenditure and related taxes should be raised, lowered or kept constant, and *not* if all public spending should be abolished! We then find that *both* simple two-sector models (see Edgar K. Browning in For Further Reading)—one sector with taxes and another without—*and* quantitative ("computable") general equilibrium models (John Shoven 1983) suggest

35

that the marginal costs of collecting one extra dollar via a progressive income tax, would have been $1.50–$1.70 at the end of the seventies in the United States.

According to studies by Ingemar Hansson (1984), the corresponding costs are as high as $3–$7 per additional tax dollar collected in Sweden, where the marginal tax rate for an average taxpayer today is about 70 percent (inclusive of *all* taxes and income-dependent transfers). Thus, increased taxes of this type should be implemented only if the spending they finance is expected to yield public goods and services worth three to seven times more than the income taken away from households in the form of tax payments. If these calculated efficiency losses, due to wider tax wedges between the taxed and the tax-free sector, are translated into GNP figures, they would during the seventies be equivalent to a reduction of the GDP growth rate in Sweden by about one percentage point, i.e., by about 25 percent. Recent studies of the marginal costs of public funds via the effects on saving decisions and asset choices also give quite high figures (see Ingemar Hansson [1985] for a survey).

It is important, however, to observe that the empirical studies made so far of disincentive effects of welfare-state policies and related taxes have been confined to only one or two of the various types of disincentive effects mentioned above. This means that *the sum* of all types of disincentive costs of higher public spending, and related tax increases, is probably much larger than the costs reported in any single study.

Marginal tax rates operate like tariffs on market transactions, breeding various types of autarchic economic behavior (leisure and do-it-yourself work, for example). It is therefore surprising that the very same economists and politicians who worry about tariffs that create wedges between social and private returns of some 10–30 percent, are often complacent about tax-induced wedges of some 100–300 percent of the after-tax returns (corresponding to marginal tax rates of 50–75 percent, inclusive of *all* taxes and income-dependent transfers).

A special complication when studying disincentive

effects, and related welfare costs, of welfare-state policies is that *the time lags* may be quite long for some of the effects. Not only may it take time for individual households (and perhaps also firms) to adjust their customary behavior, but some of the disincentive effects are transmitted via actions of various interest groups and political processes.

For instance, while the length of working time is often decided in collective bargaining, and is hence rather difficult for the individual employee to adjust, we would expect that, in a long-run perspective, the bargaining agreements themselves would also adjust to the reduction in the relative price of leisure that is brought about by higher marginal tax rates. We would also expect higher marginal tax rates to generate pressure for legislation on, say, a shorter working week, more favorable retirement conditions, and more liberal rules allowing people to stay away from work for various reasons—not only because of sickness, but, for instance, education, the care of sick children and other relatives, etc. (i.e., various types of tax-free benefits for households).

Indeed, this is exactly what has happened in some of the most advanced welfare states, such as Holland and the Scandinavian countries. Following collective bargaining and legislation, there are time lags until the effects of these events are felt; "warning signals" about disincentive effects are, therefore, often considerably delayed. That in turn may bias the system toward higher marginal tax rates than otherwise.

The role and freedom of choice of the family

Even though economists usually emphasize the efficiency costs of welfare-state and tax policies, it is conceivable that the general public will be more aware of two other separate, though related, effects: the consequences for the role of the family in society, and for the relationship between the individual and the state.

Indeed, one of the most profound consequences of the buildup of an advanced welfare state is that the

37

division of labor between households, markets and public authorities changes in a fundamental way. While high marginal tax rates by themselves stimulate home-production in general, the public provision of *specific* "private goods" such as the care of children, the old and the sick induces the transfer of such services to public institutions, away from both markets and households. This also stimulates married women to increase their participation in the labor force, usually on a part-time basis. (The latter effect would be accentuated if, as in Sweden, the assessment of taxes on income from labor is shifted from the joint income of husband and wife to the income of each individual in the family.)

Thus, in nations with advanced welfare-state systems, it is not principally the manufacturing industry that is socialized, but the household's production of services for the personal care of family members and other relatives. At the same time, household members are induced to devote more time to do-it-yourself work in the form of, for instance, painting, repairing and improving their houses, apartments and durable consumer goods. To caricature slightly: *the care for persons*, which was earlier regarded as the most important role of the family, moves to the public sector, while *the care of things* is shifted from the market to the household.

High marginal tax rates mean, of course, that the individual has limited possibilities of increasing his income by his own productive effort. If there is also far-reaching subsidizing of *public production* of services to the household (rather than of the *demand* for such services), the individual has in fact very limited choices between different ways of satisfying his demand for such services. The most important examples are probably education, medical care and (more recently) care for children and elderly parents.

As a consequence, the individual may find it difficult to influence his own life-situation as regards important and, indeed, often crucial matters of life. We will be allowed to choose between different consumer goods, but the possibility of choosing higher money income (at the expense of, say, leisure) by honest and productive work, and of choosing between different ways of satisfying the demand for important personal services may become very limited.

Thus, even though the buildup of a welfare state has improved economic security and removed economic misery, welfare-state reforms may, after a certain point of expansion, by way of high marginal tax rates and *de facto* public-sector monopolization of certain important services, considerably reduce *the freedom of choice* of the household in certain important aspects.

This is not the place to speculate about various psychological effects of all this on the individual. However, Swedish psychologist David Magnusson (see For Further Reading) has argued that a society in which the individual is systematically denied the possibility of influencing his life-situation by his own effort, creates frustration and stress, due to so-called "learned helplessness." This at least suggests that the consequences of high tax rates and monopolized public services should be studied in the context of a broader theory about what the welfare-creating factors for the individual really are. In addition to the welfare-generating factors that are traditionally analyzed in economic theory, i.e., actual leisure and consumption, it is worthwhile to examine the possibilities, or rather difficulties, encountered by the individual attempting to influence his/her own life-situation by his/her own effort.

Individual-state relations

It is not *impossible* to become rich in a society where individuals cannot easily improve their economic situation by way of honest and productive effort. The obvious method is to engage in various types of zero-sum games, such as to exploit various asymmetries and loopholes in the taxation of assets (e.g., by incurring heavy debt, with deductible interest rates, the real value of which is reduced by inflation). This means that in a high-tax welfare state it will, to a considerable extent, be the "wrong" people who become rich, from the point of view of rewarding productive effort.

In such a society, it also becomes tempting for the individual citizen to accept *offers from politicians* to do something positive for their living standard. Thus, there is a serious risk that the political conflicts between various interest groups will increase considerably. This is a reason to be skeptical about the notion that economic stability in society increases *monotonically* by reduced income differentials, even though during early phases of the buildup of a welfare state social and political conflict may indeed have been mitigated by what many people probably regard as increased "social justice."

A process of fierce political competition over the distribution of income, particuarly if combined with attempts by politicians to mitigate specific undesirable disincentive effects of the tax system, also creates strong incentives for politicians to change the tax and transfer systems frequently. As a consequence, the "rules of the game" of income formation easily become highly *unstable*. Economic decisions that yesterday seemed to have been highly rational, according to contemporary tax and transfer rules, turn out to have been mistakes when politicians have changed the rules "overnight."

These problems would be accentuated if the authorities, in order to combat unexpected adjustments of individuals, also decide to make the tax rules so *vague* that it becomes very difficult for the individual even to know in advance how the authorities would, in fact, judge his dispositions. Then, not only will the tax rate be high and the tax rules unstable, but they may also become increasingly difficult for the individual to interpret. Although such a development may not be a *necessary* consequence of a high-tax society, it is obvious that such policies will be tempting for politicians who feel that they are consistently "one step behind" private agents. That is precisely what has recently taken place in Sweden.

All this means that the traditional welfare state, designed to provide economic security and wipe out poverty, may after a while turn into a "free-for-all" competition for specific favors at the cost of the general public. Income formation may then increasingly become a complicated system of "tax, transfer, inflation, and capital-gain lotteries," which are often loaded in favor of people who are politically powerful, or well informed on financial matters, or who have high borrowing capacity and good connnections with credit institutions.

• *Taxing away honesty.* Other profound changes will occur in the relationship between the individual and the state. In particular, every tax and benefit implies, in fact, "taxation of honesty," since it usually pays the individual to give misleading information to the authorities in connection with taxes and benefits. More specifically, in societies with high marginal taxes and benefit rates, there will necessarily be strong temptations to (i) tax and benefit cheating, (ii) criminal behavior in the context of legitimate work (such as "credit fraud"), and (iii) the pursuit of illegal and tax-exempt trades and professions.

This does not necessarily mean that we should expect such activities to be more prevalent in high-tax societies than in low-tax societies. There may be a reverse causation as well, as it may have been possible to drive up taxes to particularly high levels in societies where loyalty towards the state has traditionally been strong, as in the Scandinavian countries. It may take decades to erode the "capital stock" of honesty toward the state that has accumulated during earlier centuries.

When tax evasion starts to be a significant phenomenon in a sector, market prices will be influenced in a fundamental way by the evasion, as competition and entry would be expected to drive down the rewards of the factors of production to what is normal for corresponding levels of risk-taking. This means that in such a sector, those who do not already cheat really have only two choices. Either they too have to start cheating, to get normal returns on their skills and investment within that sector, or they have to leave the sector. In the long run, tax cheating in a sector is less a problem about the distribution of income than an ethi-

cal issue and a problem of the allocation of resources:
in societies with high marginal tax rates, sectors where
cheating is relatively easy will tend to overexpand
relative to other sectors.

A more speculative point is whether increased dishonesty toward public authorities will "rub off" into
reduced honesty among private agents. If the individual does not hesitate to cheat public authorities, might
he then assume the same "right" to cheat banks, insurance companies, and other corporations and institutions, and perhaps even private individuals? If such a
spread of dishonesty should come about, most citizens
would presumably regard it as a serious matter. Honesty is a very important "collective good." It is such in
the production system, since the costs of making, im-
plementing and controlling contracts are kept down if
individuals can trust given information and agreed arrangements. But honesty is probably also a collective
good on the consumption side, or more generally in
people's daily relations with each other as human beings, in the sense that people probably enjoy honest
relations. There are thus reasons to be careful not to
construct economic and political systems that "tax
away" honesty.

Rise of the control state

The increased temptations both to cheat the authorities
over taxes and benefits, and to make "smart," though
legal, tax-induced manipulations with economic transactions is, of course, a basic reason why the authorities
in some of the most advanced welfare states have recently started to strengthen their efforts against such
activities by increased control over the activities of
individuals. Indeed, in Sweden, the development of a
strong "control state" is pronounced, with increased
reporting, inquiry and control of the lives of citizens,
and with the burden of proof of innocence more and
more shifted to the individual himself. This means that
the growth and interventionism of the public bureaucracy in a welfare state will be even more pronounced.
There is also a tendency to reallocate resources within

the legal system to fight economic crimes against the state, at the expense of the resources devoted to the protection of, and the prosecution and punishment of crimes against, individuals.

In addition to the above-mentioned effects on economic efficiency, on the role of the family in society, and on the freedom of choice of the individual, these consequences for the relationship between the individual and the state probably constitute the most profound side effects, and possibly limits, to the build-up of an advanced welfare state.

It is no doubt possible to mitigate, to some extent, the "negative" effect of the tax system discussed above, without *major* reductions in welfare programs. Obvious methods include: (1) shifts from tax-financing of some public services to financing them by fees, in particular in the case of various social security systems (by tying the value of the benefits, in an actuarial fashion, to the fees that the individual has actually paid, which removes the marginal tax wedges of the social-security contributions); (2) reduction of the ambition to redistribute income *within* middle income brackets, and possibly also between them and the upper brackets; (3) shifts from subsidizing the *production* of services by public agencies to direct subsidizing of household *demand* for such services; and (4) changes in the *structure* of taxation, such as a shift from income to consumption taxes, a closing of tax loopholes, greater symmetry in the taxation of various types of assets, and a shift from a nominal to real tax system (if the first-best solution of stopping inflation turns out not to be feasible).

Of course, most of these reforms would have consequences for the distribution of income and wealth, which means that various trade-offs between distributional considerations, on the one hand, and considerations of efficiency, freedom of choice and autonomy vis-à-vis the government, on the other, have to be faced. However, a removal of poverty in the bottom tiers of income distribution, and a comprehensive social-security system can certainly be achieved with public spending below fifty percent of GNP, and marginal tax rates below that percentage level.

However, as there are no non-distorting taxes, the basic message is that it is hardly possible to avoid serious problems concerning economic efficiency, the freedom of choice of the family, and the protection of the individual against the state without keeping *total public spending* within certain bounds. My *guess*, built on Swedish experience, is that the various problems discussed here become serious if public spending rises substantially above 50 percent of GDP, since then the after-tax rates of return start to fall rapidly for every additional increase in the tax rates.

If the expansion of welfare-state spending cannot be stopped in time, there is, in my judgment, a severe risk that other types of public spending will instead be cut substantially. That would mean that the classical role of the public sector to supply public (collective) goods may suffer seriously, as regards, for instance, justice, defense, culture and research—areas for which there are often no strong interest groups in the political process. The paradoxical situation might then arise that the private sector has increasingly to take over the provision of public (collective) goods because the government devotes so much of its resources to stimulating and directing the households' consumption of private goods.

FOR FURTHER READING

THE MARGINAL COSTS OF PUBLIC FUNDS. Edgar K. Browning in *The Journal of Political Economy*, Volume 84, 1976.

LEARNED HELPLESSNESS. David Magnusson in *Skandinaviska Banken Quarterly Review*, 1980.

APPLIED GENERAL-EQUILIBRIUM TAX MODELING. John B. Shoven. IMF Staff Papers, Volume 30, 1983.

MARGINAL COSTS OF PUBLIC FUNDS FOR DIFFERENT TAX INSTRUMENTS AND GOVERNMENT EXPENDITURES. Ingemar Hansson in *Scandinavian Journal of Economics*, Volume 86, 1984.

AN EVALUATION OF THE EVIDENCE ON THE IMPACT OF TAXATION ON CAPITAL FORMATION. Ingemar Hansson. International Institute of Public Finance, 41st Congress, Madrid, Spain, August 1985.

European Economic Review 32 (1988) 295–318. North-Holland

Joseph Schumpeter Lecture

INDIVIDUAL FREEDOM AND WELFARE STATE POLICY

Assar LINDBECK

Institute for International Economic Studies, S-106 91 Stockholm, Sweden

1. Introduction

In economic theory, the individual (or household) is basically assumed to be concerned with the bundle of goods and services which it actually obtains, including leisure and job characteristics. The *process* by which this bundle is reached plays no role for how the household evaluates it – for instance, whether the individual itself has chosen the bundle or whether the individual has instead been provided the bundle by somebody else, such as the government. This means that the issue of 'individual freedom', which is closely related not only to actual achievements but also to the process by which these are realized, is seldom squarely confronted in economic analysis. However, just such a confrontation will be attempted in this lecture.[1] As we shall see, this raises some basic issues of welfare economics and cost–benefit analysis, in particular concerning the specification and interpretation of the preference function, and even the general justification, in the context of normative economics, for the traditional partitioning between a subjective preference function and an objective opportunity set.

Generally speaking, individual freedom has to do with the tightness of various types of constraints on the decisions and actions of individuals. However, as this lecture is confined to the consequences of welfare state policy, it is not necessary to deal with the complex issue of 'freedom' in all its philosophical aspects.[2] Indeed, the analysis concentrates on three aspects: (i) *the freedom of choice* with respect to goods and services; (ii) *the predictability* of the consequences of such choice, and (iii) *the privacy* and *personal integrity* of the individual, which may be regarded as two specific types of abstract 'goods'. The reason for concentrating on these three aspects of

---

[1] I am grateful for helpful comments on an earlier draft from William Baumol, Thorvaldur Gylfason, Mats Persson, Amartya Sen, Dennis Snower, Lars Svensson, and Jörgen W. Weibull.

[2] When trying to make a useful conceptualization of individual freedom, I have found the writings of Gray (1980), Hayek (1960), Machlup (1969), Nozick (1974), Sen (1985a) and Sugden (1981) particularly useful.

individual freedom is that welfare state policies have profound consequences for each of them. It will also be assumed that the individual regards freedom per se as valuable, even though the opposite opinion is sometimes expressed, mainly due to asserted psychological disadvantages for the individual of having to choose among alternatives.[3]

By way of introduction, it is also necessary to decide what types of welfare state policies should be considered. This exposition concentrates on a collection of policy instruments that are recorded on the public budgets, namely, social security systems, money transfers to households, and government subsidization and/or provision of certain types of goods and personal services to households, such as health services, child care and old age care – as well as the financing of such programs. Macroeconomic stabilization policy and various types of regulations will basically be left outside the present discussion. An exception is that price control and related rationing will be considered – one reason being that price control has obvious similarities with subsidies, another and more fundamental, that price control and rationing are paramount in the case of public services.

When discussing individual freedom, it is important to remind ourselves that certain government-implemented limitations on freedom are a prerequisite for other types of freedoms. The most obvious example is perhaps legally imposed limitations on the freedom of one person to use force against others – i.e., government protection against 'the tyranny of anarchy'. For instance, government-guaranteed property rights and transaction rights are certainly a sine qua non for voluntary exchange, and hence for 'economic freedom'.[4] A well-known dilemma, though, is that the same government that has removed 'the tyranny of anarchy' often itself violates the very same rights, which places our societies in a precarious dilemma 'Between Anarchy and Leviathan', to quote a well-known title of a book by James Buchanan (1975).

It is also important to remember, throughout the lecture, that conceivable damage to individual freedom of welfare state policies, in particular its financing, has to be compared with conceivable gains in other respects. Indeed, it is obvious that such gains are both far-reaching and impressive in several modern welfare states: (i) in mitigating destitution among groups of citizens that would otherwise live in poverty, including physically and mentally handicapped citizens; (ii) in stimulating investment in human capital, in particular health and education; and (iii) in helping individuals to reduce uncertainty of income in connection to market risks, as well as to

---

[3]Of course, there are situations when the individual may want to commit himself in advance to certain future actions, for example to avoid that others would exploit his ability to act freely at every point of time; for game-theoretic analyses of such situations see, for example, Schelling (1960) and Lindbeck and Weibull (1987). However, voluntary decisions to commit oneself in the future can hardly be regarded as reflecting a negative attitude of the individual to freedom per se.

[4]For discussions of the importance for the individual freedom of various *rights*, see Dworkin (1978) and Kanger (1975).

smooth their consumption path over lifetime, in particular for individuals who are not able, or willing, to do that all by themselves by way of private saving and private insurances. On the basis of such achievements, I have in earlier writings characterized the build-up of the modern welfare state, up to a point, as a 'triumph of modern civilization' [Lindbeck (1988)].[5]

However, as we shall see, there is not always a conflict, as often envisaged, between such achievements, on the one hand, and individual freedom, on the other. Some welfare state programs tend to increase rather than reduce individual freedom in certain important respects, at least for some individuals; and some welfare state programs, and their financing, may, as we shall see, reduce rather than enhance economic security.

Moreover, as the relevant political issue is not if the welfare state should be *abolished* or not, but rather if it should be expanded or contracted from existing levels, we do not have to ask the 'impossible' question whether the welfare state as 'a whole' has increased or reduced individual freedom. It is usually enough for our purpose to ask about the consequences for individual freedom of *changes* in various welfare state programs. We will then occasionally find that a certain welfare state reform, and its financing, has increased individual freedom in some dimensions, at least for some individuals, and reduced it in other dimensions.

2. Freedom of choice

It is convenient to start with the freedom of choice of consumption, leisure, types of work, etc. – an aspect which may be regarded as a sub-category of the wider concept of 'individual freedom'. Such freedom of choice will be analyzed here in terms of the *opportunity set* and/or the *potential options* of the individual. The term 'opportunity set' then refers to what the individual may achieve by available resources, i.e., largely his initial wealth, possibly further restricted by non-budgetary constraints, while 'potential options' refer to states which the individual would be able to achieve if initial wealth was not a constraint. Four features of freedom of choice will then be studied: (1) the importance for freedom of choice of the 'command over resources' by way of wealth; (2) the possibility of the individual to improve his economic situation, and utility, by his own actions; (3) non-budgetary constraints on the opportunity set, such as formal or informal rationing of goods and services; and (4) restrictions on options that the individual does *not* consider to choose, i.e., removals of what may be called 'apparently irrelevant

[5]Of course, the public sector makes many other contributions to individual welfare, such as the provision of public (collective) goods, interventions in connection to externalities, etc. However, as these types of public sector activities are part of the *classical* role of government, i.e., to provide collective goods, rather than of welfare state programs, I will not discuss such actions in this paper.

alternatives'. These four features will be explained below, partly by the help of two simple diagrams.

(1) Let us first look at the command over resources by way of *individual wealth*. While there is rather widespread agreement among writers on individual freedoms that property rights and transaction rights are important for the freedom of choice, there is less agreement whether the wealth position itself should be regarded as a factor which informs us about the extent of freedom of choice. Without arguing that one definition of freedom of choice is necessarily better than another, it is certainly useful to include wealth as a factor that influences the freedom of choice when the latter, as in the present lecture, is largely analyzed in terms of the individual's opportunity set, for which wealth plays a crucial part. Then we also avoid confining the notion of freedom of choice just to *formal* rights, such as the right of both the poor and the rich to buy attractive goods or to enter excellent schools, regardless of their possibilities to finance such actions. Our terminology also implies that lump-sum taxes and lump-sum benefits will influence the freedom of choice, and that government policies which bring about *redistribution* of wealth in favor of poor sections of the population will be said to expand the freedom of choice for people who originally had little of it.[6] To the extent that welfare state policies bring about such redistribution, here is an example where welfare state policies may *increase* the freedom of choice for some people, though at the expense of others.

It is also conceivable that the attitude of the individual to constraints on his freedom of choice differ depending on *who* has imposed them. For instance, we may speculate that the individual feels that his freedom of choice is more constrained if it is *the government* that takes wealth away from him, for instance, by way of a tax increase, than if 'nature' does it, for instance, via an unfortunate ('unlucky') outcome of his own actions. One explanation may be that the individual in the former case feels that other human beings, or human institutions, have arbitrarily constrained his command over resources, while in the latter case some purely 'exogenous' force, which human beings may not be able to do anything about, is responsible. The distinction is particularly important if, following writers like Berlin

---

[6]Examples of social philosophers who object to the idea that wealth should be regarded as a component of individual freedom are Isaiah Berlin (1968), Friedrich von Hayek (1960 and 1973–79) and John Rawls (1972). They seem to regard wealth as a factor that enables the individual to get more pleasure (or more 'worth' in Rawls's terminology) from existing 'freedom', rather than as a component of freedom itself, which is then, in fact, asserted to be constrained by non-budgetary rather than budgetary constraints, such as restrictions on property rights and transaction rights. Thus, these authors make, in fact, a distinction betweeen the *ability* to buy goods and services, due to holdings of wealth (which they do not regard as a component of freedom) and the *freedom* to exercise this ability – a distinction used also by, for instance, Jensen and Meckling (1977). This distinction between budgetary and non-budgetary constraints is related to, though not congruent with the traditional distinction between 'positive' and 'negative' freedom.

(1965) and Hayek (1960), we argue that 'freedom' has more to do with restrictions on human behavior that are, directly or indirectly, imposed by other human beings, than with constraints imposed by nature. Another explanation may be that the individual, subjectively, feels that his property rights in factor incomes, which he has earned, are violated by taxes, while hypothetical increase in factor income that *could have been* earned, but have not materialized, are not connected with such subjectively felt property rights.[7]

(2) However, it is obvious that important aspects of freedom of choice cannot be dealt with solely in the context of changes in wealth, and related changes in traditionally defined utility. In particular, it is reasonable to say that freedom of choice is reduced also when the possibility for the individual to influence his situation by *his own actions* is reduced by government policies – even though the wealth position, or the traditionally defined utility, of the individual does not deteriorate. To clarify this point, it is useful to think first about the extreme situation when the marginal income tax rate is one hundred per cent, so that the individual cannot improve his income by his own effort in markets – whether the labor market or the capital market. All observers would in this case probably agree that the freedom of choice of the individual has been severely restricted by the government, in the sense that he cannot 'trade' income for leisure (in a broad sense of the latter term); indeed, taxes in this special case function like a law that forbids increased incomes from additional work effort. However, the same observers would probably also agree that a considerable reduction in the freedom of choice occurs already with marginal tax rates below one hundred per cent, as then it may be very difficult, though not completely impossible, for the individual to raise his money income by, say, twenty or even ten per cent, in spite of the fact that he could easily increase his *pretax* income at those rates by extra effort. The individual is largely 'trapped' in a certain income bracket *by government policies*, with very little possibility of changing his economic situation by his own effort, even if he is anxious to do so, and even if there are no 'natural' limitations to such a change. For instance, in the perhaps most 'advanced' welfare state in the world, Sweden, where the *average* full-time employed person has a marginal tax rate of 75 per cent (when *all* taxes and income-dependent transfers are included), it is obvious that the ability of

---

[7]It is worth noting that the so-called 'regret theory' [Loomes and Sugden (1982)] postulates just the opposite evaluation of the outcomes of exogenous events and actions by the individual itself, respectively. For that theory asserts that the individual would be unhappy (feel regret) that he did not behave differently when there is an unfortunate outcome of his own action, while no such regret would be felt in the case of an exogenous event such as a tax increase – if that theory is not widened to include regret about how the individual voted in the last elections! However, in the case of unexpectedly *positive* outcomes, regret theory asserts 'rejoice' in connection to such an outcome if it has resulted from actions taken by the individual himself.

the individual to choose freely between income and leisure has been dramatically restricted by government tax policy.

Generally speaking, it is reasonable, as a partial ordering, to talk about a government-induced reduction in the freedom of choice when *marginal* tax or subsidy rates distort individual decision-making by the creation of 'wedges' between the private and social returns on factor supplies, and effort in general. Obviously, this type of limitation on individual freedom of choice is closely connected with the traditional concept of 'dead-weight costs' of government-induced relative price distortions. We may say that traditional analysis of tax-wedges, and related dead-weight costs, in the discussion above has largely been *reinterpreted* in terms of the concept 'freedom of choice'. However, as we shall see subsequently, such a reinterpretation has some interesting consequences for normative economics.

In fig. 1, let q_1 and q_2 be the quantities of two goods, and let AB be the budget line, with the chosen point a on the highest possible indifference curve, u_1. Thus, while a deterioration (improvement) in the freedom of choice by way of a government-imposed reduction (increase) in the wealth position of the individual (even by lump-sum taxes or transfers) is simply reflected in a downward (upward) parallel shift in the budget line, reduced freedom of choice by way of a distortion of the relative price is represented as a change in the slope of the consumer's budget line. As an extreme example of the latter, letting q_1 be leisure and q_2 income, respectively, a one hundred per cent marginal income tax rate means that the individual will be stuck at a

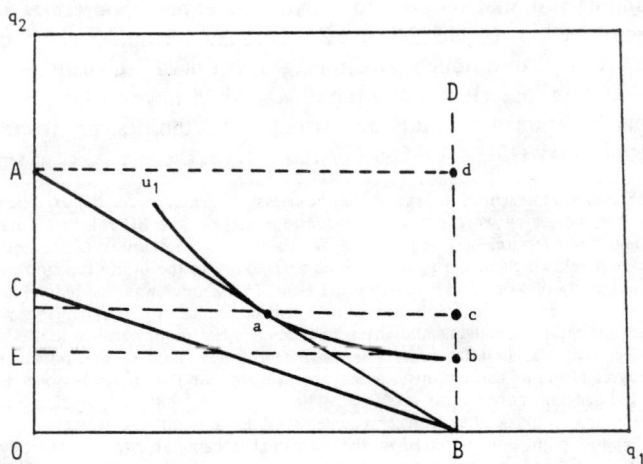

Fig. 1

point on the vertical line *BD*, i.e., at an income level where *the government* chooses to place him by way of transfer payments.[8]

For instance, if the government provides the individual with the income *OE*, the opportunity set changes from *OAB* to *OEbB*, which means, in fact, that the government places him at point *b*. Even though the individual is now provided a level of income that gives him the same, traditionally defined utility as initially (at indifference curve u_1), he is now in a situation where he cannot, by his own effort, *change* his income, while at point *a* he could do just that, if he so wanted. In this specific sense, the individual has less freedom of choice with the new budget set *OEbB* than with the initial budget set *OAB*, even though the maximum attainable, traditionally defined, utility is the same for both opportunity sets. If the individual has a positive evaluation of *the act of choosing* as such between income and leisure, he would therefore prefer to *choose* point *a* rather than being *provided* the income level *OE*. Accordingly, we may argue that there is a hypothetical income transfer, in addition to *Bb*, that would exactly compensate the individual for the loss in the freedom of choice at point *b*. Of course, we do not know, with the information provided in this example, how large this income transfer would have to be, for instance whether it would have to move the individual up to, or even above point *c*, where the level of income is the same, and leisure is larger than at the initially chosen bundle of point *a*.[9]

Though this analysis has been pursued by traditional tools of economic analysis, a modification of conventional utility functions is certainly necessary to incorporate the notion of a value of the act of choosing itself. One way of doing just that may be to include the entire opportunity set in the preference function, beside the actually consumed bundle, which means, of course, that the traditional partitioning between a 'subjective' preference function and an 'objective' opportunity set would have to be given up. The individual is assumed to value all existing opportunities, or 'advantages' in Sen's terminology (1985a, 1985b). For instance, in the special case when there

[8]This geometric representation assumes, without loss of generality of the argument, that the individual does not enjoy work per se. If he does, the vertical line *BD* will be to the left of the point of maximum leisure, or more precisely at the point where utility is maximized for the given income level, which in the simple case of separability in the utility function occurs when the marginal utility of work and leisure are the same. In a similar way, the individual's freedom to reallocate income and consumption over time will be reduced by marginal income tax rates that reduce the return on saving and investment in financial or physical capital – though not even 100 per cent marginal tax rates will *eliminate* the possibility of the individual to bring about such reallocations (by contrast to the consequences for the choice between income and leisure of 100 per cent marginal tax rate).

[9]It is tempting to argue that transfer payments of the amount *OA*, which would make the individual choose point *d*, is preferred by the individual to being able to choose freely along the budget line *AB*, as the opportunity set *OAdB* dominates the original budget set *OAB*. However, not even that assertion is self-evident, as the individual may be upset, *in principle*, by the fact that the government has removed rewards to variations in work effort.

is an unambiguous reduction (increase) in the opportunity set, in the sense that the new set is strictly inside (outside) the old, it is tempting to argue that the individual unambiguously has lost (gained) freedom of choice; (see, however, the reservation to this point in footnote 9). In the more general case, when part of the new opportunity set is inside but another part outside the original opportunity set, that simple approach does not give unambiguous results.[10]

A more appropriate way of formalizing a positive evaluation of the act of choosing in situations with price distortions may be to include the price distortion itself, for instance in terms of the size of the tax wedge, as a separate argument in the preference function. In other words, the utility function would read $U(q, t)$, where q is the consumption bundle and t, representing for instance a tax-wedge, expresses government-imposed restrictions on the ability of the individual to trade one type of good for another; $U_1 > 0$, $U_2 < 0$. For instance, a one-hundred per cent marginal tax rate would then reflect the individual's evaluation of not being able to choose income level at all, while a smaller marginal tax rate would express the evaluation of a partial elimination of that ability.

The *partial* character of this analysis should, of course, be emphasized. It is, in a more complete analysis, necessary to consider also the consequences for freedom of choice of the spending programs that are financed by the taxes under consideration. For instance, as pointed out above, such spending may increase the freedom of choice of some individuals by raising their wealth. I will give other examples later on how public spending may increase freedom of choice. It might also be argued, though I am not prepared to do so, that the individual (by rational expectations) may be aware of the possibility that lower marginal tax rates would influence factor and product prices, which in the analysis above have been taken as given by the individual, and that such changes could influence the freedom of choice.

(3) Additional light may be thrown on the issue of freedom of choice by looking also at the consequences of *non-budgetary restrictions* on the opportunity set, in the form of formal or informal rationing of goods and services in connection to 'scarcities', i.e., excess demand. The freedom of choice of the individual is then limited in the sense that he is provided a different bundle than he would choose himself at the existing budget restriction; i.e., there is a discrepancy between the desired and the provided consumption bundles at given wealth and relative prices, by contrast to

---

[10]It is in that case necessary to *weigh* each area relative to the preferences of the individual, i.e., to integrate the utility function over the areas in question. We would then argue that the freedom of choice is greater at point *a* than at point *b* if the utility-weighted area *OAB* is larger than the utility-weighted area *OEbB*. For discussions about evaluations of entire opportunity set, see Kanger (1975) and Sen (1985b, p. 21). For assertions that freedom is primarily a descriptive concept, and that it can be defined in an objective fashion, see Oppenheim (1973), Day (1970) and Parent (1974).

earlier discussed limitations in freedom of choice when markets were in equilibrium, though at distorted relative prices.

In fig. 2, let us assume that good 1 is rationed in the quantity OF The opportunity set of the individual is accordingly cut down to the area $OAeF$, which is unambiguously smaller than the initial budget set OAB; moreover, the originally most preferred bundle, a, has been removed from the opportunity set. The individual would now have to settle for the corner solution e, rather than being able to choose the original optimum bundle a. The point I want to make is that the individual in this case, *in addition* to a conventional utility loss, is 'frustrated' by not being able to achieve the consumption bundle that is optimal at existing wealth and relative prices, as expressed by the budget set OAB.

To clarify this frustration effect, let us alternatively assume that the government reduces the price of good 1 by way of a price regulation, and that the new budget set therefore is ODC in fig. 2, so that the individual now would like to choose the bundle d.[11] But suppose that he is in fact instead *provided* the initial bundle a, by way of informal or formal rationing of both goods, or simply by government decree. In other words, the opportunity set is now the bundle a. though the budget set is ODC. Even though conventionally defined utility is the same as initially, i.e. U_1, the freedom of choice has been reduced, as the individual has been robbed of alternatives.

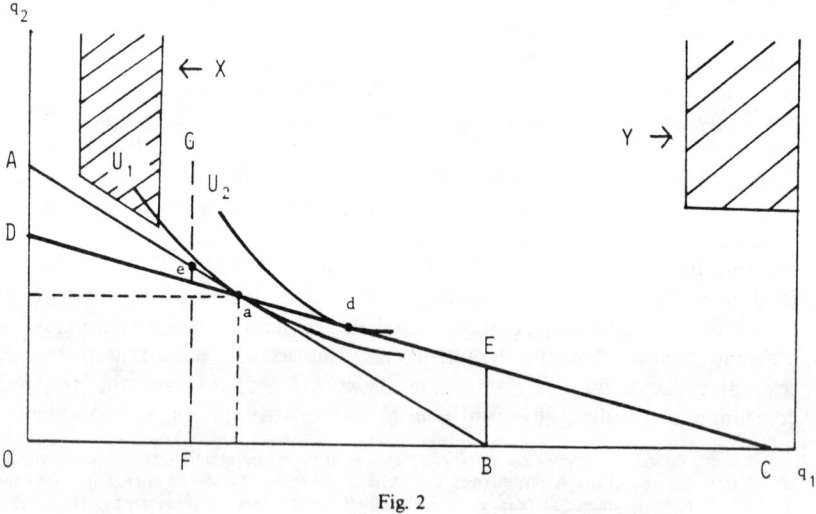

Fig. 2

[11]In the case when q_1 is leisure and q_2 income. a similar shift may be achieved by an income tax in combination with a lump sum transfer; the new budget set would then be $ODEB$ in fig. 2, where the lump sum transfer is BE.

Assuming, again, that the individual evaluates the act of choosing positively, the individual is now less satisfied than when he originally freely did choose the same bundle, i.e. point a.

Thus, my hypothesis is that the individual is 'frustrated' if he is given economic incentives to desire a better consumption bundle (such as point d in the example above), which he then is prevented from achieving because of rationing or government decree. Assuming that this frustration effect can be interpreted as a loss in satisfaction, there would, in principle, be a *hypothetical* lump-sum increase in income, which would make him indifferent between being provided with the bundle a when he desires another bundle, on one hand, and being able to choose the same bundle freely along the budget line AB, on the other hand. It is in exactly this sense that rationing may create a frustration effect, *in addition* to a possible loss in conventionally defined utility. It may also be hypothesized that the individual feels particularly 'frustrated' if he regards the rationing system as 'unfair', for instance when people with high positions in society, and good contacts, are favored, as seems to be a typical feature of many systems of rationing, in particular informal rationing, for instance in rent controlled housing markets.

One conceivable analytical representation of such a frustration effect is to postulate that not only the actual consumption (and asset) vector (q), but also the desired one (q^*), is an argument in the utility function: $u(q, q^*)$, with $u_1 > 0, u_2 < 0$, where q^* is assumed to depend on actually existing (possibly non-market-clearing) income and prices.[12] (In the example in fig. 2 above, q and q^* then depict the bundles a and d, respectively.)[13]

In other words, suppose that the individual, at the price vector p, in Walrasian equilibrium, chooses the consumption (and asset) vector q. Let us then assume that the government introduces price controls on some goods, and that the individual at the new price vector $p^* < p$ wants to obtain the vector $q^* > q$, but that he is unable to get it because of excess demand in some markets. Assume further that the government now instead *provides* him just the initial vector q.[14] We may now say that freedom of choice has been reduced, and we may hypothesize that the individual therefore feels less satisfied than initially. One *specific* analytical representation of the frustration

[12]The latter may not be a self-evident assumption when prices are non-clearing. For if the individual has 'rational expectations' concerning the alternative scenario without price control, it may be argued that he should compare the bundle that he actually gets *not* with the consumption bundle that he would like to have at the regulated price, but rather with the consumption bundle which he would choose if price control was removed and prices adjusted accordingly. In the discussion above, I have assumed that it is the existing price vector that determines the aspiration level, and then also influences the frustration effect. Maybe we can say that I subscribe to the notion of 'bounded rationality' rather than rational expectations.

[13]Formally, this specification of the utility function is similar to the analysis of 'envy effects', where q^* is then related to the consumption level of other agents.

[14]As $p^*q < pq$, we have, in order to get a consistent comparison, to assume that the government also introduces a lump-sum tax equal to $pq-p^*q$ in the case of rationing; otherwise the individual will have income 'left over' in the rationing case.

effect along this line would be the conventional consumer's surplus, measuring the utility loss to the individual of consuming the bundle q rather than q^*, i.e., the difference between utility levels U_2 and U_1.[15]

This analysis also illustrates the importance of including wealth as a factor that contributes to freedom of choice. Because, otherwise we would, in the context of the analysis above with unsatisfied demand, be forced to say that the government may *increase* the freedom of choice of the individual simply by reducing his product demand, and hence his aspiration level, q^*, (as $U_2 < 0$), by policies that reduce the individual's wealth (provided the good is a normal good).[16]

Another important example of a government-induced frustration effect is when the public sector provides *non-marketable*, tax-financed public transfers in kind, free of charge or at highly subsidized prices. The household has then to give up money income, i.e., general purchasing power, in exchange for services that cannot be resold in the market, i.e., services which have a zero market price for a potential private seller. The limitation on the freedom of choice, and the related frustration effect, consists here of the non-marketability of the provided goods, in combination with the tax-induced reduction in money-income, which means that the individual has rather limited resources to buy goods *other* than those that are provided by the government. The individual may then have too much publicly provided non-marketable goods relative to other goods. This may also mean that the possibility for the family to take care of its own children in the daytime may be eliminated, as the household may feel that it really has no choice other than to have both parents working outside the home, to obtain higher money income in order to get more of 'ordinary' goods, and to hand over the care of their children to free or highly subsidized institutions.

Exactly this has indeed happened in Sweden, due to the combined effects of high *average* tax rates and ample provision of non-marketable government services in kind. Hardly any family with children in Sweden thinks today that it can afford to take care of their own children in daytime. Even a household headed by a 'high-income' employee, like a military colonel or a university professor for that matter, in Sweden would today wind up with a

---

¹⁵This specific measure of the value to an individual of having, rather than not having the liberty to buy a desired good, seems to follow immediately from the traditional definition of consumers' surplus [Hicks (1939, pp. 38–41)]. Such a measure of the value of the right to choose freely has indeed recently been suggested by James Buchanan (1987).

¹⁶Obviously, the 'domain' for the argument in the text that freedom of choice is systematically related to the difference between desire and outcome is a limited one. I suggest that the case discussed here, where the government creates economic incentives for increased consumption but prevents the individual from realizing his new desire, is a proper 'domain' for the argument, while the 'brainwashing', via force or one-sided propaganda, of people to be content with what they have, is *not* a proper domain for the argument. In other words, the idea of freedom of choice presupposes value-pluralism and an open society in the formulation of opinions. Berlin's (1968) and Popper's (1945) conception of individual freedom emphasizes, of course, the importance of 'value pluralism' for a society to be regarded as 'free'.

money income below the official poverty level, i.e., with an income where social welfare may be received, if the household has three children and only one income earner [Du Rietz (1987)]. However, if in fact such a family would apply for social welfare payments, the family would be denied it with the argument that both parents should take jobs in the open market and hand over the children to day care outside the home, even though one parent would otherwise (at lower public spending and lower taxes) be eager to stay at home to take care of the children for some years. Freedom of choice, in a presumably very important dimension of life, has then been eliminated.

An additional frustration effect in combination to the provision of publicly provided goods may arise if the public goods are *rationed*, as they usually are in the real world; the implications of such rationing have, however, already been discussed in the previous section in connection to price control. A third type of constraint on the freedom of choice would occur if, moreover, public institutions have *monopoly positions*, or near monopoly status, in the sense that private alternatives are either legally not allowed, or discriminated against so much by subsidies to public institutions that private alternatives, which would otherwise exist, cannot survive in the market. Product variety would in these cases be reduced by government actions. Citizens who would like to have another type of health service, school, child care, old age care, or insurance than the ones that are provided by government monopolies, would then have no possibility of choosing something different – even though it is not obvious why freedom of choice among alternative products and product varieties would be less important in fields like these than, for instance, for different types of automobiles and toothpastes.

The basic reason why it makes sense to say that monopolies imply a restriction of the freedom of choice of the individual is, of course, that such freedom presupposes *alternatives* that provide substitute modes of actions for the individual. Moreover, when considering the consequences for freedom of choice of public monopolies, it is also important to remember that such monopolies remove alternative employers, and hence *varieties of job* for employees.

An analytical representation that would make justice to the idea of a reduction in the freedom of choice due to monopolies would require the same number of dimensions as the number of goods, or product varieties; the *removal* of one alternative would then be represented as a loss of one dimension. Alternately, we might want to choose a continuous representation of product variety à la Lancaster (1979), in the form of a circle of product characteristics, or à la Dixit and Stiglitz (1977), in the form of a straight line of product varieties.[17] The creation of government monopoly would then be depicted as a removal of some segments of this circle (line).

[17]More generally, D. and A. Gabor (1979) have developed a very general mathematical framework where freedom is analyzed in terms of the variety of choice in life.

In principle, it is, of course, possible to avoid such public monopolies even if there are *compulsory* insurance, and subsidization of certain types of services. In particular, private citizens could in principle be allowed to choose an insurance company even if insurance is compulsory; and subsidies may be provided on equal terms for both public and private producers, possibly in the form of voucher systems.[18]

What are the reasons for the strong discrimination against private alternatives for services like education, health, child care and old age care in many welfare state nations? 'Paternalism' is probably an important part of the answer. Indeed it is typical for the modern welfare state in capitalist countries to direct 'paternalism' towards households rather than firms – by contrast to socialist countries where paternalism seems to be directed towards both. Indeed a useful distinction between socialist states and welfare states is that while the former tend to nationalize and monopolize firms of all types, welfare states mainly nationalize and monopolize market production and household production of *personal services*, including insurance, to household members – as well as much of the factor incomes of the household, via the tax system.

One obvious explanation for such paternalism towards households is a desire among politicians to control the *quality* and the *detailed distribution* (i.e., what each individual gets) of certain services. Behind these policies there probably often lie basic objectives of avoiding social segregation of people – children as well as adults. In some countries, public services in fields like child care and education may also reflect an ambition among politicians and public administrators to 'homogenize' the population, as the family institution is often regarded as an obstacle to such homogenization, by perpetuating inequality and diversity of values and attitudes. For these various reasons, 'freedom of choice' in fields like child care, education, health care and old age care is, no doubt, regarded by some politicians and public administrators as an 'evil' rather than a value.[19]

---

[18]A complicating factor when judging the welfare consequences of subsidized public services is, of course, that such subsidies may have *distributional consequences*, in particular between three groups of households: those who would prefer the public alternative even without the subsidies, those who because of the subsidy are induced to shift to the public alternative, and those who would like to stick to the private alternative also when the public service is subsidized.

[19]It is sometimes argued that the elimination of public monopolies would reduce *the product quality* of the publicly provided good. The asserted reason would be that those who initially are induced, or forced, to consume a public good, like public day care centers, but who without discrimination of private alternatives would shift to these, usually are better educated and more vocal than those who would stick to the public alternative. In other words, it is assumed that those who choose the 'exit' option are also able to use the 'voice' option more effectively than others. [For assertions along those lines, see Hirschman (1981), Nelson and Krashinsky (1973), and Young (1976)]. On the other hand, a public supplier would get stronger *incentives* to listen to voice if exit is allowed. In other words, it is not clear whether exist and voice are complement or substitute modes of influencing product quality of this case. Thus, it is not clear at all what will happen to product quality when voice-strong people do exit. This means that the quality-argument against freedom of choice, in defence of public monopolies, is not a strong one.

(4) The asserted 'frustration effect', discussed above, was caused by a discrepancy between the desired and the provided consumption bundle. However, we may want to go a step further, and argue that the individual also regards the removal of 'apparently irrelevant alternatives' as an infringement on his freedom of choice. By that term I then mean bundles, whether inside or outside the opportunity set, which the individual does *not* consider to choose. We may then hypothesize that a removal of a subset of the original opportunity set OAB in fig. 2, but with the chosen point a retained, would be regarded as a loss of freedom of choice, even though the removed alternatives are 'irrelevant' in the sense that the individual does not want to choose them, and thus there is no 'frustration' due to a difference between demanded and actually provided bundles. For instance, an individual may regard the removal of all alternatives south-west of point a as a loss in freedom of choice, and in personal satisfaction, even though he still wants, and is still able to choose the bundle a. Indeed, these assertions tie in to the earlier discussed assumption that freedom of choice is restrained when there is an unambiguous reduction in the size of the opportunity set.

It may also be hypothesized that the individual believes that his freedom of choice is reduced when options *outside* the budget set are removed by government actions. For instance, in the context of fig. 2, the individual may feel that his freedom of choice is damaged if the government forbids the consumption of all bundles either in area X or in area $Y - X$ being a bundle that he would consider consuming at somewhat different income or relative price, and Y a bundle that he regards as being completely outside his range (forever). We may say that freedom of choice *in society at large* is reduced – in the first case for the individual itself in an alternative, quite realistic situation, and in the second case for other individuals.

The notion that options beyond the reach or interest of the individual contribute to his freedom and welfare is not unknown in the literature of philosophy and fiction, from Aristotle, via Kierkegaard and Dostojevskij to modern existentialism. Similar interpretations of the concept of freedom of choice are also found in the literature on the economic geography and spatial (urban and rural) planning – often in connection with the concept of 'accessibility'; the individual is assumed to value the existence of theater and opera in his community even if he plans never to attend a performance.[20] In a similar way, the individual may be anxious to keep a national park unexploited, even if he intended never to visit it.

One conceivable way of formalizing the importance of 'apparently irrelevant alternatives', like X and Y in fig. 2, is to let the utility function include the entire set of *options*, in society, not only those that are inside but also those that are outside the actual opportunity set – beside the actually chosen con-

[20]For a short survey, and a development of mathematical concept of accessibility, see J.W. Weibull (1980, pp. 53–67).

sumption vector. In terms of fig. 2, the entire product space would be an argument in the preference function – beside the actually obtained bundle. Of course, we are then encountered with the same problems of measurement as in the context of the earlier discussed evaluations of entire opportunity sets.

In the example in fig. 2, it was assumed that certain *quantities* of existing goods are not allowed (bundles X or Y). A more important case is perhaps that certain products, or product varieties, are entirely removed from the market. To make justice to this idea, it is, again, necessary to shift to a multidimensional representation. The elimination of certain products or product varieties, also outside the opportunity set of the individual, would then be depicted as the elimination of one or several dimensions in the product space.

An analytical representation more in line with traditional theory is to assume that the individual is uncertain about his budget equation, and/or his preference function, in future periods. In the context of such a stochastic approach, which catches at least some aspects of the importance to the individual of a set like X, bundles south-west of point a, in fig. 2, or product varieties outside the budget set, we would assume that the individual maximizes *expected* utility, with *expected* life-time wealth as budget restriction. The importance of the set Y for the individual, too, may be considered in the context of traditional utility theory if we assume that the individual is altruistic, in the sense that he wants others, including perhaps his own children (or grandchildren) to satisfy their preferences without government intervention. Thus, traditional theory can certainly cope with at least some aspects of the issue of the removal of 'apparently irrelevant alternatives'.

3. Predictability of outcome of choice

However, when analyzing the relations between welfare state policy and individual freedom, another type of uncertainty is probably more important, namely government-induced limitations on *the predictability of the consequences of individual choice*. In general, for freedom of choice to make much sense it must be possible to act purposively, which in turn requires that the individual can predict the consequences of his actions with a reasonable degree of certainty. Freedom of choice is meaningful only if there is a certain stability and predictability of the pay-off matrices for individual agents. A society with far-reaching government intervention, with laws and regulations changing all the time, tends to damage this predictability.

An important explanation for the tendency of governments to make the pay-off matrices less stable is that politicians seem to be more interested in *the outcomes in individual cases* than in the stability of the rules of the game. Moreover, there is in such societies often a tendency to introduce new legislation in order to control 'everybody' in a certain population category, or profession, as soon as 'somebody' in that category is asserted to have 'misbehaved' – either by breaking the law or simply behaving contrary to the *intent* of the law.

More specifically, when individuals adjust their behavior to government policies in ways which the government does not like, the government takes counter-measures which the individual cannot predict very well. Two types of countermeasures of the government seem to be particularly relevant and prevalent. First, in order to counteract unexpected and undesired effects of previous policy interventions, politicians make new interventions – seemingly in an endless stream of new laws and regulations. The result is *rule instability*. Second, as individuals adjust to new rules and regulations in ways which politicians do not like, these are tempted to make the rules *more vague*, to make it possible for the authorities to interpret the rules more freely, and hence to make it more difficult for individuals to escape the intended effects of the policy interventions. As a result, the rules of the game will not only be more unstable, but also *less known* at every point in time. As a consequence of both these reactions of the government, the economic system tends to become a complicated 'tax-, benefit-, and regulation lottery', with quite unpredictable effects on the distribution of wealth and economic welfare.

All this means that decisions which yesterday seemed rational to the individual, under the rules that existed then, may turn out to have been mistakes either because politicians have changed the rules overnight, or because there is a new interpretation of the existing rules – obvious examples being the frequent changes and reinterpretations of the rules of the taxation of various types of assets, as well as various rules and regulations concerning the operations of government service institutions, including the priority ordering in public queues for housing and municipal day-care centers, old age centers and institutions of higher education. (Clearly, those effects can largely be analyzed by traditional economic analysis, provided government-implemented uncertainty is introduced into the 'pay-off function' for individual actions.)

One important effect of all this is that ambitions of welfare state policies to increase economic security, after some point, may be counter-productive, as increased political and administrative risks tend to replace the market risks which the government initially tried to reduce; the stochastic elements in the 'pay-off function' of individual action may then increase over time, rather than fall as intended. This damage to the predictability of the consequences of individual choice may clearly be characterized as a reduction in individual freedom.[21]

---

[21]James Buchanan has described the situation in the following graphical terms for the U.S., where this problem most likely is much less serious than in some of the more 'advanced' welfare states in north-western Europe: 'Descriptively, we live in what might be called "constitutional

Indeed a society of this type tends to drift away from 'rule by law' to 'rule by discretion', both by exposing private agents to arbitrary changes in the laws, and by giving public officials considerable discretionary powers to interpret the laws. The Kantian 'Rechstat' is then clearly threatened, even though democratic institutions and political freedom are intact. An extreme example is the so called 'general clauses', used for instance in Sweden today, whereby formally legal actions by individuals or private organizations may be declared invalid by the court if the actions are regarded by the courts as not being in conformity with the *intent* of some legislation.

4. Individual privacy and integrity

This discussion takes us to our final point, namely, the consequences of welfare state policies for individual privacy and integrity. By 'privacy' I mean the right of the individual to withhold information about its life to others, while 'integrity' refers to the right of the individual to avoid far-reaching intervention in its life by others, including by the political authorities.

When discussing this issue, it is first of all important to note that *general* support systems, like negative income tax systems and social security systems, require less scrutiny of individuals than do *selective* support systems. Thus, the former systems, taken by themselves, are far more favorable than the latter for privacy and integrity, even though general support systems tend to create higher levels of public spending than do selective systems. This illustrates the inadequacy of assuming that individual freedom *necessarily* falls by higher levels of public spending; we have to look also at the *types* of spending and its financing. However, if more and more benefit systems are introduced, and if these become more and more generous, and the marginal tax rates higher, the gains in terms of privacy and integrity of *general*, as compared to selective support systems, will be counteracted, and even lost by the need to build up public information and control systems to fight tax and benefits cheating.

A basic reason why *privacy* is threatened by far-reaching welfare state policy, even when quite general systems are used, is that such policies, if they include high marginal tax and transfer rates, may make honesty towards the state quite 'expensive' for the individual because of the gains from giving incorrect information in connection to taxes and public benefits. And when honesty becomes expensive, there will be less of it. The government will

---

anarchy" where the range and extent of federal influence over individual behavior depends largely on the accidental preferences of politicians in judicial, legislative and executive positions of power. Increasingly, man finds himself at the mercy of a faceless, irresponsible bureaucracy, subject to unpredictable twists and turns that destroy and distort personal expectations with little opportunity for redress or retribution'. [Buchanan (1975, p. 4).]

therefore be induced to build up an elaborate system of information of the lives of individuals and private organizations.

For instance, in a dishonest society, the government has to check that people who receive unemployment benefits or sick leave compensation do not, in fact, work somewhere, such as in the 'underground economy'; and that people who are paid by the government for staying at home to take care of sick children or other relatives are doing just that rather than enjoying paid leisure. The authorities may also want to investigate whether unmarried mothers with public benefits really live alone, for instance by asking them how many nights a man stays over in their home. Some citizens, in particular if they have rather low (declared) incomes, may also be asked by the tax authorities to explain the sources of some of their spending, such as their recent vacation trip abroad, etc.

Moreover, by imposing taxes, such as value added taxes, on most economic transactions between private agents, the government will be able to get some 'double check' on transactions in the private sector, with data from both sellers and buyers, which simplifies control of individual transactions drastically. To get an additional double check the government may require private individuals to report parts of their spending to the authorities, such as the purchases of services from craftsmen. To fight false reporting, the authorities may also make private firms financially responsible for the lack of compliance among *other* firms, which they make business with.

These examples are no fantasies; arrangements like these are already a fact of life in my own country, Sweden. Moreover, information about practically all economic relations and transactions in Sweden between the individual and the public sector tend to be collected in numerous, in fact over one hundred, government data systems – a procedure that is highly facilitated by the requirement that ID-numbers of citizens be provided in all transactions with public authorities. This makes it possible for the government to check whether the individual has given consistent information about his economic situation, and life situation in general, to different public agencies, such as the tax authorities, public hospitals, public care centers, various segments of the social security systems and various public agents that provide subsidies and permits of different kinds.

A problem with these various arrangements, from the point of view of individual privacy, is that information about the private life of individual citizens will be spread out over the public administration, and also 'leak' to various public officials and other citizens. Single pieces of information which are 'innocent' in isolation may damage the reputation of an individual when hundreds of such pieces of information are combined. There is also a risk that politicians in government positions, and their supporters in the administration, may try to leak 'negative' information to mass media and to the general public about the private lives of political opponents or their relatives.

However, not only privacy but also *integrity* is threatened. If the individual is not willing and able to exploit various loopholes in the tax or benefits system, his best chance to improve his economic situation will often be to adjust his life to the desires of public authorities, hoping to get increased benefits from the government. The individual will then, to a considerable extent, be induced to consume just the goods and services that the government is willing to provide and subsidize, and to accept the division of labor between the household, the market and the public sector – and indeed also *within* the household – that the government prefers. In extreme cases, we may wind up in a 'public benefit' and 'pocket-money' society, where the amount of the provided services and pocket money, to a considerable extent depends on the willingness and ability of the individual to adjust its life to the desires and signals of public authorities.

Extensive and strongly interventionist *regulations*, outside the narrow field of welfare state policy, have similar consequences. For instance, offences against rent controls would, of course, not exist without such controls, nor would offences against building regulations exist without government restrictions on building activity. Similarly, exchange control offences would not exist without regulations of foreign exchange markets, nor violations of price controls without price regulations, or smuggling without tariffs and other trade restrictions.

Anecdotes about particular interventions and particular countries aside, the point is that the higher the marginal tax rates, and the greater the public benefits available, and the more regulations there are around, the stronger will be the incentives for citizens to cheat, and the stronger will be the temptation for the authorities to build up elaborate information and intervention systems, which is bound to reduce the privacy and integrity of the individual. All this means that an advanced welfare state, with high marginal tax and transfer rates, would, after a while, be expected to result also in an elaborate *control state*. In fact, it is typical for advanced welfare states that the government feels forced to use more and more of its legal and police resources to fight 'crimes against the state' rather than 'crimes against individuals'. As a result, the state may then not even have enough police and legal resources to protect individuals against 'the tyranny of anarchy', even though such protection was initially a basic rationale for having a state.

Thus, not only will the government indirectly, via government-imposed *incentives*, drastically influence what the individual does, and prevent him from doing what he wants. The lives of individuals will also grow ever more closely investigated and directed by *discretionary, individual-specific interventions*. 'Individual freedom' will be threatened in the sense that citizens are prevented from enjoying two very important private goods, namely privacy and integrity. Analytically, we may indeed treat this kind of loss of individual freedom as a shrinkage of a generalized opportunity set of the individual.

Of course, there is an alternative to a control state, namely to accept slack in the system, in the sense that a considerable amount of cheating with taxes, breaking of regulations and misuse of benefits are accepted by the authorities, in order to avoid tight control of individuals. Obviously, democratic societies tend to opt for some *combination* of control and slack.

5. A summing up

The traditional utilitarian argument in economic analysis for individual freedom, including freedom of choice, is 'consequentialist', or 'instrumentalist', in the special sense that decentralized decision-making is defended by its consequences for economic efficiency in production and consumption, and hence also for the actual consumption bundles of individuals. This argument is a strong one, as knowledge of individual preferences and production processes are 'contained' in millions of individual heads, and cannot be transmitted to some centralized decision-maker (a point which has been particularly developed by Friedrich von Hayek). However, this lecture has argued that the individual may be interested also in the *process* by which a certain consumption bundle is achieved, and that indeed the individual values *the act of choosing* as such, which means that freedom of choice also has an 'instrinsic' value.[22]

These considerations imply, of course, that public intervention cannot be evaluated only on the basis of their consequences for the bundle of goods and services which the individual actually consumes. In the context of the analysis that has been pursued in this lecture, it will be necessary to consider also (1) difficulties for the individual of influencing his economic situation by his own effort; (2) 'frustration effects', in addition to traditionally defined utility losses, in the case of binding non-budgetary restrictions on individual behavior; (3) the removal of 'apparently irrelevant alternatives'; (4) reduced predictability of the consequences of individual choice; and (5) losses in privacy and integrity of the individual in connection to the build up of a control state as a complement to the welfare state. If these effects are taken seriously, it is clear that conventional cost–benefit analyses of the effects of public interventions – in the form of taxes, spending programs and regulations, including welfare state programs – may have to be considerably modified.

---

[22]Of course, when there are externalities, utilitarianism may conflict with the quest for decentralized decision-making, and hence with the quest for freedom of choice and the desire of a 'private sphere' for the individual. Indeed, this seems to be the background for Amartya Sen's theorem of 'the impossibility of a Paretian Liberal' [Sen (1970)], as this theorem is derived from the assumption that outsiders' preferences concerning 'the private sphere' of an individual should count in the paretian calculation. It is also obvious that while a utilitarian position is quite consistent with government paternalism, when the individual is assumed not to act in accord with his own best interest in the view of the utilitarian observer, paternalism is clearly in conflict with the liberal notion that freedom of choice is a value in itself.

All this means that the most severe problems in advanced, high-income welfare states, in addition to productivity losses in connection to economic disincentives, probably show up in the form of *psychological* effects. This is not the right occasion – or the right speaker for that matter – to penetrate the character of such psychological effects. However, modern psychology concerning so-called 'learned helplessness' [Magnusson (1980)] reports, on the basis of experimental evidence, that individuals who learn that they cannot influence their own situation in life by their own effort tend to become either passive, or aggressive towards those who restrict their behavior. In the first case the individual expects somebody else, such as the government, to take care of them, i.e., 'passivity' and 'dependency'; in the second case they try to break the rules of the system that denies them the rights to control their own life situation, i.e., 'cheaters' or 'revolutionaries'.[23]

There has for a long time been a strong tendency among intellectuals in the west to be much more worried about direct government intervention in *intellectual or political freedom*, such as freedom of speech and expression in general, than about limitations in the 'economic freedom' of the individual. Indeed, the latter type of intervention is often, as Joseph Schumpeter (1950) once argued, applauded by these persons. Perhaps this is natural for intellectuals, who certainly are particularly active in 'the market of expression', rather than in traditional goods and asset markets. However, it is far from self-evident that other citizens regard restrictions that reduce the freedom to choose their consumption bundle, and to change their economic situation in general by their own effort, as necessarily being less important than freedom of speech and artistic expression. Such intellectuals often also seem to forget that limitations in the freedom of choice in the economic field, as we have seen, generates limitation on other types of freedom as well, such as privacy and integrity.

Moreover, *if* tax policy results in a drastic reduction in the number of large and moderate-sized private wealth holdings, we would expect not only private firms but also various types of non-profit institutions to become strongly dependent on government funds, as the availability of both private equity capital and private donations can be expected to be rather small in such a society. The most obvious effect for an economist is perhaps that centralized, politically controlled supply of capital is likely to harm the chances of the survival of decentralized entrepreneurship. However, if the public sector becomes the dominant financier of research and culture, there is also an obvious risk that *pluralism* in these fields will suffer, as researchers and artists, as well as administrators of institutions of research and culture, like people in general, may hesitate to 'bite the hands that feed them'.

---

[23]Several moral philosophers have argued that the freedom to choose also makes an individual 'a better human being', e.g., Mill (1975, ch. 3), Hayek (1960) and Nozick (1974). Maybe it could also be argued that increased 'passivity' of individuals, who have learnt that the government decides for them, will raise the psychological costs of deciding by themselves.

However, to avoid one-sidedness in the analysis, it is important to remind ourselves, again, that certain kinds of government policies, including parts of welfare state policies, may *expand*, rather than reduce individual freedom, at least for some citizens. I am referring not only to the earlier mentioned observations that government-guaranteed property rights and transaction rights are crucial for the protection of the individual against 'the tyranny of anarchy'; that freedom of choice will increase for people who gain wealth by way of redistribution policies; and that general social security systems may be more favorable for privacy than are 'smaller' welfare programs that are highly selective in the sense of requiring individual applications and bureaucratic scrutinizing of applicants. It may also be argued that compulsory social security systems, by removing market imperfections, may create opportunities, in the form of insurance programs, that did not exist before – though the compulsory character of such systems, by themselves certainly implies a limitation on the freedom of choice for some people. Another example is policy actions that increase social mobility, such as free education and government guaranteed loans to students, which may create opportunities that would not exist otherwise, as many individuals do not have either enough wealth to finance their studies, or sufficient access to the capital market because of the difficulty of using expected future human capital as collateral for borrowing. An additional example of a government action, outside the area of conventional welfare state policy, that may increase the freedom of choice of the individual is environmental policies, by way of tax-subsidy programs or regulations. As such policies may disentangle 'fixed combinations' of production and pollution, the menu of choice for citizens may be widened.

Moreover, conceivable damage to individual freedom that stems from welfare state policies should, of course, be compared with various types of gains in other respects, such as those briefly mentioned in the beginning of the lecture in fields like economic security and the distribution of wealth. Indeed, these gains may in many cases, by a majority of citizens, be regarded as dominating the disadvantage of the losses in individual freedom. Thus, it is likely that much of the paternalism that is implied in various welfare state policies is basically accepted by a majority of the population, as a reasonable trade-off between individual freedom and economic security. However, the purpose of this lecture has not been to analyze trade-offs betweeen achievements of welfare states policies and conceivable 'net' losses in individual freedom; the theme of the lecture has been the consequences just for individual freedom.

For these various reasons, there is no contradiction in applauding the build-up of a welfare state up to a certain point, but to be worried about what happens when this point is surpassed. In other words, the issue is not whether the welfare state 'as such' has served its citizens well or not, or if it has increased or reduced individual freedom, but rather *if and when* (from the point of view of certain subjective values) one surpasses the point at which the detrimental effects, including various freedom-reducing consequences, start to dominate various beneficial contributions of *additional* welfare state policy actions.

References

Berlin, I., 1968, Four essays on liberty (Oxford University Press, New York).

Buchanan, J., 1975, The limits to liberty: Between anarchy and Leviathan (Chicago University Press, Chicago, IL).

Buchanan, J., 1987, Towards the simple economics of natural liberty: An exploratory analysis, Kyklos 40, 3–10.

Day, J.P., 1970, On liberty and the real will, Philosophy 95, 177–192.

Dixit, A. and J. Stiglitz, 1977, Monopolistic competition and optimum diversity, American Economic Review 67, 297–308.

Du Reitz, G., 1986, Hushållens skatteproblem (The tax problem of households), in: Riksbankens Jubileumsfond, Skatterna – ett samhällsproblem?, ch. 2.

Dworkin. R., 1978, Taking rights seriously (Duckworth, London).

Gabor. D. and A. Gabor, 1979, An essay on the mathematical theory of freedom, International Journal of Social Economics, 330–390.

Gray, J., 1980, On negative and positive liberty, Political Studies XXVIII, no. 4, 507–526.

Hicks, J.R., 1946, Value and capital (Clarendon Press, Oxford).

Hirschman, A., 1981, Exit, voice, and loyalty: Further reflections and a survey of recent contributions essays in trespassings, in: Economics to Politics and Beyond, ch. 9.

Jensen, M. and W. Meckling, 1977, Human rights and the meaning of freedom, Mimeo., Oct.

Kanger, S., 1975, Choice based on preferences, Mimeo. Depratment of Philosophy, Uppsala University, Uppsala.

Lancaster, K., 1979, Variety, equity, and efficiency (Columbia University Press, New York).

Lindbeck, A., 1986, Limits to the welfare state, Challenge 28, 31–45.

Lindbeck, A., 1988, The advanced welfare state, The world economy, March.

Lindbeck, A. and J.W. Weibull, 1987, Strategic interaction with altruism – the economics of fait accompli, Seminar paper no. 376, Institute for International Economic Studies, Stockholm.

Loomes, G. and R. Sugden, 1982, Regret theory: An alternative theory of rational choice under uncertainty, Economic Journal 92, 805–824.

Machlup, F., 1969, Liberalism and the choice of freedoms, in: E. Streissler, ed., (Routledge and Kegan Paul, London).

Magnusson, D., 1980, Learned helplessness, Skandinaviska Banken Quarterly Review 3–4, 67–74.

Mill, J.S., 1955, On liberty (Henry Regnery, Chicago, IL).

Nelson, R. and M. Krashinsky, 1973, The demand and supply of extra-family day care, in: D. Young and R. Nelson, eds., Public policy for day care of young children, ch. 2 (Lexington Books, Lexington, MA).

Nozick, 1974, Anarchy, state and utopia (Blackwell, Oxford).

Oppenheim, F., 1973, Facts and values in politics, Political Theory 1, 54–78.

Parent, W.A., 1974, Recent work on the concept of liberty, American Philosophical Quarterly, 149–167.

Popper, K., 1945, The open society and its enemies (Routledge, London).

Rawls, A., 1972, A theory of justice (Clarendon Press, Oxford).

Schelling, T., 1960, The strategy of conflict (Harvard University Press, Cambridge, MA).

Schumpeter, J., 1943, Capitalism, socialism and democracy (Allen and Unwin, London).

Sen, A., 1970, The impossibility of a Paretian liberal, Journal of Political Economy 78, 152–157.

Sen, A., 1985a, Well-being, agency and freedom, The Dewey lecture 1984, The Journal of Philosophy LXXXII, no. 4, 169–221.

Sen, A., 1985b, Commodities and capabilities (North-Holland, Amsterdam).

Sugden, R., 1981, The political economy of public choice (Robertson, Oxford).

Tversky, S. and D. Kaneman, 1981, The framing of decisions and the psychology of choice, Science 211, 453–458.

Von Hayek, F., 1960, The constitution of liberty (Routledge and Kegan Paul, Chicago, IL).

Von Hayek, F., 1973–1979, Law, legislation and liberty: A new statement of the liberal principles of justice and political economy, Vols. I–III (Routledge and Kegan Paul, Chicago, IL).

Weibull, J.W., 1980, On the numerical measurement of accessibility, Environment and Planning, 1980, Vol. 12, 53–67.

Young, D., 1976, Consolidation or diversity: Choices in the structure of urban governance, American Economic Review 66, 378–391.

[11]

CAN PLURALISM SURVIVE?

This lecture deals with issues on the borderline between economic analysis and political ideology. More specifically, it is concerned with the relation between on the one hand the organization of our economic system, and on the other hand the possibilities of maintaining a highly pluralistic society. This means, of course, that I am forced to move outside the borders of my profession as an economist.*

By way of introduction, I would like to assert that individual freedom in the developed countries of the western world is largely based on two pillars: political democracy and pluralism. The content and prerequisites of political democracy are fairly well known. However, the same cannot, I think, be said about pluralism. What I therefore would like to do in this lecture is to show that pluralism is strongly related to the organization of our economic system, and that some contemporary trends in the economic system constitute a threat to this pluralism. I will also, in concluding, indicate how pluralism could perhaps be saved. My discussion is mainly inspired by developments in Western Europe, but the problems are, with some exceptions, very much the same in North America.

When the western countries of today are characterized as "pluralistic societies," we usually think about two particular features of these countries. First, it is observed that our societies consist of many rather independent and, at least partly, competing power groups, each one with different interests and values. Second, the individual citizens—in their capacity as income earners, consumers, producers, savers, writers, artists, and private citizens in general—have considerable freedom to "do their own thing," without asking public authorities or other strong organizations for permission. This means that the pluralism of the western world is largely based on a system of decentralized decision-making and a division of functions

---

* Some of the ideas expressed in this lecture were originally presented in a talk which I gave for Program 3 of the British Broadcasting Corporation in the series "The Art of Economics," August 16 and November 27, 1976.

7

and responsibilities between government, firms, households, and private organizations such as labor unions, political parties, and cultural associations.

In other words, our societies are characterized by a set of institutions, laws, and rules that give citizens a large scope for acting and expressing opinions individually as well as forming organizations freely. This also means that new ideas, activities, products, and production techniques have a greater chance of being launched than if one or a few centralized organizations, such as the state or some centralized corporate agencies, tightly controlled individual and group actions.

THE MARKET SYSTEM

What is then the basic prerequisite for this decentralization and division of responsibilities and the associated pluralism? Most noneconomists tend, I think, to take these features of the western societies as something "given" and unexplained. However, it is important to realize that these features are largely embedded in the organization of our economic system. More specifically, they are to a considerable extent based on a highly sophisticated and very fragile mechanism: namely the market system, or in other words the interaction between demand, supply, and prices for goods, services, capital, labor, and information in reasonably open and competitive markets.

Most people seldom think about the enormous work which we, in fact, "ask" the market system to do for us: First, to tell producers about the preferences of consumers (via their demand in markets); second, to inform consumers (via prices formed by way of competition) about the lowest costs of providing different goods; third, to give firms incentives (via expected profits) to produce the goods which consumers want to have and are willing to pay the costs for, to economize in the use of resources, and to create new products and production techniques; and finally to coordinate billions of production decisions of millions of economic agents (via equilibrating market forces) so that the outputs of all firms fit not only the final demand by consumers but also the required inputs of other firms, at home and abroad.

It is exactly the market system, with competition and free entry, that allows a rather far-reaching decentralization of economic decisions and initiatives in a world with strong interdependence between the decisions

8

and activities of various economic agents. Without a reasonably well-functioning market system, a far-reaching centralization of economic decision-making and responsibilities would be necessary; such a situation would largely destroy pluralism.

This is perhaps easiest to see if we try to visualize what the economic system would look like without markets for goods, labor, and capital. For then it would be necessary to have some central agency that determined what the preferences of individual consumers were, or should be; that told firms how and what to produce, qualitatively and quantitatively; that decided to whom different goods and services should be delivered and what new products should be introduced. And in addition to all that, the centralized authority would also have to direct labor and capital to the sector where they were regarded as needed, as well as to see that billions of decisions by millions of different production units and households were reasonably consistent, so that production and consumption would not be disrupted by severe bottlenecks in the economy. Trying to visualize what this type of society would look like helps us to understand what a heavy reliance on markets has saved us from: a strongly centralized command economy, where pluralism could hardly exist because pluralism presupposes decentralized decision-making and a considerable autonomy of households, firms, and other organizations that are engaged in economic activities, including the production and distribution of information and of what we call culture.

Some New Tendencies

What I would like to draw your attention to in this lecture is that there are under way some rather strong trends in our present societies which, if we are not very careful, will undermine the market system and hence the system of decentralized decision-making—and then in fact the pluralistic character of the present society as well. The general reason for this threat to a pluralistic society is that the traditional division of functions and responsibilities between households, firms, private organizations, and public authorities tends to break down to some extent. The main explanation is not that some "evil forces" consciously try to undermine our pluralistic society. The new trends are instead mainly rather unplanned side effects of developments which by themselves are often thought to be great advances, and in fact are often actively promoted by large fractions of the population. An important example is that services earlier pro-

9

vided by households are being taken over by institutions: in particular, services for the very young, the elderly, the sick, the handicapped, and the mentally deviating citizens.

Perhaps the major driving forces behind this development can be classified under five headings, expressing partly overlapping features. The first one is the increased and ever more detailed *specific policy ambitions* (policy targets) of governments, largely in fields such as employment, welfare distribution, and environmental quality, as well as the safety and predictability of economic life in general. The second force is connected with *general ideological factors* requiring, in principle, not only that certain services in expanding fields (such as schools and health) should be provided by public authorities, but also that more of the economic decisions taken by private firms and households should be subject to closer and more detailed political control. A third force is *increased returns to scale and mergers,* factors largely related to certain technological and institutional developments which tend to create ever larger firms and other organizations, as well as making governments more eager to finance and control them. A fourth factor, which is also closely connected with the technological development, is the increased role of so-called *externalities* of production and consumption, such as environmental pollution and hazards to workers and consumers, which also induce, and in fact require, government interventions. And a fifth force, finally, is the desire to shield the domestic economic and social system from ever stronger *international forces,* including both military conflicts (with large military sectors as a result) and increased international economic dependence and interdependence.

To summarize, the new developments which tend to undermine our decentralized economic system are related not only to ideological factors (the ambitions of politicians to control economic life and human life in general) but also to what economists call "market failures," such as economic instability and insecurity (partly brought about by international forces), inequalities in income and wealth, increased lumpiness of economic decision-making, deficiencies in the supply of collective goods, and finally external effects of economic activities.

The increasingly ambitious and ever more detailed policy interventions generated by these forces also tend to create more and more severe conflicts between objectives, not only between broad targets such as the overall distribution of income, economic efficiency, growth, employment,

10

and inflation, but also between more detailed policy targets, such as the employment level in one part of the country versus another, the incomes of some specific groups of people versus other groups, and so on.

Moreover, because of the enormous complexity of our economic system, many instances of intervention tend to lead to a deterioration in the functioning of markets and to unintended effects on the distribution of income and welfare, and thus give good reasons for new public intervention and regulations. In this way a larger and larger fraction of the government's intervention in the economy is, in fact, an attempt to counteract undesired side effects of previous intervention. Politicians are working hard to solve problems which they have largely created themselves. In other words, the more politicians and public administrators mismanage our economy and society, the more we will see detailed public intervention, and the more additional powers will go to the politicians and public administrators.

Typical examples of acts of intervention that "force" the authorities to introduce new intervention, perhaps in a never-ending stream, are price regulations and direct regulations of output or input in various sectors of the economy. Celebrated cases are, of course, maximum prices on natural gas and consequent gas shortages; rent control and the consequent housing shortage and deterioration of cities; zero-pricing for the use of street space by cars and the resulting congestion and pollution in cities; various price and quality regulations of transportation and the resulting low utilization of capacity and high costs of transport by trains, trucks, and airplanes; interest rate ceilings and a consequent strangulaion of credit and capital in some sectors, such as housing; detailed regulation of environmental and working conditions, resulting in poor incentives for innovations in those fields compared to what might be accomplished by economic incentives for good performance, for instance by way of taxes and subsidies.

The reason why the proliferation of detailed policy targets has created so many new distortions and induced so much detailed and often counterproductive intervention is not only the policy ambitions as such. Also, and perhaps above all, the methods used nearly always rely on direct regulation of inputs, outputs, production techniques, and prices, whereas good performance can often be achieved by making bad performance (such as pollution and accidents) expensive through taxes and high insurance fees, and by making good performance materially rewarding through subsidies.

11

As economists have preached for at least one hundred years, modification of economic behavior to bring it into better conformity with social purposes can as a rule be achieved at much lower costs by modifying economic incentives, rather than by using regulations that conflict with them—and that often in fact can conflict with incentives that have been created by actions of the authorities themselves. As we know, the natural instincts of legislators and administrators are directly contrary to this doctrine: they wish to forbid what they do not like and to make compulsory what they do like, rather than creating stronger incentives for "good" performance.

CONSEQUENCES OF THE NEW TENDENCIES

What are then the consequences of these new tendencies? I have already pointed out that many of them are related to developments and policy interventions which, by themselves, are backed with reasonably good arguments. For instance, few serious observers of our present societies doubt that larger firms are highly beneficial in many sectors, and that policy interventions in the market system are necessary to improve the natural and man-made environment, to increase the safety of workers and consumers, and to improve the infrastructure and the supply of public goods that the market system does not automatically provide, as well as to improve the distribution of income and wealth and the employment opportunities of various groups of people in our society, such as the handicapped, the poorly educated, or the objects of discrimination. Public support of news media and cultural affairs may also, if implemented in a decentralized and general fashion, considerably increase the diversity of information and culture, in particular in municipalities and regions with monopolistic tendencies in these fields. For it is quite clear that "unaided" market forces do not guarantee individuals a wide diversity and a reasonable freedom of choice among news media and cultural activities.

However, if we are not very careful, the combined effects of all these developments may, *largely because of the chosen methods of intervention*, be a dramatic transformation of our society that few of us would have asked for if we had seen in advance what the consequences of all developments would be in the long run. I would like to emphasize some of the different forms such effects might take.

1. First, there are the very important consequences for the functioning of markets and prices. If the mergers of firms and the accompanying concentration of market power go very far, competition will sooner or later

be hurt—with the likelihood of increased difficulty in the entry of new firms, less innovation, and a general deterioration of efficiency in the allocation of resources as a result. So far, an increase in international competition has probably largely prevented such effects, but there is a risk that an unlimited expansion of the size of firms, often in fact on a global scale, will in a later stage seriously reduce the efficiency of the market system of the western world.

Even more serious problems for the functioning of markets and prices are connected with the ever-increasing selective interventions in the market system by governments. Of course, in some cases the selective interventions will no doubt improve the performance of the price system, in the sense that the transmission of information, the creation of incentives, and the allocation of resources will be more in conformity with the preferences of citizens in general than they were before. Obvious and socially very important examples are taxes on activities that hurt the health and the environment, and subsidies that improve the education, health, employment situation, and income of disadvantaged groups in our society.

However, many of the new selective interventions in the price system are just a new version of the old protectionism and mercantilism. There is therefore, as economists have always emphasized, an obvious risk that these interventions will lead to long-term losses in efficiency and economic well-being, since many of the new interventions make prices, and hence also the allocation of resources, deviate drastically from what would be approximately optimal from the point of view of consumer preferences and realistically calculated costs. For it is quite clear that the market imperfections that motivate public interventions are sometimes trivial compared to the "political-administrative imperfections" that are introduced in their place. Housing, agriculture, energy, water supply, and transportation amply illustrate this truth. In fact, political prices for scarce resources often deviate several hundred percent from marginal and average social costs—while economists and politicians are often worried if ordinary market-determined prices deviate 10 or perhaps 20 percent from such costs.

2. Moreover, when political authorities, directly or indirectly, have more and more charge of investment and production decisions in individual industries, or perhaps even within individual firms, these decisions will in fact be made by a group of people with very little competence and very poor information about alternative products, production techniques, and sales opportunities. This factor also is bound to contribute to a major

13

deterioration in the efficiency of economic decision-making, since the bulk of the relevant information, in particular qualitative information, on these matters is carried in the heads of millions of managers, engineers, economists, and other employees in individual firms, and it cannot possible be transferred to a small group of politicians and public administrators. The problem is accentuated by the fact that the political decision-making process is often extremely shortsighted and "prestige conscious" because of the overwhelming concern of politicians for short-term party tactics. As a result politicians will buy votes from various subgroups of the population by short-term promises about public investment and subsidies, without always giving much consideration to how these activities will affect the long-term efficiency of the economy as a whole.

The losses in efficiency may be particularly pronounced if, as has already happened in some countries, we get an economic system where contacts and bargaining with government officials and politicians become more important for the successful operation of firms than the ability to pursue effective production, innovation, and marketing. A national economy will be in serious trouble if the rate of return on bargaining with public authorities becomes higher than the rate of return on market activities, because managers of firms then start to "chase subsidies and protection," instead of "chasing profits" by attempting to gain higher efficiency in production and marketing. This is exactly what happened a long time ago in countries like Argentina and Uruguay; now some developed countries in the West, such as the United Kingdom, seem to be on the same track.

An important factor behind the new tendencies is probably also an increased willingness of corporations to ask for government subsidies, guarantees, capital grants, and protection—that is, an increased inclination among managers and stockholders to want to "sit on the knees of the government." In fact government subsidies and capital grants, though often intended to protect employment in specific sectors or firms, can to a large extent be regarded also as welfare payments to stockholders in unsuccessful firms, where the stockholders "normally" would risk drastic capital losses. Thus, the tendency in many countries today for the government to bail out stockholders, rather than letting share prices collapse, means a removal of what traditionally has been part of the social function of stockholders.

14

To some extent these tendencies are a result of the increased willingness of politicians to intervene and of business managers and stockholders to try to obtain security at the expense of taxpayers and consumers. But they are also the result of increased unwillingness among labor unions to see firms make what were earlier regarded as normal profits. Low average profits put many firms in the red and make many managers willing, and in fact eager, to get equity capital, credit, and subsidies from the government, since both internal funds and external private capital tend to dry up for such firms. Thus, if profit margins and the return on capital fall below a certain level, which probably has already happened in some European countries, the only way to keep up the investment level is for the state to take over more and more of the financing—and therefore also of the allocation of investments—by way of nationalization, public capital grants, or subsidies of private firms. As we know, there have been in recent years enormous increases in such activities by governments in low-profit countries such as the United Kingdom, Benelux, and the Scandinavian countries. The process has sometimes been speeded up by increased lumpiness of investment decisions (such as in the iron and steel industries), and by the drying up of the supply of private risk capital, owing not only to a lower rate of return but also to a reduced importance of the market for shares (partly because of tax policies) for financing investment. In some countries the trend to less private risk-taking has been further accentuated by increased political uncertainty, as has happened in France and Italy.

3. However, the most drastic effects of the proliferation of government intervention are no doubt the wider political, social, and cultural consequences. The distribution of power in society will change in a complicated and dramatic way. A situation may be created where not only a small number of politicians and administrators but also some leading managers of large firms—and, in some countries, powerful labor union leaders as well—would be in a better position to act, mainly at the cost of consumers, managers in small firms, and individuals who would like to start new firms in competition with existing ones. Politicians and administrators can easily make bargains and deals with a few managers of large firms and labor unions, but hardly with thousands of small entrepreneurs, and even less readily with those who would like to become entrepreneurs. The result is to accentuate the concentration of production among a small group of large corporations, and thus inhibit new initiatives and the entry

15

of new firms, as well as many types of innovation by people outside the top echelons of established public and private hierarchies.

All this would mean that a society may be created where bargaining and the exercise of power—and even threats—become more important for the success of individuals and organizations than creativity, knowledge, and the ability to compete in markets. It also means that power in society would shift over to a small and rather closed group of politicians, public administrators, managers in large corporations—and, in some countries, also dominant labor union leaders—all of them more or less being each other's "chain prisoners." In fact, a general collaboration may emerge between these groups—not only in the sense that they will tend to share common purposes and values and to cooperate in cases where public and private activities are highly complementary—which may be all good—but that they will also bargain about various mutual favors in cases where such collaboration is not at all required for an efficient allocation of resources and a good coordination between public and private activities.

Our societies may then become dominated by a tightly knit coalition between elites representing the state, the large corporations, and the labor organizations—a coalition of Big Government, Big Business, and Big Unions. Only those who are willing to risk their careers, or who are so inexperienced that they do not understand that they risk their careers, will protest and criticize. We may then arrive at a rather dualistic society with on the one hand insiders—the new establishment—which keep together, and on the other hand outsiders who have difficulty getting the information necessary for an efficient critique. The "Silent Spring," which Rachel Carson expected in nature, may then instead arise within society.

It is difficult to predict which, if any, of the various groups making up the new coalition will in fact dominate. In some countries—perhaps in the United States and Japan—it is possible that, at least in the short run, the managers of the large corporations will dominate because of superior information and organization. In other countries—perhaps France is an example—the state bureaucracy may have the upper hand, at least for some time. However, in countries where the labor unions are strong— such as the United Kingdom, Israel, the Scandinavian countries, and to some extent West Germany—it is likely that the leaders of the large labor unions will increasingly dominate the coalition because of their unique combination of economic and political (vote-getting) strength. More generally, there is an obvious possibility that some of the organizations

16

which at the beginning of the century contributed to the pluralistic nature of our societies, such as labor unions, now tend to be so strong in some European countries that they in fact may dominate these societies and hence be a threat to the pluralism which they themselves helped to create.

The tendencies toward a rather monolithic power structure will be particularly strong if the supply and administration of capital become even more heavily concentrated in the hands of some large and centralistic organization—for example, a few giant private capital funds or the public sector—or possibly in some "corporativistic" organization like the labor union movement (as has been proposed in some countries, such as Sweden), which would mean that the labor union movement would also become the employers' association. In the latter case the society might approach what could perhaps be called a corporativistic though democratically organized labor union state, to some extent replacing the traditional pluralistic liberal state. It is important to emphasize, however, that such a development is only a future possibility, not a contemporary fact.

An alternative scenario, at least for some countries and perhaps particularly in the short run, may be a strong labor union movement *in conflict* with the government, especially in situations where the political views of the government differ greatly from those of the labor union leaders. The society could perhaps in that case be classified as dualistic rather than pluralistic.

In the case of both scenarios it would seem that a fundamental economic and political problem for our societies will be to find, within the context of a pluralistic society and traditional forms of political democracy, the "proper" role of labor leaders, who are becoming ever stronger and more ambitious for power.[1]

In the communist countries the amalgamation between the representatives of the political authorities, the state bureaucracy, the production firms, and the labor unions (in totalitarian forms) has, of course, been a fact from the very beginning, with the Party, at least so far, as the coordinator. In those systems pluralism never had a chance, even to begin with.

---

[1] Examples of this problem can be supplied from most West European countries. For instance, it was quite generally agreed in Finland that a new government could not be formed after the general election in the fall of 1975 until the elections in the union of metal workers had also come about.

17

THE AUTONOMY OF FIRMS AND INDIVIDUALS

To avoid one-sidedness in the exposition, it is important to point out that just as some of the new intervention no doubt has improved efficiency in the allocation of resources, some has also increased autonomy and the freedom of choice among some groups of the population, in particular perhaps disadvantaged groups, largely by expanding their economic opportunities. Examples of such intervention are several types of subsidies, regulations affecting working conditions and the environment, and—perhaps above all—income transfers to low-income groups, public consumption, and infrastructure expenditures. However, it is extremely easy in most countries also to point out government intervention in the economic lives of firms and households that does not have this effect or has it only to a small extent.

When one looks at developments that reduce the autonomy of individuals, it is worthwhile to make a distinction between those that reduce the sovereignty of firms and other organizations and those that increase the dependency of individuals on the government.

The first are probably perceived only indirectly and vaguely—but nevertheless strongly—by most individuals in the form of a general growth of bureaucracy and a decline in the vitality of society, perhaps even without any apparent or easily visible connection with the development of the economic system.

Individuals in general will, of course, be much more aware of regulations that directly affect their own activities. Obvious examples are obstacles and restrictions on the entry and operations of new and small firms, which may reduce the chances for individuals to be self-employed or to be owners of family enterprises; credit restrictions, which may reduce the freedom to spend; regulations governing shopping hours or the variety of goods, which may reduce the freedom of consumers to buy goods; rent controls, detailed land-use restrictions, and building regulations, which may reduce one's freedom to choose the locality and the type of home one lives in; wage regulations and closed-shop rules, which may create unemployment and at the same time reduce the freedom of the individual to choose a job; restrictions in the market for foreign exchange, which reduce the freedom to travel; centralization of the financing of education and culture, which often results in requirements for increased uniformity in

18

school systems, universities, and cultural institutions, thus tending to reduce the spectrum of cultural and intellectual life; and so on.

It is also possible that in some countries high marginal tax-transfer rates have made some citizens feel that they cannot change their economic situation by their own efforts, and hence that they are trapped and have to turn to the government.[2] This would mean not only that firms, because of low profits, would increasingly have to turn to government to grow or even survive, but also that individual citizens (households), because of high marginal tax-transfer rates, would have to rely increasingly on political actions, rather than on individual market behavior, to improve the economic situation. We would also expect the tax authorities to feel compelled to look more and more closely into the economy of private citizens, and hence into their private lives—because of the strong incentives to avoid taxes in such a society—with a consequent feeling of tighter social control among individuals.

What to Do about It?

An important question now, of course, is what can we do about all this. The previous discussion suggests quite clearly, I think, where we should look for the answers.

First of all, because the existence of a pluralistic society largely depends on decentralized economic decision-making, which in turn requires a market system, an initial prerequisite for a pluralistic society is to keep a dominant role in the economy for a competitive market system. This means that the strong tendencies to mergers of firms, the development of ever larger conglomerates, the practice of interlocking directorships in the corporate sector, and so on, must be stopped and reversed. Personally I would, in fact, strongly favor the breaking up of the largest corporations and capital funds in the world economy—say the one hundred or five hundred largest firms and capital funds—into smaller units.[3] This would

---

[2] In some countries in northwestern Europe the marginal tax rates for skilled workers in the mid-seventies were about 60 percent. On top of that, income-dependent transfers are reduced when income increases, often creating marginal tax-transfer rates of some 70–80 percent, occasionally even higher.

[3] In view of the fact that the cost curves seem to be quite flat over large ranges of output, and that relatively small firms often compete quite successfully with the giants (notice for instance the high efficiency of Swedish and Swiss firms of very modest size), the losses in allocative efficiency should be small, if any.

19

have the additional advantage of reducing the lumpiness of decisions by firms about investments and the closing down of operations. However, since corporations in many sectors may nevertheless be quite large relative to the domestic market in a number of countries, the most efficient way to bring about effective competition may often be to expose firms to international competition. In this sense, a continuation of international economic integration of markets can therefore be a crucial factor in retaining competition and decentralized decision-making in our economies.

Second, in order to save competition and a reasonably well-functioning market system, it is also important to restrict the detailed and highly selective government intervention that seriously hurts the efficiency of markets —such as extensive selective subsidies, capital grants, price regulations, import controls, licensing, and rationing systems. Otherwise more and more centralized administrative planning has to be introduced. Such a rescue of markets and competition can, in principle, be achieved if the necessary interventions are designed mainly to influence the general condition of various economic activities, rather than to regulate the activities of individual firms and households—that is, if governments "plan" the general environment of firms rather than the activities of the firms themselves. More specifically, if governments redesigned the economic incentives for firms and households by way of indirect taxes and subsidies, instead of trying to regulate against socially undesirable pursuit of self-interest, we could avoid a multiplication of detailed public regulations controlling the behavior of firms and households. Obvious and well-known examples of taxes that involve incentives to socially desirable actions are effluent charges on pollutions, instead of trying only to intervene by rules and regulations in the production technology chosen by firms; penalties (such as high insurance premiums) for firms with a high rate of injuries to their employees; fees for the use of scarce infrastructure, such as street space used by cars; subsidies for the employment of handicapped people; and so on. The suggestion above to break up the very largest corporations and capital funds would perhaps also help, to some extent, to reduce the temptation for politicians to intervene in the production, investment, and pricing operations of individual firms.

An important prerequisite for limiting government intervention in individual firms is that stabilization policy—the attempt to avoid inflation and unemployment—should be pursued more skillfully than was done during the last decade. Otherwise the demands for permanent price and wage

20

regulations will presumably increase; and if such demands are granted, the chance for a decentralized market system to survive will be drastically reduced.

A policy along the lines suggested here would, of course, be facilitated if firms would limit their habits of asking governments for grants, subsidies, and guarantees of various types. It would also help if they started voluntarily to improve their adherence to generally accepted moral codes, for instance concerning product standards, environmental considerations, and honesty in general. Moreover, the survival of a decentralized market system would be considerably enhanced if labor unions would be more willing to accept reasonably high profits and if intellectuals in general realized that the pluralistic society which they enjoy, perhaps more than other groups, is largely based on the system of decentralized markets and competition which many of them despise.

Third, the freedom of individuals and firms to act—such as the freedom to take new initiatives, including the entry of firms—depends crucially on the existence of a decentralized structure of ownership and control of financial and physical capital. In other words, a well-functioning, decentralized capital market, with many independent owners and suppliers and managers of capital, is an important foundation for a pluralistic society. This means that tendencies toward concentration of ownership and supply of capital—whether private or public—have to be stopped and reversed if the prospects for pluralism are going to brighten.

Fourth, it is important also that various types of other institutions—labor unions, cooperatives, media for information and debate, cultural and political organizations, universities, and research institutes—have a free and independent position vis-a-vis the state. This again is facilitated by a decentralized ownership structure for financial capital and a general and decentralized system of public financial support for culture, education, and research.

Fifth, a broader base for recruiting managers of the large production firms and the large capital funds—banks, pension funds, insurance companies, trust funds, investment companies, and the like—would make the economic powers of large institutional holders of capital assets more consistent with the principles of democracy and pluralism. It might also release and utilize competence among individuals who are today under-utilized in the economic system.

21

Sixth, more decentralization within firms and other organizations—what is often called "employee participation"—would help to create more pluralism inside various organizations.

Seventh, a more even distribution of income and wealth among households would make the market system—in particular profit-making—more socially acceptable. It would also contribute directly to creating and keeping a decentralized capital market. In fact, by vigorous attempts to redistribute income and wealth, pluralism could be substantially increased. In the case of the distribution of factor incomes, the most promising methods are probably a more even distribution of investment in human capital—via education, on-the-job training, and health care—and an expansion of training leading to high-income jobs. In the case of the distribution of disposable income, taxes, transfers, and public consumption programs also seem to be potentially effective devices, if properly implemented.

It is quite possible that a broadly based, decentralized participation of employees and other socioeconomic groups in the ownership and administration of capital is a necessary (political) condition for preserving an efficient, decentralized, and pluralistic society. For instance, it may be necessary in order to guarantee a level of profit high enough to make individual firms independent of government protection, subsidies, and capital funds. These arguments assume, of course, that reforms in these fields will be designed in such a way that new types of concentration of ownership and management of capital are not created—for instance, through rather centralized collective ownership by the public sector, the labor unions, or both of these. A large number of independent capital funds in competition with each other in an open capital market—"fund pluralism"—combined with personal owner-interest in these funds by individual employees may be a useful device for achieving such a guarantee. Relative to present conditions, such reforms should in fact increase the pluralistic character of our societies.

Finally, a conceivable additional answer to the problems discussed here may, of course, be a somewhat less ambitious policy. There is a risk that the attempt to create a "perfect society" will in fact give rise to a society that is not only more interventionist and bureaucratic but also more authoritarian. More tolerance of minor imperfections in our society, and of minor abuses by individuals and firms, would help to limit the proliferation of detailed government intervention. It would also mean that governments could concentrate their scarce political and administrative resources on problems that citizens really regard as of major importance—and that not even the most efficient market system can be expected to solve—rather than being bogged down into thousands, or even millions, of minor activities, many of whose effects on the welfare of the citizens are short-term and even dubious. Obvious examples of such major problems are, of course, attempts to remove poverty and to create better employment opportunities among handicapped citizens, to improve the urban and natural environment, to achieve better macroeconomic stability, and to improve the quality of the supply of collective goods. Bargaining and deals between private firms and public officials could then be limited to areas where public and private activities are highly complementary, such as those in connection with the public infrastructure: transportation, energy, and urban development.

One reason why this concentration of public programs is important is that there is an obvious possibility that the quantity of public intervention and programs is an enemy to the quality of the operations. Thus, policies in socially crucial fields could be pushed much more vigorously and successfully if the authorities reduced the number and ambitiousness of their attempts, and also made them less detailed. In other words, those of us who favor vigorous government activities in these social fields—and I belong to this group—should be the first to ask for cutbacks in government intervention in thousands of other fields, since such intervention wastes scarce administrative talents and frustrates the general public.

If recommendations of this rather utopian type were followed, it would perhaps be possible to stop the tendencies toward reduced autonomy not only of firms but also of individuals (households)—and then also to rescue a pluralistic society. Otherwise I am afraid this task will be quite difficult even if the system of political democracy as such may survive, in the sense that majority rule and free voting are preserved. The freedom of individuals—to speak, act, and "do their own thing"—requires not only political democracy but also a pluralistic economic system, based on a decentralized and reasonably competitive market economy and a system of fragmented ownership and administration of capital. Whereas many of the western societies of the nineteenth century were rather· pluralistic without being democratic, there is a risk that those in the future will be nonpluralistic democracies—unless the trends discussed in this paper can be broken. In

23

most countries of the western world today, I think, it is not political democracy that is threatened, but rather pluralism.[4]

---

[4] The most celebrated, and probably also the most criticized, exposition in which ever-increasing public interventions in the economy are asserted to undermine individual freedom is probably Friedrich Hayek's book, *The Road to Serfdom,* published at the end of World War II.

Some of the main differences between my exposition in this lecture and Hayek's discussion may be the following: 1. Whereas Hayek saw a basic threat to political democracy, I see mainly a threat to pluralism. 2. I am much more positive than Hayek about the motives behind government intervention, mainly in such fields as employment, environmental protection, and income and wealth distribution. 3. I am much more aware than Hayek of various "market failures." 4. I stress more the possibilities of reducing the risks connected with government intervention if governments choose more "market-conforming" methods of intervention (such as taxes, transfers, and subsidies) rather than direct controls (on outputs, inputs, production techniques, prices, and wages). 5. Contrary to Hayek, I suggest some new government intervention in the economic system in order to achieve more decentralization, competition, and pluralism—the breaking up of the very large capital funds and corporations, actions to equalize the distribution of income and wealth, and the creation of decentralized forms of employee participation in the ownership and management of firms. 6. I also believe that Hayek overstated some of his points.

24

[12]

Public Finance for Developing Countries

Assar Lindbeck

FROM PLANNING PARADIGM TO MARKET PARADIGM

Opinions on the appropriate role of government policy, including budget policy, in developing countries have to be based on some *vision* of what the basic mechanisms of the development process are. The specification of such a vision is crucial also for the choice of analytical techniques when studying developing countries. This is why this chapter puts budget policy, or public finance, into the broad perspective of the development process. This also makes it natural to see budget policy as a complement and/or substitute for other types of policy.

The dominant vision of the development process during the 1940s, 1950s, and early 1960s was that the market failures in less developed countries were so huge that the market mechanism could not be much relied on in such countries. This view was certainly characteristic of economists such as Gunnar Myrdal, Ragnar Nurkse, Raul Prebisch, Paul Rosenstein-Rodan, and Hans Singer, even though their emphases on specific aspects of asserted market failures differed strongly.

Various forms of "structuralism" were also popular. Developing countries were asserted to be characterized by pronounced "structural inflexibility" in the allocation of resources; in other words, low (or even zero) elasticities and long time-lags with respect to the economic incentives of the supply and demand for goods, services, and factors of production,

I am grateful for useful comments on an earlier draft from Jorgen Appel gren, Jagdish Bhagwati, Arne Bigsten, Lawrence Krause, Anne O. Krueger, Deepak Lal, Sven-Olof Lodin, Mats Lundahl, and Amartya Sen. Karl Gustav Hansson and Reza Firuzabadi have assisted with statistical computation.

102

and, indeed, of productive effort and entrepreneurship in general, were thought to exist.[1] Also based on such structuralist views of the economies of developing countries was the idea of binding saving or balance-of-payments constraints on economic growth owing to asserted weaknesses in the response of saving and investment to changes in income and interest rates, as well as of exports, imports, and long-term capital movements to changes in exchange rates, the terms of trade, and the rates of return on assets. A special variant was the "two gap" theory of savings and balance-of-payments constraints, asserting strict limits on the raising of taxes by the national government and difficulties in turning domestic saving into capital formation via the exchange of traditional export products for capital goods on international markets owing to inelastic world demand for the former (Chenery 1965, 1979).

From views like these—which were far from uniform—followed both a strong distrust of the price mechanism and, as a mirror image, considerable enthusiasm for government regulation (such as licensing systems), as well as economywide central planning of inputs, outputs, exports, imports, and investment activity. Moreover, as the manufacturing sector, in contrast to agriculture, was often asserted to be characterized by constant or even increasing returns to scale, a high propensity to save, and rapid technological progress, government-enforced industrialization at the expense of agriculture and handicraft production was usually strongly advocated. Without drastic government actions in these fields, developing countries were asserted to be doomed to "underdevelopment equilibrium traps" or "vicious circles of poverty." Also popular was the notion that the entire manufacturing sector could be treated as an "infant industry," though this notion is difficult to distinguish from general political and ideological *preferences* for industrialization as the essence of economic and social "modernization."

The recommended, and indeed often also the actual, role of *public finance* during the first decades after World War II should be seen in this perspective: (1) as helping provide an industrial base by way of heavy public investment in both physical infrastructure and manufacturing, often in the form of large-scale government projects; (2) as squeezing private consumption by increasing the aggregate saving ratio by way of

---

1. *Structuralism*, as the term is used here, is thus something quite different from the idea that the initial structures of these countries, such as the proportions between various sectors and the existence of various disequilibria among factor rewards in different sectors, are important features to recognize in a realistic analysis of both the existing state and the development prospects of such countries.

taxes, in particular on traditional exports and on the large agricultural population (though in reality agriculture was perhaps squeezed more by overvalued exchange rates and regulated output prices than by explicit land or agricultural taxes); and (3) as directing the allocation of economic resources in general by means of government enterprises, subsidies, government credits, taxes, and tariffs (import-substitution policy)—as a complement to "command," which was to be implemented by physical regulations of various types.

These ambitions made the government budget a main tool of aggregate and disaggregate "national economic planning" for the mobilization and allocation of resources—a point emphasized, for instance, by A. Waterston (1965). While attempts to direct the economy by way of taxes, tariffs, and subsidies must have been based on the idea that private agents *do* react to economic incentives—though unguided markets were asserted to give the "wrong" incentives—the recommendations for reliance on public enterprises and on command of private firms by way of physical regulations were more consistent with a structuralist view of the world (in other words, weak responses of private agents to economic incentives).

It may be argued that the policy recommendation to raise the aggregate saving and investment ratio was the most valuable feature of the predominant development paradigm during the first few decades after World War II, and that the drastic increase in saving and investment ratios to some 20–25 percent of GNP in most developing countries was the most important achievement of actual development policies. Developing countries have usually been much less successful in increasing economic efficiency, and hence in speeding up the rate of productivity growth. For instance, while output in manufacturing in developing market economies increased by 5.1 percent per year during 1960–83, the accompanying increase in labor input was as high as 3.5 percent, which implies that the increase in labor productivity was only about 1.6 percent (calculations of time trends based on data in United Nations 1983).

By itself, a strong increase in labor input is, of course, favorable from the point of view of mitigating unemployment, or "underemployment," but output growth, and hence labor-productivity growth, has certainly been much weaker than would have been possible in reasonably efficiently functioning economic systems. Indeed, even if very labor-intensive methods of production are used, labor productivity should be able to grow by several percentage points per year "simply" by the introduction of better technologies and organization, as illustrated by the experience of developed countries, and indeed also of some developing countries. Many developing countries have simply been getting too small an increase in labor productivity from their investment. We also notice extremely high marginal capital/output ratios in many developing countries, such as in Africa and Latin America.[2]

It has in fact become obvious that vastly different rates of growth of GNP, and perhaps in particular of consumption, can be achieved with about the same rates of capital accumulation depending inter alia on the allocative efficiency of investment and production. For instance, reference is often made to the success of a number of countries in Pacific Asia (Taiwan, South Korea, Singapore, Hong Kong) that have relied to a considerable extent on economic incentives and an outward-looking development strategy—though active and competent governments in these countries have certainly also stimulated growth and economic efficiency by way of institutional reforms, redistributions of assets and infrastructural investment. To some extent, these countries have been engaged in growth forecasting ("indicative planning"), and, in varying degrees, operate state-owned firms, but it is difficult to have a definite opinion about the role of these features, which they share with many other, less successful nations. What has clearly differentiated these countries from many others is that governments have tried to *support* rather than restrict the activities and initiatives of the private sector.

It is for these various reasons natural that the emphasis in analytical discussions of economic policy in developing countries has gradually shifted to issues relating to the allocation, and not just the total volume, of investment, and indeed to *the allocative efficiency in general of production activities.* This is probably an important explanation for the increased respect for decentralized decision making by way of markets, price signals, and economic incentives, and, as a mirror image, an increased skepticism about the usefulness of direct government regulation and central planning.

2. These observations do not, of course, mean that when countries strive for better allocation of investment this will have to occur at the expense of the aggregate volume of saving and investment. There is not necessarily a conflict between high and efficiently allocated saving, as witnessed by, for instance, Japan. Indeed, several countries that have experienced particularly poor economic performance have been unsuccessful with both the volume and the allocative efficiency of saving—obvious examples being countries like Bangladesh, Chad, Ghana, Mali, Sudan, and Upper Volta, with gross saving rates in the neighborhood of zero or even with negative rates; see World Bank, 1985.

More generally, it has become increasingly understood during the past few decades that, contrary to previous assertions, both the aggregate and the "fine" (disaggregate) micro structure of the economies of developing countries respond quite strongly to economic reward, including profitability prospects and relative prices and wages—if governments allow such a response.[3] This is perhaps what we should expect, as poor people have no less reason to respond to the opportunities for improving their economic situation than do more affluent people, perhaps rather the reverse.

Moreover, after having brought about large infrastructural investments, and in some cases a considerable mobilization of resources, it is natural that problems of economic efficiency, and hence resource allocation, become more interesting. It has also become clearer over time that the potentialities of import substitution in manufacturing are rapidly exhausted in most countries owing to the smallness of domestic markets. It would also seem that the attractiveness of the Soviet planning model subsided when it became more widely understood that this was more of a "mobilization model" than a prescription for economic efficiency— indeed, that the model stimulated inefficiency.

When relying on markets, governments must, of course, help ensure that the market signals are "right," in the sense that prices reflect opportunity costs and preferences. However, it is also crucial that the price signals "work," in the sense that various institutional "filters" in society do not distort, or even "abort," the information and incentive content of market signals. Thus there is a potentially important role for the government both as regards improvement of the information and incentive structure and helping strengthen (and perhaps, at an early stage of economic development, even helping create) market-oriented institutions.

In broad terms, the main contribution of *public finance* to the economic development of market-oriented developing countries would then probably be (1) to provide infrastructure and public goods; (2) to help relative prices reflect opportunity costs and preferences, which is

3. Jacob Viner (1952), Gottfrid Haberler (1959), Theodore Schultz (1964), and Peter Bauer (1971) were pioneers in making these points, and early support for outward-looking strategies was provided by Hla Myint (1967). J. N. Bhagwati (1966) was also early in noting the potential importance for economic development of a relative price structure that is conducive to allocative efficiency. Similar views have more recently been reflected in, for instance, Little 1982 and Lal 1983, where liberal references are provided to research into the role of relative prices and economic incentives. However, the "watershed" book, symbolizing a shift among economists in general away from a regulation-and-planning paradigm to a market paradigm emphasizing outward-looking strategies, is probably Little, Scitovsky, and Scott 1970.

often more a question of avoiding and removing distortions previously introduced by the government itself than of fighting "spontaneous" market distortions; (3) to contribute to the redistribution of income and wealth (according to certain values concerning equity) by methods that are as market-conforming as possible; and (4) to contribute to the development of market-oriented institutions that respond satisfactorily to market signals, for instance, in the fields of finance, trade, labor markets, consulting, and the transfer of technology. However, it is also important to emphasize the crucial role of (5) macroeconomic stabilization policy, as failures in that field have often been extremely damaging to attempts to liberalize the economies of developing countries.

If governments start to rely more on markets for the supply of ordinary goods, the public sector can increasingly concentrate on those activities, mentioned above, that only the government can pursue, or where government at least has a comparative advantage relative to private agents. The administrative resources that are then released in the public sector can instead be used to improve the quality of the public sector's remaining functions, to the extent that such resources are not simply transferred to the private sector. This is an important consequence of the shift of a developing country to a more market-oriented system, as the majority of these countries are characterized by a shortage of competent civil servants. Administrative "overload," which has recently been much discussed in developed countries, is an even more characteristic feature of most developing countries—a problem that could be mitigated by a shift to a more market-oriented system. Indeed, managers of firms would then also be able to devote more time to "ordinary" business, rather than bargaining with government officials, or "rent seeking" (Krueger 1974), whereas today the latter often yields higher returns than do attempts to improve efficiency within firms. A removal of regulations could change that.

More generally, in market-oriented economies, the role of government planning and public finance is largely to "plan" the physical and psychological *environment* of private agents rather than to plan what those agents are supposed to do.

METHOD OF ANALYSIS

On the basis of the dominating view in the early post–World War II period that private agents in developing countries react (if at all!) completely differently to economic incentives than do agents in developed countries, and that markets in developing countries will not be able to function properly in the foreseeable future, there followed a profound skepticism about traditional methods of economic analysis. Developing countries were often asserted to be "different kinds" of economies, requiring both new tools of analysis and different behavior assumptions; indeed "development economics" was often asserted to represent a *new and separate branch of economic analysis.* By contrast, this chapter is based on the assumption that there are great enough similarities between behavior patterns and economic mechanisms in general in developed and developing countries to make standard economic analysis relevant for the latter type of country as well.

It is indeed quite easy to illustrate the relevance of standard economic analysis for developing countries. For instance, in a similar way as in developed countries, "overvalued" currencies, by keeping down profitability, tend to reduce output and employment growth in the tradable sectors, which often also results in (increased) budget deficits owing to the negative consequences for the tax base.[4] Moreover, it is well established by now, not only for developed but also for developing countries, that high real wage rates, in particular when combined with low real interest rates, tend to favor capital-intensive methods of production. Regulated wage rates tend to accentuate unemployment for certain types of labor (for instance where minimum wage rates are binding), while for other types of labor more or less permanent vacancies tend to prevail. Pegged interest rates create credit shortages, with "arbitrary" credit rationing and an inefficient allocation of credit and capital as a result. High tariffs and large subsidies to specific sectors tend to expand these sectors at the expense of others, in particular sectors for which government regulations have kept down prices, such as agriculture. Rent control hits house building, creates housing shortages, and results in a deterioration of the housing stock as well as a reduction in labor mobility.

We also note that, as in developed countries, regulations breed new regulations, as politicians and public administrators try to fight the unintended, and, for them, often unexpected, side effects of previous regulations. And, probably even more than in developed countries, regulation is "the mother of corruption," as corruption presupposes that politicians and administrators have "something to sell"—such as licenses, tax concessions, tariffs, or subsidies. Indeed, there is most likely

---

4. There may, of course, also be causation in the other direction—from budget deficits to cost increases that result in overvalued currencies (in fixed-exchange-rate regimes).

also a "reverse causation": corrupt politicians and public administrators have a strong self-interest in promoting regulations.

Moreover, the possibilities of substitution between labor and capital, and indeed between inputs in general, have come to be regarded as much more promising than they were earlier thought to be—a development that in economic theory is symbolized by the replacement of the rigid Harrod-Domar growth equation with more flexible aggregate growth models à la Solow and (in more detailed and quantified form) Denison. Such possibilities of substituting labor for capital in developing countries have proved to be particularly promising in multiple-shift operations and in ancillary services, such as maintenance, and handling of material and other transport services, such as packing (Morawetz 1976; White 1978).

My conclusion is that it is quite appropriate to regard "development economics" as an application of the standard tools of economic analysis (whether at micro- or macroeconomic levels) to long-term growth and development issues for *all* types of countries, in the same way as trade theory is the application of micro- and general equilibrium theories to issues of international trade regardless of what types of countries are studied. In particular, the traditional microeconomic theories regarding prices, markets, and incentives are probably no less useful for the analysis of developing countries than for that of developed countries. This also means that the entire arsenal of tools and insights from applied fields of economic analysis such as industrial organization, money and banking, labor economics, and, as illustrated by this chapter, public finance, can be put into operation in analyses of developing countries and not just of developed ones.

Of course, it is important to take into account various institutional peculiarities in the analyses, though by treating institutions not as insurmountable obstacles to development, which was typical for early postwar development theories, but rather as the "filters" through which incentives, as well as commands, necessarily have to pass. However, that cannot be done by assuming some kind of "standard" developing country institutional setup. Owing to the wide variations in institutional conditions among developing countries—heuristically speaking, with stronger variations than among developed countries—the institutional conditions have to be specified separately for each country.

The main contribution of the earlier evolution of economic analysis for less developed countries as a specific field of economics is then mainly that it has increased awareness of the importance in economic analysis (of both developed and developing countries) of watching out for various institutional peculiarities and the changes in these over time.

However, when discovering "institutional peculiarities," which sometimes makes markets look unfamiliar, it is important to realize that what in the light of traditional models may (superficially) appear as a "market distortion" may in fact be a simple reflection of costs that are not apparent when examining only conventionally defined production costs. It is, for instance, well known that price differences between apparently similar goods, services, or factors may reflect differences in risk, information costs, or "interlocking" markets (Stiglitz 1985).

Concern for the interaction between incentives and institutional conditions is important also in the field of politics and public administration, and not just in markets. Indeed, if it is agreed that differences in government policies are responsible for much of the variation in economic performance among nations, it must be a research topic of the uppermost priority to try to establish which institutional circumstances are conducive to various types of policies. More specifically, policy recommendations that do not rely on a realistic assessment of the functioning of the political systems and of the administrative capabilities of the countries concerned often do more harm than good. In particular, policy advice that is based on the assumption that governments and public administrators behave like well-informed, competent, and highly "benevolent guardians of the public good," maximizing some asserted social welfare function, are bound to lead to disappointing results. Indeed, it may be argued that a policy advisor should base his advice on a hypothesis about the *effects* of his advice on the actual policies (Lindbeck 1973).

Against this background it is important to include in the analysis not only traditional concepts of static efficiency and Pareto optimality, but also broader ideas about the functioning of the economic and political system, such as J. M. Clark's vision of competition as a dynamic process ("workable competition"); Joseph Schumpeter's idea of competition as "creative destruction" (when new kinds of competition, technologies, and products threaten existing ones); Friedrich von Hayek's view of competition as a decentralized search for ways of using existing knowledge more efficiently; Harvey Leibenstein's vision of X-efficiency, reflecting other types of economic efficiency than traditional allocative efficiency; and Herbert Simon's theory of "satisfying behavior," "bounded rationality," and endogenous changes in the aspiration levels of agents.

For instance, rather than taking the production function as given, it is important to analyze the process by which the production function is chosen or developed, not only via research and investment in physical and human capital, but also through organizational modification, innovation, and entrepreneurship. And when analyzing economic policy it is necessary to regard political and administrative decision making as an endogenous process with its own patterns of behavior, as suggested by the Public Choice School (Buchanan and Tullock 1962) and others. The latter point also emphasizes the importance of studying constitutional rules and political culture, including not only the distinction between democracies and authoritarian regimes, but also the rules of election, the degree of political centralization, the character of party competition, and the use of referenda (Lindbeck 1985). Moreover, Amartya Sen (1981) has argued that the existence of a free press and an active political opposition has helped prevent crop failures from resulting in starvation for various population groups.

In other words, analyses of the development process and appropriate government policies, including budget policies, have to include much broader, though often less rigorous, aspects than those on which formalized general equilibrium theory and optimization analysis are built. Institutional conditions and institutional change, the political and administrative processes, and the environment for human creativity and entrepreneurship are factors that seem to have played too small a role in economic analysis of both developed and developing countries.

This methodological point also implies that it is important that the genuine complexity and diversity of the development process are taken into consideration, and that evaluations of the performance of both markets and governments are made against much less ambitious benchmarks than perfect competition, perfect information, Pareto efficiency, and the maximization of social welfare functions. That we shall do below.

GOVERNMENT EXPENDITURES

If a country starts to rely more heavily on markets, economic incentives, and decentralized private initiatives, the "classical" roles of government spending for the allocation of resources come to the forefront: (1) *infrastructural investment* in physical and human capital, including the supply of goods that are produced with particularly high fixed costs relative to the variable costs, such as harbors, bridges, and some other transportation systems; and (2) the supply of *public (collective) goods*—including the legal system, education, basic research, and environmental protection. Moreover, as poor people in developing countries cannot be much helped by tax reductions, government expenditure policies become crucial also in (3) *redistributional policies*.

Infrastructural expenditures hardly need advertisement today. However, as the low productivity level in developing countries derives to a considerable extent from the lack of human capital, it may nevertheless be worth advertising infrastructural investment in the form of the accumulation of *human resources in a wide sense of the term*—including not only education, but also health, sanitation, and, in many countries, food supply to particularly poor sections of the population.

As it has been increasingly recognized that the social rates of return in most developing countries are higher for primary education and vocational training than for most forms of higher theoretical education (Psachropoulous 1981), a change in the composition of public spending on education in favor of the former seems to make sense for many developing countries. It is also important that public policies in the field of education and training recognize the need to build up competence that is relevant at the *microeconomic* level in society (for example, and in particular, within individual firms). This would probably be greatly facilitated if firms, rather than government institutions, were largely in charge of vocational training programs, so as to make them practically applicable and strongly market-oriented—the latter being particularly important in economies that follow a market-oriented strategy of economic development. However, as firms have suboptimal incentives to provide general training, owing to the mobility of labor between firms, it is natural to recommend combinations of general schooling provided by public institutions and specific training within firms, though the latter, too, could be at least partly tax-financed. Modified to fit the specific conditions in the countries concerned, the apprenticeship system in West Germany may be a model worth following.

It is also conceivable that the import and domestic dispersion of technology could be stimulated by government initiatives, even if the actual import is certainly best done by individual firms. For instance, government initiatives to help establish private import and service firms in the field of technology may be worth pursuing for a while in the least developed countries.

In many fields of technology it would certainly be useful if research could take place in the countries of the Third World themselves—though in many cases in cooperation with institutions and individuals in developed countries. The rationale is to increase the probability that the research will be relevant for the developing countries. Such activities could also perhaps, at least for a while, be stimulated by government initiatives. Obvious examples of such fields are aspects of agriculture and health care, such as tropical agriculture, soil analysis, integrated development in arid areas, aquaculture, and tropical medicine. As the results of research and development in these fields are characteristically public goods owing to the smallness of the firms and the externalities in the ecological systems, government spending programs have a particularly important role to play here. For instance, the experiences of agricultural extension services, financed by the government, often seem to have been rather good. Indeed, the atomistic structure of the agricultural sector makes it important that governments take initiatives to help establish such services in precisely this sector.

Beside basic general skills and technological competence, one of the most important bottlenecks in the area of human resources in developing countries is *managerial skills*—in the private as well as in the public sector. The role of managerial skill is not only an issue of the competence of managers at the top of organizations. Particular attention must probably be focused on middle-level management, supervisory staff, and people providing specialist services at the middle level—for example, procurement and inventory management; production management; control research; marketing; advertising; tool room service; raw material and product testing; machine assembly; equipment maintenance; staff recruitment; and project development. Government initiatives to stimulate training in such fields are clearly a promising type of government investment in developing countries.

Whereas the various types of training mentioned above are relevant for all types of developing countries, the buildup of *entrepreneurial capabilities* is particularly important in liberalizing developing countries. Experience from many countries over long historical periods illustrates the enormous role of entrepreneurship in the development process, not least in small and medium-sized firms and newly started firms. Because of the difficulties involved in formalizing and quantifying the role and importance of entrepreneurship, it easily "disappears," not only in economic theory, but also in domestic development plans and political and administrative discussion, which has often concentrated on existing firms and large firms. However, all developing countries that opt for industrialization and modernization along market-oriented lines are strongly urged to facilitate the emergence of vital entrepreneurship not only by way of formal education in business, but also, and in particular, *by allowing and stimulating entrepreneurial initiative*. Indeed, in addition to land, capital, and labor, it is reasonable to regard entrepreneurship as a fourth factor of production of crucial importance for economic development—a factor the government may promote by stimulating the buildup of facilities for the training of entrepreneurs and by deregulation, which tends to release entrepreneurial skills.

So much for the "creation" part of Schumpeter's vision of "creative destruction." It is, of course, also important that politicians allow the "destructive" part of the process to operate by avoiding subsidizing contracting or even "dying" sectors, firms, and production processes, even though the "demand" for such protection is certainly one of the most powerful forces in the political process in most countries. An important "constitutional" issue is then what types of political decision-making rules are conducive to preventing more subsidization than the electorate, and a majority of politicians, *on reflection* would like.

The stimulation of entrepreneurship is also an issue of the political and social attitudes in society toward entrepreneurial activities. Indeed, the attitudes in society toward entrepreneurship may be regarded as an important collective good in a private enterprise economy.

In the context of government expenditure policies, it is often also important to look over the rules, incentives, and practices of the management of publicly owned firms and agencies, which play an important role in many developing countries. Indeed, if governments of developing countries are serious about the shift to a more market-oriented system, it is important that this shift incorporate state-owned enterprises too, in the sense that these are either handed over to the private sector or given the same incentives and freedom of action as private business—and that they also feel the same need as private firms, by way of competitive pressure, to react to market signals. The withdrawal of "automatic" government financing of losses of government-owned firms is crucial from that point of view.

This chapter is not designed to deal with issues related to specific production sectors. However, it is nowadays well understood that the modernization and industrialization process is easily damaged, or may even fail completely, if *agriculture* is neglected, which may also have serious consequences for the distribution of income. "Negative" illustrations of this thesis are provided by several South American and especially African countries, while positive examples are found in several countries in Pacific Asia—countries that have also been strikingly successful in manufacturing.

Widespread experiences suggest, for instance, that government marketing boards in agriculture tend to destroy incentives. Such boards usually do not have either the competence or the incentives to create a level and structure of producers' prices that is even remotely rational for economic efficiency. Moreover, they tend to direct the rents from agriculture to inefficient and highly protected manufacturing firms by way of import-substitution policies. Thus, as a way of improving the production incentives for farmers, it is, as a rule, useful to abolish government marketing boards in agriculture. This would also contribute to the allocation of the rents and profits of agricultural production via market mechanisms rather than by bureaucratic fiat and government subsidies.

Favorable production opportunities in agriculture are important also for achieving a geographically dispersed income growth in society— among both regions and population groups. Obvious policies to promote this, besides a reasonably conducive price policy toward agriculture, are a decentralized public infrastructure and regionally dispersed public services in rural areas in general. Of course, this is something that is important regardless of whether the economy is liberalized or not. However, as decentralization of decision making may in some cases accentuate regional income differences, at least for a while, there is a case for conscious government attempts to speed up the process by which higher income in the national economy as a whole raises incomes in regions that lag behind.

This raises the general problem of poverty and income distribution. Considering the enormous misery among a minority at the bottom of the income distribution, humanitarian values should certainly make us emphasize redistributive actions in favor of the very poorest members of society, in the same way as redistribution policy in the presently developed countries started with "poor laws" even before the Industrial Revolution. On the expenditure side of the budget, such programs could very well to a considerable extent consist of what has been called a "basic needs strategy" for the purpose of providing basic food, shelter, water, sanitation, health, and education to the very poor, which is perhaps to some extent most effectively done by way of transfers in kind. Indeed, experience suggests that it is possible for a country to achieve substantial improvements in a number of "social indicators" at relatively low levels of per capita income (Balassa 1983), examples being life expectancy, infant mortality, and child death rates.

Thus there is evidence of the usefulness of "direct" attempts to satisfy some "basic needs" in nutrition and health, even at low levels of per capita income. A "basic needs approach" is therefore quite compatible with a growth-oriented approach based on economic incentives, provided that neither is pushed to the extreme. Indeed, a great number of studies indicate that increased spending on health, nutrition, and education—up to certain levels—may give considerable boosts to productivity growth (Balassa 1983).

So far, it has been typical for developing countries to provide income support via indirect subsidies of commodities rather than via direct transfers. One reason has certainly been administrative feasibility. However, another reason has simply been that strong pressure groups in the urban centers have "demanded" low food and housing prices, which has not only reduced production incentives in agriculture and housing but has often also assisted people with income levels considerably above those of the rural poor.

Sooner or later, when the "modern sector" starts to dominate the national economy, we would expect the same types of demands for social security systems for a broad section of the population as in developed countries. This is, again, not something which is confined to market-oriented systems. But market-oriented systems are certainly often blamed for creating inequalities and insecurities. Thus, in order to maintain their legitimacy among broad sections of the population, such systems need not only to pursue redistributions to the very poor, but also to provide social security systems for the population as a whole, though powerful urban pressure groups may benefit the most from such systems.

Indeed, while social security spending is only about 1.2 percent of GNP in low-income developing countries (with per capita income below $400 in 1983 prices), the figure is as high as 6.6 percent in upper-middle income countries (per capita incomes above $1,600); see figure 3.1. (Other categories of public spending do not differ much between developing countries with different per capita incomes.[5])

Eventually, of course, public spending programs may raise the same type of welfare state incentive problems that are intensively discussed today in most developed countries. Indeed, there may be a risk of the creation of "premature welfare states," in the sense that the economic

5. These statistics, covering "central government," are compiled from World Bank 1986, table 22, and International Monetary Fund 1985. A study by Tanzi (1986) indicates that total tax revenues of all levels of government, i.e., "general government," in developing countries are only slightly (one or two percentage points) higher than the figures for tax revenues of central government that are reported in fig. 3.2. (The countries are not exactly the same in the two samples, however.) Perhaps we could assume that the difference between general and central government is also on the expenditures side.

foundation for an elaborate system of social security, transfer payments, and redistributions of income among large population groups does not yet exist (Uruguay is often mentioned as an example). "Early" attempts to create elaborate social security systems may not only create severe incentive problems in the private sector; they may also strain the taxation system so much that governments will not be able to provide what they have a comparative advantage in supplying: collective goods and infrastructure facilities. These points lead directly to the problem of taxation.

TAXATION

The level and structure of taxes, subsidies, and tariffs differ so much between various developing countries that generalizations about their taxation problems are difficult. However, the general level of taxation in this group of countries is still usually much lower than that in developed countries—typically 10–25 percent of GDP, as compared to about 30–55 percent in Western Europe, 33 percent in the United States, and 25 percent in Japan. Among eighty-two developing countries for which information is available, the average tax share of GNP seems to have been about 18 percent in the early 1980s (Tanzi 1986), with taxes on goods and services and foreign trade playing a much more important part than in developed countries. (Figure 3.2 provides statistics for "central government" revenues; figures for "general government" are probably, on average, one or two percentage points higher.) Thus disincentive problems for private agents, owing to a *generally* high level of tax rates, cannot possibly be a serious problem in most developing countries. However, these figures underestimate the "tax bite" for those sectors that actually pay the bulk of the taxes. (For instance, if we assume, as an extreme case, that agriculture pays no taxes at all, the average tax rate for the rest of the economy would be about 24 percent as compared to 18 percent for the entire economy.)

One dilemma, though, is that a given level of taxes (as a percentage of GDP) may "hurt" people more in a poor than in a rich country by depressing an already very low level of private consumption. However, this is not really a problem of economic disincentives for private agents, but rather an issue concerning the ability, or disability, of the political process to generate a reasonable allocation and distribution of resources between private consumption, public consumption, and investment. However, it is also an issue of the efficiency of the allocation of investment.

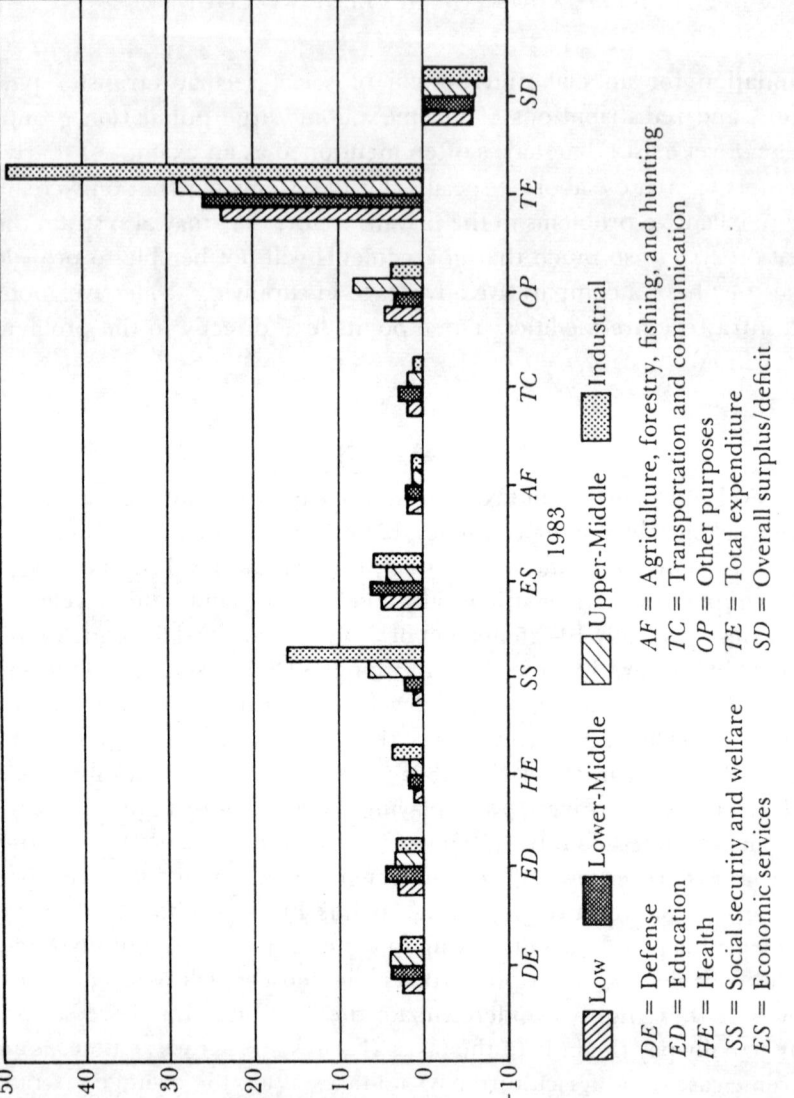

Fig. 3.1 Central Government Expenditure for Low, Lower-Middle, Upper-Middle, and Industrial Economies

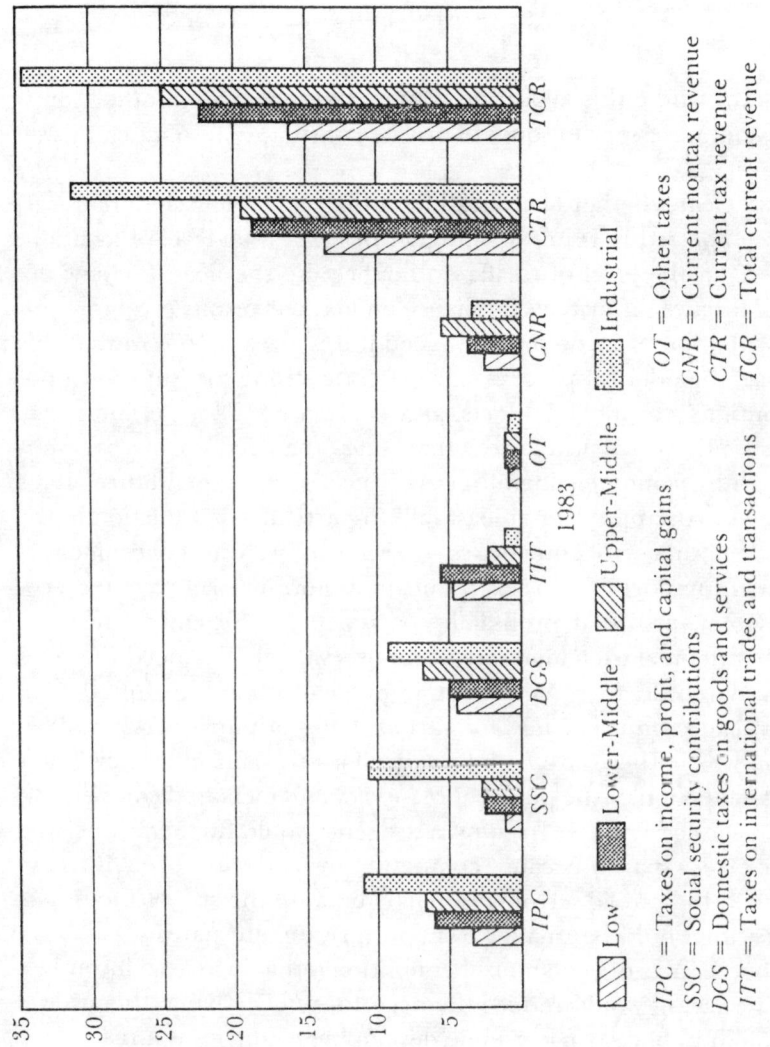

Fig. 3.2. Central Government Current Revenue for Low, Lower-Middle, Upper-Middle, and Industrial Economies

□ Low ▨ Lower-Middle ▨ Upper-Middle ▨ Industrial

IPC = Taxes on income, profit, and capital gains   *OT* = Other taxes
SSC = Social security contributions   *CNR* = Current nontax revenue
DGS = Domestic taxes on goods and services   *CTR* = Current tax revenue
ITT = Taxes on international trades and transactions   *TCR* = Total current revenue

In a country where this allocation is more efficient than in other countries, it is not necessary to squeeze private consumption so much by way of taxes.

It is not clear whether liberalization of the economic system requires, or can be expected to result in, a higher or lower total level of taxation. Reductions in the level of tariffs no doubt raise the need for new tax sources. Moreover, if increased reliance on markets results in a more uneven distribution of income, and indeed if it is already *believed* that this is the case, the political process may generate strong pressure for more redistributions via public budgets, and hence a need for tax increases.

However, there are also factors that *reduce* the need for taxes in connection with economic liberalization, since some expenditure items would tend to disappear, or at least fall. In particular, a reduction in the need for subsidies to enterprises—private as well as government—would be an important part of a shift to a more market-oriented economic system, provided profitability is kept up sufficiently, which requires that the real exchange rate is not overvalued. The need for taxes would also recede to some extent if public authorities shifted to a greater reliance on users' fees for various types of public services, a reform for which there are well-known allocative and efficiency arguments. A reduction of the public bureaucracy and increased competition for public service agencies from private agents would further reduce the need for taxes—partly because competition would most likely increase efficiency in the public sector, and partly because the size of the public service sector would be smaller owing to private alternatives.

Another feature of economic liberalization is that increased incentives for private saving would reduce the need for public saving, though the recent fall in public saving in some developing countries is a reason for not advising the authorities to make substantial tax reductions on this ground.

However, even though the level of taxes in most developing countries cannot be regarded as excessive, or "harmful," the *structure* of taxes, subsidies, and tariffs is certainly already a serious problem. It is hardly necessary to say that high and strongly selective tariffs and taxes on foreign trade—*export discrimination policies*—often result in suboptimal foreign trade, and hence in an underutilization of the gains from the international division of labor. Indeed, it is today quite well established that such policies, often designed to promote "import substitution," when pursued for long periods (such as several decades), have been highly detrimental to most developing countries that have pursued them.

It is also quite clear that highly selective commodity taxes, as in fact implemented, have often created inefficiencies in the allocation of resources in the private sector, on both the consumption and production side, without always providing advantages in terms of the distribution of income. And in cases where selective taxes and subsidies have actually improved the distribution of income (on the basis of certain values), the same improvements could perhaps in many cases have been achieved by a structure of taxes and subsidies with smaller efficiency costs.

Severe distortions may also come out of some other taxes. The provision of accelerated depreciation for investment and subsidies to some investment, in combination with payroll taxes on labor, may contribute to raising the wage/rental ratio—though recent increases in interest rates may have reversed this feature in several countries. Moreover, some developing countries do have quite high statutory *marginal* income tax rates for high-income groups, and sometimes also for middle-high income earners—such as households with two or three times the national average. For instance, according to a study by Sicat and Virmani (1986) referring to the situation in the early eighties of married couples with one earner and a "standard" number of children (three), about half out of fifty developing countries studied had marginal income tax rates above 30 percent for incomes three times the average, and about a third of the countries had marginal income tax rates of at least 40 percent for that (relative) income bracket. (The mean marginal rate was 34 percent for that income bracket, as compared to 19 percent for the middle-income bracket.) If separate statistics had been available for the formal sector in urban areas, we would certainly have found much higher figures. Of course, legal avoidance and illegal evasion mean that many taxpayers do not in fact pay those rates, even remotely. However, the statutory marginal rates are an indicator of the incentives to avoid and evade, which is part of the process by which marginal tax rates distort the allocation of resources and human effort.

Of course, an overhaul of the tax system makes perfectly good sense even without a shift to a more market-oriented system. However, a reform of the price and incentive system is clearly more significant for a pronounced market-oriented system than for a highly regulated and centrally planned system, as the gains of shifting to a more market-oriented system cannot be fully achieved without reforming the price and incentive system in conformity with efficiency criteria. Indeed, this truth has been well illustrated in recent decades by the attempts of socialist countries in Eastern Europe to rely more heavily on markets and economic incentives. Moreover, if capital movements too are liberalized, it is important to adjust capital taxation to levels that make domestic and foreign wealth owners and firms willing to invest enough in the country in question, rather than abroad—and to allow remittances of earnings, as well as providing guarantees of property rights in general. Stability of the domestic currency is, of course, also crucial in this context. Indeed, the problem of "capital flight" in developing countries is to a large extent a "confidence problem" concerning property rights and the value of the domestic money.

What, then, are the most important specific changes to be considered in the tax system when an economy shifts from regulations and central command to increased reliance on markets? Some economists may want to base their policy advice on sophisticated calculations of *optimal* tariffs, taxes, and subsidies. There is no doubt that the literature on optimum taxation has helped us understand the general problems of taxes and subsidies in cases where compromises have to be made between the requirements of tax revenues, on one hand, and the losses of economic efficiency owing to the "excess burden" of positive marginal tax rates on the other. The literature on optimum income taxation has, for example, given precision to the old idea that marginal tax rates should be higher, the smaller the elasticity of effort with respect to rewards is, *ceteris paribus*. And the literature on optimum commodity taxation has formalized old views among economists about how to make a compromise between the allocative efficiency of consumption and concern for the distribution of income. While in the interest of economic efficiency tax rates should be relatively high on goods and services for which the demand and supply elasticities are small, the rates should, for distributional reasons, be high also on goods and services that play a relatively important part in the consumption pattern of groups of households that are supposed to be discriminated against in redistribution policy; these groups are often, of course, high income earners. Taxes should, *ceteris paribus*, also be high on goods and services that for the consumers closely complement untaxed, or indeed untaxable, goods and services, such as leisure. Quite complex formulas have in fact been derived to strike a balance between these different, often conflicting, aspects, using a Social Welfare Function as the criterion for the trade-off (Atkinson and Stiglitz 1980; Stern 1984).

However, there are strong objections to the strategy of using such calculations *as a basis for actual policy advice* in developing as well as in developed countries:

(1) First, formulas of optimum taxation catch only one, or possibly a few, types of mechanisms for adjustment by the individual agents, such as a shift between leisure and work, and/or between the consumption of different commodities. In reality there are, of course, myriads of other adjustment mechanisms for taxes, such as variations in the amount of do-it-yourself work and the intensity of work; adjustment of the level of saving and the composition of portfolios; changes in the level and type of investment in physical and human capital; changes of profession, workplace, or location of residence; emigration across national borders; the use of more time to search for tax loopholes, or even for cheating with taxes. Formulas that would simultaneously reflect all such major adjustment mechanisms, or most of them, are quite simply beyond the range of useful analysis.

(2) Second, even to derive an optimum tax formula that takes into account just *one single* type of adjustment mechanism, such as the choice between leisure and income, or between different consumer goods on the demand side, it is in fact necessary to rely on extremely special assumptions, such as identical preferences of all individuals, and special forms of the production function, such as Cobb-Douglas functions.

(3) Third, all optimum tax formulas, even rather modest ones, require statistical information that is not very reliable. Not only do we need an "arbitrarily" chosen Social Welfare Function, but also information about individual capabilities and preferences specific enough to quantify the sensitivity of the response to contemplated tax rate changes of the various types of adjustments that are supposed to be covered in the study. On most of this we shall never get sufficiently reliable information. This is serious, as the tax rates that are derived from optimum tax formulas are very sensitive to alternative specifications of the various functions and the statistical parameterization.

Indeed, if all the necessary information on individual capabilities and preferences that is required for empirical application of the theory of optimum taxation were available, we would not be too far from the type of knowledge that is necessary to design lump-sum taxes and transfers, and hence avoid the economic distortions that are the reason for choosing an optimum tax approach in the first place! More specifically, in order to design optimum tax systems, we would need information about both individual abilities and preferences, whereas it is simultaneously the difficulty in obtaining information about matters like these that is the basic reason why we are not able to use lump-sum taxes, and hence why there is a case for a second-best solution by way of "optimum taxation."

(4) Applications of the theory of optimum taxation are also confronted with a severe aggregation problem. More specifically, the tax rate that is assigned to a specific product in the context of an optimum tax formula depends crucially on the degree and type of aggregation of commodities. For instance, if furniture is put into the group of durable consumer goods, it gets one tax rate, but if it is put into some other group of goods, it would get a different rate—or even a zero rate or a subsidy. In other words, the tax rate of an individual good will be highly arbitrary depending on which other goods and services it is lumped together with. This means that optimum taxation will to a large extent be "arbitrary taxation." It is in reality also difficult to group the goods in such a way that only consumers' goods are included in the tax base. Many inputs in the production process will in fact also be taxed, which means that distortions of the allocation of resources will arise from the production side as well, without these distortions being considered in the calculation of the optimum tax structure. Attempts to differentiate the tax rates of one and the same type of good when used for direct consumption and when used as an input in the production process are bound to raise severe problems of administration and evasion.

Several of these difficulties with optimum taxation are, of course, well known by the adherents of optimum taxation. But it seems to me that they have not taken these problems seriously enough when ruling out "traditional" principles of uniformity of commodity taxes and tariffs, as well as "comprehensive" income taxation with similar tax rates for all sources of income (for instance, the so-called Haig-Simons principle).

(5) However, there is an even more fundamental objection to using optimum taxation as a basis for policy advice. There is no reason to assume that politicians and public administrators would follow advice that is based on calculations of optimum taxation by the help of some (assumed) Social Welfare Function. Politicians have their own targets and ambitions, which may not bear much relation to the ideas that lie behind calculations by economists of opti-

mum tax or tariff structures. Indeed, this is exactly the background for various attempts in recent years to endogenize the behavior of politicians and public administrators, as well as for suggestions tying the behavior of politicians to various types of "rules." More generally, there is no reason to assume that tax rates that are the outcome of political processes—with conflicts and compromises between various political parties and interest group organizations—would be much correlated to the tax structure that some economists may derive from optimization calculations.

This point about political behavior is important regardless of whether the main ambition of politicians is to satisfy some strong interest group, to increase the probability of being elected, or to adhere to some personal or ideological idiosyncrasy. Politicians and public administrators, with the help of their economic advisors, can always present some reasonable-sounding argument for their particular choice of a differentiated structure of taxes and subsidies—for instance, by referring to aspects that have not been considered in the calculations of the optimum tax specialist, or by exploiting the wide choice of "reasonable" elasticities of the demand and supply responses to taxes. The fact that calculated "optimum rates" for individual goods depend crucially on how goods are aggregated also opens the possibility of various interest groups arguing about the "proper" way of aggregating goods in official statistics.

If optimum tax theory then is not the most appropriate basis for tax policy advice in developing countries (or in developed countries for that matter), what types of considerations should be used instead? The general answer, in my judgment, is that it is better to rely on approaches that are less ambitious and less demanding concerning knowledge about private behavior patterns, statistical information, and administrative competence, but instead more ambitious with respect to basic insights about the functioning of the political process. In other words, it is important to focus on more "pedestrian," practical, and "commonsense" aspects than those emphasized in the optimum tax literature. For instance, the following types of tax reforms are worth considering in a great number of developing countries:

(1) As several developing countries, in particular those in Latin America, often have high and highly variable rates of inflation, an

adjustment of tax assessment and tax collection to inflation is often crucial. Though inflation functions as an implicit "inflation-tax" on the stock of money and government bonds (with less than fully adjusted interest to inflation), inflation often also implies that the government loses "explicit" tax revenues in real terms owing to the timelags in tax collection (the so-called Oliveira-Tanzi effect). Inflation often also erodes the tax base because of the deductibility of *nominal* interest rates, which in an inflationary situation means that part of the amortization of the debt, in real terms, can be deducted from the tax base. If the latter two effects dominate the former, inflation will generate (or accentuate) higher budget deficits (in real terms), which then often feed back into even higher inflation rates. Obvious reforms to solve these problems are to shorten the time lags in tax collection; make inflation adjustments to the tax rates (or tax brackets); and redefine the tax base in order to make a distinction in real terms between (deductible) interest payments and (nondeductible) amortization.

(2) As the tax base is often very narrow in developing countries, the tax rates are often relatively high for certain sectors and groups of taxpayers. For instance, in many developing countries today income taxation is, in fact, mainly a tax on public servants and the employees of large corporations rather than on capital owners or on employers and employees in agriculture or in the "informal" urban sectors. The tax system is also plagued with other types of "asymmetries" with respect to the effective tax rates for different agents and sources of income, and these asymmetries are often accentuated by inflation. These asymmetries could, of course, be mitigated by moving in the direction of a Haig-Simons type "comprehensive" income tax, with uniformity between different sources of incomes, different assets, and different types of income earners. Basically that would mean a broadening of the base and a lowering of the rates—as has recently been tried in some developed countries. The tax system would then most likely be improved in terms both of efficiency and equity (and perhaps even equality), whereas attempts to differentiate based on optimum tax formulas are likely to be exploited by various interest groups. In other words, uniformity, as the basic rule of taxation, is probably less vulnerable to manipulation by powerful interest groups than is the principle of "differentiation" according to optimum tax principles.

(3) As the small degree of household saving that exists in most developing countries largely takes place among the very top income earners, attempts to redistribute income from these groups *on a large scale* are likely to conflict with ambitions to stimulate private saving and to increase the supply of risk capital. This is a reason for being careful about heavy increases in income and wealth taxes for upper-middle and high income groups. Moreover, as corporate saving plays an important part in aggregate saving in some developing countries, and could play an even more important part in the future, there is a strong case also against raising taxes drastically on corporations.

Superficially, it may be argued that tax increases that reduce private saving are not really a problem, as it does not matter if saving is done by private agents or public authorities. However, this argument is seriously flawed for two reasons. First, it neglects imperfections in the political process in the sense that tax increases originally designed to increase public saving often, in fact, release increased public consumption or subsidies of private consumption. Second, public saving is *not* a perfect substitute for private saving in market-oriented economies, as private saving contributes to a decentralization of decisions regarding investment, the entry of new firms, and innovation. To keep down private consumption is not the only purpose of saving; another important role, which it plays in market-oriented economies, is to allow and stimulate the emergence of a system of *decentralized decision making,* and hence to help channel resources to alternative types of assets in an efficient way.

Indeed, it may be argued that one of the most important prerequisites for a successful shift to a more market-oriented economic system is just this, namely the stimulation of private saving—a conclusion that follows from *informal* commonsense views on the functioning of markets (such as those of Hayek and Schumpeter), rather than from formalized general equilibrium theories.

In fact, the history of economic development in the West during the past few hundred years illustrates vividly the importance of private saving and private supply of capital for the entry and growth of new firms, for "entrepreneurship," and hence also for innovation. In other words, it is difficult to preserve an important role for the entrepreneur if the private capitalist is "destroyed"—partly because these are often the same persons. Thus, while both centrally regulated economies and market-oriented economies have to be careful not to destroy incentives to work, it is also important in market-oriented economies to watch out for disincentive effects on private saving and entrepreneurship. This means, of course, that certain "sacrifices" have to be made in the ambition to redistribute incomes from high- to low-income groups—though less so in the case of redistributions from economically "passive" groups, such as "traditional" wealth holders who keep their assets in idle land and various types of collectors' items.

What, then, are the conclusions for indirect (commodity) taxation? My basic assertion is that if we opt for a reasonably nondistorting structure of taxes, tariffs, and subsidies, it is advisable to choose, at least as a starting point, a uniform structure (same tax rate on every commodity and the same tariff rate on every importable), rather than attempting to find some optimum tax structure. The rationale is simply to avoid a situation where something even further away from an optimum structure will in fact be implemented by way of party competition and the influence of strong interest groups. It is difficult for voters to judge if a highly differentiated tax structure reflects an attempt to implement "optimum tax rates" or if it is simply designed to assist politically powerful pressure groups. It is probably easier for voters to judge on this matter if the norm is a proportional structure of indirect taxes rather than some *asserted* optimum structure.

Moreover, it is likely that highly selective taxes and subsidies, like direct regulations, breed both corruption and "rent seeking" via political lobbying (Myrdal 1968). This means that while a liberalization of the economic system in developing countries is most likely a *necessary* requirement for a drastic removal of rent seeking and corruption, this outcome could partly be jeopardized if highly selective taxes and subsidies are introduced as suggested by proponents of optimum tax theory.

An obvious objection to this reasoning is that it may, in fact, be difficult to induce politicians to follow a norm about uniform indirect taxes and tariffs. However, it is well known that politicians sometimes may find it in their own interest to "straightjacket" themselves by accepting various types of norms—obvious examples being international GATT rules on tariffs. Indeed, commitment by way of binding rules has been discussed frequently in game theory in recent years, emphasizing that this may be a method of preventing various groups in society from exploiting the difficulties experienced by government, without such rules, in committing itself in advance to a policy it would like to pursue.

A braver strategy would be to use a uniform tax structure as the basis for the tax system, but to allow some additional selective taxes on goods for which there are really strong and uncontroversial reasons to believe

(1) that the supply and demand elasticities are very low, and (2) that the goods are consumed proportionally much less among citizens with low incomes than among high-income groups (assuming that an improvement in incomes of low-income groups relative to high-income groups is desired). Of course, there is then an equivalent case for deviating from the basically proportional tax structure by low tax rates (or even selective indirect subsidies) on goods and services that there is overwhelming reason to assume have the opposite characteristics.

Such a modification of a strategy of uniform indirect taxes would be a modest attempt to accomodate some of the basic ideas of the optimum tax theory without using that theory as the basic foundation for tax policy recommendations. It differs from the idea of optimum taxation in the sense that (1) attempts to adjust tax rates to differences in demand and supply elasticities would be the exception rather than the rule, and (2) considerations of the functioning of the political process would be paramount.

However, in a short- and medium-term perspective, the most important aspect of tax reform in developing countries is probably *to improve tax collection and tax compliance*. Not only is the administrative capacity of the tax authorities often weak, but in addition, firms are often small and difficult to control, and loyalty to the national state is often rather limited in some developing countries owing to historical experience. Greater uniformity and less differentiation in the treatment of different taxpayers, products, and sources of incomes may often facilitate both tax administration and tax compliance. Moreover, it may be advisable to use a sales tax on wholesale trade rather than a comprehensive value-added tax or a sales tax in retailing. Reductions in the element of "arbitrary discretion" by local tax collectors may also help to increase voluntary tax compliance, as would implementation of the earlier suggestion about a broader base and lower rates.

To summarize my general points on tax policies: policy that relies on (1) sophisticated analytical techniques, combined with (2) extreme oversimplifications of the functioning of the economic system, (3) enormous requirements of sophisticated statistical information, and (4) total neglect of the functioning of the political and administrative system is likely to create more distortions than simple rules of thumb using uniform and broadly based taxes and tariffs—possibly modified by selective taxes or subsidies where the case for such a modification is particularly strong. Thus, there is a strong case for the "traditional" recommendation in public finance of a "comprehensive" income tax with uniform rates between different sources of income assets and types of income earners, and a similar case for uniformity of the tax rates for commodity taxation as the basic starting point, though exceptions may be made where strong cases can be put forward.

GROWTH, DISTRIBUTION, AND POVERTY

Allocative efficiency and economic growth should not, of course, be regarded as "ends in themselves," but rather as means of raising the material well-being of "the ordinary man," and in particular of the poorest fraction of the population. This observation raises the classical question of the relation between the distribution of income, on the one hand, and allocative efficiency and economic growth on the other, hence highlighting the celebrated conflict between equity and efficiency—"the Big Trade-off" in Arthur Okun's terminology (Okun 1974). However, it is also obvious that equity and efficiency considerations are in many cases complementary rather than conflicting objectives. Indeed, it is important to try to find strategies and instruments of growth and redistribution policy for which such complementarities exist.

The most solid empirical observation on the relation between growth and distribution is perhaps that the fruits of economic growth, at least after a while, tend to become dispersed enough to result in an increase in the standard of living of both the great majority of the population and of the bulk of low-income groups (Kuznets 1955, 1963). Thus "immiserizing growth" (Bhagwati 1985) seems to be quite unlikely in a long-term perspective.

However, there is also rather strong evidence from time-series analysis that the *relative* overall distribution of income (as measured by, for instance, the Gini coefficient) often becomes more uneven during the very first decades of economic growth, with a reversal of this tendency later on. This is, of course, the empirical background to the celebrated "Kuznets' Law" about the inverted U shape of the relation between per capita income and the inequality of the overall distribution of income. Indeed, for a given point of time, cross-country studies, too, support the hypothesis of such an inverted U relation (Ahluwalia 1976 and references in Bigsten 1986).

The usual theoretical explanation for this asserted empirical regularity is that economic growth to begin with tends to be concentrated in the initially very small "modern" sector of the economy where per capita income is higher and more uneven, and often also tends to rise more rapidly than in the traditional (usually rural) sectors. When, later on during the growth process, the modern sector becomes a larger share of the total, and the intrasector distribution of skills tends to become more even, the overall distribution of national income, too, tends to become more even—possibly also more even than in the "initial" situation before the "take-off" of modern economic growth (Bigsten 1986).

A similar pattern seems to hold if we look at the relative position of low-income groups (such as the very lowest income deciles) rather than at measures of the overall distribution of income: though low-income groups often seem to gain absolutely also during the very first few decades of economic growth, they usually seem to lose ground relative to other groups during that phase of economic development.[6]

Thus, though there is hardly any reason to be pessimistic about the possibilities of raising the standard of living of low-income groups by way of economic growth, both concern for the relative positions of people during early phases of economic growth and an eagerness to help the very poorest certainly make a case for deliberate policy actions to help the fruits of economic growth spread to the poorest fraction of the population. Thus Kuznets' Law should be regarded as a "tendency" of given economic and social policies, rather than some "iron law of distribution" that cannot be repealed by appropriate economic and social reforms.

When discussing such reforms, it may be useful to distinguish between four (closely related) aspects: (1) attempts to redistribute the ownership of human, financial, and physical assets in favor of low- and low-middle-income groups; (2) removals of institutional obstacles keeping these groups from participating in the process of income growth; (3) redistributional considerations when designing general economic policies; and (4) fiscal policy actions specifically designed to improve the living standards of people in the above mentioned groups.

(1) It is true (and practically tautological) that a relatively even *initial* distribution of human and physical capital, in particular of land, helps to spread the fruits of growth widely. However, it would seem that successful land reforms have to fulfill two requirements: they should opt for private ownership, largely in the form of family farms, and they have to be once-and-for-all actions, so

---

6. It would seem that only a very modest part of the variations of the distribution of income among developed countries can be statistically "explained" by the level of per capita income. According to Bigsten (1986), about 80 percent of the inequalities remain to be explained by other factors.

that the owners of land can be sure about their property rights. Otherwise a serious conflict between equity and efficiency considerations easily arises in agriculture. We would also expect educational reforms during a process of growth to even out the overall distribution of income, in particular if there is a strong emphasis on literacy and vocational training for broad population groups.

(2) Obvious examples of methods to remove *institutional* obstacles to a dispersed distribution of the fruits of economic growth is the stimulation of the buildup of credit market institutions that reach low- and low-middle-income groups, in particular in rural areas. In the case of farm families characterized by ample availability of labor and scarcity of land, it is also important to remove legal and institutional obstacles for additional land tenure (such as the leasing of land). It is also obvious that the possibilities of poor farmers participating in the process of income growth may be drastically improved by government infrastructural investment, both to increase the productivity on the farms (for example, by irrigation systems) and by creating a favorable infrastructure for nonfarm activities in the countryside, where family labor may get additional earnings.

(3) The distributional consequences of alternative general policy strategies is a more difficult and controversial matter. However, both casual observations and systematic research indicate that a shift to an outward-oriented growth strategy tends to favor not only overall economic efficiency, but also employment and redistribution of income to unskilled labor (Krueger 1978; Bhagwati 1978). One of the explanations is that import protection in manufacturing turns the terms of trade against agriculture, where the majority of poor people are to be found in most developing countries. Another explanation is that such policies tend to increase competition and hence reduce monopoly profits. However, even more fundamentally, an outward-looking growth strategy in labor-abundant countries favors labor-intensive sectors and labor-intensive production techniques simply because free trade tends to allocate factors of production in conformity with comparative advantages, which tends to turn the composition of national income in favor of labor income, in particular for low-skilled workers. Poverty will then tend to be reduced, as there is overwhelming evidence that increased employment is of utmost importance of the removal of poverty (Fields 1984). Indeed, as

pointed out by Ranis (1978, 407), "The only sure method of achieving a sustained improvement in equity lies in hastening the advance of commercialization, i.e. the end of the labor surplus conditions."

The importance of high demand for labor for an even distribution of income, and for the mitigation of poverty, also creates a strong case for fighting various regulations in the labor market that keep low-skilled labor unemployed. Obvious examples are minimum-wage legislation and wage policies by unions with similar characteristics, though such legislation and policies do help some low- and middle-income employees—if they do not lose their jobs by way of such actions. Here then is another illustration that efficiency and equality do not always conflict.

However, when stimulating employment, it is, from the point of view of distributional considerations, important to avoid using methods, such as aggressive demand expansion, that generate high and fluctuating inflation, which easily hurts low-income groups. This is particularly important as inequalities generated by inflation are usually "nonfunctional," in the sense that they do not contribute to efficient economic incentives (probably the reverse), in contrast to inequalities that are caused by differences in productive effort. As high-inflation economies tend to get large distortions of relative prices, including the real exchange rate, here is another example where allocative and distributional aspects are complementary.

The upshot of all this is that those who, for efficiency reasons, are in favor of outward-oriented development strategies have certainly no reason to be shy about their position from the point of view of the distribution of income—rather the opposite. Recent experiences in countries like South Korea and Taiwan illustrate this point. There countries have demonstrated the possibility of reconciling efficiency and distributional considerations *both* by choosing an outward-looking development strategy *and* by making early redistributions of the ownership of land and human capital. Thus, even if examples are easy to find where specific tools of egalitarian policies, such as high marginal tax rates, do harm economic growth, there is no presumption of an unavoidable negative reverse causation, according to which increased economic growth would necessarily be unfavorable for income equality even in a short- and medium-term perspective.

The situation is more complex for countries with abundant natural resources rather than labor, as a growth process based on comparative advantage in this case tends to result in high rents. It is then often important to achieve institutional conditions, including a well-functioning capital market, dynamic entrepreneurship, and tax and expenditure policies that help these rents to flow to other sectors where the country has a comparative advantage, rather than using these rents for subsidies to import-substitution production.

(4) Of course, various arguments for institutional reforms in favor of low-income groups, redistribution of assets, and an outward-looking development strategy do not rule out the possibility of more direct policy actions specifically designed to improve the consumption of poor people. As pointed out in the section on expenditure policies, one obvious example is the provision of water, sanitation, health care, and food. It is, however, important to warn countries against choosing methods of redistribution that harm growth, as after a while economic growth usually tends to be accompanied by an equalization of the overall distribution of income.

PROBLEMS OF TRANSITION AND MACROECONOMIC INSTABILITY

So far our discussion has been confined to various aspects of the allocation of resources and the distribution of income. However, when analyzing public finance, or economic policy in general for liberalizing developing countries, there is a strong case for emphasizing *stabilization policy* aspects as well. For instance, greater reliance on foreign trade, which is an expected consequence of more market-oriented economic policies, would be expected to accentuate the size of "imported" disturbances from world markets, though at the same time domestically generated disturbances will have smaller effects on the domestic economy, as part of the effects "leaks out" through the balance of payments.

However, it is conceivable that a market-oriented and outward-looking country will be so much more flexible than a highly regulated one (with the emphasis on import substitution) that the *effects* on the domestic economy of foreign shocks will not be greater in the former than in the latter type of country. Indeed, Bela Balassa (1984) asserts that a number of highly "outward-oriented" economies, in particular in Pacific

Asia, though being exposed to greater international shocks than most other developing countries, have recently been able to "absorb" the shocks better than more regulated, "inward-looking" developing countries. However, it is equally striking that attempts to liberalize the economies of some developing countries, in particular in South America, have backfired because of their inability to deal with problems of macroeconomic instability during the period of transition to a more market-oriented economic system. These important issues will be dealt with below.

One obvious problem during a period of transition to a more market-oriented economic system is that the redistribution of income and wealth, which is induced by the accompanying shifts in relative prices, profitabilities, and the composition of demand, will be resisted by various interest groups in society. New market uncertainties will often also be created during the transition period. One reason is that when an economy is originally in a situation characterized by pronounced disequilibria, which is a characteristic feature of a regulated economy, it becomes difficult to predict what will happen to various relative prices, demands, and supplies when the economy is liberalized. It is therefore important that there be confidence among private agents that the shift of system is *permanent,* as otherwise economic agents may not be willing to fully adjust their activities, in particular their investment, to the new information and the new incentives that are transmitted via the market system. An important explanation as to why the economic liberalization in West Germany in 1947–50 and in Pacific Asia in the 1960s and 1970s was so successful is probably just that there was considerable confidence that the shift to new rules of the game was permanent. More efficient market-oriented institutions in product and factor markets would also help smooth the transition, obvious examples being highly flexible credit institutes and labor exchange agents. It would also be useful if the government could adjust the public infrastructure rapidly, if possible even in advance of the liberalization of product and factor markets.

Another obvious transitional problem is the emergence of severe risks of large increases in frictional and structural unemployment, as the requirements of reallocations of labor may outstrip the ability of the labor market to achieve this smoothly. Thus, it may be hazardous to liberalize product markets without at the same time removing important obstacles to the flexibility of the factor markets. From that point of view it would be wise if, for instance, minimum-wage regulations and interest-rate ceilings were removed before, or simultaneously with, a liberalization of the product market. Recent studies indicate, however, that severe unemployment problems have not been caused by the liberalization attempts during the seventies—except in a few countries that pursued stabilization policies that severely damaged the employment situation (Michaeli 1986).

Indeed, experience suggests that the most important transition problem concerns macroeconomic instabilty—the difficulties of avoiding fluctuations in capacity utilization, inflation, and the balance of payments. For instance, inflation and balance of payments problems will most likely be accentuated when price controls and other types of regulations are removed. Indeed, this is exactly what has happened when socialist countries have experimented with a freer system of price and wage formation. The obvious, and generally accepted, conclusion is that a liberalization of the economic system has to be combined with increased concern for the management of stabilization policy—with fiscal, monetary, and exchange-rate policies as the main tools.

However, many years of experience in developed countries certainly show that even rather well designed macropolicies may not be enough to prevent high, and perhaps even rising, inflation. A main reason for this is that the mechanisms of wage formation are characterized by a pronounced inflationary bias in most, perhaps all, of the world's market economies. Some adjustment of these mechanisms is therefore worth considering when developing countries plan to liberalize their economic systems (in the same way as such modifications are today discussed in various developed countries). This argument may carry particular weight in countries with fairly strong labor unions, as in some Latin American countries.

Obvious candidates for such reforms are: removals of price index clauses in wage contracts, and the introduction of new contract forms with bonus systems that tie wage increases to productivity increases or profits. When developing countries introduce unemployment insurance systems, a strong case can also be made for letting unions and firms in each separate sector bear the bulk of the insurance costs, rather than shifting these costs onto the taxpayers. The idea is, of course, to internalize the negative consequences on the employment level of aggressive wage increases. Clearly, government budget policy has a direct responsibility for the rate of wage increases in the public sector, which in some developing countries has an important bearing on wages in the entire labor market. However, in some developing countries, where labor unions are weak, general macroeconomic policy—with a concentration on getting the budget surplus, the monetary aggregates, and the exchange rate right—may be not only a necessary but also a sufficient condition for reasonable macroeconomic stability if international disturbances are not too large.

In countries with large fluctuations in the terms of trade (owing, for instance, to heavy exports of raw materials), there is also a strong case for pursuing monetary and fiscal policies that avoid large swings in the real exchange rate for nontraditional exports to prevent a "Dutch disease" in that sector in connection to export booms. The "sterilization" of extreme export earnings (for example, by taxation) or of their consequences for domestic financial markets (by monetary policy actions) to reduce instability in the real exchange rate is a crucial aspect of a successful stabilization policy for such countries.

There are also a number of specific transition problems connected to the liberalization of foreign transactions—trade as well as capital movements. For instance, as a tariff reduction initially reduces the prices of import goods ("importables") relative to both export goods ("exportables") and nontraded goods ("nontradables"), both domestic absorption of importables and the production of nontradables are stimulated. In other words, there is an appreciation in the "real exchange rate." In combination with the reduced competitiveness of domestic production of importables, we would, in short-term perspective, expect temporary unemployment problems in that sector, and most likely also an increased current account deficit. This is, of course, the rationale for the traditional policy advice to devalue the currency in connection with a general tariff reduction—implying a slowing down (or reversal) of the appreciation of the real exchange rate. An additional complication is that the inflationary effects of the devaluation may dominate the deflationary effects of the tariff reduction, which is, of course, a reason to suggest that the devaluation be combined with restrictive demand management policies.

As direct regulations regarding imports are often more disruptive to the efficiency of the economy than tariffs, it is worthwhile starting a process of import liberalization not only with an "evening out" of the structure of tariffs between different groups of commodities but also with liberalizations of direct import controls. Attempts to reduce the *average* level of tariffs could then be delayed somewhat if rapid devaluations prove to be difficult.

With sufficiently restrictive management of domestic aggregate demand, the combination of tariff reduction and devaluation could then, in principle, bring about the desired shift of resources not only from less to more efficient parts within the tradable sector, but also from the nontradable to the tradable sector, with an expansion of foreign trade without a deterioration of the current account and without increased inflation.

However, if nominal wage increases (owing, for instance, to explicit or implicit indexation of wage rates) follow price increases closely, the result may be both stagflation and (with fixed exchange rates) a gradual disappearance of the gains in competitiveness that the devaluation was designed to provide. What would then remain of the entire operation would be a more efficient level and structure of tariffs, and hence a more efficient allocation of resources, though at the cost of more inflation and possibly also a deterioration in the current account of the balance of payments. Both the higher rate of inflation and the increase in the current account deficit then easily release political forces that result either in the reintroduction of a protectionist stance or in strongly restrictive unemployment-creating policy actions. *All this highlights the importance of an appropriate combination of trade liberalization and macroeconomic policy during a transition period.*

Of course, an increased current account deficit could, in principle, be financed by capital inflows, which are facilitated by the liberalization of capital movements, in particular if domestic interest rates are initially higher than the rates on world markets. However, such a development requires both high confidence in the permanence of the liberalization of capital movements and a sufficiently high real rate of return on domestically held assets, implying an appropriate and stable real exchange rate. As such conditions cannot always be taken for granted, a country that is about to liberalize foreign exchange should build up its reserve and/or lines of credit in advance, for instance by way of foreign borrowing by the government.

It would seem that the unsuccessful liberalization attempts in some countries in South America—in particular, in the so-called Southern Cone countries, Chile, Argentina, and Uruguay—in the late seventies and early eighties were closely connected with serious deficiencies just in short- and medium-term macropolicies. These policies were simply not "consistent" enough with the liberalization attempts (Khan and Zahler 1984). An overexpansion of domestic aggregate demand, often via a large budget deficit and a rapid increase of the money stock (partly to finance the budget deficit, partly owing to large capital inflows), during the process of liberalization contributed both to inflation and to rising current account deficits, which then resulted in severe liquidity and confidence problems for the national economy.

In these countries expansion of domestic aggregate demand pulled up prices in the nontradable sectors and wages in the entire economy, which with fixed exchange rates severely harmed production and employment in the tradable sectors. This also illustrates the dangers of trying to fight inflation with a fixed exchange rate if domestic aggregate demand policies are not kept under control—in particular, if wages are indexed to the domestic price level for consumer goods (with a strong component of nontradables). The experiences of Argentina and Chile during the late seventies illustrate this point.

Thus, the most important aspect of the transition problem is probably to avoid combining a liberalization of trade and capital movements with (1) an expansion of domestic aggregate demand by way of big budget deficits and a large expansion of the monetary aggregates, and (2) unstable real exchange rates, in particular heavy appreciations, for instance, owing to rapid wage increases with fixed (or lagging) exchange rates. Such policies have, of course, particularly serious consequences in an international environment characterized by drastically increased interest rates, a deterioration of the terms of trade, and a cyclical weakening of foreign markets, as in the early eighties.

However, it is also difficult to introduce trade liberalization in a situation in which the government tries to bring down inflation by restrictive demand policies, which will accentuate the unavoidable disturbances in the labor market resulting from the trade liberalization programs. This dilemma has induced some observers to suggest that a trade liberalization program has to be postponed until inflation has been brought down substantially (Bruno and Sachs 1985). It is also obvious that the order of trade liberalization is important. For instance, the experience of Argentina illustrates the danger of liberalizing imports before exports, and the experience of Chile illustrates the risk of liberalizing capital movements at an early stage of the liberalization process if effective action is not undertaken to prevent inflationary effects from capital inflows.

Finally, it is also important to avoid destabilizing macropolicies after a period of transition to a more market-oriented economic system, as both allocation and growth policies are likely to fail if the macroeconomic policy is not pursued with reasonable skill. An open economy, in particular a small one with large foreign trade, will be disrupted if aggregate demand is much too high, or much too low for that matter, and if the most important relative price of all—the real exchange rate—is excessive. Experience shows that this simple point cannot be stressed too much.

REFERENCES

Ahluwalia, Montek T. 1976. "Income Distributions and Development: Some Stylized Facts." *American Economic Review* 66 (May): 128–35.

Atkinson, Anthony B., and Joseph E. Stiglitz. 1980. *Lectures on Public Economics,* chaps. 12–14. New York: McGraw-Hill.

Balassa, Bela. 1983. "Public Finance and Social Policy—Explanations of Trends and Development: The Case of Developing Countries." In *Public Finance and Social Policy,* 41–58. Proceedings of the 39th Congress of the International Institute of Public Finance, Budapest.

———. 1984. "Adjustment Policies in Developing Countries: A Reassessment." *World Development* 12 (September): 955–72.

Bauer, P. T. 1971. *Dissent on Development.* London: Weidenfeld & Nicholson.

Bhagwati, J. N. 1966. *The Economics of Underdeveloped Countries.* New York: McGraw-Hill.

———. 1968. *The Theory and Practice of Commercial Policy: Departure from Unified Exchange Rates.* Essays in International Finance no. 8. International Finance Section, Department of Economics, Princeton University.

———. 1978. *Foreign Trade Regimes and Economic Development: Anatomy and Consequences of Exchange Control Regimes.* Cambridge, Mass.: Ballinger.

———. 1985. "Growth and Poverty." Lecture delivered at Michigan State University, East Lansing, April 4.

Bigsten, A. 1986. "Poverty, Inequality and Development." University of Gothenburg. Mimeographed.

Bruno, Michael, and Jeffrey D. Sachs. 1985. *Economics of Worldwide Stagflation.* Cambridge, Mass.: Harvard University Press.

Buchanan, James M., and Gordon Tullock. 1962. *The Calculus of Consent: Logical Foundations of Constitutional Democracy.* Ann Arbor: University of Michigan Press.

Chenery, Hollis B. 1975. "The Structuralist Approach to Economic Development." *American Economic Review* 65 (May): 310–16.

———. 1979. *Structural Change and Development Policy.* London: Oxford University Press.

Fields, G. S. 1979. "Decomposing LDC Inequality." *Oxford Economic Papers* 31 (November): 437–59.

———. 1984. "Employment, Income Distribution and Economic Growth in Seven Small Economies." *Economic Journal* 94 (March): 74–83.

Haberler, G. 1959. *International Trade and Economic Development* Cairo: National Bank of Egypt.

International Labor Organization. 1976. *Employment, Growth and Basic Needs.* Geneva: ILO.

International Monetary Fund. 1985. *Government Finance Statistics Yearbook.* Washington, D.C.: International Monetary Fund.

Khan, M. S., and R. Zahler. 1984. *Trade and Financial Liberalization in the Context of External Shocks and Inconsistent Domestic Policies.* IMF Document DM 84/44. Washington, D.C.: International Monetary Fund.

Krueger, Anne O. 1974. "The Political Economy of the Rent-Seeking Society." *American Economic Review* 64 (June): 291–303.

———, ed. 1983. *Trade and Employment in Developing Countries*. Vol. 3, *Synthesis and Conclusions*. Chicago: University of Chicago Press.

Kuznets, S. 1955. "Economic Growth and Income Inequality." *American Economic Review* 45 (March): 1–28.

———. 1963. "Quantitative Aspects of the Economic Growth of Nations: III: Distribution of Income by Size." *Economic Development and Cultural Change* 11 (January): 1–80.

Lal, Deepak. 1983. *The Poverty of Development Economics*. Hobart Paperback no. 16. Washington, D.C.: Institute of Economic Affairs.

Lindbeck, Assar. 1973. "Endogenous Politicians and the Theory of Economic Policy." Seminar Paper no. 35. Stockholm: Institute for International Economic Studies.

———. 1985. "What Is Wrong with the West European Economies?" *World Economy* (June): 153–70.

Little, I. 1982. *Economic Development: Theory, Policy and International Relations*. New York: Basic Books.

Little, I., T. Scitovsky and M. Scott. 1970. *Industry and Trade in Some Developing Countries: A Comparative Study*. London: Oxford University Press.

Michaeli, M. 1986. "The Timing and Sequencing of a Trade Liberalization Policy." World Bank papers prepared for conference in Lisbon, June 15–22. Mimeographed.

Morawetz, D. 1976. "Elasticities of Substitution in Industry: What Do We Learn from Econometric Estimates?" *World Development* 4 (January): 11–15.

Myint, H. 1967. "Economic Theory and Development Policy." *Economica* 34 (May): 117–30.

Myrdal, Gunnar. 1968. *Asian Drama: An Inquiry into the Poverty of Nations*. New York: Twentieth Century Fund. Reprint, Penguin Books.

Okun, A. M. 1974. *Equality and Efficiency: The Big Trade-Off*. Washington, D.C.: Brookings Institution.

Psacharopoulos, G. 1981. "Returns to Education: An Updated International Expansion." *Comparative Education* 17:321–41.

Ranis, Gustav. 1978. "Equity with Growth in Taiwan: How 'Special' Is the Special Case?" *World Development* 6 (March): 397–409.

Schultz, Theodore W. 1964. *Transforming Traditional Agriculture*. New Haven: Yale University Press.

Sen, Amartya. 1981. *Poverty and Famines: An Essay on Entitlement and Deprivation*. New York: Oxford University Press.

Sicat, G. P., and A. Virmani. 1986. "Personal Income Taxes in Developing Countries." World Bank. Mimeographed.

Stern, N. H. 1984. "Optimum Taxation and Tax Policy." *IMF Staff Papers* 31 (June): 339–78.

Stiglitz, Joseph E. 1985. *Economics of Information and the Theory of Economic Development*. NBER Working Paper no. 1. Cambridge, Mass.: National Bureau of Economic Research.

Tanzi, V. 1986. "Quantitative Characteristics of the Tax System in Developing Countries." In D. Newberg and N. Stern, eds., *Modern Tax Theory for Developing Countries.* Washington, D.C.: World Bank.

United Nations. 1983. *Industrial Yearbook.* New York: UN.

Viner, J. 1952. *International Trade and Economic Development.* Lectures delivered at National University of Brazil. Glencoe, Ill.: Free Press.

Waterston, A. 1965. *Development Planning: Lessons of Experience.* Baltimore: Johns Hopkins University Press for the World Bank.

White, L. J. 1978. "The Evidence on Appropriate Factor Proportions for Manufacturing in Less Developed Countries: A Survey." *Economic Development and Cultural Change* 27 (October): 27–59.

World Bank. 1985. *World Development Report, 1985.* Washington, D.C.: World Bank.

——— . 1986. *World Development Report, 1986.* Washington, D.C.: World Bank.

Name Index

Subject Index

Economists of the Twentieth Century

Monetarism and Macroeconomic Policy
Thomas Mayer

Studies in Fiscal Federalism
Wallace E. Oates

The World Economy in Perspective
Essays in International Trade and European Integration
Herbert Giersch

Towards a New Economics
Critical Essays on Ecology, Distribution and Other Themes
Kenneth E. Boulding

Studies in Positive and Normative Economics
Martin J. Bailey

The Collected Essays of Richard E. Quandt (2 volumes)
Richard E. Quandt

International Trade Theory and Policy
Selected Essays of W. Max Corden
W. Max Corden

Organization and Technology in Capitalist Development
William Lazonick

Studies in Human Capital
The Collected Essays of Jacob Mincer, Volume 1
Jacob Mincer

Studies in Labor Supply
The Collected Essays of Jacob Mincer, Volume 2
Jacob Mincer

Macroeconomics and Economic Policy
The Selected Essays of Assar Lindbeck, Volume I
Assar Lindbeck

The Welfare State
The Selected Essays of Assar Lindbeck, Volume II
Assar Lindbeck

Classical Economics, Public Expenditure and Growth
Walter Eltis

Money, Interest Rates and Inflation
Frederic S. Mishkin

The Public Choice Approach to Politics
Dennis C. Mueller

The Liberal Economic Order
Volume I   Essays on International Economics
Volume II   Money, Cycles and Related Themes
Gottfried Haberler
Edited by Anthony Y.C. Koo

Economic Growth and Business Cycles
Prices and the Process of Cyclical Development
Paolo Sylos Labini

Economic Theory and Market Socialism
Selected Essays of Oskar Lange
Edited by Tadeusz Kowalik